MW01156444

Bagpipes in Babylon

From reviews of Glencairn Balfour Paul's *End of Empire in the Middle East:*

'His account of Britain's complicated final years in the Middle East is elegantly written and gives a balanced picture which should commend it to experts and amateurs alike.' – Peter Tripp, *British Journal of Middle East Studies*

'Balfour-Paul's elegant style and his eye for apt quotation brings to life a vanished age.' – Wm. Roger Louis, *Times Literary Supplement*

'A valuable and original work in a lively and often witty style.' – Yousif Choueiri, *Journal of Islamic Studies*

'Perceptive and elegantly written – particularly worth reading in the light of the Gulf War.' – Keith Robins, *International Affairs*

'His perceptive treatment of personalities and an urbane sense of humour illuminate a lively narrative and thoughtful reflections. This wise book is very readable.' – A.R.H. Kelly, *Middle East International*

Bagpipes in Babylon

A Lifetime in the Arab World and Beyond

GLENCAIRN BALFOUR PAUL

I.B. TAURIS

LONDON · NEW YORK

Reprinted in 2006 by I.B.Tauris & Co. Ltd.
First published in 2006 by I.B.Tauris & Co. Ltd
6 Salem Road, London W2 4BU
175 Fifth Avenue, New York NY 10010
www.ibtauris.com

In the United States of America and in Canada distributed by Palgrave
Macmillan, a division of St Martin's Press, 175 Fifth Avenue, New York NY 10010

ISBN 1 84511 151 6
EAN 978 1 84511 151 9

A full CIP record for this book is available from the British Library
A full CIP record for this book is available from the Library of Congress
Library of Congress catalog card: available

Set in Monotype Dante by Ewan Smith, London
Printed and bound in Great Britain by TJ International Ltd, Padstow, Cornwall

Contents

Illustrations | vii   Foreword | ix
Introduction | xi   Maps | xiii–xvi
Family Tree | xviii–xix

THE PAST

1   Family Origins and Oddities   3
2   My Parents' Generation   21

GROWING UP

3   Childhood   37
4   Adolescence   50
5   Oxford   62

THE WAR YEARS

6   Colchester and Tillicoultry   71
7   *Regione Inesplorita* in Abyssinia   76
8   In and Around Kufra Oasis   87
9   Libya and the Near East   98
10 Kaimakam in Tripolitania   108

SUDAN POLITICAL SERVICE

11 The Blue Nile   119
12 Darfur   137

DIPLOMACY

13 New Pastures (FCO and Chile)   155
14 The Lebanon   171
15 Dubai   190
16 Bahrain and St Antony's   201

EXPERIENCES AS AMBASSADOR

17 Iraq   215
18 Jordan   226
19 Tunisia   240

RETIREMENT REVERSED

20 Starting Again: Middle East Association and
   Academia   251
21 More Excursions and Occasional Alarms (Yemen,
   Dubai, Oman)   261
22 Jaunts and Jollities (North Yemen, Peru, Egypt,
   South Yemen)   271

FURTHER TRAVELS WITH JENNY

23 Off Again: Morocco, Thailand and Laos   283
24 Pursuing Indigo into Mali's Dogon Country   289
25 Dramas in India and Bangladesh   298
26 Following Footsteps in the Marquesas Islands and
   Southern India   309

   Index   323

Illustrations

1 The Lyon's clan. Sir James BP and his descendants down to Glen-cairn (aged four) on his mother's lap. Taken at St Boswells, Scottish borders, in 1921.   6

2 Grandfather (Sir James BP) in his tabard as Lyon King of Arms.   8

3 Pilrig House, seat of the Balfours, where Robert Louis Stevenson frequently stayed. (Built 1638, reconstructed in the 1980s after it burnt down.)   10

4 Jack (John William) BP after losing an arm in the Boer war in 1901. (Taken in Colombo.)   24

5 Muriel Monteith as bride of Jack BP in 1908.   28

6 GBP revisiting Cakemuir in 2002. Its rear face from the garden.   42

7 Specimen pages from dictionaries and magazines in the *Lob* language, invented by Scrap, Ian and Glencairn as children in 1925.   44

8 As Lieutenant in the Argyll and Sutherland Highlanders, en route for the Middle East. (Photographed in Cape Town by French host and hostess.)   78

9 Tagiura village in Tripolitania sketched by GPB in 1943, when Kaimakam in HQ.   110

10 Arriving back at starting point in north-west Darfur from Ennedi exploration. GBP with Ann and Alison in boxes on either side of his camel.   148

11 Sudanese notable Muhammed Ahmed Abu Sinn, staying with the BPs in Beirut in 1962, holding Cati.   180

12 Sheikh Rashid bin Sa'id al Maktoum, ruler of Dubai, with Political Agent GBP in 1965.   196

13 Marnie with her four children, Ann, Alison, Cati and Jamie in Bahrain, 1967.   202

14 Sheikh Shakhbut's palace in Abu Dhabi in 1966.   204

15 Reed-built *mejlis* of a sheikh of the Marsh Arabs in southern Iraq on visit by BP family in 1969.   220

16 Glencairn and Jenny at their marriage in Devon, September 1974.   230

17 Ambassador GBP and Jenny meeting King Hussein and the visiting Shah of Persia (and their wives) in the palace in Amman, 1975.   232

18 Cricket match against King Hussein's XI. GBP bowling to General
    Zaid bin Shakir. The King at the bowler's end.   234

19 Jenny on St Simeon's shrunken pillar at Qala'at Sima'an in Syria, on
    the way home in 1976.   236

20 Jenny's drawing of British Ambassador's Residence at La Marsa.   242

21 The Tassili mountains in Algeria. Jibreel, their last and only
    inhabitant, with our guide Kandoweess, squatting to right of
    photograph, 1977.   246

22 Sana'a medina, Yemen.   264

23 GBP in 2002 in Anaho Bay, Nukuhiva (where Robert Louis Stevenson
    anchored and stayed for three weeks en route for Samoa).   310

24 Amazing fourteenth-century fishing nets at Cochin in Kerala.   317

25 Jenny, Hamish, Finella and Glencairn at the wedding of Toni
    Evennett and Jez Waites in Exeter, 2004.   321

Foreword

GLEN Balfour Paul's unusual and memorable book can be read in at least
three different ways. First and foremost it is an account of forty years' experience as a soldier, as an Administrator in the Sudan Political Service, and as a
diplomat in the Middle East. It is also a work of literature, for he is a poet
as well as a gifted writer of prose. Last, and perhaps above all, the book will
take its place among inspired twentieth-century accounts of travel in virtually
all parts of the world.

It is useful to bear in mind the stages of his life, not least his Scottish
family background. He was born in 1917. After Magdalen College, Oxford,
he served in the Sudan Defence Force 1939–45 and was instantly obliged to
wear the insignia of a Turkish-Egyptian Lieutenant Colonel – this was not
entirely a matter of merit: even the youngest British officers were automatically elevated to make them senior to almost all Sudanese officers. His account
of his years in the Sudan Political Service will command the attention of
those interested in the history of the British Empire (much later in life he
became a contributor to the *Oxford History of the British Empire*). He entered
the Foreign Office in 1955 on the eve of the Suez Crisis, which he regards
as destroying at one stroke Britain's standing in the Middle East. His career
perhaps reached its peak as Ambassador in Iraq (1969–71). He recalls Saddam
Hussein essentially as a thug, but initially as an impressive politician. He later
served in Jordan (1972–75) and Tunis (1975–77). After 1977 he pursued a dual
career as historian and traveller.

The key to his outlook on life, and the reason for the distinction of the
book, is Balfour Paul's belief that human experience is never complete until
it finds expression in writing. I wrote in reviewing his *End of Empire in the
Middle East* in *The Times Literary Supplement*: 'Balfour Paul's elegant style and
his eye for apt quotation bring to life a vanished age.' Those words are just
as valid for the present book. His political observations are acute. He draws
lasting lessons from his experience in the Middle East. But what will impress
the reader most of all is his essential humanity and his view that 'life is too
serious not to be taken lightly'. In the accounts of his travels with his wife
Jenny he comes close to comic genius.

Wm Roger Louis

Introduction

MAY I begin by explaining first what this book is not and then what it is.

During my years as a Research Fellow at Exeter University I applied myself in a small way to the serious writing of history. The outcome was *The End of Empire in the Middle East* (CUP, 1991), the Middle East chapter in the *Oxford History of the British Empire* (OUP, 2000), and a string of articles and chapters in journals and books.

What I have sought to present in these memoirs is not 'history' in that sense. Rather, my aim has been to record my own modest involvement, seldom significant and sometimes ludicrous, in the course of events over the past eighty years. As originally envisaged, my reminiscences were to be jotted down simply for the entertainment of my family and descendants, but I was urged to seek a wider audience. So I started again, and have described in some detail the shattering developments that have occurred during my lifetime and the principal personalities involved, so far as they were personally known to me. The experiences of one ordinary man and his reactions to them, as the history of his time unfolded itself, do not – quite rightly – figure in serious history books; but however unimportant in themselves, they are none the less a genuine element in the story of those times and an account of them may throw a slightly different light on some of what was going on.

To start with, however, I have set down something of the world from which I myself sprang, different as that was from the world I came to know in my turn and sought to keep pace with as it changed into the world of the next generation on its bewildering way into the twenty-first century. But the long dead live on, in the sense that all generations carry with them willy-nilly the imprint of their progenitors; and it is right that each generation should learn something of those who, however impalpably, contributed to their own make-up. Two thousand years ago Cicero made the same point more forcibly: '*Nescire autem quid antequam natus sis acciderit, id est semper esse puerum.*' In English, 'Not to know what happened before you were born is to remain for ever a child.'

What follows may here and there descend to triviality. But I wrote over the years a lot of poetry, and in one of the poems I have allowed myself to quote in these pages I expressed my belief that 'the Trivial makes the world safe for the Sublime'. The twentieth century may have manifested little sublimity, but in setting down these reminiscences I am not ashamed of exploiting my belief in the value of triviality.

One of my weaknesses, if it *is* a weakness, is that I have always shared the view expressed somewhere by Aldous Huxley that no experience is complete until it is reduced to words. Such reduction to words necessarily involves some element of re-creation, not to say imagination, every time we relive an experience in this way. Much, of course, depends on the extent and validity of the re-creation. King George II, I recall, told so many audiences over the years how he had led the final charge at the Battle of Dettingen that he ended up believing it himself. But if for him experience was re-created *ex nihilo*, that is in no sense the case with me.

Just after I joined the Foreign Office (aged forty) my immediate boss rushed into my room to show me with great hilarity a report from Washington of the fate of a blueprint for a new American fighter plane, submitted to the US Secretary of Defense for his approval. Across the blueprint the Defense Secretary had simply scrawled in red ink the words 'SIMPLIFICATE. ADD LIGHTNESS'. I have done what I can to follow this admirable principle, if only by considerably reducing the size of the original version. What those American aircraft designers did to meet their Minister's terse requirements I do not know.

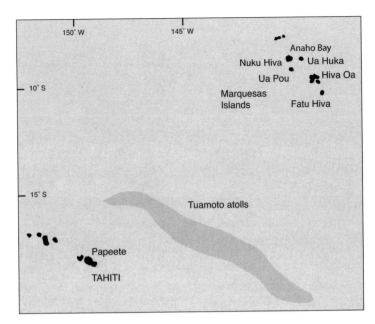

French Polynesia (Tahiti and the Marquesas Islands)

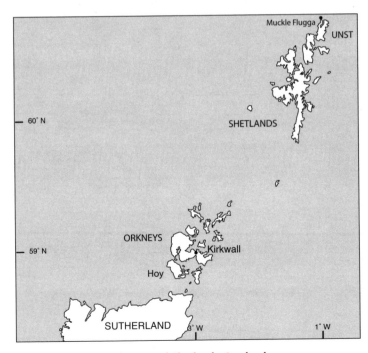

Orkneys and Shetlands, Scotland

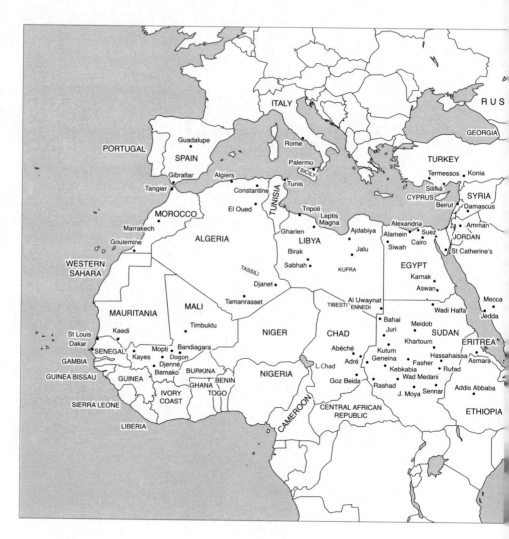

Sketchmap showing the main places in the text

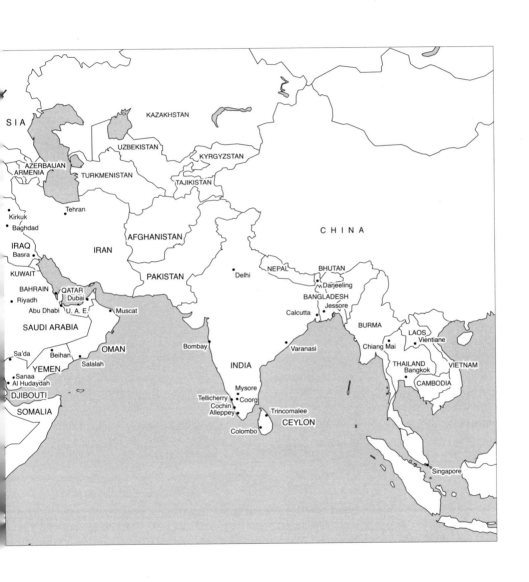

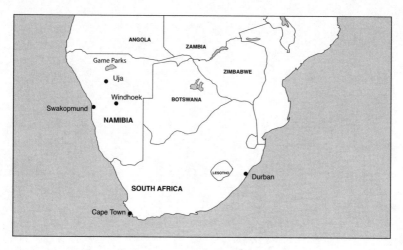

Namibia and Southern Africa

South America

FOR JENNY, WITHOUT WHOM NOT

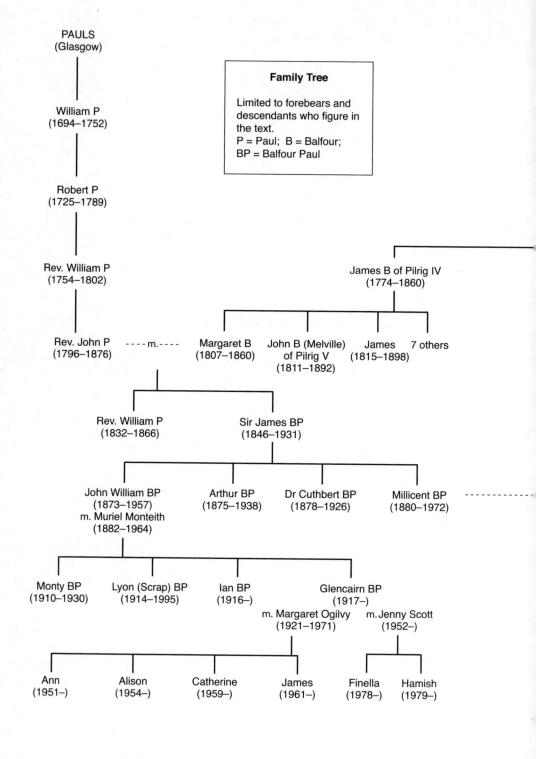

PAULS
(Glasgow)

William P
(1694–1752)

Robert P
(1725–1789)

Rev. William P
(1754–1802)

Rev. John P   ---- m. ----   Margaret B
(1796–1876)   (1807–1860)

James B of Pilrig IV
(1774–1860)

John B (Melville)   James   7 others
of Pilrig V   (1815–1898)
(1811–1892)

Family Tree

Limited to forebears and
descendants who figure in
the text.
P = Paul; B = Balfour;
BP = Balfour Paul

Rev. William P   Sir James BP
(1832–1866)   (1846–1931)

John William BP   Arthur BP   Dr Cuthbert BP   Millicent BP   ------------
(1873–1957)   (1875–1938)   (1878–1926)   (1880–1972)
m. Muriel Monteith
(1882–1964)

Monty BP   Lyon (Scrap) BP   Ian BP   Glencairn BP
(1910–1930)   (1914–1995)   (1916–)   (1917–)
                                                       m. Margaret Ogilvy   m. Jenny Scott
                                                       (1921–1971)   (1952–)

Ann   Alison   Catherine   James   Finella   Hamish
(1951–)   (1954–)   (1959–)   (1961–)   (1978–)   (1979–)

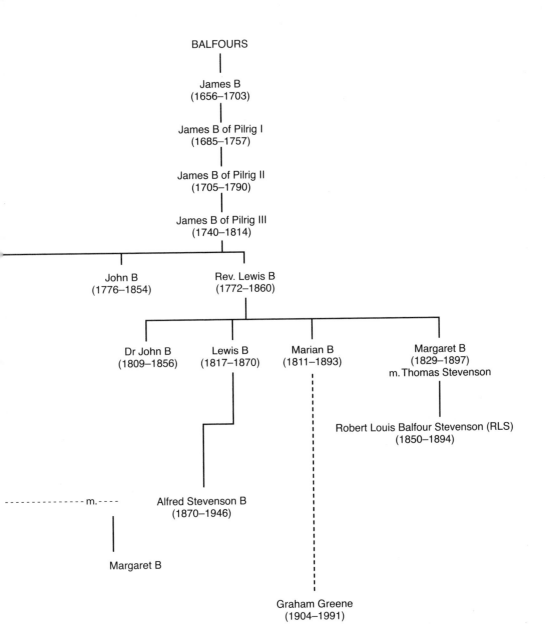

BALFOURS

James B
(1656–1703)

James B of Pilrig I
(1685–1757)

James B of Pilrig II
(1705–1790)

James B of Pilrig III
(1740–1814)

John B
(1776–1854)

Rev. Lewis B
(1772–1860)

Dr John B
(1809–1856)

Lewis B
(1817–1870)

Marian B
(1811–1893)

Margaret B
(1829–1897)
m. Thomas Stevenson

Robert Louis Balfour Stevenson (RLS)
(1850–1894)

----------- m.----

Alfred Stevenson B
(1870–1946)

Margaret B

Graham Greene
(1904–1991)

The Past

Family Origins and Oddities

SADDAM seized me by the shoulders and marched me by his side in a sort of embrace, saying, 'Can't you British understand that there is nothing in the world I detest more than a Russian Communist – except an Iraqi one? It is London's foolish hostility that has compelled me to turn to Moscow. Get that through to your government.' That was late 1969. The occasion was the first audience I had with Saddam Hussein. (We talked in Arabic, since he would never use an interpreter.) He was coldly businesslike for half an hour, but when I spoke of my government's opposition to Iraq's cosying up with Soviet Russia, he jumped from his chair and started pacing up and down his office. I rose to my feet as protocol demanded, and found myself in the embrace described above.

Not all of my experiences as an Ambassador were as melodramatic as that one. Saddam had not yet come out in his true colours as a tyrannical thug, and I thought he made good enough sense and that we could, by a change of approach, get along usefully with him. But history, and Saddam, took a different course. We now know how Saddam came to grief, but history hobbles on.

Before I relate other curious experiences in my life, well before, during and well after I went in for diplomacy, I should start off with an account of my origins, the sources from which I sprang. Many of my ancestors deserve description as unusual, indeed sometimes even eccentric, characters.

In 14 Belgrave Crescent, Edinburgh (my parents' last home), my father would sometimes display a fat volume put together by my grandfather, Sir James BP, setting out in stupendous detail the family tree. As I recall, it started with Malcolm III of Scotland and Edward the Confessor and ended, in the bottom right-hand corner of the final page, with *me*.

Being the last small fruit on the family tree did not always prove a source of pride. It presumably explains the appellation I long suffered at the hands of my parents and my three elder brothers as 'The Wee Man'. To be fair, by the time I was ostensibly adult, or at least a commissioned officer in HM Armed Forces, my father substituted the slightly less pejorative 'Young Fellah' (or YF on his old Yost typewriter, to which he always addressed himself in the standing position).

The first documentary account of my progenitors that came my way was an anonymous booklet entitled 'Some Pauls of Glasgow and their Descendants'. This must have been the work of my grandfather, and evidently composed in 1910. Here are a few of its more entertaining contents.

The early Pauls of Glasgow, other than those who took the cloth, are in sundry cases described as having been 'gardeners' by profession – promoted once or twice to 'botanists'. It is just possible that the terms were still synonymous, for I learnt recently that the distinguished botanists who have directed the world-famous Chelsea Physic Garden since its foundation in the fourteenth century have always been entitled 'The Gardener'. Most of the later Pauls were in trade and therefore, in social terms, little better by the standards of the time. Banking was perhaps a little classier, and there were lots of Paul bankers too. One of them, Robert Paul (1788–1866), who was a founding member-manager for many years of the Commercial Bank of Edinburgh, deserves a passing tribute for the signal, not to say heroic, part played by his ghost in my brother Scrap's precarious financial life. For one day in the fifties Scrap approached the Commercial Bank in Tobermory, Mull, for a small loan. Its manager, on discovering that Scrap must be a descendant of the great man whose portrait hung behind his desk, declared that he would be honoured to lend him any sum he cared to name. Scrap settled for a modest £50,000.

This Robert was the second son of the Reverend William Paul, who, as minister of St Cuthbert's for many years, was held in such esteem that his death in 1804 was announced all over the city by 'bills hawked about the streets'; and he was painted posthumously by his distinguished parishioner, Raeburn – the sort of treatment reserved today for pop stars.

Another of the Reverend William's sons, John (1795–1873), also became minister of St Cuthbert's and was Moderator of the Kirk in 1848. But a more relevant distinction is that he married Margaret, eldest child of the fourth James Balfour of Pilrig. Hence, in accordance with the Scottish practice of the time, the assumption of Balfour into the family name by my grandfather, their second son. The Balfour connection was reinforced later by the marriage of his daughter, my Aunt Millicent, to her cousin Commander Alfred Stevenson Balfour. He, my Uncle Alfie, was a grandson of the Reverend Lewis Balfour, a brother of James Balfour of Pilrig. Another of his grandsons was Robert Louis Stevenson, for the Reverend Lewis's youngest daughter, another Margaret, married a Thomas Stevenson and RLS was their child. (RLS spent much of his childhood in the Reverend Lewis's manse in Colinton and writes movingly of the old man in his *Memoirs and Portraits*.)

Thomas Stevenson, along with his father, his father's brother and a cousin, became famous for designing and building – against appalling odds – ninety-seven lighthouses round the dangerous coasts of Scotland and elsewhere.*

---

* *The Lighthouse Stevensons* by Bella Bathurst (HarperCollins, 1999) is a riveting read.

It was Thomas Stevenson's intention that his son Robert Louis should join this alarming family business. But after a year or two's experience of it, RLS defected and devoted himself to writing books instead – 'thus', as he himself put it, 'not serving humanity so well'. RLS thus descended on his mother's side from a string of Balfours of Pilrig. Hence the prominence in both *Kidnapped* and *Catriona* of the half-fictional David Balfour and the wholly factual Pilrig House. Yet another descendant of the Reverend Lewis Balfour was Graham Greene, a great admirer of the works of his Stevenson cousin.

The Balfour element in my ancestry had a more distinguished history than the Pauls'. This was written up in great detail by one of its offshoots, Barbara Balfour-Melville, and published by Constable in 1907. She traces the family back to (and beyond) the Alexander Balfour who in the fifteenth century was King James IV's *cellerarius*, i.e. Master of Bottles. Most of Alexander's direct descendants, however, were ministers of the kirk, and one of them (James again) was one of the eight staunch divines who led the vigorous protest against King James VI's endeavour, on acquiring the throne of England in 1603, to impose episcopacy on the Scots. After nine months of fearful argumentation, the eight were summoned to London in the King's vain attempt to secure their submission. They were eventually allowed to return to Scotland, but not to preach – though the citizenry of Edinburgh paid the Reverend James his stipend until his death in 1613. His less orthodox grandson (James, of course) made quite a pile out of soapworks and glassworks in Leith and from the monopoly he acquired for the manufacture of gunpowder at Powderhall. But nemesis struck when he invested it all in the notorious Darien Scheme, of which he was the principal promoter. Its purpose was for Scotland to make money, as England did, out of plantations in the West Indies. The total collapse of this 'South Sea bubble' in 1700 resulted in the loss of *half the liquid capital of Scotland* and all James Balfour's. The poor man lay down and died, but not before composing a long poem on the subject which was found years after in an iron chest (with a secret lock) in Pilrig House, along with a list of all those he had prevailed upon to contribute to the scheme. Fortunately for his son (yet another James) the government of England, which had sabotaged the Darien Scheme out of resentment, decided in 1707 to compensate the Scots for their losses, since England was by then seeking Scotland's agreement to the unpopular Act of Union. It was this James Balfour's share of the huge English bribe so paid that enabled him to buy as the family seat the property of Pilrig for £4,222 4s 5½d from Lord Rosebery in 1718. Pilrig was a fine house just outside Edinburgh with a private avenue that in those days led through its own farmland right up to Leith Walk. But by my own early days it had become an oasis in factory land, occupied by two great-aunts whom I was taken to visit as a child. They were its last family occupants. Left empty on their death, it was set on fire by vandals and completely gutted.

That James Balfour's eldest son (James!) gave the family its only claim

1 The Lyon's clan. Sir James BP and his descendants down to Glencairn (aged four) on his mother's lap. Taken at St Boswells, Scottish borders, in 1921.

to academic distinction by receiving in 1754 the Chair of 'Moral and Pneumatic (!) Philosophy' at Edinburgh University. His rival candidate for the Chair was none other than the celebrated David Hume, author of the sceptical and empiricist *Principles of Morals*, with which, in his strict but undistinguished orthodoxy, James Balfour disagreed, as did the orthodox electors to the University Chair. Professor James received the more lasting distinction of several mentions by RLS in *Kidnapped* and *Catriona*.

James Balfour, my great-great-grandfather, had two other distinctions. First, his wife Annie Mackintosh descended in a direct line, and with a nice Shakespearian touch, from both a twelfth-century Duncan Thane of Fife and a thirteenth-century Thane of Cawdor. Second, the eldest of their children was the Margaret who united the Balfours and the Pauls by marrying in 1830 the Reverend John Paul and producing my grandfather, Sir James.

To him I now turn – on bended knee: bended in shame for not having bothered until 1991, sixty years after his death, to learn anything of his diverse and remarkable singularities. I was, of course, aware, when he was still alive, that he had revived, if not reinvented, Scottish heraldry, becoming Lyon King of Arms in 1890 and a knight in 1900, and that his eight-volume *Scots Peerage* was only a fraction of his literary output. I knew too that he had been raised in George Square (then the best address in Edinburgh) and had at some point moved 'across the water' to the New Town, as did many of the Edinburgh nobs a bit earlier in the nineteenth century, and had settled for the rest of his life in 30 Heriot Row.* But that was about the extent of my knowledge. My own childhood memories of him were not such as to inspire me to investigate further. I have grim recollections of being taken to call, and once to stay, at 30 Heriot Row – and especially of morning prayers in its oak-panelled dining room. I can still *hear* the maids rustling in to stand behind us in their starched uniforms and can still *see* the butler slipping discreetly forward to place a blanket over the parrot's cage – presumably in case it squawked 'Amen' in the wrong place or burst into some inappropriate sea shanty. It seems curious that he should have kept a parrot at all – or was it the property of Her Ladyship, as my grandmother was always reverentially entitled? She predeceased her husband in 1929 and I barely remember her at all, but I recall 'The Lyon', as he was always called, quite vividly. To me he seemed an unsympathetic, indeed grumpy, little old man, half hidden behind a sandy red moustache and always wearing spats. My last visual memory is of his chauffeur tucking a large motoring rug with animal fur on the inside round the Lyon's white-spatted ankles, as he settled into a big car outside a hotel in St Boswells. That was where in the 1920s he spent ritual summer holidays and where we were taken reluctantly to touch our caps. Indeed, it was evidently there that the ceremonial photographing of the Lyon surrounded by his whole clan took place in 1921. I recall nothing of the occasion save the big buttons on my desperate pale mauve costume.

The best story I ever heard about the Lyon was related in 1990 to my brother Ian by none other than George Macleod, the greatest Scots cleric of the century and founder of the Iona Community. The Lyon was thought to be on his deathbed and George, a close friend of the family, paid him a visit. The old man was lying speechless with closed eyes. George offered to say a prayer for him. The offer was not visibly rejected, so George decided to go ahead. Unable, however, to think of any suitable wording, he limited himself to repeating the Lord's Prayer. There was a pause, and then one eye was half opened and the figure on the bed produced the following memorable whisper: 'Thank you, George, thank you. You always did tell good stories.' Only a minister of George Macleod's quality would have enjoyed dining out on the incident for sixty years.

I learnt from family papers in Scrap's keeping something of the Lyon's standing as an entertaining and formidable Edinburgh figure. He was also, according to one of my father's rare family reminiscences, capable of righteous rages. One such he displayed on receiving London's reply to the letter he once sent there proposing a coat of arms for the Borough of Wick. The rousing

---

* Thomas Stevenson and family moved to 17 Heriot Row in 1857. This was a few doors along from number 30.

2 Grandfather (Sir James BP) in his tabard as Lyon King of Arms.

motto that the Lyon had devised – WICK WARKS WEEL – had been dismally amended in London to WICK WORKS WELL. Nothing, of course, and here I would agree with him, sounds as good in English as in Scots.

But my trivial impressions of my grandfather were totally transmogrified by borrowing from Scrap in 1990 *A Lyon's Tale*, his unpublished 420-page memoirs. This finally revealed to me what a singular man of parts the Lyon had been and how wide ranging his interests. (His scholarly tastes are all the more impressive in view of the lamentable quality of his education, which he describes in detail, at the old Edinburgh High School.) *A Lyon's Tale* is fascinating reading for anyone interested in nineteenth-century Scottish history; and since there exists only one copy (typewritten and bound) I insert here some of the highlights.

Until he reorganised it on his appointment in 1890 to the unpaid post of Lyon King of Arms – or Lord Lyon until he modestly dropped the bogus ennoblement since revived by his successor – it was a pretty undemanding sinecure. Earlier incumbents had done no serious work, lining their pockets with whatever they could get from the sale of dubious coats of arms, matriculations and patents. His immediate predecessor had been rather better intentioned but had kept no files and had simply stuffed scribbled bits of paper in drawers in a poky office in Parliament House. James BP changed all that, moved the office to dignified quarters in Register House at the top of Princes St, redesigned the uniforms for himself and his three heralds and three pursuivants, got the court and its staff remunerated from the Civil List, and set about recasting the whole operation. Under his aegis heraldry became an art form and pedigrees a matter of scholarly investigation, provoking in Edwardian days widespread interest. All four of his contemporary Kings of Arms in England were knighted, and the Lyon was a little surprised that even the newcomer of Ulster (his personal protégé), who did little, received a knighthood earlier than he did himself (in 1900). A photograph of 1894 shows all five Kings of Arms – only one of them, I notice, then a knight.

Quite apart from his prolific publications, he was an active member and often chairman of a dozen or more learned societies and much in demand as a speaker. He was chosen one year to give the prestigious Rhind Lectures on archaeology, which were published and much admired.

But his private hobbies are perhaps of greater interest. He was, for instance, a tremendous bicyclist, pedalling on average 1,500 miles a year all over Scotland and England. He was still maintaining this habit in 1896, by which time the penny farthing (which he tried) had been replaced by the rubber-tyred 'metallic horse', as the new bicycle was called. He frequently cycled on his 'metallic horse' from Moffat to Edinburgh, and records his pride at having done it one year in five and a quarter hours, which included a stop-off for lunch with friends, having set out earlier in the day from Windermere. He was already King of Arms but presumably did not mount the 'metallic horse' in his tabard. The Lyon records with regret that he was obliged to give up bicycling in 1908 because the motor car was, with its dangerous drivers, making Scotland's narrow roads hazardous for bicyclists. The London to Edinburgh and back motor-car race, he says, had begun in 1900, and these new machines filled the good people of Scotland with amazement.

3 Pilrig House, seat of the Balfours, where Robert Louis Stevenson frequently
stayed. (Built 1638, reconstructed in the 1980s after it burnt down.)

He was also a keen horseman, or at least an enthusiastic driver of equine
transport, tandems, post-chaises, etc. He even drove a stagecoach round Scotland for fun. Curling was another of his passions, a sport he particularly
relished since it 'brought together all sorts and conditions of men in complete
equality … The best player, whoever he may be, takes the lead, and a peer
may have to obey the commands and suffer the objurgations of a poacher.'
Curling was a sport for which the Edinburgh climate gave much scope, since
the winters in those days were always frost-bound; and one year (1895) he
says the ice remained solid from the last day of December to the middle of
March. We all, of course, believe that the rivers froze over every winter in
the old days. See, for instance, that marvellous passage in W. H. Auden's *The
Sea and the Mirror*, where Caliban attributes to his audience the following plea:
'Carry me back, Master, to the cathedral town where the canons run through
the meadows with butterfly nets and the old women keep sweet-shops in the
cobbled side-streets … back to the years where beer was cheap and *the rivers
really froze in winter.*' We have at least my grandfather's word for the truth in
Scotland of the words in italics.

More unexpected is his passion for the theatre. 'In my father's house of
course the theatre was tabooed.' (I like the 'of course'.) Once grown up he
went to every play going – eight, he records, in a single week (two matinées and
six evening performances) on one of the many visits he and my grandmother
paid to London. He never missed a play in which his friend the great Henry
Irving was performing. For years he was the theatre critic of Edinburgh's

arts newspaper, the *Courant*. Moreover, he and Grandma took leading parts themselves in no fewer than seventy amateur productions. In those days almost all theatre productions outside London were put on by amateurs.

Odd as it might now seem, his father's taboo on theatre going did not extend to the pantomime or the circus. The pantomime, to be sure, was a different kettle of fish in those days. The first or 'literary' part of this annual Edinburgh diversion was written by public figures like the Justice Clerk, and the rest consisted always of the jolly adventures of Harlequin, Columbine, Clown and Pantaloon, ending in a standard fairy-like Transformation Scene. The performers, moreover, were often out of the top drawer; and Henry Irving himself, regarded as the greatest actor of the century, took the part of the Witch one year. 'But the day of Pantomime', the Lyon writes, 'is alas! gone. Now it is merely a lot of music-hall turns, abounding more in vulgarity than fun.' Would he, I wonder, have been equally dismissive of the great Edinburgh pantomime comic of my own early youth, Tommy Lorne, whose annual appearance as the 'Dame' was the high spot of my Christmas holidays? So far as vulgarity went, I recall only one faintly risqué joke – at which I observed my mother glancing at my father along the row with a quick conspiratorial smile. A particularly vivid recollection is the take-off Tommy Lorne did one year of the weather forecasts just introduced by Daventry Broadcasting Station, the forerunner of the BBC. He kept running onstage over and over again to announce dramatically, 'It is still rraining in Aiberrdeen.' (Brother Ian and I have greeted each other for sixty years by repeating Tommy Lorne's announcement of the Aiberdeen weather.) As for the circus, which the Lyon regularly attended in his youth, that too was a different art form in those days. The clowns, for instance, 'did nothing so vulgar as paint their faces', relying entirely on their witty patter.

As for the public mores of upper-class Edinburgh 100 to 150 years ago, he records how the introduction of smoking cigars at the end of dinner gravely reduced the consumption of claret, since the smell ruined the bouquet of good wine and the men were obliged to abandon the dinner table and join the ladies as soon as cigars or pipes were lit. Many of the endless banquets it fell to him to attend were also ruined by the length of toast-making speeches. Fourteen such toasts were not unusual, and some went on for over an hour, like the sermons in church. As to the latter, he was (of course) an elder for half a century in St Cuthbert's great grey kirk in Princes Street, where his father, grandfather and great-uncle Moncrieff had all been ministers; but he writes critically of the long sermons, which always dealt with theological nuances and never, as he judged they should, with human behaviour. Anything under forty minutes was considered to be 'trifling with the congregation', by whom an hour was expected. Kirk services in the Lyon's childhood must have been dour as well as lengthy. The singing of hymns, and for that matter the practice of kneeling to pray, was regarded as unacceptably Episcopalian.

(Even in my own youth children in the Canongate used to dance up and down the pavement chanting: 'Piskie, Piskie, Aymen,/Doon on yer knees and up again.') And there was strong resistance to the threatened introduction of the organ. The account he gives of the half-yearly communion weekend is positively startling. It involved, at least for a son of the manse, four consecutive days in church – full services on Friday (the initial fast day), on Saturday, on Sunday (right through to 8 p.m.) and on Monday. All shops and businesses were closed throughout in order to encourage attendance. These prolonged church celebrations were, however, increasingly treated less as holy days than as holidays, and towards the end of the century were replaced – sensibly in the Lyon's view – by the spring and autumn bank holidays. St Cuthbert's parish, incidentally, was then the biggest in Scotland, the minister's glebe lying where the Lothian Road now runs; and his cows (says *A Lyon's Tale*) were frequently milked by 'invading pauper women'.

He proves to have been an avid collector of coincidences, mysterious happenings and (low be it spoke) funny stories. One of these relates the behaviour of a neighbour in George Square – a Miss Jeannie Wauchope, who in later years always 'wore a man's tall hat' and was a famous character. One Sunday, when she was an attractive young thing, Henry Cockburn (author of *Cockburn's Memorials*, the best book ever written about early nineteenth-century Edinburgh) was staying with the Wauchopes, and after lunch was sent off with Jeannie to the kirk by her old father. In passing through a garden on the way they were seduced by the excellence of the gooseberries and, at Jeannie's suggestion, stayed there munching them all afternoon instead of going to church. At dinner the old gentleman asked his daughter what the text of the sermon had been. 'Ah, Father,' she replied, 'you know I have never been good at minding texts. You'd better ask Mr Henry.' 'Well, Henry, what was the text?' 'The text, sir,' answered Cockburn, nonplussed only for a moment, 'the text was in Genesis.' 'Very good,' said Wauchope, 'but what were the words?' 'The words, sir,' replied Cockburn, 'so far as I can remember, were these: "And the woman whom thou gavest to be with me, she gave me of the fruit and I did eat."'

But the story (also ecclesiastical) I like best was related to the Lyon by a friend who had just been visiting St Petersburg. On a Sunday morning he had attended the service in a great Orthodox church and had been dumbfounded to hear the tall-hatted priest, as he passed by him down the aisle from the iconostasis swinging his censer at the worshippers, audibly muttering in broad Scots, 'It may na dae ye ony guid, but it'll dae ye nae hairm.' The priest proved on subsequent enquiry to have come from Haddington, his farmer father having been imported into Russia by Tsar Nicholas I to instruct his subjects in the mysteries of East Lothian agriculture; and since the Tsar forbade him to leave, his four sons on growing up had to follow whatever professions were available, and for the youngest that meant the Church.

As for mysterious happenings, one of those he records was a ghostly experience of my mother's. She told him how, before her marriage, she had gone to look after a sick aunt in a large old house in Dumfriesshire, where over the years the old lady had constantly heard heavy footsteps coming along the corridor to her bedroom between midnight and 3 a.m. and a knocking on her door. She had ceased worrying about this inoffensive ghost until she fell ill and the ghostly visitor got on her nerves. My mother therefore decided to sit up all night in the old lady's bedroom and see what happened. Sure enough, at 1.30 a.m. she heard footsteps and three loud knocks on her door. Bravely she jumped up, seizing a candle, flung the door open and found – nothing. The visitations ceased for a long time thereafter and the old lady recovered before they intermittently started again.

My mother, in parenthesis, was curiously prone to ghostly experiences. When she was packing trunks on my parents' final departure from Ceylon in 1921, a large flat-iron suddenly flew across the room from its shelf and narrowly missed her head. The only explanation she could think of was a large snake, but none was to be found. The malevolent iron was thrown out and left behind. Unpacking the trunks months later in Scotland, she was amazed to discover the iron between neat layers of her underclothing.

As will already be evident, the Lyon's predominant passion was for travel, especially where it enabled him to study historic architecture. For much of his life he undertook an annual trip to a new area of the Continent, and he comments knowledgeably on dozens of its architectural splendours. European travel for those of modest means was an exacting business in the nineteenth century. The public 'diligence' in which he and Grandma travelled to Italy was ambushed one year by highwaymen on top of the Alps; but though taking all the government's money they found in the coach, the brigands considerately took none of the foreign visitors'. The Lyon was not much impressed by the inhabitants of the Continent. 'The ignorance of the native population', he remarks, after doing the chateaux of the Loire, 'is extraordinary.' This was in the immediate aftermath of the Franco-German war of 1870; and the barbarous damage wilfully done to many of France's architectural treasures by the invading Germans (still occupying much of the country) aroused his lifelong detestation of the 'Huns' – the Prussians, that is, not the harmless German tribes of the south and west. His detestation of the Prussians redoubled, of course, in 1914.

His first visit to London (in 1868) was made on SS *Trident*, 'a big broad roomy paddle-steamer', sailing from Granton to Wapping. The voyage took three days. Reading his account reminded me of the last visit my father undertook to London in the 1950s, when Marnie and I were living at 20 Essex Villas in Kensington. His letter setting out his plans for this enterprising expedition covered all possible modes of travel but he ended up choosing to do it by boat from Leith to Kent and (as he put it) 'getting into England that way'. It sounded like Julius Caesar planning an earlier invasion of England.

The Lyon's architectural expertise no doubt explains both his constant invitations to the great houses of Scotland to advise on their improvement or restoration and his involvement in designing the Chapel of the Order of the Thistle (at St Giles), opened by King George V in 1911 with tremendous éclat. (The Lyon himself was a member of the Order.) For the King's visit the Lyon himself drew up the ceremonial programme, reintroducing for the occasion the ancient practice whereby state processions were led by the Lyon's court on horseback. He got together for his own appointed steed 'a decent set of housings with a shabraque' (whatever that may be).

Though obviously a workaholic, he regularly took his wife and, when these appeared, his children for summer holidays in houses all over the country. One of the earliest of these (in 1878) was at Bamburgh on the Northumberland coast, where he joined in games of tennis, then just coming into fashion. It was played on the beach, 'using small round racquets and bare india-rubber balls, the court being marked afresh when the tide ebbed'. Some of the houses he rented were in Galloway. One of them (in 1881) was Hastings Hall in Moniaive, where he made the acquaintance of the minister, Mr Monteith, 'living in the beautiful manse with his still more beautiful wife, a maid of Kent. And here we saw in her cradle a lovely baby destined to become my very dear daughter-in-law, Muriel. She and her sister grew up', he goes on, 'to be two of the prettiest girls one could meet with on a summer's day.'

It was from Hastings Hall that year that the Lyon had to pop up (perhaps by bicycle?) to Edinburgh to attend, as a member of the Royal Bodyguard, a military review of 40,000 troops by Queen Victoria, which I mention here for a minor point of historical interest. It was the wettest day imaginable. The troops were over their ankles in glutinous mud and virtually unable to march at all. The Queen, says the Lyon, 'sat it out in an open carriage, a succession of more or less dry umbrellas being handed to her by her servant, a *bumptious and unpopular Highlander*, John Brown'. Her Majesty would not have relished this (italicised) description of her notorious favourite at Balmoral; but historians might do so, as would those who have seen that popular film of 1997, *Mrs Brown*.

Twenty-seven years after that occasion the Lyon rented Ballochmorrie, a house in Ayrshire with a small grouse moor to provide his eldest son, back on leave from Ceylon, with some shooting. But (he says) 'Jack's interest in shooting rather evaporated, as he got engaged to a very beautiful girl who was staying with us – Muriel Monteith, whom we first saw in her cradle at Moniaive ... It was not for want of asking that she had not married long before, as she might [he adds mysteriously] have been a very great and influential lady, had her heart inclined that way.' He does not disclose why she had been invited to stay at Ballochmorrie; but we may guess.

In 1890 the annual migration to a different holiday house was ended or interrupted by the Lyon's purchase, from his uncle Lord Moncreiff, of Tullibole in Kinrosshire – 'a fine example of a Scottish laird's house of 1608' – as a permanent country cot. In the Lyon's time this was an alarmingly sociable area. Scarcely a day passed in summer, he records, without their attending a garden party within the requisite horse-drawn distance of eight miles.

When for some reason he ended his memoirs in 1917, he felt strongly that the kingdom's great days were over. Here is what he wrote on the point:

> I cannot but be glad that I shall not see much of its future. The country has till now been on the whole under the guidance of men of marked ability, but signs are not wanting that it will pass into the hands of mere blatant and vociferous demagogues, each fighting for his own hand without any regard for the welfare of the country as a whole. There are not a few men in the House of Commons whom I would not trust with the management of a sixpence ... It is sad to see the country drifting from bad to worse and to note the inordinate devotion to pleasure which has prevailed so much in late years. The whole aim of many people, both young and old, is to 'have a good time' without regard to the calls of either duty or religion. The lack of parental control and the increase of juvenile crime, fostered to a large extent by the Cinema mania, is a bad augury for the future.

(Not many changes needed, perhaps only the substitution of TV and computer screens for the cinema, for his text to apply today!) There I must leave him. He had assuredly 'warked weel'.

My paternal grandmother, I should add, was the daughter of John Nairne Forman W. S. of Staffa. Whether she was raised on that boggy rock in a house or even a cave – rock formations resembling Fingal's Cave being the island's only known attribute – I do not know. She certainly suffered much from asthma and fevers.

Before moving on to my mother's ancestry, there is one remaining paternal forebear who deserves a full paragraph, though I had never heard of this great-uncle until I read *A Lyon's Tale*. This was the Lyon's adored brother (his elder by fourteen years), the Reverend William Paul. Among the family papers is his 'Financial Daybook' as minister of Whitekirk and Tyningham (near Haddington) from November 1863 to September 1866, written in his faultless copybook hand and entitled 'Whitekirk – State of Affairs of Reverend W. Paul'. It is a revealing document on the lifestyle of an unpretentious minister of the kirk in the mid-nineteenth century. Every minutest expenditure, down to the pennies given to beggars, sailors and people wrecked at Cockburnspath, is carefully recorded on the side marked 'Application of Income'. The income available for such application is of interest too. It derived from stipendiary payments of £333 15s 9d in all by the three 'heritors' of the living (the Earl of Haddington, Sir David Baird of Lennoxlove and a Mr Laidlay of Seacliff, a retired indigo planter), from the interest on a substantial loan to Lord Southesk, from his investments in Scottish railways, and from the sale of the produce of his glebe at Whitekirk, and finally from an allowance for having no glebe at Tyningham. But it is his expenditure which most enchants: 'A dozen red herrings, 7^d, ... Gutta Percha tube for carriage, 10/6^d ... Cords and Pulleys for Dovecot, 4½^d ... To see Design for the Prince Consort's Memorial, 6^d ... Charity to The Old Poor, 1/-', etc. If we overlook the substantial sum of £29 paid to his wine merchant one year, his only conscious extravagance, indicated by an exclamation mark, is 'Croquet, 30/-!' He must have played a lot of croquet, for nine months later the balls are repainted for four shillings.*

One quaint feature of his accounts is his resorting to French terms in his expenditure on journeys. Entries for his frequent train fares to Edinburgh, for instance, read 'Linton à Edin^h, 1ème [sic] cl., 3/11$^{d'}$, preceded by 'Cab à la station 1/-' – though at one point in 1864 we find him sinking to '2ème cl.' and inserting a protest which reads (and invites our sympathy today): 'The fares are raised a little! Shame! and under the pretext of accommodating the public.' Similarly when, as often, he is exposed to toll charges on his way to preach in neighbouring parishes, the entry reads: 'Toll en allant à Dunbar (Aberlady, etc) et à retour ...' (Was this habit a personal quirk or a reflection of Scotland's erstwhile French connection?)

The Daybook accounts are occasionally interspersed with riveting non-monetary entries, e.g.: 'Poor Papa [the erstwhile moderator, John Paul of St Cuthbert's] was taken very ill with stranggury ... the result of over-exertion and over-anxiety on the Sacramental Sabbath.' (Stranggury, if I am not mistaken, is the painful urinary infection by which I was troubled in the 1980s myself – though not from the same cause! The poet Horatius Flaccus – Horace – suffered from it too two thousand years ago.)

The entry on the last page of the Daybook, dated 30 September 1865, reads 'carried over to a new book'. But alas it wasn't, for he died the following year aged only thirty-three. His church at Whitekirk, described by the Lyon as 'one of the most beautiful old churches in Scotland', also came to a premature end. For he records that it was burnt to the ground in 1912 by 'militant suffragettes' – surely not their usual kind of activity? It had housed a rose window designed and installed by the Lyon in his brother's memory. This and the whole building were reconstructed after the suffragettes destroyed it.

So much for my father's ancestry. I know much less of my mother's. She was the fourth of the five handsome children of the Reverend John Monteith,

---

* For those to whom the old currency is unfamiliar, a pound consisted of 20 shillings, a shilling of 12 pence. The sum of 30 shillings (i.e. £1 10s 0d) in 1864 would today equate to about £130, so the croquet was indeed an extravagance. On the other hand the Daybook shows that the Reverend William's total income in 1864 was £792 19s 3d, a substantial sum then – and very much higher in real terms than my own income at his age!

minister of Glencairn (Moniaive) from 1870 to 1886, and Ellen née Neve, the Lyon's 'beautiful Kentish maid'. Both died before my day – the Reverend John in his forties when trying to stop the carriage of a parishioner whose horse had bolted. He clearly had a sense of fun, however, for he must have been the source of the story (picked up by brother Ian) about one of his awkward ex-parishioners. Dissatisfied with the Church of Scotland, the man severed connections with it and joined the Wee Frees. This did not satisfy him either and he soon transferred his allegiance to the Methodists. But not for long, for he shortly declared to my grandpa, 'I think I shall have to give up religion altogether and join the Episcopalians' (the Anglican Church in Scotland).

My grandparents' house in Moniaive, Barbuie, features in paintings by their friend and neighbour, James Paterson, RSA. He was a well-known painter, and a museum about him was established in his house in Moniaive by one of his descendants, Anne Paterson Wallace, but it recently folded and its exhibits were dispersed. Another of these descendants, Sheila Glencairn Bishop, came up to me after a poetry presentation in Exeter in 1991 to ask why I bore the same forename. She told me that all her own family, descendants of James Paterson, were given Glencairn as their middle name. An old lady living a mile from our present West Country home proudly told me that she too was born in Glencairn. If one small village in Dumfriesshire has spread its offshoots all over Devon – and there is even a house called Glencairn in the small fishing village of Port Isaac in Cornwall – it is no wonder that the Scots have been running England (unobserved by the English) since 1707, just as they ran most of the British Empire! Indeed, the residence of the British Ambassador in Dublin bears the name 'Glencairn'. Come to that, 'Glencairn' whisky can even be found on sale, at least in Egypt.

But back to my mother, of whom a guest at my first wedding said to me, 'I always thought her the most beautiful woman of her generation.' Though information about her ancestors is scanty, of two of her lateral ancestors a good deal is known, and both deserve coverage. Her Uncle Willie (Neve), known as Nunc, was a distinct 'character'. His profession of architecture must have brought him money, though that is not easy to understand if all the houses he built were like Glenluiart (where I was born) in Moniaive or the flamboyant West Court, Bray-on-Thames, where he lived himself. But tastes are evidently changing, for in 1997 Glenluiart was, to our astonishment, listed Grade A and sold for £260,000. As for West Court, on the river side you stepped out on to croquet lawns (Nunc claimed to have played croquet for Kent) and in the orchard on the other side he kept a flock of golden pheasants. He was a great joker, not always in impeccable taste. It is recorded that he once invited the whole corps de ballet from a London theatre to spend the day at West Court, and after lunch he suggested to the twenty girls that they might enjoy a swim in the river. Alas! they said, they had not brought bathing costumes. Nunc said he had plenty for all in the house and distributed fetching little models. The girls popped them on with delight and plunged in. In the water the costumes rapidly dissolved into nothing. Nunc, of course, was standing on the lawn, heaving with merriment.

Bill Monteith and I used to go over from Magdalen College in the late thirties and spend a night with Nunc from time to time. The rituals included the following. First, he always made his butler serve us at supper with chocolate éclairs made of cotton wool, and at breakfast with fried eggs made of rubber, and he chortled with delight at the consternation we knew it was our duty to display. Second, being an enthusiast for port, he always had two decanters on the dinner table, one of the best for himself and one of inferior stuff for Bill and me.

Nunc died in January 1943, reputedly of a surfeit of port and oysters, both forbidden by his doctors. Since he was unmarried and our richest relation, his death was a matter of considerable family interest; and it was a cause of some dismay when the share received by my mother, his favourite niece, proved to consist of little more than his garden swing-seat (which I nicked from Cakemuir in 1946 and which has stood in all my gardens till today), together with a bag of used tennis balls and a box of old 78 rpm dance records. It may be that Nunc did not in fact have much liquid capital since his wealth is said to have been invested in the ownership of half Southampton docks and a chunk of the East End of London, both of which were flattened by Hitler's bombers. This may well be a family fiction, though a lot of liquid assets (but none of his port, which was all gone) were found in his cellar and were claimed by his rascally butler as having been left to him. I should add to this summary account of Nunc by recording that the sofa cushions in his drawing room bore embroidered representations of a man on the gallows, said by Nunc to be an ancestor hanged for sheep-stealing.

The other Neve relation of distinction was Margaret Ann Neve, my mother's great-aunt. She was born in Guernsey in 1792, and having been widowed young she spent the last fifty years of her life in the family mansion of Rouge Huis in St Peter Port. My interest in this remarkable lady was first aroused by finding in the family archives an account in the local *Times* of her 107th birthday. For the celebrations she invited 'the Town Council, the *jurats*, officers of the staff, and about 250 leading residents' to the three-hour lunch party she gave. A fairly exhausting experience, one might suppose, at the age of 107, but the *Times* correspondent recorded finding her the following morning busy making marmalade.

I learnt much more about her later. *A Lyon's Tale*, for a start, records my mother telling the Lyon that this great-aunt of hers had never been ill until she had flu aged 105 and bronchitis aged 108. The doctor whom she then admitted insisted on a fire being lit in her freezing bedroom. While he was outside the room giving instructions to a nurse, the old lady leapt out of bed and noisily pulled the whole fire out of the grate, declaring, when they rushed in, that she 'had never had a fire in her bedroom and was not going to have one *now*'. My mother evidently knew her well enough to send congratulations on her 110th birthday and to receive from her in reply a neatly written card and photograph. She had already become known as 'the oldest person in Europe', and Queen Victoria is recorded as having asked whether she could keep the photograph sent to her in that connection. Shortly before her death in 1903, when she was on the point of reaching 111, she was briefly 'lost' in an apple tree, up which she had climbed to pick a marvellous apple. She explained that apples were much tastier when eaten straight off their tree.

The archives subsequently revealed several further articles about her. For her education – unusually good for a girl two hundred years ago – she went from Jersey to Bristol by sailing boat (which was driven ashore somewhere on one alarming occasion). Her teachers there, poets named Cottle, enabled her to meet and talk to such distinguished literary friends of theirs as Coleridge, Southerne, De Quincey, Lamb and Hazlitt. She then went on to what would now be called a 'finishing school' in Brussels in 1815, and was eventually able to converse as fluently in French and Italian as in English, and well enough in German and Spanish; and she constantly read the New Testament in Greek. Belgium was also the scene of her most remarkable experience, namely being taken by her headmistress to the field of Waterloo shortly after the battle. 'The girls', says a press article, 'did not see any corpses lying about.' They picked up, however, some interesting relics of the dead, including in Margaret's case the brass waist-plate of a member of Napoleon's Imperial Cavalry of the Guard. She showed it years later to the Prussian Field Marshal Blucher, whose timely participation in the Battle of Waterloo had enabled Wellington to win it, when she was presented to him on a visit he paid to London.

She was certainly an adventurous traveller all her life. An obituary says that by the mid-1850s she and her younger sister, Mrs Huyshe, had travelled round most of Europe 'before railways became general'. Another article states that she went round the world aged ninety-three with her sister. Yet another speaks of her travelling in her nineties to Russia and then, as a personal tribute to the great Polish patriot Kosciuszko, to Crakow to visit the monument to him there. Maybe Mrs Neve inherited the travel itch from her mother, who, she used to tell people, 'was one of the very first ladies to venture to travel in a railway-train', and she herself well remembered the caricatures of tea kettles and saucepans jerking along, which the pictorial humour of the day headlined as 'Puffing Billy'. Her own travels abroad, the earlier ones anyway, were horse-drawn.

When Jenny and I popped over from St-Malo to Guernsey in September 1999 after seeing the start of the Tall Ships Race (with our daughter Finella on board the brigantine *Eye of the Wind*), our object was to see what more we might discover of Margaret Ann Neve on her own island. The Priaulx Museum and Library there proved to have a whole shelf on her. Not much new, however, apart from a splendid photograph of her taken on 28 May 1901 on her 109th birthday 'at 3 p.m. as the Solar Eclipse began'. Among other details we collected in the museum was a note that two days before she died she recited to her adoring niece the whole of the Ninetieth Psalm in French. The flags in Guernsey were lowered to half-mast on her death in 1903: but the cemetery in which her tomb stood 'for all to see' is now totally overgrown and locked.

It was a relief to me to establish definitively that the oldest woman in Europe was only a Neve (i.e. my mother's family) by marriage and was therefore 'nae drap's bluid' (as we Scots put it) to me, so there is no danger of my having inherited her genes and thereby following her example into a 111th year. Sadly she was childless.

CHAPTER 2

My Parents' Generation

OF the Lyon's four offspring the eldest – John William, my father, b. 1873 – will feature frequently in later pages. At this stage I will set down only a little of his history before I entered it.

Of his schooling in the 1880s at Sedbergh in West Yorkshire we were told little, save that he came first in the Mile Race and (though this must surely be part fiction) that he once walked from Edinburgh to Sedbergh carrying his school trunk on his head. Thereafter, apart from intervals for wars, he planted tea in Ceylon on Oodoowerry Estate, Nureilia. In today's anti-imperialist age it is doubtless taken for granted that the British tea planters there ground the faces of the suffering natives; but even if, as I like to believe, some of them didn't, it was a sufficiently profitable occupation to enable my father to retire when he was fifty. The long names I once knew well from the map of Ceylon pinned on the door of the downstairs lavatory at Cakemuir have all faded from my memory. The map was replaced in 1936 by 'The Proclamation of the Abdication of Edward VIII', the sonorous opening words of which, after gazing at them daily for the next three years, I can still recite. ('Whereas by an Instrument of Abdication dated the tenth day of December instant his former Majesty King Edward the Eighth did declare his Irrevocable Determination to renounce the Throne for Himself and his Descendants ... ') All these royal proclamations had to be read out by the Lyon's three heralds at historic locations; and it fell to my father to read this one on the pier at Leith. How, with his one arm, he managed even to unroll it in a high wind is one of the family's treasured conjectures. But since his only audience was the breakers of the Firth of Forth, maybe it didn't much matter. Another memorable occasion was when he was photographed by the *Edinburgh Evening Dispatch* queueing for herrings in his herald's tabard outside a Dalkeith fishmonger's, and looking as though this was nothing odd.

In his early days in Ceylon he lost several fingers of his left hand. One he accidentally cut the top joint off, another he shot off by pulling the trigger of what he thought was an unloaded gun with his finger over the spout, and I believe a third went missing somehow else. But this at least meant that when he lost the whole of his left arm in the Boer War, it wasn't as much of a loss as it would otherwise have been.

As to that last point, it needs explaining that many of the planters were volunteers in the Ceylon Mounted Rifles (set up in 1883); and as soon as the Boer War broke out, this curious body sent a squadron to take part (as they again did in 1914 when the First World War broke out). A copy of the history of the Ceylon Mounted Rifles, which my father wrote long afterwards (in 1938), survives in the family archives and includes an account of its participation in that grotesque conflict with the Afrikaners in South Africa. The contingent eventually sailed from Colombo on 1 February 1900 in SS *Umkazi*, my father being designated a corporal and therefore spared the appalling conditions on board endured by his fellow planters not carrying a (fairly bogus) rank. On reaching Cape Town a fortnight later, they were marched off to camp in 'some desolate stretch of sand and dust', where they slept in the open in torrents of rain with no tents, no water cart and of course no doctor, before moving up country to the area of fighting. Conditions were gruesome. They were ordered to leave behind all their spare clothes and even their razors, so that they soon looked, as my father put it in a letter to the Lyon, 'a disreputable bunch of vagabonds'. They all became rapidly lousy and severely reduced in numbers by 'enteric, malaria, veldt-sores, casualties, etc'. At one stage no more than three officers, three sergeants and twenty-nine other ranks out of the squadron's strength of 150 were able to parade. Various 'actions' took place, during one of which, to everyone's horror, their commander's pipe was rudely knocked out of his mouth by a Boer bullet. Rations consisted of 'one and a half biscuits a day, plus what porridge we could make out of mealies, the biscuits occasionally giving place to a handful of flour, carried in one's helmet, wherewith to concoct chupatties. Matches were unobtainable and one could only get a light for a pipe by chasing a veldt-fire or making improper use of a stick of cordite.'

The course of the war and the '15 major engagements' the contingent took part in are irrelevant here until their final disastrous battle at Noitgedacht ('Never-to-be-forgotten') on 13 December 1900, at which, among many other British casualties, my father's arm was shattered. He and three others* spent the next three days in a 'Kaffir kraal' and managed to stop being shelled by their own side's artillery only by finding a reasonably white pillowcase, painting a red cross on it in their own blood and hanging it out. They were then transported 20 agonizing miles over anthills and other bumps in a mule-drawn cart to a 'field hospital' – actually no more than a simple dressing station – at Reitfontein. My father managed to pencil a short letter on 18 December to his mother. Characteristically throwaway, its main sentence reads, 'Am hit in the left arm – bone smashed – explosive bullet … am feeling v. fit.' On a stretcher mounted on four sticks he was kept alive for a fortnight with a daily

---

* They included his mate and fellow corporal Sturdee, who survived to become a prominent Edinburgh painter. He painted the Lyon in his tabard.

bottle of champagne by the two New South Wales corporals who manned the dressing station, but being unable to do anything else, or even clean him up, they then sent him on another 20 miles to the Yeomanry Hospital in Pretoria, where the month-old dried blood covering him was at last washed off and his arm was removed. The telegram that he dispatched to Heriot Row on 10 January simply reads: 'Arm amputated – progressing favourably.' After another fortnight he was sent on the Base Hospital in Deilfontein where he wrote to his mother on 18 February, 'Arm still suppurating. Am getting rather sick of the delay but am v. well otherwise.' It was another week (since the Boers had cut the railway line) before a train took him to Cape Town; and when he was judged fit to travel he was put on a ship to London on 29 March. Brother Ian, who was later regaled with some of the story's unpleasant details, used to tell his biology classes at Merchiston School how the surgeon had had to start the amputation (without anaesthetics) by scooping out a cupful of lively maggots which, though unappetising, had saved his father from death by gangrene. Much worse things, to be sure, happened in the next war of 1914–18. I record the above simply because of my father's involvement and his stoic reactions.

He then went back to planting tea. In 1908, after meeting Muriel Monteith on a leave home, he sent her anonymously on his way back a parcel of chocolates. Her thank-you letter of 29 June 1908, when she had established who must have sent them, begins, 'Dear Mr Balfour Paul, Is this a bribe to increase trade with the tea plantations in Ceylon? Do you have to propitiate all your clients in this way? It was very nice of you to include me, seeing as I have been brought up on cold water. It very nearly induced me to drink your health in two cups of strong tea. However, I thought better of it and ate it in chocolates instead … ' (Reading between the lines, one may guess that their acquaintanceship was already well advanced.) On his next leave home (1910) he married her in Moniaive, the main village in the parish of Glencairn. It was not, one supposes, the facial charm of this rather bizarre figure with his large nose, comic-opera moustachio, cocked hat and empty sleeve which won her heart. But it was a love match that lasted a lifetime.

After their marriage, off they went to Oodoowerry. What life was like there can be deduced from the lecture my mother gave some years later in Scotland over and over again. I say 'over and over again' since the original manuscript begins, 'Thirteen years ago …', the figure thirteen being amended successively in the margin to seventeen, eighteen, twenty, twenty-five, twenty-seven, thirty (thus almost equalling the number of Jenny's lectures nearly a century later on indigo). Its tattered text is much more dramatic than anything in my own life. I summarise or quote from it below.

Oodoowerry, 6,000 feet up from Colombo, was 3 miles from the nearest road (and 1,500 feet above it) and 23 miles from a railway. During a spell of seven months after arriving there my mother saw only two white women

4 Jack (John William) BP after losing an arm in the Boer War in 1901.
(Taken in Colombo.)

– quite a change for a girl accustomed to the social round of Moniaive (see below). But the view from their house was breathtaking. Improving and enlarging the thatched bungalow – some of whose thatch 'had been there for over 100 years and you can imagine there was some dust flying around' – took them a whole year. Whereas stones were plentiful all around, everything else had to be carried up the three steep miles from the road, she says, 'on the heads of coolies or on the backs of little bulls – except for cement, which came up in barrels dangling by ropes from elephants' mouths'. The elephants, she adds, 'got to know us and wouldn't leave without a present of some Edinburgh Rock'. Inside the house she 'could sit in a chair under the cloth ceiling and watch the movement over it of ratsnakes chasing rats'.

They had, to be sure, servants in plenty, 'though not as many as in caste-ridden India, for in Ceylon the man who cleans the knives will also black the boots'. Over her five initial years there only two had to be got rid of. One was an assistant cook who was discovered making soup out of the dirty bath water; the other was her top cook, who was constantly drunk and kept throwing eggs at the other servants. Rice curries were the standard diet. These were often excellent, 'though one rather draws the line when it comes to the cook rifling the sacks of dried manure for bits of dried fish to add to the curry'. Her next cook, however, was a 'treasure'. He loved decorating cakes with mottos, 'one of his particularly heavy iced cakes being inscribed with the highly appropriate words PREPARE TO MEET THY GOD'. His only drawback was his wife, who on one occasion hurled a brick at his head, resulting in a week's hospitalisation.

She gives impressive accounts of the natives' indifference to pain. One of their workers, for instance, suffered grievously when a tree was sawn down and fell on him, necessitating the amputation of his foot on the spot. When infection spread, he had to be taken to hospital, where he was told he would have to have his leg cut off right up to the thigh. The night before the operation was to be done, he escaped from the hospital and 'hopped six miles back to Oodoowerry and was soon working on the estate again'. The tea crop had to be plucked every eight or nine days – a task not helped by the savage rainfall, 'on one occasion twenty-seven inches in three days' (surely outdoing even Moniaive or Aberdeen).

There were many wild beasts around – buffaloes, jackals, leopards, monkeys, porcupines, two sorts of deadly snakes, and 'fish that walked for miles'. On one occasion they motored through 11 miles of solid yellow butterflies and had constantly to get out and clear them off the windscreen. Once a leaping leopard missed their car by a few feet, and was followed by a 'less successful buffalo'. (Only a smashed lamp and dents in the ironwork resulted.) Insects were a far greater problem. Apart from mosquitoes, scorpions, leeches, stinging ants and 'eye-flies', the big trouble was white ants. When they returned to Oodoowerry after four years' absence in the First World War, the white ants had eaten 'two or three dozen linen sheets, thirty three bathtowels and piles of other things ... Of a leather portmanteau full of the children's toys we found only the brass buckles.' Worse still, their large library of books, which they had packed away in 'tin-lined boxes coated with ant-proof solution', was no more than a pile of dust. (White ants were to give me trouble thirty years later.) But she loved her time in Ceylon.

Meanwhile, in 1910 Monty (Cuthbert Monteith) was born and carried around in appropriate state. In April 1914 number two followed. It was christened – more kindly than Cuthbert Monteith – Lyon (just Lyon); but he soon received from his four-year-old brother the description that was to stick for ever, namely 'What a funny little *scrap*'. Four months later the outbreak of another war enabled my father to return home and put on uniform again, commissioned as second-in-command of the 7th Battalion of the Dorsetshire Regiment, training teenagers at Fovant. (In 1916 Ian was born at Bournemouth on St Valentine's Day.) In April 1917 he suddenly received at Fovant a telegram telling him to report at once to the embarcation officer at Folkestone – nothing more informative, though it clearly meant France. When he landed there, no job for him was apparent, but after some days he chanced to meet a General who was a friend of the family and showed an active interest. The upshot of this quaint procedure was that he found himself in the 14th Battalion of the Labour Corps in an area where front-line troops were being massacred in the mud. The functions of the Battalion, of which he later became the Commander as a Lieutenant Colonel, were clearing up the messes, stretcher-bearing, collecting and burying the dead, etc. In a letter to Heriot Row of this time (also preserved) he describes two quite awful atrocities. Moving into the remains of a French village from which the Germans had just been driven out, he saw a kitten nailed to a door, alive and screaming, and told some of his men to go and release it. They tried. It was booby-trapped and five of his men were killed. Later, collecting the dead from no man's land, his men sought decently to collect the German dead as well. Some of these too, if one can believe it, were booby-trapped ...

(Whatever may be true of German soldiers, I'm not suggesting that British troops are all decent folk. At Tillicoultry in early 1941, my Platoon Sergeant, whom I had previously liked and who had recently returned from France where his Argylls Battalion had been decimated, showed me privily his treasured possession. This was a chocolate box full of German testicles. God save us all.)

The war ended and my father joined my mother at Glenluiart (the house that Nunc had built in Moniaive). Their final war baby, whose sex was a grievous disappointment, had already made his appearance there on 23 September 1917. Regrettably he inherited his father's facial genes rather than, like Scrap, his mother's.

The Lyon's second son, known mysteriously as 'Mouse', inherited his father's passion for architecture. One of his partners in Edinburgh was Basil Spence, who gained fame for designing the post-war Coventry Cathedral and the whole of Sussex University. As for his three daughters, I recall an embarrassing childhood experience with the third of them. We three younger boys were taken to Mouse's home, Peffermill, to share baths with his three girls and thus discover the difference between the sexes. This was the nearest my parents ever came to discussing sex with their offspring – apart from an abortive incident with my father, to be related later.

The Lyon's third son was Cuthbert (Uncle Cub), a prominent surgeon in Carlisle, where a hospital ward is still named after him. When barely fifty he developed blood poisoning in his leg from rusty barbed wire when shooting in Belgium. Faced with the alternatives of having the leg off or dying, he chose death. He had been a great family favourite, joining in our pillow fights at Glenluiart (where we used to assemble for Christmas) with great abandon.

The fourth of the Lyon's family, my Aunt Millicent (b. 1880), never seemed a close intimate of my father's, despite – or perhaps because of – her dedication to watercolours. Her sailor husband, Uncle Alfie (RLS's first cousin), was also for some reason regarded as rather a figure of fun. Their only offspring, Margaret, played harp solos on the BBC, which we philistines evidently regarded as going a bit far. She married a Brigadier Daunt, and when he was Acting Governor of Malta just after the war, their first child was tragically killed when playing in the Residence garden by a random slate falling off the wall on to her head.

I turn to my mother's family. Until the early death of their father in 1886 the five Monteith children – Jack, William, Maud, Muriel and Hugh – lived blissfully at the family home of Barbuie in Moniaive. Amateur dramatics had already gripped my mother, and there are splendid photographs of her, lavishly costumed, taking the part of Romeo's Juliet when she was at school at St Leonard's in St Andrews. She was much given to writing high-minded but sometimes amusing poetry. She learnt, she used to tell us, the whole of the metrical psalms of Tate and Brady while combing her hair before breakfast. Much time was also spent walking the three miles to Glencairn Church, along which route the Reverend John had planted an avenue of trees – still standing – to shade his dutiful parishioners from the (infrequent) sun. At the end of 1902 the family moved to Glenluiart, which architect Nunc had by now completed. There is a fine watercolour by James Paterson of the house still under construction.

The 'Glenluiart Journal' (of which I possess the original) was maintained diary-fashion by William and Muriel and their mother from January 1903 to August 1907 and is as revealing about the goings-on of a reasonably well-to-do household in a Dumfriesshire village as is the Lyon's account of social life in Edinburgh fifty years earlier (see above). The Journal was open to entries by all members of the family, but Jack was by now commissioned in the army, Hugh was largely away at Cambridge (getting his Blue at rugby football), and Maud was not given to such things.

There were never fewer than a dozen people staying or calling at Glenluiart every day. My mother refers to it as 'Glenluiart Hotel with its non-paying

5 Muriel Monteith as bride of Jack BP in 1908

guests', and the social round is horrific. 'Seventeen callers, quite enough for one afternoon,' writes William, who was at the time 'chewing indigestible Hebrew roots', preparatory to his passing in November 1903 the exam for admission to ministership in the Church of Scotland.

Visits were constantly exchanged with, for example, the Lauries of Maxwelton, where the 'braes are bonny'. The words and tune of the famous song 'Annie Laurie' (so I recently learnt) were written not, as I had always imagined, by Robert Burns but by Lady Jane Scott, sister-in-law of the Duke of Buccleuch, in 1834. When publishing the words she lamentably rewrote the last verse, which in its traditional form was much finer and read: 'She's backit like a peacock/And breastit like a swan./She's jimp aboot the middle,/her weist ye well will span./Her weist ye well will span,/And she has a rolling eye,/And for bonnie Annie Laurie/I'll lay doon ma heid and die.' Annie (1682–1764) was the daughter of Robert Laurie of Maxwelton.

Members of the Glenluiart family, separately as a rule, paid on average four calls a day on families in the neighbourhood, either on horseback or by bicycle, and generally in the rain (11 inches, for instance, in the month of October 1908). But not all the dinner parties attended were relished. Of one William writes: 'Every minute seemed like ten, every hour like three weeks, while the conversation scintillated like a deserted coal-mine on a starless night.' Muriel also records that she and Maud were often 'condemned' to playing bridge with neighbours – 'an iniquitous institution which should be put down by law'.

But the main form of entertainment at Glenluiart was music-making and singing. William writes of one such 'matinée musicale' that 'everyone within the radius of ten miles who was not present is hardly worth mentioning, and two or three of those who *were* present are not worth mentioning either'. A quartet formed by William, Maud, Muriel and the new minister of Glencairn was constantly giving performances in Glenluiart and other houses. Much tennis was played at home and elsewhere, for example at Caitloch 'on a court closely resembling a Gruyère cheese', with curious square-ended rackets. (My own first recollection of tennis, I may insert, is of the famous world champion Suzanne Lenglen competing at Gleneagles in about 1924. She wore a ground-level skirt and green eyeshades and she served underhand.) In winter, curling was popular, but the only time the two girls went to watch (on Maxwelton pond) a kindly but overweight doctor who chaperoned them fell through the ice and the girls fell in too and nearly drowned. Much pride was felt at Glenluiart when Jack was given a staff appointment in India, and Hugh was capped eight times for the Scottish rugby XV. Reporting on a match against Ireland, the Edinburgh press wrote admiringly of Monteith's performance, not least because he dislocated his shoulder at the beginning of the second half and went on playing till the final whistle.

But the main diversion in the winter of 1903 was the performance by the Monteiths and their friends in the village hall of two plays – oddly entitled *Freezing a Mother-in-law* and *Ici on parle français* – raising £15 (a huge sum) and 'a cordial reception from critics and commoners alike'.

After two years ministering to the Scots in Buenos Aires, William came home and contributed further to the Journal. But in August 1907, alas, production ceased. Though the record is often amusing, Edwardian upper-middle-class life was not full of excitement by today's standards. Most of the domestic drudgery was done by servants, and the ladies had little to do but exchange visits and carry out, if they were so inclined, good works (to which Maud was much given). Only on one occasion did the two girls do the cooking – a banquet of eight courses for a party of fifteen. But relations with the 'underclasses' (at least at Glenluiart) appear close and affectionate. Since I have recorded in these pages snatches of my own poems, I will do my mother the courtesy of quoting one of hers, dedicated to their much-loved washerwoman, who was never happy unless up to the shoulders in soapy water. It is entitled 'The Tale of a Tub'. Here are its Tuesday and Saturday stanzas and the final one:

> When Tuesday's sun shines
> There are clothes on the lines
> 'The washing this week was *so* big'
> Oh, how she would grieve
> If like Adam and Eve
> We wore but the leaves of a fig.

> Next day, though, her daughter
> Finds her back in the water
> And happy – tho' growing depressed,
> For tomorrow it's Sunday,
> She can't wash till Monday,
> 'Oh the wearisome long day of rest!'

> Up to Heaven I know
> She will not want to go,
> For she can't play the harp, nor yet sings;
> Though the angels don't dress
> Nor get much in a mess
> She'll be washing and folding their wings.

I move on ten years to the next family tragedies. The First World War broke out and very soon both Jack and William were killed at Loos in France in the same week of September 1915, before the birth of their only sons. (These were respectively Jack, who ended as a prominent soldier and Colonel of the Black Watch, and Bill, of whom more anon.) The third brother, Hugh Glencairn – my unofficial godfather, though I recall only one half-crown resulting – survived the war as a RAMC doctor. Jack, William and Hugh were a handsome trio, as is evident from photographs and portraits done just before the war.

Hugh married a London society deb, whom I eventually liked greatly; but he went off to St Ives towards the end of his life to turn himself into a painter in oils, to his great enjoyment but no great success. They had two predictably good-looking children: Ronnie, who was killed in the next world war, and Cynthia Glencairn, who was used as the advertisement for Kolynos toothpaste. She married the undesirable Max Aitken (Lord Beaverbrook's son), who deserted her when she suffered damage in a car accident. Her second husband, Ben Welles, was the journalist son of an American politician who was then Ambassador in London and later Secretary of State.

Jack junior's widowed mother, Jane (née Wilson), remarried in 1932 Lieutenant General Sir Reginald May, who had been the second-highest General in the British army. I stayed with them several times after the Second World War in their handsome flat overlooking Kensington Gardens. Sir Reggie clearly found my aunt colossal fun and teased her endlessly, not least for her Glasgow accent and her economical Scots habit of insisting that everyone turn off every light that ceased to be essential in getting round the flat. Uncle William's widow, Aunt Moolie (née Cox), was not the sort to remarry, though I do not doubt that many men would have jumped at the chance, for she was the most engaging of all my aunts, well rounded in every sense and bubbling with fun. It was she, though no blood relation, who was entrusted with us lot when my parents returned to Ceylon after the First World War for their final few years there. More of this anon.

Of my mother's siblings we are left with her elder sister. Aunt Maud was somewhat less beautiful than my mother and never married, though when she was very young an ardent admirer wrote a long poem about her entitled 'Maud of the Manse', which was published in *Chambers Journal* in 1883. Having met her again sixteen years later, he wrote to her very affectionately, signing himself 'Your old sweetheart'. But he married someone else. Towards the end of her life Maud sold her house at Ascot and returned to Moniaive, settling finally in a cottage where she had gnomes on the road frontage. She died there in about 1948, and as I was the only male relative available I was involved in clearing up her effects. All I remember of this, apart from the gnomes, was a drawerful of photographs taken at spiritualist gatherings in London, in which faces loomed out of cotton-woolly mist. Thinking them somewhat *malsains* I burnt the whole lot, or thought I had. One, however, which she had lent to the editor of the *Greater World Christian Spiritualist League*, survived.

Maybe my revulsion to those photographs was unjust, for in 1999 I came upon two letters from Aunt Maud to my mother in the family papers. In one, dated 7 May 1933, she describes a spiritualist meeting she had just attended and says, 'The medium, Mrs Hurst, went into a trance and soon described mother and father (and my own life) and then Jack and Willie with messages for them all … then a boy and a great noise of some machine and a crash.' (My eldest brother Monty was killed in 1930 when his motorcycle collided with a lorry in Cambridge.) 'The medium got from the boy the name Len (i.e. Lyon), saying he was looking after him. She (Mrs Hurst) is the only medium our Monty has come through.' The second letter, undated but evidently later, reports a similar gathering – this time with 'Arthur Ford, one of America's finest mediums, who receives messages clairaudiently from the other side'. On this occasion every message but one (she writes) was recognised by different people in the audience. The medium then declared that 'someone called Monty who had gone over through an accident, and who had with him someone called Will in uniform who had passed away in the War, asks his aunt to give his mother his love and tell her how happy he is over there'. Assuming that neither of these mediums had any personal knowledge of Aunt Maud and her family, or even of her presence in the audience, it appears inescapable that some form of communication from the dead is possible. So there we are.

One other document in the archives relating to Aunt Maud is of interest historically. It consists of a postcard sent by her to Monty in Ceylon on 8 September 1911 by the 'first ever Aerial Post' – an experiment requiring the sender to 'affix adhesive stamps for 6½d'. Aunt Maud, however, put on only two halfpenny stamps. Yet it reached Monty successfully three weeks after she posted it.

There I must leave my ancestors, though my parents and Aunt Moolie will reappear in these pages when I joined them. But before turning to my own generation I will reproduce the verse tributes I paid long after to the pair who brought me into the world. The first, written as recently as 1991, was a late attempt to do justice to my father's efforts to get through to his sons. These were barely appreciated at the time, but my own sadly inadequate record as a father made me turn back, in sympathy, to his. The other, written immediately after the burial of my mother beside him in Crichton churchyard in 1963, is a tribute of a more direct kind.

Filial Journey

Sorting the attic in the family home
We came on a clutter of sawn softwood
Dustburied in a corner, and beside it
A pile of rusted nails and a dried-up gluepot.

Sixty years back, in secret (though we knew),
Our long-dead father had battled to construct
A box for road maps as a birthday prize
For one of us. But with his single arm
(The other sawn off in a Victorian war)
Carpentry was a craft he could never manage.
Before a bigger box took up his time
With brass handles, he must have left the stuff –
The unfinished keepsake – lying hidden there.

It had been like that with many one-arm's-length gestures.
Love in an empty sleeve. Bundles of sawn-up signals
He never could articulate into shapes
To square with ours, our rough-edged endgrain always
Awkwardly standing proud of his blunt-planed jointings.

But shouldn't we now, a generation later,
Melt back the glue, collect the wood and the nails
And hammer through time to reconstruct the object
The old man had intended as a memento
For his young? – A filial journey aiming to narrow,
Before those old maps fade and are forgotten,
The distance between begetter and begotten.

Crichton Churchyard, 18.4.1964

So the last of them is gone, the generation
From whom we sprang (or shambled),
And now their upper lips are stiff for ever.

Difficult even with brothers, communication
Was barely audible as the belfries tumbled;
And now the line is cut with them for ever.

Not ours the judge's part. Each age devises
Its own best epitaph on the obstinate stone
Before the uncaring moss muffs it for ever.

Theirs had at least the virtues of its vices,
Coherent, round, not random like our own.

Roundness surely is honourable, whatever
Corners it cuts. By Heaven, before the burning
Of the family papers, may our sons discover
The missing maps ourselves discovered never.

So now I turn and leave you, this April morning,
Most brave, most beautiful, most loved, my mother
Under the trumpeting daffodils for ever.

Roundness surely *was* honourable, whatever corners it cut. The rest of this compilation will be centred on a more angular generation, and mostly on myself.

Growing Up

CHAPTER 3

Childhood

MOST people claim more sensational 'first memories' than I can. Mine –
recalled, I expect, because it was the first occasion I was conscious of being
laughed at – was of the arrival at West House, Elie, of my parents on their
penultimate leave from Ceylon. I was three. Asked, as they dismounted,
whether I could remember my father, I naturally claimed to do so. The
resulting enquiry, 'How?', was a poser; and my mumbled answer, 'By his
stockings', aroused humiliating adult ribaldry. My father (D from now on, as
my mother will be M) wore, incidentally, until he died knee-breeches with
stockings knitted in heather mixture by M.

The incident took place at Elie because, as already related, it was to the long-
suffering Aunt Moolie that Scrap, Ian and I were entrusted until our parents'
final retirement from Ceylon. (Where Monty was I do not know.) She was the
perfect foster mother, having in addition to her unflappable gaiety a son (Bill)
of Ian's age. She kept D and M posted with accounts of our goings-on and
memorable observations, illustrating her letters with such drawings as 'Intellectual Ian and Bashful Bunty'. Being known as Bunty became a humiliation.
Being the youngest child – and a failed daughter to boot – induced a sense of
inadequacy in many ways. For instance, when Scrap, Bill and Ian went to Miss
Campbell's pre-school at the far end of Elie beach, I had to walk there with
them. Being too young myself to qualify, I used to watch them going in with
envious mortification and wend my lonely way home.

We were lucky to spend our earliest years alongside the best beach in
eastern Scotland, West House standing right on its breakwater. Not that I
remember bathing then (or ever) in the North Sea with any pleasure. The most
excruciating ritual years later at Cakemuir was the annual family expedition to
bathe near Dunbar – the whole party wearing those long dark blue bathing
dresses that flapped round the thighs, and gnawing wet, gritty sandwiches
among the spiky knobs of grass with sand blowing up our nostrils. How I
hated it! But I suppose we must have pretended it was fun or it wouldn't
have gone on as a summer treat.

It was in my childhood that I first manifested my lifelong weakness for
producing Deathless Lyrics. Two of those I composed aged five were preserved. The first ran:

> For fear of mumps
> The mousie jumps
> To get some lumps
> Of apple dumps.

The other, more interesting since it reveals a precocious feeling for visual rhyme, went:

> By Jove
> My glove's
> In the stove.

Oddly I have no recollection of our final departure from Elie, probably because we so often went back there. It was to Moniaive that we first went, to occupy the rat-ridden Ardnacloich (later occupied by the famous poetess Carol Rumens). But Ardnacloich was only a brief interlude in my parents' long search for the Ideal Home. Their respective criteria, as we understood in course of time, differed; indeed were almost incompatible. For D insisted on 'a historic house with battlements and a hill to start the car on', while M would not accept one with a basement and without 'comfortable servants' quarters'. Life consequently became nomadic, Ardnacloich being followed by Amesfield near Dumfries, then by Linplum near Gifford in East Lothian, then by Moreland in Kinrosshire, and – after six months in Edinburgh while Uncle Mouse did up our final destination – by Cakemuir. There was even, in my own memory (though regarded by my brothers as fiction), a brief period between Amesfield and Linplum when we occupied a house in Biggar called Dottyville. No wonder it has been dismissed from the family's memories. Indeed, it is difficult to believe that D would ever have headed a letter from a house called Dottyville, or even 'Dottyville Castle'. ('Cakemuir', as it figured on M's writing paper, was 'Cakemuir Castle' on D's.) Bill Monteith (who died in 2004) was the only relative for whom it rang a bell, for 'The Dotties of Dottyville' was, he recalled, the title of a play we performed in (or about) a house of that name.

Of my recollections of Amesfield I will record only one. This is of endlessly collecting blackberries along the lanes in a wheelbarrow; and there was one unforgettable afternoon when the gardener's child, a boy with a hole in the roof of his mouth and consequently no great articulator, met us as we returned with a barrowful of blackberries and proceeded to pee on the lot. I remember how vexed I felt, being by nature mean even in those days, when we were ordered to throw the whole barrowload away. Poor gardener's boy, he was immortalised in the family scriptures for once declaring that what he most wanted in the world was a 'splut hat like the Kurrnel's' (or Colonel's). It seems a curious yearning, for the 'splut hat' (or Homburg?) never struck me, particularly at the rakish angle he preferred, as doing the Kurrnel's image much good.

We were still at Amesfield when Miss McD (Gladys McDermid) arrived as our governess and was to remain with us in house after house, retaining our great affection throughout. In Miss McD's old age it was characteristically Ian who saw to her welfare, setting her up in a little house at Kelmsley, Yorkshire, where he frequently visited her. I to my shame found it possible to do so only once, with Jenny. Yet it was I who profited most from her services, partly because, as the younger pupil, I was forced (in the horticultural sense) and partly because in those days I was quite bright and even enjoyed mastering Latin conjugations at the age of six.

Linplum was Victorian and large, though (as I discovered when visiting the place sixty years later) nothing like as large as childhood memory presents it. But it was nicely set, tree-girt over a valley, with a long lawn stretching all the way to the lodge gates, on which we played golf. This activity gave rise to a permanent family expression, 'From here to the Lodge' – D's ecstatic description of a modest putt, five feet perhaps, which he successfully managed. D was a born exaggerator. 'From here to the Lodge' became our standard way of describing shortish distances hyperbolically. Miss McD's game, however, was tennis, which she tirelessly taught Ian and me on Linplum's bowling green. This was low lying and always spongily damp, and the balls we used were not the hairy felt kind but a goose-pimpled rubber model – perhaps a relic of those used by Grandfather Lyon on the beach at Bamburgh in the 1870s (see p. 14).

But it is Miss McD's theatrical productions at Linplum which retain special vividness. The first was 'The Madhatter's Tea-party', in which (inevitably) I was cast as the Dormouse and Scrap and Ian had enormous fun stuffing me into a huge teapot. Then, equally inevitably, we did *Alice in Wonderland*. But the most ambitious of her productions was *A Midsummer Night's Dream* – the whole of it, or so it must have seemed to the gardener and his wife, who were press-ganged into attending along with M and D. The cast consisted only of Ian and me and Miss McD (who was about our size); and we had to dodge about from placard to placard among the laurel bushes to indicate which of the dramatis personae we momentarily represented. On another occasion Ian and I gave a lifelike but mercifully briefer rendering of 'Tweedledum and Tweedledee', costumed in saucepans. I may as well add here the last McD production at 19 Northumberland Street in Edinburgh. This was Tennyson's 'Lady of the Lake', an ambitious venture in the drawing room, with a lake of blue crêpe paper made to billow by a pair of concealed fire bellows. From beneath the lake I had to push up D's Boer War sword through a hole. I can still recite part of my part: 'Clothed in white samite, mystic, wonderful ...' (I never learned what samite was until Jenny enlightened me seventy years later.)

Another beneficial pursuit into which Miss McD inducted us was collecting wild flowers. There was then a countrywide competition for children.

You were issued with a big blue ledger containing in columns the name, in Latin too, of every wild flower under the sun; and you had to record the place and date of all those you found and send in the completed ledger at the end of the season. The Balfour Pauls, needless to say, were scrupulously truthful, but the system invited dishonesty. Ian and I were convinced that the Ogilvies, who lived near by, won the competition by the most nefarious false entries. But at least we knew for a time the names, even in Latin, of lots of wild flowers. The only one D learnt by proxy, and relished since he too enjoyed the sound of words, was ramping fumatory. He had one equally resonant garden flower by heart as well. This was *Mecanopsis bailleyi*, the blue poppy that mysteriously grew at Cakemuir. He would toss it off proudly in the manner of G. K. Chesterton, who relates in his essay 'Showing the Garden' how he used to impress many visiting old ladies by introducing them with a wave of the hand to what, ever since I read the essay, has been my favourite flower. 'Ah, that,' he would tell them, no matter what they were pointing at, 'that is bishop's bigamy.' Bishop's bigamy has grown in all the gardens I have ever had.

D's consuming interest at Linplum was trying to coax our old red Ford up the long steep hill to the lodge gates without changing gear. With his one arm he had a natural disinclination for gear changes, and climbing this hill in top gear was asking a lot of an old Ford. Usually it petered out well before reaching the top, despite the furious 30 mph at which he approached it. Our job was to leap out when it stalled and shove a sizeable stone behind a wheel. Old teapots, topped up as required, were permanently stationed at various points up the hill for refilling the radiator when it boiled.

D's driving was always a matter of interest, not to say concern. In later years, when he decided that a gear did need changing, this meant removing his hand from the wheel and steering with his left knee. This was just about all right on the straight, not so all right on corners. Things became even more alarming towards the end of his life when distances had to be judged with his one remaining good eye. It was always, to be sure, the other person's fault if he consequently hit someone or something on rounding a corner – for example, the traffic policeman at the Mound corner in Edinburgh when his right eye and his left knee misjudged between them the turn. Fortunately he never drove faster than about 30 mph and there were never any fatal casualties, police or other. But even driving into the commodious garage at Cakemuir could be problematic. On one occasion he went smack into the door and was heard booming, 'What's that damned door doing THERE?'

It was from Linplum that we used to be press-ganged to Winton Castle (the Ogilvy chateau, near Haddington) to be taught Scottish dancing. For me this was pure nightmare. I used resolutely to take my knitting in a bag and sit on a dumpy executing endless coloured dishcloths which were sewn together (dropped stitches and all) into blankets and consigned to the suffering poor. It was many years and in other pastures before I mastered even the eightsome and began to see merit in any kind of dancing. (It was also many years before I began to see merit in any kind of Ogilvy.)

Our move to Moreland was in that sense a relief. D of course knew Moreland from his early years at Tullibole (see p. 15); but why such a house in this rather desolate area of Kinrosshire should have attracted my parents I do not know. It had no particular merits – certainly no battlements and not even enough of a hill to start the car on. Maybe it had nice quarters for the servants. But it did have merits for us children – good bicycling country, trees to build houses in and not too many neighbours. It was here that the construction of a house-in-the-wood first absorbed our interest. Scrap's notebooks describe and illustrate the high tech involved. But, much more important, it was at Moreland that Scrap, Ian and I invented the *Lob* language, which became so central a feature of my childhood.

I don't know how it became known as *Lob*; it was in fact the *Vu* language, *Vu* meaning 'wood' while *Lob* was just 'the', its full title being *Lob Vu Hognóboli*. (Those who do not enjoy languages must surely find *Hognóboli* an appropriate word for them.) *Lob* had its own written characters, somewhere between Pharaonic hieroglyphs and Babylonian cuneiform. Four of the dictionaries we compiled have survived, none of them consistent with the others. In one, for instance, the basic preposition 'on' had to be rendered by nothing less than *snubbligogilfat*, whereas in a later edition this was replaced by the more manageable *haft* or *ugi*. The purpose and therefore the lexicology of *Lob* were of course bound up with the activities we pursued at Moreland under Scrap's command, such as *ronborn canternob* ('go to hunt for mushrooms'). A notebook of Scrap's sets out with professional illustrations 'Things to do in summer'. These were: 'Baith in Pow Burn', 'Give some guinea-pigs away', 'Make path down ravine more firm', etc.

Many of the entries in the lexicon became and remained for ever part of the whole family's ordinary language, such as *Squubbery Jimpo* ('Badger Camp', our house-in-the-wood, abbreviated to *Squubbo*), *nimfez nebbicuke* ('fish and chips'), *slobjig* ('rather wet and muddy'), *slushwinks* ('very wet and very muddy') – the distinction was obviously important – *canibonáka* ('bad luck'), balanced by *glosgotanto* ('good luck'). The meaning of some words was complex, for example *rampárnocan* ('bicycling to Powmill to buy sherbet'), *ramtoti* ('go to see dam and make it more firm and see if there are any fish in it'), *rolgoberkin canternob* ('going to hunt for wharps' nests'), *rintonto* ('if you tell nobody') – obviously an important concept. One of the standard works I read years later at Oxford was *The Meaning of Meaning*. In it I learnt with a flashback of delight that it is a characteristic of primitive languages to have simple terms for complex but familiar operations, and that in Guatemala, or somewhere like that, there was a single word that meant 'To watch a negro jump over a hedge by moonlight with a pumpkin under his arm' – something the Guatemalans

6 GBP revisiting Cakemuir in 2002. Its rear face from the garden.

evidently do, or did, constantly; much as we three boys repeatedly 'bicycled to Powmill to buy sherbet' (*rampárnocan*). More of *Lob* later.

It was also when we were at Moreland that my parents identified on the top of the Lammermuirs in Midlothian the ideal home they had long been looking for. Cakemuir certainly had the four requisite qualifications (see p. 38). As a sixteenth-century border keep it had fine battlements; and standing quite high up on the desolate Fala moor, it had an ample hill to start the car on. It also had, as M demanded, a comfortable servants' hall and no basement. While architect Uncle Mouse was doing it up we moved as an interim measure to 19 Northumberland Street in Edinburgh. The latter has few memories for me, apart from 'The Lady of the Lake' (see p. 39), but I can still smell the baps that Ian and I used to run to buy before breakfast at the corner shop for a bawbee (the old halfpenny) apiece.

To Cakemuir, then, we went, after five moves in five years, in 1926. A special attraction for D was that, as with almost every castellated building in middle Scotland, Mary Queen of Scots was said to have once taken refuge there. Moreover, hidden in the corner of the low and ill-lit 'Queen's Room', which naturally became D's study, was located that other historic mark of Catholic occupancy, a 'priest's hole' (opened up in more enlightened days). From the square keep extended a pleasant eighteenth-century extension with 'good rooms' on three floors; and at right angles to this had later been added 'comfortable servants' quarters'. The large lawn at the back was supervised by a huge Douglas fir, on top of which (for it was easy to climb) we frequently ate *nimfez nebbicuke*. We may well have written out up there the third of our surviving *Lob* dictionaries, for the meaning of *slibberygob* has changed from 'Moreland Wood' to 'Cakemuir Wood'. The new *slibberygob* followed the Cake burn up towards the grouse moor. The top end of this wood, where the new *Squubbo* was sited, became the centre of our lives (by now aged thirteen, eleven and nine).

Squubbo's walls were made not of gingerbread but of Venetian blinds salvaged from the house, and an old wooden baker's van was somehow manhandled there to add a bedroom. Alongside we hacked out a small fenced garden where gooseberries (*jousels*) were the main crop, and unripe goosegogs boiled in our dirty hankies were the cause of some parental apprehension. The burn (*bo*) down below was just big enough to be dammed into a batheable pool (*durnto*).

A much bigger *durnto*, some hundred yards from *Squubbo* down in the haugh, had trout (*globbery*) in it and duck in the adjoining bog. SS *Mantelpiece* – so called after Captain Reece of the Mantelpiece in W.S. Gilbert's *The Bab Ballads* – was constructed out of a wooden crate and launched into the pool. Ian has a vivid memory of us two venturing out in it one Sunday afternoon. We soon seemed to be sinking. Just then the shepherd on the farm chanced to pass by. We shouted at him to come to our rescue and save us from drowning. His only response consisted of the words 'Not on the Saaabath day'. But we evidently survived unaided. Scrap, however, would sail around it endlessly catching the trout and shooting the duck. The rest of the day he spent playing the bagpipes round the battlements. In the evenings, while Ian and I were expected to play auction bridge in the drawing room until the nine o'clock news began or M fell asleep over the knitting of heather-mixture stockings (or both), Scrap would be up in the 'mess room' modelling and painting marvellous little figures out of some special sort of clay. How I envied Scrap's individualist manner of life! He could never be bothered with tennis, which the rest of us played endlessly.

Periodical *Lob* magazines (roughly 3 inches by 2) were issued at Cakemuir. Any new words required were prescribed by Scrap, the illustrations were done by Ian, the clerical work by me. Only one of these magazines is now traceable. It must have been edited at our prep school, since its leading article, painstakingly deciphered by me, reads: 'The ... went back to school on Thursday, the ... of January. Bad luck' (*lob ... woddy laurin halp subto lob ... grubo lut, canibonáca*). 'We left *Squubbery Jimpo* in good condition' (*It absod Squubbery Jimpo dey glosgo scrampot*).

A more interesting article in that issue of the magazine, deciphered more recently, reads in translation: 'When we went a little way to the house, suddenly through the mist we saw the most terrible thing we had ever seen,

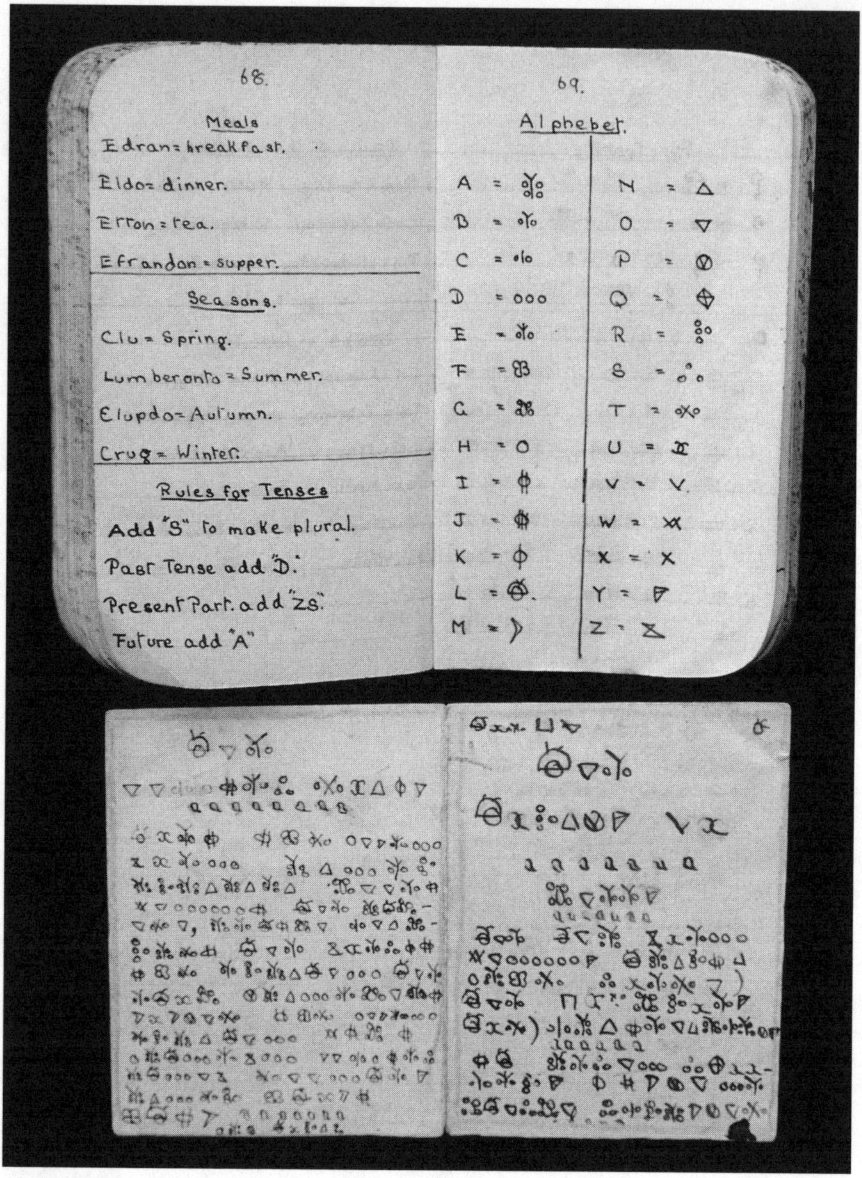

68.

Meals

Edran= breakfast.

Eldo= dinner.

Erron= tea.

Efrandon = supper.

Seasons.

Clu = Spring.

Lumberonto = Summer.

Elupdo= Autumn.

Crug= Winter.

Rules for Tenses

Add "S" to make plural.

Past Tense add "D."

Present Part. add "ZS."

Future add "A"

69.

Alphabet.

A = ⅝
B = ⅝
C = ·|o
D = ooo
E = ⅝
F = ⅜
G = ⅜
H = O
I = ⌀
J = ⌀
K = ⌀
L = ⌀.
M =)

N = △
O = ▽
P = ⊘
Q = ⌀
R = ⅜
S = ⅜
T = oⅩo
U = Ⅱ
V = V.
W = ⅩⅩ
X = Ⅹ
Y = ⅂
Z = Ⅹ

7 Specimen pages from dictionaries and magazines in the *Lob* language, invented by Scrap, Ian and Glencairn as children in 1925.

oochies running round a fire.' I couldn't find *oochie* in any of the *Lob*–English dictionaries. The nearest was *goochie,* meaning 'turnip'. But though the sight of turnips running round a fire would have been unusual, it would hardly have struck terror. Then only yesterday, leafing through our one English–*Lob* dictionary, I happened to notice *oochie*. It meant 'bogey'. But what can these bogeys have been?

One other literary work survives, on four rather bigger pages and in a totally different and more beautiful script, resembling Hindi. Scrap evidently had a *hognóboli*, or perhaps just a script, all of his own, into which Ian and I were never initiated.

And there I must say goodbye to *Lob*. The new world of children, their imaginations trussed by television, is not drawn to enterprises of that kind. (*Canibonáca!*) The passion of the young for *nimfez nebbicuke*, however, has survived the telly.

Why Miss McD was still around is not clear, for even I had by now followed in my brothers' footsteps to Mrs Crosthwaite's quaint educational establishment at Wetheral (see below). Perhaps she came only to help look after us in the holidays. But she vanished eventually. This followed the sad collapse of her hopes of marriage – a circumstance I recall largely because it transpired that her young man was the mate on the ship appointed to sail to the Cocos Islands and find the buried gold at Point X – a scandalous con which had attracted D's spare cash and, worse still, that of some acquaintances he had persuaded to contribute. This 'South Sea bubble', though not as catastrophic to Scotland as the Darien one (see p. 5), was pricked quite quickly, but not before Miss McD's young man had disappeared for ever on this bogus quest. (The Cocos Islands scandal did not, incidentally, prevent my gullible father from losing some more cash in another grotesque project, the mining of masses of gold rumoured to be located in some mountain in Wales. Though D's enthusiasms of this kind were infectious in their way, I think the rest of us felt, even at the time, that if there *was* any gold in a Welsh mountain the wily Welshmen would have got at it long before my father could.)

D was inordinately proud of Cakemuir. His main outdoor preoccupation was raking the gravel in front of the house with an enormous rake. The gravel was jealously protected from disturbance by any but the most important visitors' cars. Bill Monteith recalls that whenever Aunt Moolie and he arrived on a visit my father would be standing where the gravel began, with the rake raised, ordering them to keep off it and park farther up the bumpy slope. When indoors D would stand typing with one finger on the ancient Yost that stood chest high, his typescript being notoriously cavalier. His other activities in the Queen's Room consisted of making lampshades with the family coat of arms copied on to vellum, and composing the history of Straitton Church in Ayrshire, a literary work (all of eight pages) with which he was greatly pleased and which he had printed. It was displayed to all comers for years.

Bill Monteith once described D as 'a most lovable freak', a quality which his own children never quite recognised. Aunt Moolie was the only person who knew that teasing him was the best way of bringing out his freakish qualities. I remember him giving signs of aggrieved dismay only once. This was when he had stood for election to the County Education Committee. His canvassing CV was mostly about the part he had played in the Boer War and suchlike qualifications, which proved to have less appeal to the electors than he thought proper. He was not elected.

There was not, I suspect, so much competition for posts he did obtain. He was a member of the Archers, the Royal Bodyguard for Scotland – though he would not have guarded the royal body very effectively with a bow and arrows and one arm. I do not know whether there was competition for his heraldic appointment. There was certainly none for his appointment as County Commissioner of Boy Scouts. The best story I know which relates to his long continuance in that role was unexpectedly told to me many years later by a man squatting next to me in the outpatient corridor of the Bahrain hospital (of all places) in 1967. This fellow outpatient, having established my antecedents, regaled me with an incident at a scout function attended by my father thirty years before at the man's home, Loanhead in Midlothian. A public urinal, in whose construction the local scouts had taken part, was being ceremoniously opened by the Loanhead Provost (Scots for mayor). The climax of the Provost's speech had been this: 'Weel, boys, I hereby declare Loanhead's urinal is open. All we need noo is an arsenal.' No such embarrassing addresses, I'm sure, were faced by M in her equally long tenure as District Commissioner of Girl Guides.

For all its merits Cakemuir was not an ideal home for the young. The keep itself, with its fifteenth-century spiral stone staircase, was dispiritingly damp, and the central heating engine in the dungeon (as it was called) had to be plied with anthracite and frequently went out. There was no mains electricity until much later, and the daily corvée of starting the primitive generator, up by the garage, usually involved tying a rope round and round its axle and running with the end of it over and over again across the yard, come rain come snow, until with luck it rumbled into life. Cakemuir was distinctly isolated from 'civilisation', as a border keep obviously would be, and an inward-turning place to grow up in.

Why Lime House, Wetheral, away down near Carlisle, was the prep school we were all four sent to I never discovered. It was run by the ninety-year-old Mrs Crosthwaite and her rigorous daughter Miss Eleanor, assisted only by Mr Binns, who never changed his one dark baggy suit, and by the equally uncharismatic Mr Goss. The latter taught us history by reading out from a scuffed exercise book disconnected questions, such as 'What was the date of the Defenestration of Prague?' I mastered by this process the date but never learnt – and still haven't – why someone was once thrown out of a window in Czechoslovakia. Our letters home on Sunday evenings were all submitted to Miss Eleanor for approval before their envelopes could be sealed, so naturally no suggestion of discontent appeared in them. Mine consisted of little but cricket scores. The only one preserved records my scoring 128 not out against Carlisle Prep (who were all out for 12) and being presented by Mrs Crosthwaite with a cricket bat for so doing. Those were the days! My more lasting achievement on the cricket field was to receive a fast ball on my nose which successfully broke it and turned it from Roman to straight. The impact was unfortunately not powerful enough to shorten it as well.

Lime House was conservative in every sense. It was taken for granted that anyone who sent their children there would, or should, vote Tory; and I recall that at the general elections of 1929 the whole school was paraded along the road front to cheer the Tory candidate driving past – except for the two unfortunate boys whose father was heterodox enough to be standing as the Labour candidate. They had moreover the name of Weber, which was clearly foreign and made things worse. They were small, gentle and clever, and for all these reasons too were not well treated by anyone.

I have to confess I enjoyed school. My enjoyment was doubtless due to my being in those days good at things – except swimming. The Monday-morning train journey to the stinking swimming baths at Carlisle established my life-long dislike of swimming baths, and almost of swimming itself. The journey was redeemed only by my one remembered venture into wickedness. This was when Ian and I, awaiting that Carlisle train in Wetheral station, privily inserted a penny in a slot machine, extracted one cigarette, cut it in two with a penknife, and each smoked his half behind the ticket office, inserting a pin to hold it by. Thirty-five years later, when passing through Wetheral, I made a pilgrimage to the station to visit that slot machine. But it had gone. Indeed, the station had long been closed altogether. On the footbridge the glass headpiece of the gas lamp (also of course defunct) was smashed – but its mantle, touchingly but inexplicably, was still intact.

When Ian was due to leave Wetheral in 1929 Miss Eleanor urged that one of the four Balfour Paul boys should go to a *'good'* school (not Sedbergh). Poor Ian was therefore consigned to Wellington, where he collected beetles, played for the First XV,* and did the school record for the Plunge – indeed, turned round, so he claimed to us, on reaching the end of the baths and floated some of the way back too. In what other respects Wellington proved an improvement on Sedbergh is not clear!

The last of the Balfour Pauls at Wetheral was a revoltingly good boy. I won all the prizes – the *victor ludorum* twice – receiving them from the hands of my mother, who always seemed to be invited to present the prizes at the school sports day. She was constantly being asked to make speeches everywhere

---

* Ian retains the text of a poem about the First XV composed by his fellow pupil Gavin Ewart, who became in the 1990s one of the runners-up for the post of Poet Laureate. The passage he proudly quotes is: 'And Balfour Paul,/Good in the scrummage and quick on the ball.' Ian is certainly the only member of the family immortalised by a near-Poet Laureate – though none of Gavin Ewart's seven published collections includes the poem concerned!

and was always physically sick with apprehension, even when it was only the Pathhead WRI (Women's Rural Institute) she had to address.

Does the Pathhead 'Rural', as it was called, still go on, I wonder, as it did when M ran it? Do the old 'bizzoms' still hobble gaily arm in arm up and down the village hall singing 'The Grand Old Duke of York' and hold inexorable competitions for the best ankles? For that matter do the stout old ladies of the 'Rural' in the neighbouring village of Blackshiels, which M also patronised, still conclude the weekly talk on 'Porridge-making in the Open Air' or some equally stirring subject by singing such songs as the one I once heard from outside the window waiting to drive M home? Its refrain ran 'Ye canna shove yer grannie off the tram'. I suppose it was this weekly draught of incantatory nonsense which enabled the members of the 'Rural' to return refreshed to their damp cottages and their drunken husbands for another week of drudgery.

The only misdirection (as Miss Eleanor saw it) I followed at Wetheral was to learn the ukulele from the brash young Mr Alp, who had joined the staff. This was, for me at any rate, better than nothing, for my parents had shown no inclination to introduce me to anything more musical than the Sedbergh school songs, which D used to sing (roughly) when stropping his cut-throat razor in the mornings, and on which Miss McD was required to accompany Ian and me on the piano after breakfast. They had put Monty to the piano for a short time but he was never able to distinguish (in the family jest) between 'God save the Weasel' and 'Pop goes the King'. Scrap took, on his own initiative, to the bagpipes, and was later to win first prize in the national Pibroch Society's annual competition year after year. Ian was, in musical terms, in Monty's mould. So no attempt was made with the last in the row. Being sadly unadventurous I never sought to do anything about it till I went to Oxford, when I started getting piano lessons from a teacher in Walton Street. This initiative coincided with my adoption of the then trendy Hay Diet, which forbade the eating at the same time of any combination of proteins, carbohydrates and vegetable matter. As I had time to pursue music only during the lunch break, I used to bicycle to Walton Street with a bag of Brussels sprouts and oranges and eat them in between playing scales, whenever my tutor was not alongside guiding me painstakingly through my one 'piece', a waltz from the musical *Bitter Sweet*. One day I was careless enough to leave a pile of orange peel on the lower keys of his piano and was rightly adjured on my next visit not to darken his doors again. Undeterred I hired a piano and squeezed it into my room in Magdalen College; and every afternoon about 3 p.m., when even its lazier denizens were, or ought to have been, out strolling round Addison's Walk and admiring the fritillaries, I would practise away at my waltz. And then one afternoon the College 'scout' (manservant) responsible for my quad knocked at my door and said, 'Professor Dickson's compliments [Professor Dickson was the Pure Mathematician who lived above me] and would Mr Balfour Paul mind changing the tune?' As I knew no other, I couldn't, and gave up the piano.

The ukulele, being a less demanding instrument, was more up my street (or cul-de-sac), and I kept it up for some years at Cakemuir after leaving Wetheral, hiding myself in a small spare bedroom under the back stairs, or in summer in the sentry box on the battlements, singing the simpler folk songs while I strummed away.

Not long before I left Wetheral Miss Eleanor called me in to tell me that my brother Monty, then at Cambridge, had been killed when his motorbike had crashed into a lorry. I pass over the dark cloud that inevitably enveloped the family. His bedroom at Cakemuir was never again entered or touched; and M would be found in the freezing gunroom every Sunday morning year after year, making a wreath to put on his grave in Crichton churchyard.

At the end of the summer term in 1931 I left Wetheral with a host of useless trophies and a hopelessly immature make-up. It must have been that year that I became a 'King's Scout'. This final badge was acquired by the horrendous procedure of conducting my County Commissioner father round Crichton Castle, enumerating as I went its architectural derivations such as 'fifteenth-century Italianesque', unintelligible to me but learnt by rote. At the end of that summer holiday and on the eve of my departure to the 'grown-up world' of Sedbergh I was carving the V-shaped top of a home-made scout stave in my bedroom when D paid me an unexpected visit. Clearing his throat nervously, he said, 'I suppose you ... er ... know how you were born?' I didn't, save in the haziest way, but the prospect of enlightenment from my father was so alarming that I mumbled, 'Yes, I think so.' 'Oh, good,' said D, and beat a hasty retreat.

CHAPTER 4

Adolescence

THIS chapter will mean little to anyone who did not go to a boarding public school, but that experience may account for some of my own characteristics.

The first thing a new boy had to do in Hart House, Sedbergh, was to stand on a chair in the common room and, under the unsympathetic gaze of the assembled house, sing a song. This, I suppose, was a ritual invented to put in their place boys who may have formed an undesirably high opinion of themselves as elder statesmen in their prep schools. It was only one of the impositions immediately placed on them. Another was to learn by heart the names and initials of all those symbols of majestic power, the school prefects. I can still remember many of them, especially N. S. Mitchell-Innes, captain of the school cricket XI (and subsequently of Oxford and Somerset. He was later my colleague in the Sudan Political Service, when I regarded him with less veneration.) Other features of a new boy's initiation were observing the prohibition on doing up the top button of one's mackintosh until one had been there a year, and learning the proper response to hearing one of the five prefects in the house bellowing 'FAG!'. The sort of tasks that fell to the last fag to arrive were cleaning the prefect's football boots with a penknife and dubbin until they shone all over (bottom included), or taking a note, folded in a standardised way, to the housemaster reporting that such and such a boy, often enough oneself, had been caned. Caning – or beating, the masculine term used – involved bending over the end of a bath in the senior changing room, with one's trousers down, and receiving a specified number of whacks with an OTC cane. The practice probably did more harm to the psyche of the giver than that of the recipient. Nevertheless I have to admit that I felt a slight grievance when our new enlightened house master, Frank Chawner, abolished caning by prefects the very term I became one.

The only credit I quickly acquired among my contemporaries was the skill I developed for forging the signature of the then house master, F. A. M. Brown. This was particularly valued on half-holiday afternoons for counterfeiting 'Leave to enter an inn', without which signed document it was dangerous to be caught in one by the prefects (who didn't need permission). I also acquired more slowly the knack of minimising my misfortunes by turning them into self-deprecatory verbal jokes: bad jokes of course. Psychoanalysts would probably say that this habit of self-mockery symptomises a private conviction that one is in fact a mighty fine fellow and that making oneself deliberately look a fool, so far from reducing one's self-esteem, actually reinforces it. I wouldn't go all the way with that, for the habit has stuck and in times of personal depression has proved a valuable defence mechanism.

The main trouble about going to Sedbergh was that it destroyed my easy admiring relationship with Scrap. He was a house prefect but his new boy brother was put on arrival in the form above him, the Classical Lower Vth, he himself never getting beyond 'Remove', the curious designation of the form below mine on the 'Modern' side. It must have been a humiliating situation for him. A related absurdity for myself was that there were only two forms, Upper Vth and VIth, ahead of me in the five years I would be there. The inevitable consequence was that by the time I was in the top form, aged fifteen, I thought I was clever; and during my second-last year I was allowed to spend much of my time in the gallery of the school hall, supposedly studying the classics, instead of in a classroom. In fact I passed the hours reading any old rubbish and writing doggerel. The headmaster, G. B. Smith, a good historian, had already suspected that I was not educating myself properly, and one day he took me off to his study in School House and lent me his copy of Philip Guedalla's *Second Empire* to read. I never opened it, but weeks later I spilt a bottle of ink all over it in my study. I am ashamed to record that I was too pusillanimous to hand it back to him with apologies but slipped furtively into his house when he was out and stuffed it into his bookshelves. He must have discovered but never mentioned it. Another shrewd act of his, of which I learnt only three years later when the boy concerned came as a science scholar to Magdalen, was the following. The boy had developed such a crush on me, ludicrous as that seemed even to him, that he went spontaneously to the headmaster for what would now be called 'counselling'. The advice he received was to write a sonnet about me! The attempt and the absurdity it revealed produced a complete cure.

G. B. Smith retired at the end of my last term, and in the Hart House magazine (*The Jay*), of which I was the editor, I published a snap I had taken of him, quoting beneath it a line of Virgil which I intended as a tribute: '*Forsan et haec olim meminisse juvabit*' (Perhaps one day it will be pleasant to remember even these things). But my knowledge even of Virgil was so defective that I was unaware that the line concerned was Aeneas's way of encouraging his weary shipmates with the idea that one day they would enjoy looking back on the horrors of the past and those that had caused them, and thank heaven they were over. Fortunately GBS was no classicist.

One earlier memory does him no credit at all. Interviewing me with other twelve-year-old candidates for an entry scholarship to Sedbergh, he predictably asked me what books I read. Acting on my father's prior advice I confidently answered, 'Stevenson and John Buchan.' GBS's response was, 'Ah well, don't limit yourself to that sort of writer.' (Stevenson is widely regarded nowadays as the finest writer of his time.)

Despite the headmaster's efforts, the only thing that revealed to me my academic inadequacy was that I failed two years running to win a scholarship to Oxford. The notoriously hearty Brasenose College did offer me an exhibition the second time simply because I was good at games, having captained the Sedbergh rugby XV and the cricket XI. But I declined it, largely to avoid being laughed at by Greig Barr, one of my cleverest friends.

Despite the awkwardness in my relations with Scrap, while all this was going on, Sedbergh did not affect my continuing admiration of his individualist lifestyle. By now he was known in Edinburgh as 'The Debs' Delight' – a reputation which, coupled with his old red hoodless car (the Flying Lavatory, as it was called) and his kilted bravado, filled me in my unsociable teens with envy. Indeed, I have gone through life accepting without question his superiority as a social figure and an interesting character. Being asked whether by chance I was 'a relation of Scrap Balfour Paul' is an experience that dogged me all over the world. The most unexpected illustration of this was vouchsafed in the remote oasis of Brach in the Fezzan in Libya in 1944. I was engaged in the curious task of reconnoitring, for the potential benefit of Sudanese troops in Tripolitania, a possible route for sending them more expeditiously on their annual leave by directing them through the middle of Africa and round the bottom of the Tibesti massif instead of right across North Africa, up the Nile and across the deserts of Kordofan (which took about three months out of the twelve). When my small caravan reached the Brach oasis, occupied by Free French soldiery, the tough-looking French *Commandant* was visibly taken aback to see stepping out of the leading jeep to inspect his guard of honour a pipsqueak of schoolboyish appearance dressed up as a Full Colonel (i.e. wearing the jacked-up insignia of a Sudan Kaimakam). It was only after supper that the atmosphere eased, when he unexpectedly put the familiar question, 'Are you related to a certain Scrap Balfour Paul?' I proudly declared that I was his brother. '*Vous êtes le frère de Scrap! Alors ... *', and we clinked glasses in new-found amity. I cannot remember how M. le Commandant and Scrap became mysteriously acquainted. They did not even have a language in common. But nothing of the kind – with the standard question resulting – ever surprised me.

Reverting to Sedbergh and my facility at games, my selection to play rugby one year for the English Schools against the Welsh, and the next year for the Scottish against the English, no doubt led me to think myself the cat's whiskers, excused thereby from developing my mind. Games, of course, were more important in school perspectives in those days than they are now; but I would not have wished any child of mine to be as absorbed as I was in pursuing the bubble reputation as a games player – unless perhaps he was genuinely talented. The superficiality of my own skill at cricket was quickly demonstrated when I went to Oxford and scored two 'ducks' in the Freshmen's Trial. As for rugger, an amusing muddle in the full coverage given in those days in *The Times* to the Oxford Rugger Trial gave me some momentary glory. In the match I followed my usual practice of positioning myself as full-back in such a way as to minimise the risk of having to tackle opponents bigger than myself, and my general performance was dismal. But *The Times* mixed up the names of the two opposing full-backs with the result that the brilliant things done by the other one were credited to Balfour Paul and the dismal things done by *me* were attributed to *him*. The selectors, however, were not misled.

I was incidentally still at Sedbergh when my prep school precocity at running and jumping was revealed to be fraudulent, for I turned out to be no good at athletics of any kind. On the other hand I did – however incredible it now seems – once win the school heavyweight boxing competition. The only partial explanation of this oddity is that at the age of fifteen I weighed 11 stone 5. (Indeed, I continued at that exact weight till middle age, when I started shrinking. Today I can reach 10 stone 5 only by weighing myself fully clothed.)

The food at Sedbergh was awful and would cause an uproar in these dietetic days. Nothing after lunch but bread and butter and stewed Tetley's at 6 p.m., eked out with anything one bought at the tuck shop. I once invited over to visit Hart House a twenty-six-year-old labourer from Kendal, met at a Rover Scout Moot in Stockholm. The memorable description of our supper he volunteered was this: 'Coop o' tea and a worm. Bring yer own worm.' He couldn't believe that the nobs at public schools were fed so atrociously.

Incidentally that Rover Moot at Stockholm was the occasion of my only appearance in a rugby 'international', playing for Britain's Rovers against the whole of Sweden (where only four clubs existed). We won 57–0, owing largely to the charming habit of the Swedish players, whenever they happened to tackle you or knock you down, of courteously picking you up and apologising. This must have been the basis of my belief, still not wholly evaporated, of the moral superiority of the Swedes.

Much more important in things that mattered at Sedbergh was the influence of the man who took over Hart House for my last two years. Frank Chawner (who was also the school's assistant head of music) had the special gift of laughing at my jokes – even then my basic criterion of virtue – and we became close friends. He tried with little immediate success to interest me in classical music, but he sowed the seeds. I mention him to illustrate the one genuine value of boarding schools as opposed to day schools. For though there are instances enough when individual teachers at day schools have been able to influence permanently for good the lives of individual pupils, the process is very much easier in boarding schools where housemasters and their assistants are always on hand to detect, encourage and develop their pupils' interests. Such influence can of course be used for bad as well as good. But Chawner was the right kind and I owe him much. He came to stay one year at Cakemuir and agreed to deputise at the Crichton Church organ for the minister's wife, who had fallen sick at the last moment. Characteristically, and simply from memory, he chose to play as a voluntary a melody then popular with the young, 'When I grow too old to dream, I'll have you to remember'. The old folk who had struggled to the kirk and who were unaware of the song's wholly secular nature declared it a wonderful spiritual experience. Chawner, I should add, was not a homosexual.

I do not know whether D was equally moved by that voluntary. Indeed, his religious beliefs were never expounded to his children. (What father's *are*?) I suspect they were fairly undemanding, unlike M's. But he loved singing 'O God of Bethel' whenever its turn came round at Crichton, always had the Reverend Macnab to lunch on Christmas Day and, when Macnab died, quietly bought his widow a nice house in Pathhead. Apart from that, his regular church attendance was always marked, as the sermon began, by the audible crackle (eagerly awaited by the small congregation) as he unrolled a Fox's Glacier Mint across his knee – not actually so easily done with one hand. I also remember him, one Sunday when the local scouts were paraded, standing beneath the pulpit to read the Old Testament lesson. 'Remember now thy Creator in the days of thy youth,' he confidently began. This was followed by an awkward pause. Then he turned round, passed the good book up to the minister and boomed at him, 'Can't read it. Too damned dark.' His somewhat patrician view of the church may be illustrated from a letter I once had from him – and his letters were the nearest he got to intimacy – in which he described disdainfully how the lessons at Crichton had been read by 'some visiting lay-reader, the sort that lick their finger to turn the page over'. It may be relevant to add that it was D who drew my attention early on to Charles Murray's Scots poem 'Gin I was God'. ('Gin', I should perhaps explain, has a hard G and is Scots for 'if'.) It is one of the few poems of all those I once had by heart that I can still recite (and often do!) without effort. Since it is not easily traceable these days I will insert the text here, prefacing it with English equivalents of terms that may not be understood:

(Darg = hard work. Deeved = deafened. Pooshan = poison. Sheet = shoot. Fell = slaughter. Birlin' = whirling round. Sark = shirtsleeve. Hale hypothek = whole business. Dicht the sklate = Wipe the slate. Brod = brood.)

Gin I was God, sittin' up there abeen,
Wearit nae doot noo a' ma darg was deen,
Deeved wi' the hairps an' hymns oonendin' ringin',
Tired o' the flockin' angels hairse wi' singin',
Tae some clood edge I'ld daunder forth an', faith,

Look ower and watch hoo things were gaun' aneath.
Sine, gin I saw how men I made masel'
Had stairted in tae pooshan, sheet, an' fell,
Tae reeve an' rape, an' fairly mak a hell
O' my braw birlin' earth – a hale week's wark! -
I'ld cast ma coat again, row up ma sark,
An' ere they'd time to lench a second ark,
Tak back ma word an' send anither spate,
Droon out the hale hypothek, dicht the sklate,
Ain ma mistak, an' aince I'd cleared the brod,
Start a' things ower again, gin I was God.

Metaphysically archaic, perhaps, but we can all share the feeling.

Not that D was a great reader of poetry – Kipling, of course, excepted. 'Dayspring mishandled', he often used (disturbingly in retrospect) to quote to us, 'cometh not again.' Kipling's was the prose he used to read, too. Indeed, I have the impression he never stopped, starting again, like the painters of the Forth bridge, as soon as he got to the end. M, on the other hand, read whatever she happened to pick up – anything, I suspect, to keep her going while she knitted those stockings after supper in her low chair by the fire. Everyone, ourselves especially, adored her. It is strange that it is always my father I keep running on about.

Indeed, I may as well insert here some more examples of the things he loved (or was loved for), not least his passion for wearing uniforms. For instance, the Lyon King of Arms (his father) had three subordinate 'Pursuivants' or 'Heralds' with splendid costumes, and my father became the Falkland Herald in 1927, the Albany Herald in 1931 and the Marchmont Herald in 1939. He enjoyed relating an occurrence at an official luncheon at Galashiels. He had been standing by his place card at the table when a lady burgess, looking for hers, saw his card as she passed by and was heard to mutter, *'Albany Herald? Albany Herald?* Whit paper's thaat?' To have been thought a representative of anything as vulgar as the press was (he implied) a hideous experience. In fact, he clearly enjoyed it. There were costumes of a less dignified kind than a Herald's that he liked wearing on appropriate occasions. I think particularly of the press photograph of him playing in the World One-armed Golf Championship on the Royal Golf Course at Barnton. (He was paired off against the one-armed champion of Poland, but any one-armed beginner would have had equal ease in winning every hole.) He wore for this sporting occasion his Boer War khaki shorts and smoked his pipe even when driving off. Even his crimson tweed knickerbockers, which were his usual daily attire, began over the years to look a trifle bizarre. But he loved official uniforms even more. Membership of the Archers, the King's Bodyguard for Scotland, enabled him to wear a striking green velvet model and a cocked hat. We suspected that he also became a Commander of the Order of St John of Jerusalem not from any passionate concern for the Holy City but because this too carried with it a jolly uniform to be donned occasionally. It may even be the case that the attractions of being County Commissioner of the Scouts lay in the panache of wearing a kilt and a hat of nostalgically Boer War pattern. There is so much about D in retrospect to endorse Bill Monteith's description of him as 'a lovable freak'.

Before reverting once more to Sedbergh I will insert here a different illustration of D's cast of mind. It was about this time that I began to display what he liked describing as my 'prowess with the gun'. He had provided me in my early teens with an old-fashioned sixteen-bore hammer gun. Contrary to all the rules it was my practice to shut my left eye and use the hammer as a foresight; and for some reason this resulted in my seldom missing even a driven grouse. Just before the war, the barrels of this blunderbuss became so thin with wear that he replaced it with an ordinary model with no hammers. From then on I could never hit even a sitting rabbit – a fall from grace that the war prevented my father from ever discovering. But it was the faint risk of killing something which led me in later years to give up shooting altogether.

I was no sooner in the Classical VIth at Sedbergh before Holy Joe, the school chaplain and a good classicist, started awarding me prizes for composing Greek and Latin verses. I can't think how I could have achieved this by cheating, but it was certainly by cheating that I won, two years running, the English literature prize – also judged by Holy Joe. The precocious familiarity I displayed with nineteenth-century English poetry to win the prize was contrived by learning by heart during the preceding holidays selected short introductions on each big name in my mother's dusty copy of Ward's (three-volume) *English Poets*, along with two or three lines from their work, and trotting them out in the exam. A rank deceit, for that was all I read of them. To my surprise someone who turned out to be Holy Joe's daughter came up and greeted me warmly when I was giving a poetry reading at Pitlochry in 2001. She was married to the great Scots linguist H. S. Lorimer, and presented me with four copies of his translation of *Macbeth* into Scots. 'Unstieve o will, gie me the bityach', etc. Both Ian and I have been distinctly 'unstieve o will' (infirm of purpose) struggling through its Scots language, the bityach (dagger) not least.

To be fair to myself, my interest in more modern poetry was in fact awakening, helped by two chance experiences. One was reading T. S. Eliot's 'Lovesong of J. Alfred Prufrock' in my first study (a two-man sanctuary on the top floor of Hart House, which I shared with 'Icy-Creamo' Stowell, whose interests lay elsewhere). I doubt that I understood much of it at fifteen, but its haunting cadences remained very much part of me for ever after. The other happening was a lecture to the sixth forms by Humbert Wolfe, a now almost forgotten poet of the thirties, in a floppy bow tie. The high point of the lecture was his reciting De La Mare's 'Here lies a most beautiful lady'. The revolutionary beat of this astonishing lyric, he told us, had altered the whole course of English poetry. The way he slowly read it, with a slight break after 'lies' and 'beaut-', etc., was quite magical. Of Humbert Wolfe's own work, which I then read (with moderate enjoyment), I can quote only two quatrains from his *Uncelestial City*:

> You cannot hope
> To bribe or twist,
> Thank God, the British
> Journalist.

> But seeing what
> The man will do
> Unbribed, there's no
> Occasion to.

I cannot claim that my own doggerel took a turn for the better as a result of those happenings, but it was at this time that my tall, shambling Jamaican friend Hal Lindo appealed to me to help him write an Ode to Sleeplessness for his prep. The sonnet I tossed off for him led his form master to suspect that behind Lindo's unpromising exterior lay a literary genius trying to get out. His poem was instantly reproduced in the school magazine. I can recall only two of its lines, addressed to the imp that keeps us awake at night:

> Go paddle nutshells in the lazy stream
> Of Lethe, where the tall bulrushes grow.

Some of my verses in those days had an old-fashioned imperial theme (further evidence, no doubt, of D's mysterious influence). One, which I put anonymously in the house magazine of which I was then the junior of the two editors, began:

> They were clustered round his bed,
> The spectres of the dead,
> The men who died in glory long ago …

Imagine my dismay when the magazine appeared and alongside my passionate lyric was a crushing comment on it, also in verse, by the senior editor, Tom Smith, the head of house. It started thus:

> O bald and hearty Britisher
> Of worse than bulldog breed …

After that I kept my imperialist musings to myself, and perhaps even began to question their propriety. Tom Smith, incidentally, became Scotland's leading legal expert on rape and was knighted for it. I met him fifty years later at a British Academy annual dinner. He had scarcely changed but enjoyed my recalling the humiliation he had inflicted on me.

Also at that dinner, and also incidentally, I found myself seated opposite the philosopher A. J. Ayer (knighted in his case for *Logical Positivism*, the epoch-making book that he was said to have composed during the hours he spent in the war in a sentry box outside Buckingham Palace). I had sat nervously at his feet at Oxford, but tonight he was less imposing, being distinctly drunk. His evening's contribution to the Higher Truth (the British Academy's *raison d'être*) came as the guest of honour was approaching the climax of his high-minded speech. At this point the speaker was interrupted by Sir Alfred Ayer shouting 'BALLS!' before collapsing under the table.

Reverting to Sedbergh, one of my embarrassments arose from the fact that as the youngest son I always inherited Ian's cast-off shiny blue suits. One watershed day before the summer term of 1933 – I was to be in the Colts XI again and suffered from knowing how smartly its other members dressed up for away matches – I summoned up the courage to ask my parents whether I could have a suit of my own. This was generously conceded. 'What colour are you thinking of?' they asked. I hadn't actually got that far and mumbled at random, 'Purple.' So I was taken to Edinburgh to have one made; and my 'Purrrple Suiting' – always pronounced in the Doric with three Rs – became throughout the many years I wore it another subject of unseemly family jest.

Sedbergh – DURA VIRUM NUTRIX, the hard nurse of men, as it proudly called itself – never nursed much hardihood in *me*. I was never one for fell-climbing, much less for running huge distances; and the unwritten law that every boy should enter at least once for the 'Ten', the gruelling annual 11½-mile race ('up every airy mountain, down every rushy glen'), filled me with foreboding. I naturally put it off until my last year; and then, as the dreaded day neared, four boys went down with meningitis (one of them dying) and the school was closed down for the rest of the term. No 'Ten'.

I did, however, acquire the habit of getting up at 6 a.m. in the summer term and running with a few others to bathe in a nearby river before early prep. The consequence of this *Dura Virum* bravado was that I regularly fell asleep in the afternoon lessons, thereby (a) never getting beyond litmus paper in the weekly science period to which the Classical VIth was rightly subjected in the summer term, and (b) learning less of the Impressionists than I might have done from the weekly lectures by Lyons Wilson, the art master.

Lyons Wilson deserves a paragraph to himself. He had been a 'tommy' in the trenches in the First World War and had there developed an aptitude for drawing pictures of the soldiers lying around him in the mud. Surviving the war, he had married an engaging redhead and gone to live in a barn on a hill in Wensleydale. There he painted watercolours which he persuaded the local pub-keeper to hang up in the bar for sale. One day Neville Gorton (who later married the girl for whose hand Frank Chawner was the defeated rival and who later still became Bishop of Coventry) chanced to drop into the pub concerned for a drink. 'Gortie', who was then a Sedbergh housemaster, once told us how a broad Yorkshire wool merchant from Bradford had come into the bar just after he did himself and had been struck, as was Gortie, by the paintings on the wall. The wool merchant had gone round the room, pausing in front of each and shouting to the barman, 'Lap that oop!' ... 'Lap that oop!' He had then gone off with all but one of the paintings wrapped up (or lapped oop) in newspaper by the publican. The one he rejected was a rather different picture, not of the Wensleydale landscape but of Abraham on the point of sacrificing Isaac. The wool merchant had pointed to it disparagingly, adding the memorable words, 'And wot's this 'ere? Toop stoock in't thicket?' (A toop or tup is of course a ram.) The outcome of all this was that Gortie had got Lyons Wilson appointed assistant art master at Sedbergh. He did indeed paint enviable watercolours (one of which hangs before me as I write), but was also an early exponent of abstract oil painting in England. Just after the war I went on a watercolour course at West Buckland (the only time I entered Devon before Jenny entered my life) run by Lyons Wilson, who was then art master at nearby Blundells. My attendance was largely due to Monty Christopherson, who had taught me the Classics in Lower Vth, was quite an accomplished painter, a lover of long words, and the only beneficent influence other than Frank Chawner that Sedbergh vouchsafed me. 'That was a pyrotechnical display,' he once said to me in his memorable growl as I untied my pads after scoring a number of boundaries in a school match – perhaps one of those matches for which my life-long friend Michael Adams served as scorer in the pavilion. Michael was two years my junior and declares that I was (then) his hero! He was later to reverse these roles and become one of mine for his dedication to the Palestinian cause throughout his adult life which sadly ended in 2005.

Monty Christopherson was also Commandant of the OTC but saw no reason to congratulate me on my performance in *that* field. I did rise briefly to the rank of Sergeant; but one field day I had the brilliant, not to say pyrotechnical, idea of surprising the enemy infantry by ordering my platoon, which was taking cover behind a dry-stone dyke, to take off their steel helmets and lay them cleverly along the rough top of the wall. We then dodged round behind another wall and (as I saw it) defeated the enemy by a surprise attack from the flank. I should, I thought, have been promoted on the spot for this ingenuity, but the umpires judged it facetious and I was reduced to the rank of Corporal.

Misfortune dogged me in another field of activity, my participation in a series of school plays. In a production of *The Late Christopher Bean* I was cast as the Welsh maidservant. This involved not only acquiring a Welsh accent from Garnons Williams (who taught the Classical VIth and came from Tenby,

Pemby), but also being painted in oils by Lyons Wilson wearing a black wig and peeling carrots. The portrait was needed as an important prop in the play. (I learnt later that it had been purchased by the Bradford City Art Gallery, and I have always wanted to go there and look for it – 'lapped oop' no doubt in a basement.) I was also cast (more shades of 'Bunty') as Gwendolen in *The Importance of Being Earnest* and am still haunted by the visible distaste displayed by X (a tough centre-row forward in the XV) at having to kiss me in front of the whole school. In two other performances disaster also befell. As the messenger in Euripides' *Medea*, in Gilbert Murray's translation, I had to rush on and reveal in a moving speech the dreadful fate of Medea's daughter, looking (as Ian Spalding said to me afterwards) 'like a Stone Age boy scout'; and my appearance reduced the audience to hearty laughter. I was no more successful as the Fairy of Education in some operetta. Gaily caparisoned in a yellow tutu, I had to skip on and sing:

> I'm the Fairy of Education,
> Friend of the rising generation.
> Here I present to charm your hearts
> The Fairies of the various Arts ...

At this critical moment in the aria I did an extra skip forward and caught my foot in a wire leading to the footlights, collapsing in an unfairylike heap. More general merriment.

In view of these dramatic misadventures it is curious that on reaching Oxford one of my first acts was to seek a part in the 1936 OUDS production of *Macbeth*. At the audition parts were allotted indiscriminately round the assembled aspirants. What fell to Mr Balfour Paul was the messenger in Act III Scene 2. Eagerly I turned the pages of my Shakespeare to see how the part would enable me to be recognised as the next John Gielgud. Alas, I found that all the messenger did was to enter and announce, 'The King comes here tonight.' As the audition proceeded, I practised these five words *sotto voce* over and over so often that when the great moment arrived I was totally unable to articulate at all.

I seem to have moved ahead to Oxford without a farewell tribute to Sedbergh. It was not a very distinguished school. Indeed, one of its features was that it had then produced almost no one of distinction (other than W. W. Wakefield, who captained England's XV). I remember hearing of the difficulty experienced in trying to find a titled Old Sedberghian to be chairman of the governors. They did eventually find someone who, though expelled from school for some grave offence, had later been knighted (no doubt for another) and the problem was solved.

My days there, though not the proverbial 'happiest of my life', were, at least in retrospect, good fun thanks to Chawner and others who laughed at my jokes. I also owe to my schooldays my old facility for learning words, poetry mostly, by heart and retaining them for years. Garnons Williams, indeed, made members of the Classical VIth each choose and learn over the weekend a piece of English verse or prose and recite it to the form on Monday mornings. This had no obvious relevance to mastering Greek and Latin, but how right he was! It is one of my criticisms of today's schooling that the practice of making the young learn passages of great literature by heart seems to have been abandoned.

The only mentionable hardship I suffered was collapsing with frequent violent migraines. These were by no means of the Jane Austen type. They involved first an inability to see straight, then a fierce headache and finally much vomiting. And they often struck at awkward moments, such as when being confirmed into the Church of Scotland or in the middle of a key rugger match. At home, my parents took me from time to time to specialists in Edinburgh, but always 'They answered, as they took their fees, "There is no cure for this disease".' (There still, I believe, isn't.) It was not till I was in my thirties that I finally grew out of them.

But there were frequently brighter things to look forward to at Sedbergh. For instance, those were the days when – to quote again that marvellous passage from Auden's *The Sea and the Mirror* – the rivers always *did* freeze over in winter. Three winters out of my five the lake on the road to Kendal froze solid enough for the headmaster to declare special half-holidays and everyone played ice hockey there till darkness fell. It was in many ways a memorable landscape to grow up in. PULCHRA (if not DURA) VIRUM NUTRIX.

CHAPTER 5

Oxford

AND so to Oxford in autumn 1936 – as a commoner (having failed those scholarship exams) in Magdalen College, where my cousin Bill Monteith was in his third year surrounded by his awe-inspiring Wykehamist friends. My own immaturity was a living demonstration of the folly of not spending a year between school and university to discover something of the real world first, as well as something of oneself. My main anxiety was to find friends. Kenneth Smith, whose rooms adjoined mine in Longwall Quad and who four years later in the war smashed himself up at Habbaniya in Iraq by driving his RAF fighter into the back of a lorry, became one for life. So, in his teasing way, did Greig Barr, who arrived with me from Sedbergh (where he had been head boy) as a history scholar. He proceeded to win university history prizes without, infuriatingly, doing a visible stroke of work. Indeed, he flopped on to my sofa one evening in 1937 to announce his relief that a seventh cinema had opened in town, so that he had something to fill his one otherwise vacant evening. Towards the end of the war, when he was a Lieutenant Colonel in the Gunners in Burma, he was snapped up by Exeter College (Oxford), becoming in due course its Rector.

Outside the College – apart from Ian Spalding, another history scholar from Sedbergh, who will figure prominently in Chapter 9 – I was mysteriously adopted by two second-year scholars in Oriel College. One was the handsome classicist David Elias, who had been head boy at Rugby and who composed beautiful songs on the piano. But he eventually went down the drain by briefly marrying the louche blonde-bombshell daughter of the notorious Labour MP Ian Mikardo and by teaching at Dartington, then a distinctly way-out school! The other was the witty William Clark, who was to make his name in many fields. He was Prime Minister Eden's Press Secretary and resigned over Suez, founded the Overseas Development Institute and became number two in the World Bank, remaining throughout an enormously entertaining friend. He developed cancer (making light even of that) and died at seventy. I spent a summer vacation with the two of them near Oberammergau in the monastery at Ettal, whose monks lived off making liquor from the local gentians and selling it to tourists. But I was no intellectual match for either of them, and David's affection did not survive. The last time I saw him, when the war ended, he told me how he had run into Evelyn Waugh at Caen after the Allied landings in France and had asked him how much money he had. Waugh's characteristic reply had been, 'About three quarters of an hour.'

I was something of a compulsive swot, having realised how much I needed to catch up as a result of my idleness at Sedbergh; and this hard work gained for me an (in-house) exhibition from the College. But I failed to get a first in Honour Mods (the exam in Classics taken in the fifth term of the four-year course). Actually I failed, so I learnt, only because of the poor mark received in the first paper, Latin verse composition; and I was able to attribute this to having followed the advice of the cognoscenti by relaxing over the weekend before exams. My 'relaxation' had taken the form of playing thirty-six holes of golf on the Sunday and developing as a result so severe a headache that when the Latin verse exam took place on Monday morning I could barely distinguish between a dactyl and a spondee.

I longed to speak in the Oxford Union debates but could never summon up the courage. Less (or is it more?) conventionally, I fell in love – with Valerie Lloyd George, the great man's beautiful niece. Thereby hangs a tale of sorts. Valerie was on the committee of the University Pacifist Society, which I therefore joined. Membership was small enough to enable me to sit with her on its central committee. My devotion even led me to accompany the president and address the world on pacifism from a soapbox by the pond on Hampstead Heath – in the belief that Valerie would be present. We had some difficulty in manipulating our unwieldy soapbox on the Underground through London. It was midwinter and snow was falling. There was only one other soapbox there, occupied by a resolute and bearded ideologue of some kind; and the total audience consisted of one old lady under an umbrella and a policeman to keep order. What was infinitely worse was that Valerie didn't turn up. On return to Oxford I wrote her a graceful Horatian ode (in Latin) commemorating the occasion. Its last line, *Audiebat exiguissima multitudo* (There listened a most exiguous multitude) struck me as especially felicitous. But it was of no avail in advancing my cause, for Valerie knew no Latin. She ultimately married an economic statistician in Jesus College ...

Coincident with all this I also joined, in my desire to learn to ride a horse, the University Cavalry Corps. This involved the ludicrous practice of sword drill and attending horse parades before breakfast. Having missed the first of these owing to my failure to get out of bed in time, I was instructed to fall in the following morning. By a supreme effort I got there, only to find that this was the day for the advanced squad. We were required to canter without stirrups round the field, jumping over alarming obstacles; and I ended up ignominiously under my horse's head clinging to its mane. But the end of my career as a cavalryman came about for a different reason. The Commandant of the Corps, having heard of my pacifist involvement, wrote me a stiff letter saying that I was in honour bound to choose between the two. I naturally opted for pacifism (and Valerie). His terse reply read memorably, 'Sir, You have broken a gentleman's agreement. Kindly return your breeches to the Armoury.'

After Honour Mods I moved on to the second part of 'Greats' (Lit. Hum., or in translation 'the more humane letters'). I was tutored for this by an ancient historian and a philosopher. My historian, Michael Parker, was interested in me initially because his father had been a close friend of the Lyon, but we became genuine friends and I twice stayed with him in his cottage (opposite the Duke of Argyll's larger one) on Loch Fyne. He regularly sent me throughout the war parcels of books.

My philosophy tutor, *per contra*, scared me stiff, not only because Kant and suchlike, as I struggled round their peripheries in German, seemed impenetrable, but even more because the dreaded John Austin never let me read out more than the first paragraph of my weekly essay before tearing it all to pieces. Imagine my astonishment when in the summer of 1939, at the end-of-term ritual that involved filing up to the College President to hear one's tutor's reports on one's progress, John Austin said, 'I see no reason why Mr Balfour Paul should not obtain a first'! Fortunately the war then broke out and saved him from having committed for once in his life a total misjudgement. The last I saw of this brilliant Aristotelian, who had half a dozen eastern European languages at his command as well, was at my medical examination when I was called up for military service. There was this great intellectual employed by our inscrutable government to hand urinal vases to recruits. How on earth, as I asked myself on many occasions over the next five years, did we ever win a war? Or did the Germans employ people like Kant for similar abject purposes?

I mentioned above my vain struggles with Kant in the original language. This needs explaining. I had soon found that the most important books on ancient history as well as on philosophy were all written in that dreadful tongue and I concluded that I must at least acquire a nodding acquaintance with it. So I used to spend my lonely winter holidays at Cakemuir walking over the moors learning German word lists; and fortified with this I spent one summer in Dresden and the next in Bonn, staying with German widows who taught the language. Dresden was full of jackbooted young Prussians striding around and exchanging Nazi salutes. The Jewish doctor who lived in the flat below and had looked after my hostess and her family for years was by now disdainfully ostracised by them as untouchable. But not even this aroused in me any serious political concern, and I had no qualms about going to Bonn the following summer (1938). This was precisely when Neville Chamberlain reached his controversial 'Peace in our time' agreement with Hitler, and most British residents in Germany (so I learnt later) wisely cut and ran. I simply stayed where I was, engrossed in the attempt to master Goethe and Schiller. Had it not been for Chamberlain's postponement of hostilities I would doubtless have spent the war interned in a German prison camp.

My other venture into the foreign languages of Europe was melodramatic in a more amusing way. At a tea party (in John Masefield's house!) on Boars Hill I met a rather dazzling Italian girl from Florence, who looked almost as romantic as her name, which was Angelina Nannarone di Santa Vittoria. She told me she was trying to find students to teach Italian to, in order to buy her ticket home. I gaily said I would find lots. I found none, and felt morally obliged to fork out 2s 6d an hour for lessons myself. She became ostensibly attached to me and asked whether she could come and spend a fortnight at Cakemuir. ('What's that?' said my father. '*Foreigners* in the house?') She came, and we spent several days stretched in the heather at a proper distance from each other, practising irregular verbs. On what turned out to be the last of these occasions she rolled over and astonished me by saying, 'What pretty eyelashes you have!' (Mine are in fact short and boring.) And she followed this up with, 'You don't know what you're missing.' To my credit (if anyone can believe this) I didn't. Anyway, the following morning at breakfast a telegram came for her. She opened it and went rushing out of the room in tears. My mother solicitously followed her – and the truth came out. In Italy, she told my mother, she had been under pursuit by a Neapolitan duke whom she detested. To escape his attentions she had flown to Bournemouth, letting it be known indirectly to her pursuer that she had gone to Madras. In Bournemouth she had received from the indefatigable *duca* a letter forwarded from her home address, saying '*Sono in Madras. Dove tu?*' (I'm in Madras. Where are you?) She had of course not replied but had judged it discreet to decamp to Oxford. In Oxford another letter from her pursuer reached her in the same way from Bournemouth. And this was why, fearing that the pursuit was getting uncomfortably close, she had asked whether she could come to Cakemuir. The telegram she received at that dramatic breakfast, which M brought down and showed us, was from Oxford and read, 'Carissima, I will have you, dead or alive.' D, who had a soft spot for any young lady who was not, in his own expression, a 'scone-faced wench', bought her an air ticket to Florence. Then the war began, and Angelina passed out of my life. The whole episode confirmed my belief in the oddity of the Latin races and may explain why I was always able to speak my halting Italian – unlike my equally halting German and French – with complete abandon, feeling the whole exercise to be pure *opera buffa*.

Moving out of College (to revert to 1937), I shared lodgings with Kenneth Smith. He disapproved of my slogging away at nights on such esoteric problems as 'The dating of the Battle of Plataea from primary sources'; and while I struggled with them, he would be on his knees on the carpet propelling a shoehorn in and out of the legs of my chair and grunting '*Shoo*-shoo-shoo-shoo … *Shoo*-shoo-shoo-shoo'. He was assuredly an influence for good.

However much I may, despite Kenneth, have slogged away in the evenings and zealously attended lectures in the mornings (acquiring thereby a genuine love of Horace and Aristophanes), I cannot have done much academic work in the afternoons. Apart from other activities, I spent endless hours on the college cricket field. Indeed, I captained the college XI and even took it on a tour of England, playing against the 'Gentlemen' of sundry counties and almost scoring a century in Yorkshire. I also enjoyed punting on the Cher, though so incompetently that I once knocked my bicycle out of the punt into the muddy depths and had to buy a replacement. More enterprisingly I made the joint purchase with Greig Barr of an old T-model Ford for £25 and explored a lot of Oxfordshire in it. In the manner of Toad of Toad Hall I once loaded it into a rowing boat to cross the Thames in a remote area and found I had punctured a tyre in the process. It was no simple job collecting enough local farm hands to lift it bodily out of the boat on to dry land. Our ancient Ford was one of those long-forgotten models in which gear changes were operated with a rackety noise by means of a long handle outside the driver's door. We called it 'Wi Tin Po', which Ian Spalding insisted was the name of a character in Somerset Maugham's play *The Moon and Sixpence* – also performed at Sedbergh – of whom another of the characters made the memorable announcement (so Ian said), 'Wi Tin Po also died drunk, he tried to embrace the moon in the Yellow River.'

But my Wi Tin Po died in a less romantic manner. He was lent one summer holidays for a tour of Scotland to Julian Symonds (the president of the Pacifist Society, with whom I had addressed the world on Hampstead Heath), for Greig didn't need it and I was away in St-Malo studying Plato and improving my French. Into my room there one morning walked Julian Symonds. A young man of high principle (later becoming one of Gandhi's private secretaries), he had flown from Britain to confess to me that Wi Tin Po had expired on the summit of Glencoe. Even a Scottish mechanic had declared it 'not worth salvaging'. And there, I imagine, it still is, rusting in the heather. Greig, who had money, bought himself a Rover, while I reverted sadly to my bicycle.

On another disturbing morning in St-Malo when I was closeted with Plato, I found I couldn't see to read. My hostess advised me to visit an optician in the town. The optician told me I needed spectacles and sold me an impressive tortoiseshell pair. I wore them dutifully for the next five years and then, passing through Cairo as a soldier, I broke a lens. I took them to an Egyptian optician (see p. 100 for the quite separate melodrama that resulted), who examined them to establish what magnification they had. They turned out to be simple bottle glass. By this time I did need real spectacles for reading, but I have never trusted French opticians since.

During my years at Oxford I was patronised by the remarkable Dacre Balsdon, a Roman historian of Exeter College, perhaps because he had originally taught at Sedbergh and felt a loyal concern for its products. His preference for the male sex, though not disclosed to *me*, was evidently common knowledge in Exeter College, for in 1991 Greig Barr (then its Rector) told me a disgraceful but amusing story of how the Queen of Spain had recently dined in the College hall. In his speech of welcome the Rector had observed that this was the first time a queen had dined there. At this a voice from the back of the hall had shouted, 'What about Dacre?' And everyone, except the Queen of Spain who was wholly unsighted, had burst into wicked laughter. Dacre fortunately had died a year before.

But he was a notorious wit, circulating or inventing many famous Oxford stories. One that I recall him telling me was of an aged Balliol professor who was pathologically terrified of the motorised traffic that had for some decades invaded the centre of his ivory world. He had consequently never ventured to cross Oxford High Street in living memory. Then one 11 November (Remembrance Day) he had received a summons to attend a luncheon in Christchurch College in honour of a royal visitor. A posse of Balliol dons ingeniously herded him across the High Street during the two minutes' silence, when the custom then was for all traffic to stop as an act of Remembrance. But no means, Dacre alleged, were ever found of getting him back again.

With one year to go before my dreaded finals I was sitting by the window of the mess room at Cakemuir in late September 1939 reading Broad's *Mind and Its Place in Nature*. I was at page 531 when Scrap walked in and remarked in a throwaway manner, 'Well, it's begun.' What had begun was the evacuation of children from the cities of Britain on the eve of the declaration of the Second World War. I placed a scrap of paper at page 531 of Broad, imagining that it would be some time before I would be in a position to finish the book. I was never to open it again.

The War Years

CHAPTER 6

Colchester and Tillicoultry

ONLY a few days had followed Scrap's throwaway announcement before I received a call-up summons to report for medical inspection in Oxford. It seemed a curious policy to mobilise and train as officers the youngest adult age group first, with the result that boys like me were to find themselves senior in rank to older age groups called up later. Presumably the object was to avoid disrupting industry and the social services for as long as possible. Having passed the medical test (filling the urinal vase handed to me by my philosophy tutor – see above), I was dispatched to an OCTU (Officer Cadet Training Unit) at Colchester to experience for three months a mixture of hell and hilarity. Somehow my adolescent disdain for regular officers as failed adults had to be reconciled with my boy scout devotion to King and Country. The swing from ridicule to recognition of the seriousness of the profession of arms took time. At the start there was plenty of ridicule.

Almost the first thing we were taught – trench warfare being the expected mode – was how to dig by numbers: 'On the command One, HANDLE LOW. On the command Two, SWING AND FILL. On the command Three, SWING AND THROW.' I knew I could dig a trench in Flanders or wherever far better without the complication of having to do it by numbers. At bayonet drill, when we were faced with a row of stuffed sacks disguised as men or women, I was, for lack of imagination, more responsive. 'At the Left Breast, point and remain – Point!' Around me other undergraduates, on that order, simply fainted and fell into the snow. (It was a dreadful winter.) But not the valiant Balfour Paul.

He had, however, other problems in common with the rest of the trainees. One consequence of the wintry conditions was that all the loos in our barracks froze and were nailed up. What could one do after breakfast but use a slit trench? Unfairly, I still think, I was put on a charge for being caught committing this offence. For a crime of a different kind I was also arrested a little more reasonably. For during such leisure hours as we were granted it was my habit to wander through the streets of Colchester reading a paperback, oblivious to all around me; and in these circumstances I was arrested one day on the curious charge of 'Saluting an Officer with a Penguin' under the catch-all Section 40 of the Army Act (Conduct Prejudicial to Good Order and Military Discipline).

In general I promised poorly as a military figure. I suffered especially from my inability to project my reedy tenor farther than about 20 yards; and having to drill the whole company on the vast parade ground was a regular terror. On one such occasion it fell to me, standing isolated beside the implacable Sergeant-Major, to shout orders to the whole parade as they marched this way and that. A climax was reached when the company in 'Extended Order' approached the main road at the far end of the parade ground. 'Tell them to about turn,' said the Sergeant-Major. 'About turn!' I screamed. No response. Another 10 yards and thirty promising future officers would be mowed down by lorries thundering past. 'ABOUT TURN! ABOUT TURN!' On they marched. Two yards left. At this point, just as they reached the pavement, the impassive Sergeant-Major, without so much as raising his voice, barked 'About turn!' – and about they turned. The Sergeant-Major looked at me standing in my pool of sweat ... and sucked his teeth. This fearful experience still goes on in my nightmares. The Charge of the Light Brigade was by comparison the merest frolic.

After a month of this and other traumas we all had to file into the Company Commander's office for our first reports to be read out to us. This was mine: 'Balfour Paul. Dirty in appearance and also, I think, in mind.' Smartness of appearance was indeed difficult since all our civilian clothes had had to be handed in on arrival in exchange for a pair of second-hand slacks and a battledress jacket. But I never discovered what justification Captain X thought he had for the second part of his report. We were then graded by merit into three platoons. My place was second bottom of the bottom section in the bottom platoon. Below me was only Woodrow Wyatt, the notorious future Labour MP and Tory lord, who was so obstinately unmilitary that he was, I believe, never commissioned at all.

I was gradually to redeem myself, by luck rather than merit. At a Quiz of Military Knowledge my platoon was stood in line (myself, of course, second to the end of it) for questions to be fired at us. If the man at the top didn't know the answer, the question was repeated down the line and the man who gave the correct answer moved to the top. At one point the question fired was 'How many Lance Corporals are there in a mobile bath unit?' Everyone above me in the line shook his head. 'Two,' I barked, snatching a number out of the empty air; and Balfour Paul moved to the top of the platoon amid murmurs of admiration for his detailed knowledge of army structure. The distinction didn't last, of course; but in the last week before final success or failure was to be announced, I was allotted the role of Company Commander in a TEWT (Tactical Exercise Without Troops). The orders I gave for the company's attack were judged battlesome and I scraped a commission in HM Armed Forces. Whether relevant or not, my Platoon Sergeant told me that I had obtained very helpful reports from him and the other regular NCOs by having knitted a pair of braces for each of them embroidered with marigolds down the front.

Before departure we were filed in again and asked which 'arm of the service' we would prefer to join. I still didn't quite know what 'arm of the service' meant, and all I could think of saying was 'The Argyll and Sutherland Highlanders', simply because I liked the noise the words made. This wasn't the kind of answer required, but the fact that someone actually *wanted* to serve in the PBI (the 'Poor Bloody Infantry') was evidently such a pleasant surprise that off I was sent early in January 1940 with a Second Lieutenant's badge on my shoulder to the training wing of the Argylls, at Tillicoultry in the now vanished county of Clackmannanshire.

There didn't seem to be anything very demanding to do there. I was put in charge of the officers' mess hens. I read a lot of Baudelaire in the library of a friend of Aunt Moolie's who lived in the village. Then I was detailed to take command of a newly invented thing called the tank-hunting platoon. This suited me down to the ground, since I and my merry men were issued with bicycles, rolls of concertina wire and wooden imitation anti-tank mines tied together with string; and all we had to do was to bicycle around the county hiding these absurdities in suitable locations and then taking them away again. I gained favour with my platoon by so planning our exercises that we always ended up in a pub, where we played a card game I had laboriously invented to teach us to identify different species of German tank. But I doubt whether my tank-hunting platoon would have greatly inconvenienced a panzer division if the Germans had landed in the Firth of Forth. That was something we had to discourage in a less agreeable way at night-time by occasionally manning sandbag emplacements overlooking the Firth, armed with imitation rifles made of wood. There weren't enough real ones to go round in Scotland. We wouldn't have proved much more of a deterrent than the LDV (Local Defence Volunteers), rechristened the 'Home Guard' by Churchill, and later rechristened again 'Dad's Army' by the BBC. (My own dad was a stalwart member of it; indeed, he apparently commanded its Midlothian battalion.) *They* were armed with a few shotguns and medieval pikes commandeered from stately homes. It was a bad day in D's life when in 1943, having turned seventy, he was superannuated even from the Home Guard. But at least he became chairman of the Scottish–Polish Society, for which he received from the Polish government-in-exile the Commanders Cross of *Polonia Restituta*.

Major Crystal, the Irish Fusilier who commanded at Tillicoultry, was the first regular officer to win my heart. This he did one evening at supper in the mess when, hearing that I had a weakness for poetry, he took a silver pencil from his pocket and wrote on a paper napkin a line of poetry he had learnt in Burma. He pushed it across the table to me, saying it was the best line ever written. It read: 'And all the pathways of the birds are filled with rain.' Not bad really. It was about this time, incidentally, that Henry Reed entered, so to speak, my life when I read in the *Spectator* his spoof 'Wartime Broadcast by T. S. Eliot', entitled 'Charred Whitlow'. It begins:

As we get older we do not get any younger.
Seasons return and today I am fifty-five,
And this time last year I was fifty-four,
And this time next year I shall be sixty-two.

He goes on to adjure listeners:

There are certain precautions, though none of them very reliable,
Against the blast from bombs and the flying splinter,
But not against the blast from Heaven, *vento dei venti*,
The wind within a wind, unable to speak for wind:
And the frigid burnings of Purgatory will not be touched
By any emollient.
        I think you will find this put,
Better than I could ever hope to express it,
In the words of Kharma: 'It is, we believe,
Idle to hope that the simple stirrup-pump
Will extinguish Hell.'
        Oh listeners,
And you especially who have turned off the wireless
And sit in Stoke or Basingstoke listening appreciatively
                            to the silence ...

Henry Reed, who went on to write his immortal infantry lyrics 'Naming of Parts' and 'Judging Distances' (in *Lessons of the War*), must surely have done as much for the national morale as did Winston Churchill in *his* wartime broadcasts.

In Tillicoultry in particular morale may have been thought to need boosting, for 'Tillie' became famous at the time as the chosen butt of the runaway traitor 'Lord Haw-Haw' in his broadcasts from Berlin. The troops in Tillie were barracked in two disused and rat-infested wool mills of such squalor that 'Haw-Haw' used them in his broadcasts as an illustration of the misery of the downtrodden British soldiery, hoping thus to destroy our national morale. Morale was in fact curiously high in Tillie, though it dropped a bit when the Eye-tie (Italian) who ran the village ice-cream shop was carried away into internment with the rest of the harmless Italian immigrants, and there was no more ice cream.

The months passed, along with the retreat from Dunkirk in May 1940 and then, from July to October, the Battle of Britain. This was the time when, in Churchill's memorable words, 'so much was owed by so many to so few', to the extent that the threat of German invasion began to relax. Throughout this critical period I still soldiered on inconspicuously with my tank-hunting platoon at Tillicoultry. This seemed odd since all the young Argylls officers commissioned with and after me had been posted to the regiment's two battalions in France, and some never returned. This account of my own war is a collection of the merest trivia, but I did not live through Dunkirk and the summer of 1940 without realising something of the gravity of what was going on.

Then one day in October, on a training exercise when I was crawling under a barbed-wire fence in my kilt, I raised my behind – for it was horribly muddy – higher than was authorised by the Infantry Training Manual, and tore my kilt. As I couldn't contribute usefully to the war effort with one hand holding up a train of tartan, Major Crystal sent me off to the regimental headquarters 20 miles away in Stirling (which I had never previously visited) to indent for a new kilt. He also entrusted me with a letter to the Adjutant; and when I diffidently entered the Adjutant's office and saluted he looked up and said, 'Who are you, sonny?' I gave him my name. He rang for the Regimental Sergeant-Major and said, 'This boy says he's in the regiment.' The RSM went off and came back a few minutes later to report that there was no sign of anyone of that name on the rolls. I had evidently been mislaid all those months (my pay, such as it was, being issued extra-regimentally by the Command Paymaster in Perth). After some telephoning my bona fides were established, and the Adjutant then said, 'Better send you out East.' And so it was that the tearing of my kilt on that barbed wire changed the whole course of my life.

CHAPTER 7

Regione Inesplorita *in Abyssinia*

THE first boat I was put on at Liverpool in December 1940 to convey me and several thousand others 'out East' was one captured from the French (who had surrendered in June to the invading Germans). 'We hadna been a league, a league,/A league but barely three' when it conked out. Fortunately it did not sink and we did not, like Sir Patrick Spens, 'wet our cork-heeled shoon' but managed to make it back to Liverpool. Two dreary months followed at the West Yorks barracks in York, until another convoy was assembled in Liverpool in February 1941. So off I sailed in SS *Stratheden* with a couple of destroyers protecting the convoy from German U-boats.

I should explain that from then until August 1958 all my personal experiences were recorded in letters sent home and to other recipients. What follows, therefore, over the next seventeen years, has been checked for veracity against the carbon copies, which I made as a sort of diary and still have, of all those letters.

I pass over the tedium of the voyage out round the Cape of Good Hope. I must have bored the company of West Yorks for whom I was given responsibility by subjecting them to lectures on such subjects as the Minoans of Crete, the only period of Mediterranean military history I knew anything about. Also, if you (or I) can believe it, I taught German every afternoon to a group of military policemen who, my letters record, were already doing the choruses from Goethe's *Faust* in my third lesson!

The tedium was broken only by one or two excitements at Cape Town. We were all allowed ashore for three days – all, that is, except for a party of macho Australian soldiers who had been misbehaving. Undeterred, however, they apparently pinched some pistols from somewhere and got themselves ashore by firing them from the top of the gangway until the guards at the bottom took cover. As for myself, I was whisked off to be entertained first by General Smuts's erstwhile private secretary and then by a French painter and his wife. Even more inexplicably I heard the wife whispering to her husband, before she discovered that I had some French, '*Qu'il est joli, le jeune officier!*' No one had ever said anything similar about me since I played in the ladies' match at Wetheral, aged eight. Nor has anyone since. This French lady took a snap of me and sent it to my parents, who preserved it, no doubt thinking it might be their last vision of their youngest son.

When our convoy was off Durban it suddenly split in two. Half of the boats – almost, it seemed, of their own volition – turned east and (so we heard later) docked in Singapore. The surrender of Singapore to the Japanese in February 1942 – 'the worst disaster', in Churchill's words, 'and the largest capitulation in British history' – may have meant that many of the troops in these unlucky ships spent the rest of the war in Japanese prisoner-of-war camps. The other boats, including fortunately SS *Stratheden*, steamed straight on up north. We had of course no idea of our destination. It proved to be Geneifa in the Suez Canal. It was intended that we should replace casualties in our various regiments in Libya, but maybe there was a lull in the slaughter there, and as a preliminary form of training we spent our time running up sand dunes in full battle order and getting distinctly bored. Other boatloads kept docking at Geneifa, including one (so I was assured) carrying sandbags from Britain already filled with good English sand. I stole away for as many meals as I could to eat with a Greek battalion camped near by to learn some demotic Greek.

Then another military muddle altered once more the course of my life. A notice on the mess board invited subalterns to volunteer for something called the Sudan Defence Force. Most of the two hundred subalterns were by now so bored or so anxious to survive that they sent their names in. I, not having read the notice and for that matter not knowing where the Sudan was, was one of the few who didn't. But I was one of the eight names posted up to go. This seemed par for the course – until I chanced across another subaltern whose name was Paul, who spoke Arabic and had volunteered. He was obviously the Paul intended, so we went together to the Garrison 'A' Branch and pointed out the mistake. The Major in charge said it must have been a typing error and rang the 'A' Branch in Cairo to get it put right. We heard a booming voice coming through his receiver, saying, 'Mistake? We don't make mistakes. Whatever we said stands.' So off I went with the other seven up the Nile to where the Sudan proved to be (while my Arabic-speaking namesake was probably posted to Finland). Mistake or not, this fortuitous posting may well have saved my life since it prevented my replacing one of the innumerable casualties the Argylls were soon to suffer in Libya and becoming one myself.

Those born since the war may not be aware of the desperate situation facing Britain and her allies all over the world from 1940 to 1943. Even those who lived through it may (like me) have been barely aware at the time of the scale of the disasters that befell us one after another, or they may have forgotten some of them since. So here is a summary account of the course of events in those three fateful years.

By May 1940 Hitler's forces, having swung destructively through Holland and Belgium, had reached the Channel coast around Calais, and his planned invasion of Britain looked imminent. In June the hazardous and humiliating

8 As Lieutenant in the Argyll and Sutherland Highlanders, en route for the
Middle East. (Photographed in Cape Town by French host and hostess.)

evacuation of our army through Dunkirk took place. As a result Mussolini
brought Italy into the war the same month, and the French government
capitulated. German air raids on Britain mounted, and in September the blitz
on London began. Only the courageous performance of the RAF persuaded
Hitler to postpone his planned invasion across the Channel. But in April
1941 his forces overran Greece and a month later compelled us to evacuate
Crete too. Two unexpected developments in the rest of the world saved our
bacon.

First, in June Hitler made the grave mistake of invading Russia (hitherto
his inactive ally). His campaign there began with devastating successes. But he
had lost enormous numbers of men – as of course had his opponent Stalin
– by the time the Russian forces eventually turned the tables on him; and
in February 1943 his troops surrendered at Stalingrad. The other major and

equally unexpected development was the Japanese assault on Pearl Harbor in December 1941. This crucially brought America into the war, but before this began to make a big difference on the ground our new Japanese enemies inflicted on us a series of disasters by land and sea. Having quickly occupied Hong Kong, they drove us out of Malaya and its valuable resources in January 1942; and the following month (as already recorded) 100,000 allied troops in Singapore surrendered. The Japanese then proceeded, overcoming opposition as they went, towards the north-west frontiers of India itself. And all this time shipping losses in every ocean were increasing Britain's shortage of vital supplies.

What meanwhile, in this perilous period, was the situation in North Africa? In February 1941 Rommel, the cleverest General in the German army, was posted to Tripoli to complete the expected defeat of the Allies. He took some time reversing the latter's recent gains, but by May 1942 he was advancing with his Italian partners and by June they had driven us all the way back to the frontier of Egypt, recapturing the key Cyrenaican port of Tobruk in the process. (Mussolini was busy in June striking medals for his expected triumphant entry into Cairo; see p. 113.) The vital confrontation, just inside Egypt, between Rommel and Montgomery, who had replaced Auchinleck as GOC of the British forces in August, was now approaching. Montgomery's amazing victory at El Alamein in November was a turning point in the whole war, though plenty of savage fighting across North Africa (and of course elsewhere in the world) was still to come before the final expulsion of the Axis from Tunisia in May 1943.

Well before these critical developments ensued, I and the seven other sub-alterns designated for secondment to the Sudan Defence Force had 'escaped' up the Nile. On arrival in Khartoum in April 1941 we reported to army head-quarters. I was instructed to join 2 Motor Machine Gun Group in Abyssinia. The staff officer concerned took me over to an Italian map on the wall (since they had no other) and pointed to an area in the middle of Abyssinia across which was printed in big letters 'REGIONE INESPLORITA'. 2 MMG Group was, he thought, somewhere about 'there'. He had no particular views on how I might find my way to this unexplored region many hundreds of miles away. Then someone mentioned that 2 MMG Group's second-in-command, Kaimakam Gus Powell, was expected in Khartoum shortly to buy necessities (such as whisky and gin) for the officers of the Group (i.e. Battalion) and could doubtless give me a lift as far at least as Asmara, the capital of Eritrea. Asmara, 200 miles north of the unexplored region, was apparently where his duties normally kept him.

I spent the intervening days getting myself issued with the equipment of a Sudan Defence Force officer, including a campbed, folding chair, canvas washbasin on a tripod, pressure lamp, mosquito net, and – most grotesque of all – the insignia of a Bimbashi or Lieutenant Colonel, the rank to which even the youngest British officers were automatically elevated to make them senior to virtually all Sudanese officers. That done, I was given two extraordinary tasks. One was to go to the SDF training centre in Omdurman and select recruits for my Battalion – an odd responsibility for an absolute newcomer with no language in common. Fortunately a young Sudanese officer was on hand to help. He told me he had returned when war broke out from a course in England, during which he had been playing football for Arsenal in bare feet. The opposing teams had complained so often that having no boots on gave him an unfair advantage that he had been obliged to buy a pair of the beastly things.

My second task was odder still. This was to attend the disembarkation at Khartoum railway station, from the guard's van of a train from Asmara, of a coffin-shaped box dispatched from there by a British officer returning to Khartoum on leave. It was rumoured to contain the body of an Italian lady with whom the officer concerned had fallen in love; and it was suspected that before popping her secretly into the box he had put her to sleep with a hypodermic syringe. It seemed an unlikely story; but when the box was prized open on the platform, there she dramatically was, surrounded by flowers and looking rather like the drowned Ophelia. (I learnt later that the officer's impropriety was overlooked. Indeed, he married the girl and they lived happily ever after.)

Gus Powell (wearing a Kaimakam's insignia of a full Colonel) then turned up. I was instantly terrified. He was a portly six-foot-two Major in the Marines with an air of authority and a bushy moustache. When we set off together in his well-stocked van, accompanied by a truckload of Sudanese soldiers, my uneasiness was not diminished by his conversational gambits. He kept making remarks, as we gazed over the featureless desert, such as 'Reminds me of the Kyles of Bute'. 'It does rather,' I felt it incumbent on me to mumble in reply. But after some time I realised that he was just making a monkey of me, and I began to enjoy him. (He became in the two years we spent together a special friend. He died, alas, in 1968, having been on the shortlist to become GOC of the Marines.) We stopped for the first night in the middle of nowhere. After breakfast, being uncertain how to manage such things in a flat desert, I put some loo paper in my sporran (for I was still wearing my kilt) and walked away from our camp until the natural curvature of the earth's surface rendered some of me invisible to the Sudanese soldiery. When I returned, Gus asked me what I had been up to. I explained. 'Ah,' he said, 'I always send the soldiers into the desert and use the bumpers of my car.'

Gus warned me, as we approached Asmara in June 1941, that most people went off their heads there owing to the height above sea level. The top British military police officer, for instance, had just been found to be collecting bars of gold in his bedroom drawer and had had to be transferred. So on arrival I awaited personal developments with apprehension. But the nearest I came to lunacy proved to be my wearing on my breast a badge reading 'INTERPRETE', meaning that (thanks to Angelina Nannarone di Santa Vittoria) I spoke some Italian. This cost me dear, for in the Asmara transit camp, where I awaited some means of pushing on into the unexplored region, two senior officers unexpectedly invited me to lunch in a classy restaurant. They proved to have reserved a table for five and we were soon joined by two Italian blondes. I realised that my presence had been sought simply because the badge I wore had led them to assume that I would be able to translate for them. In fact I hardly understood even in English the uninhibited propositions I was called upon to convey to the lady guests; much less did I know the Italian for them ... That night, with my scissors, I removed the interpreter's badge from my tunic.

In due course I was informed that a small convoy was shortly setting off south carrying loads of Maria Theresa dollars for the Abyssinian 'Patriots', i.e. those tribesmen who had opted for the King's Shilling in preference to the Duce's Lira. They were said to be operating, under the command of a lone British officer, on the Gondar plateau 50 miles beyond the village of Adi Arcai, where 2 MMG Group were understood to be based. So I hitched a lift from the amiable Sergeant in charge of the truckloads of bullion. Maria Theresa dollars made by that formidable eighteenth-century Empress of Austria were now being manufactured in Birmingham and elsewhere bearing the original date of 1780. They were the only currency, being pure silver, that the Patriot forces would accept. The Sergeant said it was the best job he had ever had, since he would hardly be blamed if a box or two never got delivered.

Once past Axum with my bullion Sergeant, the Abyssinian country turned into sensational mountains and valleys, and by the time we reached Adi Arcai I was ready for anything – even Headquarters 2 MMG Group. Lieutenant Colonel H. H. Deane, with the crown and three stars of a Miralai disguising him as a Brigadier General, was as frightening at first sight as his second-in-command, Gus Powell, had been. He was short, stout, red haired and Irish. He allotted me to No. 5 Company to replace the only officer casualty the Battalion suffered in Abyssinia (or thereafter) – killed on a patrol sent to investigate, of all things, a cow tethered by the Italians in their entrenched position on the mountains overlooking the Group's forward Company at Debivar.

One of the odder aspects of life in the SDF was immediately made manifest by my Company Commander, Captain (Bimbashi) Simms. This was that since a small number of British officers living side by side for a long time got on each other's nerves, each was required to employ his own civilian cook and eat separately in his own quarters. As a concession on my first night, since it would be difficult to find a civilian cook in the mountains of Abyssinia in a matter of minutes, Captain Simms invited me to share his supper. Apart from telling me that he could recite the whole of *The Winter's Tale* by heart, having no other book in his baggage, he revealed to me over the meal some of the practicalities of SDF life. For instance:

a) It was the only army under British command not issued with rations. We had to just live off the land, commandeering sustenance from the local peasants in exchange for Maria Theresa dollars. The one item that *was* issued was rum, at 1 fluid ounce or something per head. And since the Sudanese, as good Muslims, didn't touch it there was always plenty for the British officers.

b) The Sudanese were almost all colour blind. At the recent watershed battle of Keren in Eritrea the orders issued to the waiting troops were that if a green Verey light was discharged they should seize their muskets and charge the Italians; if a red Verey light went up, they should 'pile' their muskets and sit down again. Since the Sudanese confused the two primary colours, the resulting muddle had been dramatic. But somehow they had helped to win this decisive battle.

c) For six months before the advance into Eritrea, when Mussolini's many divisions were poised to invade the Sudan, two battalions of the SDF were all that manned about 100 miles of the frontier. Fortunately the army intelligence of the Italians was so defective that they believed we opposed them in such colossal strength that they did not risk invading. In fact there was only about one Sudanese soldier every 200 yards and one British officer every 2 miles. The latter sat contentedly on their folding chairs at their trek tables, each under his own acacia tree, supplied at breakfast by the daily train from Khartoum to Kassala with kippers and Cooper's Oxford marmalade without which, Frankie Simms declared, any serious contribution to the war effort was unthinkable.

He was a marvellous raconteur, was Frankie Simms, and like other regular officers I served under, visibly efficient despite his debonair manner. He contrived soon after this to be returned to his British regiment and was killed in Italy.

I had to set about learning Arabic as the only means of communicating with the troops (though the Sudanese officers spoke some English). After about a fortnight during which I had mastered such essentials as 'Good morning', 'Stand at ease', and 'Bring me my fish pie' (for I had mysteriously acquired a civilian cook), I was detailed to fall in with a squad of Ombashis (Corporals) being instructed by a Shawish (Sergeant) on the finer points of the Vickers machine gun. The system of instruction was that the Shawish (who was of course illiterate but had the training manual by heart) recited the relevant section – 'Points before Firing', for example – and simultaneously went through the motions on the gun. Each member of the squad had then to rise to his feet and repeat as much of it as he could remember. I was treated no differently, and my attempts to reproduce the noise which meant 'body-locking-nut-securing-pin' or whatever produced cascades of happy laughter. I used to recover from these humbling experiences by drawing pencil views of the elephant-grey peaks soaring up around us, their legs swathed in mist.

The Arabic for body-locking-nut-securing-pin has stayed with me ever since, though it has never proved of much conversational value. But my beautiful drawings have vanished.

After a month we changed places with No. 3 Company in their forward position 10 miles farther south at Debivar, with the Italians huddled in their caves and sangars at the top of the soaring Gondar Pass looking down at us. We had our tents pitched in the lea of a foothill, so that such Italian shells as were discharged at us were bound to overshoot. In any case many of them didn't explode. So we spent the time collecting strawberries (a legacy of the Italian colonists), which grew round about in abundance, playing bridge in the evenings and consuming 150 rations of rum while doing so. The question arose as to whether we oughtn't to send another patrol up the mountain, despite the fatal British casualty on the previous one, to see what the Italians were up to. The proposal got far enough for Frankie Simms to say to his two subaltern officers, 'Which of you would care to lead it?' It was decided that we should toss for the honour. The other subaltern won the toss and to my great relief felt honour bound to lead it. No doubt to *his* great relief, Hal Deane quashed the idea as unnecessarily risky. But this was as near as I got to enemy fire in six years of war.

The decision was taken soon afterwards by GHQ in Cairo to try to persuade the unhappy Italians to capitulate by a more imaginative military enterprise. This took the form of flying a platoon of the Argyll and Sutherland Highlanders all the way down from Libya to dance around frenziedly on our foothills in their kilts. This terrifying spectacle was calculated to induce the Italians to give up the struggle. The Argylls duly came and performed their eightsomes with loud whoops. But it was misty and pouring with rain; and the Italians, even if they heard something strange, could see nothing and went on drinking Chianti in their caves. The Argylls got their kilts thoroughly soaked and were flown back in disgruntled mood to where they had come from.

One happy encounter at Debivar was with Oliver Gurney, a friend of Aunt Moolie's and normally a lecturer in Hittite at Oxford. He had mysteriously been posted as a Gunner Officer in the SDF battery that shared our camp, perhaps because the War Office confused the Hittites with the Hivites, Jebusites and other Old Testament tribes that, the War Office may have fancied, lived in Abyssinia. Oliver did not favourably impress his Battery Commander, a one-legged cotton planter from the Sudan, since his academic training always prompted him when given an order (for example, to fire his 25-pounder at something) to ask 'Why?' – a question to which there was seldom an answer. But he certainly impressed *me* during the hours we spent together, closeted in a convenient hideaway, discussing such important military issues as Homer's familiarity with the Hittites. Oliver, however, was not unexpectedly sent away to be turned into a Staff Officer. On the resultant training course (so he told me in a letter) he aroused grave suspicion by taking his notes in Greek. But he survived the war and remained a Reader in Hittite studies until he died in 2001.

My life during these months was darkened by constantly going septic whenever I had scratched myself or been bitten by a mosquito. The doctor from HQ had to be called up to examine me. He declared that my fungoid growths appeared to be 'vegetable', but the diagnosis served no purpose other than arousing the interest of my fellow officers, whose diet was deficient in legumes. I was confined to my campbed from time to time reading the *Aeneid*, but so many bits of my anatomy were inflamed with sepsis that this was less enjoyable than it might have been.

Then Miralai Deane (HHD from now on), who was the one and only British officer in Group HQ – Gus Powell being away in Asmara most of the time – decided in August 1941 that he needed an Adjutant. The lot fell to *me*. HHD told me later that his original intention had been to appoint the other young Bimbashi in No. 5 Company, who, he said, was more intelligent and efficient than me but (if possible) less entertaining. I was to remain his adjutant for two and a half years.

He began by telling me I had better acquire a typewriter, since his HQ, not being given to literary excesses, had hitherto kept no copies of correspondence. His practice, he said, was to write his replies to incoming signals on their reverse side in orange chalk and, once the text had been morsed off by the Signals Officer, to hang them in the jakes (army term for the loo) to be put to good use. But this procedure, he felt, was becoming outmoded. How I acquired the small portable Olivetti which served me faithfully throughout my Adjutancy (and for long after since I grew to consider it my own) I do not remember. Doubtless we got it, like all the group's food and much else, in exchange for Maria Theresa dollars, which HHD kept in a sack under his bed.

Two years later, in Tripolitania, a signal from GHQ in Cairo was brought to my tent demanding the submission of detailed accounts for the expenditure of MT dollars issued to us in the East Africa campaign. I was appalled, since no accounts had ever been kept and the bullion had been put to all sorts of questionable uses. Wondering whether it would mean being cashiered or just reduced to the ranks, I ran through in a great state of nerves to HHD with the signal. 'Don't worry, Beep,' he said ('Beep' was what I was called in those days), 'I'll deal with that.' I sat apprehensively in my tent until I was able to see the carbon copy of his reply (not now hung in the jakes). It read:

> Your signal xxx
> Bulls for the Troops.
> H. H. Deane.

This rather summary accounting for six months' expenditure of limitless MT dollars was evidently regarded as satisfactory. At any rate no comment was ever received.

Back to Adi Arcai. The most memorable thing that happened during the time I shared with HHD the best and only undamaged house in the village was the following. The wife of Ras Saiyoum, the sister of the Emperor Haile Selassie, was being evacuated from some more dangerous area and was to rest for a few days in our village on her way. We received instructions to prepare accommodation for her, her eighteen-year-old son and their retinue. No building other than ours had more than three walls still standing. On her arrival our distinguished guest was conducted by a Sudanese officer to a house that at least had most of its roof. That evening HHD and I were sitting on our veranda, our tumblers in our hands, when up the driveway swept the Emperor's sister in her grey tweed two-piece, accompanied by her son and followed by her large and fierce-looking entourage. She had come to protest at the infamous accommodation provided for her. Diplomacy was not HHD's strong point, and after some unprofitable exchanges (in French, translated by me) she demanded to be put in immediate touch by telephone with Anthony Eden, Britain's Foreign Secretary. HHD brushed this aside on the reasonable grounds that all the local telephone wires had been dismantled by the retreating Italians. She was scarcely mollified, and in the ensuing impasse I stepped in bravely with 'Was there anything we could do for *Madame la Soeur de l'Empéreur* to make her stay in Adi Arcai less disagreeable?' She turned to her son in his immaculate dark suit and conferred with him in Amharic, before turning back with the one word 'Gin!'. We brightened up. 'Anything else, madame?' After renewed consultation she said, 'Sardines.' We were thus able to part amicably and conduct her back up the drive furnished with two bottles of Cypriot potato gin and some tins of pickled pilchards.

We were shortly withdrawn to 2 MMG Group's peacetime base at Kassala in the Sudan's east. It was there that on my way to Asmara with Gus Powell I had deposited my kilt, and I hurried to see that it was safe and sound. I opened the relevant drawer and there was nothing, but nothing, there save the two glass eyes of my badger sporran gazing up at me. The rest had been totally consumed by white ants.

During our few weeks' rest to recuperate from our valiant efforts in Abyssinia the incident I most vividly recall nearly cost me my Adjutancy. As commander of the Eastern Arab Corps HHD was high enough in the Sudan hierarchy to receive a personal, numbered copy of a top-secret circular from the Governor General's office in Khartoum setting out the subversive activities of the recently formed 'Sudan Graduates Congress', warning him to keep a sharp lookout for local sympathisers, and instructing him to burn the document after reading and report action taken. He lodged the document with me for safe-keeping overnight so that he could study it again in the morning. At breakfast he told me to go and fetch it. I couldn't find it in my security cabinet where I thought I had lodged it. I must therefore have left this highly sensitive circular on my office table. But it wasn't there. HHD was properly furious at the thought that his personal copy of a top-secret letter might have found its way through my gross negligence into subversive hands. The troops were immediately confined to barracks, the civilian clerk in our HQ was put under preventive detention, and anyone who may have had access to my office was sternly interrogated – all without effect. At midday I was ordered to draft a telegram to Khartoum reporting the facts. I sat at my desk wondering what to say, when I suddenly noticed the corner of a top-secret document peeping out from under my blotting paper ... It was a long time before HHD entrusted his Adjutant with any more top secrets.

I was issued at Kassala with a new batman. This was a tall Beja tribesman who told me, when we had reached a measure of understanding, that he had changed sides several times during the fighting, depending not on whether we or the Italians looked more likely to win, but on which of us paid better. Though perhaps a soldier of questionable loyalty to iron the trousers of an officer as careless with top secrets as myself, he continued to iron them for the next two years.

CHAPTER 8

In and Around Kufra Oasis

WE then set off for our next assignment – at Kufra, a lonely oasis in southern Libya, a thousand miles or so from Kassala, 600 miles west of Wadi Halfa on the Nile, and a little less south of Tobruk on the Mediterranean. It sounded a safe enough distance from the enemy (or from anything else). We were to relieve another SDF Battalion, taking over their transport at Wadi Halfa on the other side of the Nile. This consisted of open vans with machine guns mounted behind the driver's seat, and armoured cars. The hand-over took place in orderly fashion but then disaster struck. HHD had had the Battalion Commander's baggage van brought specially across the Nile to be loaded with his many personal necessities. My job was to get it safely back to the other side. We reached the far bank successfully on a sort of raft and tied up. The driver then put it by mistake into reverse and all my Commanding Officer's creature comforts disappeared for ever into the Nile. There was hell to pay. But he still didn't sack me.

The 600 miles of desert between the Nile and Kufra were virtually un-mapped and there were only two sources of water on the way. When we reached the first, at Selima, the three carrier pigeons, which the Royal Corps of Signals had entrusted to our Signals Officer with a view to testing their reliability as a means of carrying messages back to Wadi Halfa, were to be released. We were sceptical of their value as compared with our old Morse-tapping machines, but were assured they were well trained for the purpose. Accordingly they were extracted from their mobile dovecote, messages were tied to their legs and they were loosed into the air. We watched them fly off into the moonlight. But instead of flying straight back to Wadi Halfa, what did they do but circle round and round above our heads, finally coming down to land on the bumpers of their mobile dovecote. HHD snorted derisively and had them served up for supper.

Apart from our MMG Group, Kufra was occupied by the headquarters of the famous LRDG (Long Range Desert Group, set up in 1942) and also by a platoon of Free French. General Leclerc, who had captured Kufra from the Italians a year before, had insisted that thirty of his *méharistes* (camel soldiery) should remain there indefinitely as a symbol of Free French valour. As Garrison Adjutant to HHD, who was formally overall Commander, my writ, so to speak, ran everywhere. The LRDG of course hardly needed to take any notice. Perhaps the bravest thing I did in the war was to address its members (those who were resting from their courageous raids behind enemy lines hundreds of miles up north) on the qualities of the Sudanese soldier. They lay around in the dark, bearded, silent and properly scornful even of my jokes – reacting much as a body of Muslim mullahs might react to a talk on the qualities of the Anglican Sunday school. I did, however, pick up one day in the sand dunes north of Kufra an abandoned bedding roll, marked as the property of Colonel David Stirling – founder of the SAS but attached for some time to the LRDG, which was presumably when he lost his bedding roll. I kept it for years.

But the Free French were less frightening. Their Platoon Commander, a lecturer in philosophy at Bordeaux University, lent me a lot of French poetry. In a very French, and conspicuously non-British, way he had furnished his dungeon-like quarters up in the fort with delicate silk hangings, bright cushions and objets d'art; and I used to sit among them at his feet when off duty and have civilisation explained to me. His successor was an asset of a different kind, looking like de Gaulle when young. He even played football with us (a game hardly then known in France), wearing his kepi throughout. And though he knew none of the rules, he would shout at the referee whenever his opponents scored a goal, '*Un tout petit peu offside, non?*'

As Adjutant I had under my personal command the Headquarters Platoon. One day its only efficient Ombashi, an unpopular disciplinarian, found the bolt of his rifle missing. Losing the bolt of your rifle was a court-martial offence and HHD ordered me to try the case. At this point the Ombashi pleaded with me to call in the services of the local Fiki, or holy man, an Arabic-speaking Tibbu tribesman, whose magical powers would assuredly reveal which of the soldiers had stolen his rifle bolt. I fell for this proposal (but did not of course disclose this to HHD, who would have snorted 'Don't be a fool!'). Half an hour before sunset (the appointed time) I was present to watch the conjuring. The platoon was sitting there in a circle round the Fiki, who stood in the centre pointing a long wooden tent peg at the sun. I squatted down with the soldiers in eager anticipation. The holy man then nuzzled the point of the tent peg into the sand and poised a hammer above it, alternating blows with verses of the Koran and glances at the sun. It became clear that the blow driving the tent peg finally into the subsoil would be timed to coincide with the sun's final disappearance – at which, presumably, the guilty soldier would produce the stolen bolt from his pocket with a sob. The sun's chin cut the horizon. The peg still had two inches to go, and the sun about the same. Bang, bang, bang, bang. Tent peg and sun disappeared together … There was no movement among the soldiers and no sound of sobbing. In the hush the holy man suddenly said, '*Goomu fog!*' (Get up!). The soldiers all leapt to their feet. I myself, whose calves were not designed for squatting Arab-fashion with the legs bent double and the heels on the ground under one's bottom, was by now so numb with pins-and-needles that I couldn't move. The Fiki turned and silently pointed his accusing finger at *me*, rooted like the tent peg to the ground. Everyone – except the Ombashi – expressed hearty relief. It took me some courage to reveal to HHD what had been going on, and to persuade him that in the circumstances the court martial would have to be called off. The Fiki charged me 50 piastres for his divination. Ordnance charged the Ombashi a good deal more for a new rifle bolt, and the whole embarrassing affair was generously hushed up. Good order and military discipline – if not my good standing with HHD – were gradually restored.

One of the strange features of Kufra was the salt lakes that shared the oasis with palm trees. Their salt content was reputedly higher even than the Dead Sea, where, as I was to learn from later experience, you can't sink and can read *The Times* lying comfortably on your back in the water. Shortly before our arrival in Kufra a visiting RAF Corporal, unaware of the prohibition on bathing in them, had dived into one and been unable to get his heavier top half up again, drowning in consequence. Another oddity about these salt lakes was the inexplicable fertility of the sand around them. HHD took it into his head to plant radish seeds along the edge of the lake nearest the mess. In a matter of days he came prancing in with a 6-inch white radish on the end of his shooting stick. We harvested the crop for weeks.

Jenny should recognise that even then I had one of the qualities for a future partner. For I went one day to the Kufra market. 'One would expect to find', as I wrote in a letter home, 'in an Arab *suq* separated from civilisation by several thousand miles of sand all sorts of articles of ethnological interest, such as richly-dight carpets of goats-hair, gourd vases etched with primitive charm, pottery reminding the classicist of the Mycenaean period, and the bones of infidels cunningly wrought into salt-cellars and prayer-lockets. But all I found were bales of gaudy poplin from Tokyo, a pile or two of cheap Manchester metal-ware, and endless little bottles of odious Cairo scent. I returned disillusioned with three vegetable marrows.'

A more grievous discomfort was the appalling headaches I began to suffer. They came on every day at 11.15 a.m. and went on till precisely 4 p.m. I sat gloomily in my office, 'composing [so I bravely wrote home] Sperm Whale Returns while Italian Generals are three a penny across the Sands of Dee' – a breach of security that may at least have caused confusion to the censors reading our mail in London. Eventually I went to consult Henry Richards, the garrison doctor. He said that after years of hospital administration in the Sudan he had forgotten all the medicines he ever knew, but 'Try some of *this*!' He reached for a bottle of white powder on the shelf behind him and told me to mix a spoonful of it with some non-alcoholic fluid whenever the pain came on. I did so. Relief was instantaneous and the headaches soon stopped oppressing me. Two years later in Tripoli I had a recurrence of the same unidentified trouble. Henry Richards was now our divisional head doctor, so I asked him for some more of the magical cure he had prescribed for me in Kufra. He couldn't remember what on earth it could have been (nor did he before he died in the 1980s). If he had, he would assuredly have made a fortune, for what I was suffering from, like millions in the world, was later diagnosed as acute frontal sinusitis. The only thing he could think of prescribing by now was Alka Seltzer.

Our six months in Kufra came to an end and we set off on the long trek back to Wadi Halfa (and thence to Kassala). It started well, for we stopped after a day or two at the Oweinat outcrop. It proved immensely exciting as the site of prehistoric rock paintings of fauna now vanished from these desert latitudes – zebras and lions and elephants. I had long hankered for a career in archaeology. Homeric archaeology had been my special subject at Oxford, taught by the great Miss Lorimer. (She was an eccentric character and very thin. It was her habit to sleep out in summer, and on one occasion the grass in her college quad was so dewy that she moved her sleeping bag on to the dry earth path. An undergraduate bicycling back to his room in the small hours felt a distinct bump on the pathway and found on dismounting that the bump was Miss Lorimer. She did not even wake up. Such sterling qualities are typical of many female archaeologists, with some of whom I was later to collaborate.) At Oweinat an old man, almost the sole survivor of the tribe that had once lived there, led me to the cave paintings.

But the rest of the journey to Wadi Halfa was less enjoyable. There can be few more humbling experiences than developing amoebic dysentery in a column of motorised troops moving across a flat desert. I will omit the sordid details. After a time HHD judged that his Adjutant would soon be dead, and he nobly decided to abandon the convoy and drive me in his staff car, accompanied by a machine-gun van, the remaining 250 miles. At breakneck speed he headed roughly east, having no time to use a compass, with me doubled up and groaning beside him. He got properly lost but eventually hit the Nile not more than 20 miles off course. I remember no more than waking up a day or two later in Halfa hospital.

On my eventual release from hospital I was instructed to go and recuperate at Erkowit, the Sudan's summer health station 800 miles away in the Red Sea hills, where I was to lodge in the local hostelry. When I somehow reached Erkowit, there was no room in the inn, and I learnt to my dismay that I was to lodge instead, as a guest, in the Governor General's 'summer palace', where he and his wife and daughter were in residence at the time. I had nothing in which to dress for dinner except my one SDF battledress, my steel helmet and my gas mask, and in any case felt hardly up to social niceties of any kind. General Sir Hubert Huddleston was an imposing figure for someone like me to dine with at the best of times. Obviously they were enormously kind, but the only light relief was when their prankish twelve-year-old daughter fell through a skylight on to the breakfast table, scattering the crockery with peels of merriment not shared by her parents. One morning desperation led me to tell Lady Huddleston that I had arranged to ride down the mountain on a camel the following day to visit Suakin. (Suakin is Sudan's ancient Red Sea port, already at this time a museum piece, trade having moved up the coast to deeper water at Port Sudan.) To my horror Lady Huddleston declared that she would come too. This was a double embarrassment since my camel story was pure fiction, my intention being simply to escape and doss down under a bush at a safe distance from the palace. Now, however, there was nothing for it but to find some camels and cameleers in quick time, and with great luck I managed to do so. At lunch Sir Hubert was apprised of his wife's plan and to my enormous relief put his foot down. But since the camels were mustered, there was no way out of escaping on them myself.

After lunch I sat on a rock gazing down apprehensively towards my distant destination. Here is part of the lyric I broke out into. (It should be remembered that in 1942 we were visibly losing the war.)

> As gull on rock watches the ranging waves
> Shoulder their long relief map to the shore,
> Sit crosslegged on this ledge, here where the graves
> Of men whose spears were not afraid of bullets*
> Obstruct the cropping unparticular goat,
> > And watch these pilgrim hills
> Trekking to Mecca. On their bony shoulders
> The tattered shadows of the clouds are clinging,
> > As on these nearer boulders
> Five ragged lizards (look!) spreadeagled ...
>
> Now let the uncondemning eye
> Pace up the silent shore towards Suakin,
> That grey shirt hanging on the line of sky.
> The emptying city under siege to time
> Faces the slow impenetrable hosts
> Of minutes. The tall houses turn to tombs,
> > And all too hot for ghosts.
> Thither we English on a sceptical camel's
> Hump tilting shall tomorrow tread
> To pay a pilgrim tribute from the threatened
> > To the more nearly dead.**

---

* A reference to the bravery of the Mahdist Osman Digna and his followers, who fought the British here in 1891. ** The late David Burnett (see later), to whom I must have sent this poem, suddenly produced it in 1978 from a drawer in his desk at Hay's Wharf, and gave me a copy (I had lost the original). Hay's Wharf in the Pool of London, of which he was managing director, had been for several generations the property of the Burnett family.

Whatever else may be thought of it, this forgotten poem shows that despite the triviality of these reminiscences I was not unaware in 1942 of the then threatened end of civilisation.

It proved a memorable pilgrimage. My 'Fuzzy-Wuzzy' guide (the British referred to the Beja tribes thus because of their curly hair) and I stilted down the mountain in the morning. He did not allow a halt until nearly midnight, when we dossed down under the stars. By midday we were approaching the causeway leading into Suakin (which is an island in a lagoon) and were preparing to cross it through 'Kitchener's Arch'. Some eight people, the whole population roughly, turned out to watch this unusual spectacle. Passing through the eye of a needle proved too much for this rich man's camel, which reared up on its hind legs and discharged me through the air into the arms of a stout lady. Winding the rest of my way sweatily on foot through the tall deserted houses with their beautiful *mashrabiyas* (projecting alcoves of see-through carved wooden slats), I reached the white fort where Kitchener and sundry Turkish commanders had once had their headquarters. It overlooked the frabjous lagoon, and I made straight for the water, warned by the old man who looked after what was now a resthouse to avoid the black and poisonous porcupine-plants growing on the rocks beneath its surface. I plunged in among the exotic fish and had the bathe of my life. Getting out, as anyone reading this will have foreseen, I pushed my left foot plumb into a porcupine-plant, securing a number of its quills in my big toe. A medicine man from the mainland was hastily summoned. His equipment proved to consist of a brazier full of live coals and a lump of animal fat. He wrapped the fat round my toe, melting it on by the simple expedient of putting my foot into the brazier for a bit, and assured me that quite soon the poisonous thorns would be sucked out. I lay down on a bed and went to sleep. When I woke up, white ants had eaten the lard and, apart from some inflammation where my foot had been thrust into the brazier, the treatment had had no visible effect. The quills remain to this day embedded, as far as I know, in my toe. Maybe they account for my in-growing toenails.

The rest of my sojourn in Suakin was pure delight, either wandering among the empty houses with their upstairs balconies leaning together over the twisted streets as if gossiping, or lying on the curving breakwater to watch the polychrome fishes darting this way and that.

By the time I regained Erkowit, the Huddlestons had gone but now there was room in the inn. There I made the acquaintance of Robin Hodgkin, on leave from teaching in Gordon College, Khartoum, and spent much time learning from him about the Eternal Verities (and Fallacies). When he was at Oxford in 1935 he went up Mount Everest with Hugh Boustead and others and lost the ends of his fingers and toes from frostbite. Not that this deterred him from scrambling up rock-faced mountains at Erkowit, and making me scramble after him. I spent a night with him twenty-five years later when he was headmaster of a Quaker school in Staffordshire. He had just returned from climbing Mont Blanc with Edmund Hillary and another Tenzing. On the way down he had lost his footing in a blizzard and hung over an abyss with Hillary and Tenzing at the ends of the rope, holding him so poised for long enough (he told me) for him to say to himself, 'What on earth am I doing here, with a wife and three children in Staffordshire?' He was saved and never climbed a molehill thereafter, a splendidly rounded person whose friendship I cherished. He even wrote in 2000 the Preface to my book of poems *A Kind of Kindness*. He died, alas, in 2003.

My convalescence over, I returned to 2 MMG Group at Kassala. My letters in the sweaty heat pursued their frivolous way. One of them (London being at the time subject to heavy German bombing) reports my reading Benvenuto Cellini's autobiography, in which he describes the siege of Rome in 1510. He relates how he saved the crops from rotting and the Romans from starvation by directing his Roman artillery (gerfalcons and swivels and demi-culverins) at the storm clouds, blowing such holes in them that the sun got through and dried everything up and the crops matured. Churchill's speeches were, I suppose, a species of gerfalcon or demi-culverin for those besieged in London.

My own facetious outpourings, though almost indecent in view of what was going on in the bloodstained world at the time, may at least have helped to sustain morale at Cakemuir. The facility of my then prose style, typed out on my old Olivetti, arouses in me today something like envy. This is my only justification for reproducing some random extracts here. For instance:

My main warlike activity here is tennis. I hasten to add that tennis at Kassala bears roughly the same relation to tennis at Wimbledon as croquet in *Alice in Wonderland* bears to croquet at Bray-on-Thames. I do not mean that we beat about the bush with 13 oz Slazenger flamingoes or even with the more tightly-strung and homely bustard. But in other respects the similarity is close. Things like Cheshire Cats grin at one out of the bushes, occasional hyenas lope across the fairway, and one feels that at any moment the part of the Red Queen shouting 'Off with his head!' will be played by HHD. For not only do the labourers who act as ball-boys thoroughly deserve beheading but the Commanding Officer would be almost within his rights to behead them, for they are all prisoners from the local gaol serving life-sentences for some unspeakable African crime. When one asks them for a ball, they tiptoe up with the delicate fervour of a child bringing a Ramping Fumatory to its governess and reverently lay it with a melting smile at one's feet. Most of the time they merely chase the Commanding Officer's rococo serves until they locate them in a distant ha-ha or irrigation channel. Nothing will make them understand that the rectangular area marked out with lentils from the Quartermaster's stores is reserved for players or batsmen. One really feels that these criminals are too harmlessly stupid to have committed any serious crime. The tennis net, however, is a tribute to their ingenuity. Like all nets, but more so, this one consists of a number of holes tied together with string. But the one respect in which *these* holes resembled each other is that they are all just large enough to allow a tennis-ball to pass through. The effect of this is good or bad depending on whether you are playing with or against the Commanding Officer, for it is he who does the scoring.

And so on for endless effortless pages. Or this:

I have done nothing sensational recently to win the War but conduct an armed raid on the nearby population of bedouin Fuzzy-Wuzzies. This involved getting up before dawn, something I have not done since I was a cavalry-man at Oxford, and careering up steaming riverbeds and through prickly forests until a cluster of nomadic tents was sighted, dismounting thereupon and surrounding them. One patriarch whose house I invested, advancing at the head of my troops with my revolver at the ready, protested that his wife under that pile of rags was in the last stages of child-bearing and must on no account be disturbed. At that moment a *soi-disant* midwife darted forward, fumbled in the lady's parts, and withdrew bearing a suitable-sized bundle. Suddenly the baby in the bundle clinked unmistakably. My Sudanese Serjeant gave chase and returned with a broad grin and a bagful of .303 bullets. And then without more ado he advanced and with practised hand stripped the pregnant lady naked in a twinkling. Before I had half adjusted my bearings to this development, he had delivered her of a fine Lee Enfield rifle. Mother and father, I hear, are not doing well.

We set off shortly for a second six months defending King and Country in Kufra. During our week's pause at Wadi Halfa, it was the habit of the officers of Battalion HQ to dine in the mess in their pyjamas. One night, having struggled hiccuping back to my tent after the usual session of poker dice, I was stung painfully in my right big toe by a colossal scorpion. As I lay groaning I realised that my right leg was going numb from the toe upwards, inch by inch. I stumbled out to find the Tumergi (Medical Orderly) and woke him up. He seized a razor blade and proceeded to make incisions in my big toe, presumably intending to squeeze out the poison where it had got in. This was even more painful than the sting itself. I decided to jump in my van and drive helter-skelter to the Halfa hospital a few miles away. It wouldn't start. Nearing despair, I hobbled into HHD's saloon car (for he was away at a conference in Khartoum) and drove shakily off. The numbness, in *both* legs now, had reached my middle. Nearing the hospital and attempting to change gear with my dead extremities, I overturned the car in the ditch. Past caring, I dragged myself out and covered the remaining quarter-mile on all fours. At last I crawled into the hospital, was injected with some magic potion and my dead body came alive again. I then remembered that HHD was due back from Khartoum on the 8 a.m. train and would expect his car and his Adjutant to be waiting at the station. So I explained to the Matron that I must be off. 'No!' she said (she was a proper old battleaxe). 'No patient may leave until the doctor does his rounds at eight a.m.' I pleaded with her, but to no avail. There was nothing for it, once she had gone, but to escape under the remaining half-hour of dark. I climbed unseen out of the window, slid down a drainpipe and ran at top speed in my pink pyjamas to where the Colonel's car lay on its side in the ditch. The citizenry were just stirring. I rounded up six of them and we succeeded in lifting the car bodily back on to the road the right way up. To my relief it still worked. I whizzed back to camp, and after a fitter had hastily straightened out the only telltale dent and washed off the mud, I summoned the Colonel's driver and as the clock struck eight I was at the station, properly dressed and able to salute HHD nonchalantly as he stepped off the train. It was some weeks before I was brave enough to tell him of that night's adventure.

Soon I was back in the same old Garrison Adjutant's chair that I had occupied in Kufra six months before – the 600 miles of intervening desert by now well enough marked by tyres to prevent us getting lost. Not that this prevented a subsequent Service Corps convoy from Wadi Halfa, bringing our Christmas mail and goodies, from doing just that. Owing to its non-arrival we set ourselves to intercept the successive radio signals its Commander kept sending to his HQ. The last one we bothered with, about ten days later, said, 'Have found stone marked LOCUST EXPEDITION 1924. Where am I?' It transpired that he was away up near the Egyptian oasis of Kharjah, some 250 miles off course. We never received our Christmas comforts.

For some time there was little new to report in my letters home, and I will only record one interesting discovery I made. This was when HHD had sent his motorcycle orderly with a 100-piastre note to buy him something in the market. He duly returned with the required purchase and handed HHD the change. The change consisted of two pairs of bootlaces and a tin of 'Griffin's Old-fashioned Oxblood Paste'. This obvious relic of the days before coinage had penetrated these remote areas aroused my antiquarian interest in traditional mediums of exchange, when the currency must have consisted of tins of Griffin's Oxblood Paste. And how many bootlaces, I wondered, went to one camel?

But my investigations of this topic were rudely swept aside when HHD suddenly decided, for reasons he did not divulge, that I was to set off with him forthwith to explore the various small oases in the desert to the north. They were the only things, apart from latitudes and longitudes, on our handkerchief maps. (These latter were a splendid invention of the Sudan Surveys Department, widely used by us as tablecloths, lampshades, face towels, turbans, etc., and had the added advantage that, unlike the folding paper maps still used everywhere today, they did not tear or disintegrate.) It would be a useful experience for me, said HHD, to practise using the Bagnold compass to find our way. This involved constantly referring to things called azimuth tables, an art I never really mastered, though reluctant to admit it. All I did know was that correct interpretation of them enabled one to shift one's sun-compass round a bit every fifteen minutes to keep pace with the sun. Off we went, with me at the wheel of the front jeep, ostensibly marking our progress on my map board, and HHD driving another jeep behind. I assured him glibly when we stopped for the first night that this kind of orientational geometry – 'dead reckoning', as it was called – was proving no problem. In the morning I found I had lost my watch, an essential instrument for use with azimuth tables. But this didn't save me from having to do the navigation since HHD arranged to catch me up in his jeep every fifteenth minute and give a sharp toot on his horn to remind me to make the necessary adjustment on my sun-compass. How we survived this six-day trip and even found several small oases remains a mystery.

In one of them I had my first experience of the humbling generosity of the Muslim poor. The oasis was 50 miles from any other and tiny, just a rocky outcrop, a salt pool, palm trees and a handful of inhabitants in three palm-branch huts. The oldest of the men welcomed us in courteous fashion – though he had no idea what country we hailed from, much less that we were engaged in a world war. We were simply guests in his tiny kingdom; and after some sort of exchange of pleasantries (he spoke only Tibbu) he insisted on presenting us as we climbed back into our jeeps with one of his kingdom's four goats and its only visible hen. Our cars, I need hardly say, were already stuffed for our week's nourishment with tinned goodies that would have kept the whole oasis in luxury (if they had a tin opener) for a year. But by this time I knew that to have refused the generosity of a Muslim host, however poor, would have been an affront to his dignity.

Crossing uncharted sand seas exercised a powerful fascination for me (and still does). Most of this desert seemed never to have been disturbed by wheeled transport. Bagnold, the inventor of the sun-compass, whose splendid *Libyan Sands* I had by now read, describes in it how tyre marks vanish totally from sight after a few years of wind, but that if you chance to cross where wheels had once passed you will feel a small but unmistakable shudder. He himself, exploring in the twenties an apparently virgin area of desert, had occasionally felt that shudder just where his researches indicated that X had passed ten years before. No such thrilling flashback to the past was vouchsafed to me on this trip, but I experienced it more than once later.

In the last oasis we found our way to there was actually a small house – once the property of the Senussi King whose regime had been suppressed by the Italian colonisers, but now a lonely Libyan police post. No one, we learnt later, had visited it for months, and the sudden arrival of visitors from the other side in the war they were ostensibly engaged in was quite an occasion. I drew up ahead of HHD and could see through the closed window of the house a half-naked body struggling to its feet. He opened the door and ran to greet me. I explained that His Excellency the General was just behind, having come from the ends of the earth to pay a visit. A look of terror crossed his face and he made like lightning for the door to go and smarten himself up. The door, alas, was one of those that lock themselves automatically when allowed to swing shut, and he had left the key inside. There was a sudden crash, and the only glass window for hundreds of miles was sacrificed to the honour of the Libyan police force. Thirty seconds later 'His Excellency the General' drew up and gave a martial blow on his horn. The door of the house opened and a now fully clad Libyan policeman (with all the regalia that implies) emerged and presented arms. 'Pray Allah, Your Excellency will come in,' he said, and turned to open the door. Poor man, it had swung to again and the key was still inside. By the time he had got it open by diving once more through the smashed pane in full regalia, the Sergeant in charge and his other man arrived and took over. After the usual courtesies the Sergeant said to HHD in Arabic, 'Has Your Excellency seen any Laurel and Hardy films lately?' I could conceive of few questions less to be expected in an isolated Libyan oasis in the middle of a world war, and it almost knocked even HHD off his pivot. It transpired that the man had been captured at Sidi Barrani in Wavell's successful occupation of Cyrenaica in 1941, taken a prisoner to Cairo and quite soon released as posing no danger to the Allied cause – but not before he and his fellow captives had been entertained with the only English film he had ever seen. Whether Laurel and Hardy had convinced him that Britain would surely lose the war and that consequently his best plan was to hurry back and serve the Axis as a Libyan policeman was something we forbore to pursue.

Almost as soon as we got back to Kufra, HHD took me off to 'do another Bagnold', as he put it. This time we went to the south-east, perhaps to counter any suspicions of the secret plan (which he still could not reveal to me) under which we were shortly to launch from Kufra a full-scale attack on Jalo, a big and strategic oasis farther north and still occupied, as General Montgomery began his advance in November 1942 after the battle of El Alamein, by the enemy. Our objective on this second 'Bagnold' was the isolated waterhole dug ten years before by the Senussi King's followers when they were driven even out of Kufra by the Italians. The water, so the story went, had been vouchsafed in answer to the Senussi King's prayer at a depth of 75 feet, and had enabled some of his followers to survive this appalling journey. Since then the miraculous waterhole had opened a new, though hazardous, caravan route for smugglers. When (thanks to my dead reckoning!) we found it, the sand all around was littered with the bones of thirsty camels that had presumably drunk too much and died. Even the cairn built there was constructed of them. The gruesomeness was in no way diminished by the protrusion from the littered sand of a human foot and lower leg.

CHAPTER 9

Libya and the Near East

IN fact, the secret attack on Jalo never took place. This, as HHD told me when its cancellation enabled him to disclose what the plan had been, was because a number of indiscreet officers in the famous Shepheard's Hotel in Cairo had talked at the bar about it. It had therefore ceased to be a secret and had been called off. This was certainly a blessing, for when Jalo was visited some weeks later, as Montgomery was pushing the enemy out of Cyrenaica, it was found to have been not casually defended by unsoldierly Italians but made resolutely impregnable by Germans. An assault on it by 2 MMG Group would have been a fearful shambles.

Shortly after this, as the Axis armies retreated west, we received orders in January 1943 to take the battalion and ancillary units due north from Kufra to Agedabia, 550 miles away on the Mediterranean. This was not accomplished without dust and heat since HHD entrusted me, after all my experience on the Bagnold compass, with the navigation. There was nothing in the middle of our handkerchief maps to take a dead reckoning on, except one spot marked 'Crashed Aeroplane'. I took a scholarly bearing on it, but as the days passed no one was less surprised than me that the crashed aircraft didn't show up. I navigated fearlessly on, buoyed by the thought that, provided we went roughly north, we were bound to hit the Mediterranean *somewhere*. But when I led the convoy, including eight 3-ton trucks of petrol, into a soft hollow where the whole lot got stuck up to their differentials in the sand, HHD's confidence in my navigation finally evaporated and he decided to take over the sun-compass himself. While the vehicles were being slowly dug out and rafted on to metal 'sand channels', I walked off in a sulk to sit on a sand dune. What should I find at my feet as I sat down but a prehistoric pot containing flint arrowheads? My morale was instantly restored and I rushed back to show my find to HHD. His only comment was, 'What's the bloody use of *that*?'

Eventually we did, under his guidance, hit the Mediterranean quite near Agedabia. As we neared the coast, flowers of all kinds appeared in the sub-desert and the Sudanese, who had never seen anything like it, leapt off their transport and threw themselves into the scented flora, gurgling with delight.

By this time the 8th Army was well into Tripolitania and we were instructed to push on behind them along the coast road. When we reached the outskirts of Tripoli, by now safely in Allied hands, HHD and I went to report to the man appointed to govern the captured province (a top member of the Sudan Political Service, in fact). As we dismounted at the doors of the Villa Volpi, previously the Italian Governor's residence, we saw through the drawing-room window the great man slip in and take position at the grand piano. He was playing Chopin as we were ushered in.

We then took the battalion on up into the mountain range south of Tripoli to occupy (unopposed) the town of Gharian. We arrived after dark, and it was a great moment when I woke in the morning to find that my campbed stood in the atrium of a Roman villa among mosaic tesserae. Once we had distributed our companies farther along the mountain range (but still at a safe distance from the retreating enemy and very picturesque) our first task was to liberate the Libyan prisoners from the Italian gaol. They were all very annoyed at being liberated, protesting that living there at no cost to themselves had been the nicest time of their lives.

The Berber tribes up here were troglodytic, living underground in 'houses' about the size of gasworks cut downwards into the soft rock and entered by sloping tunnels from ground level, the rooms being carved round the perimeter of these subterranean gasworks. One effect of this was that their villages were invisible above ground, and the ignorant became aware of them only by falling into them (some 20 feet). On one occasion I was invited in to tea by the occupants of a house. The teapot was brought in ceremoniously with a tea cosy on it. On the upturned oil drum on which it was placed stood a silver-framed colour photograph of their son in glamorous full Italian army uniform. I might have been taking tea in Corstorphine, Edinburgh, though it would have been unusual for a Corstorphine hostess to seat her guest on the cushioned handle of a huge kettle as the seat of honour or to provide the cream for his tea by sending a child to fetch a goat and milking it at his feet. The only change in these troglodyte villages when Jenny and I visited them thirty years later was that the whereabouts of each dwelling were now revealed by a television aerial protruding from its depths.

Perhaps my most alarming assignment in Gharian was an instruction from HHD to draft standing orders for the Battalion with the help of his own (Welch Regiment) model, 200 pages long, which he carried throughout the war in his knapsack. The Welch Regiment, if you can believe it, gave such valuable guidance on good order and military discipline as the following: 'All ranks will wear in their Service Cap on St David's Day a leek of REASONABLE size. Leeks will be worn on the lefthand side of the headdress with the root to the rear. They will not be pinned to the headdress but will be under the chinstrap.' And in a later section dealing with the regimental mascot, I came across this: 'The Goat's horns will on no account be scraped or rubbed with sandpaper. Should the Goat be off his feed, the drummer in charge will immediately make a written report to the Adjutant ... The Goat will always kneel during the playing of the National Anthem.' As can be imagined, I included comparable (but spoof) sections in my draft standing orders for 2 MMG Group.

Perhaps to spur me on in this *magnum opus*, I was sent by HHD on a course at the Infantry Training Centre in Cairo. I went there by aeroplane, the first such experience in my life. The prospect of flying thrilled me – the only time (as I wrote home) I would be anywhere near heaven except for the afternoon at Oxford when Valerie Lloyd George came to tea. The aeroplane proved to be a wobbly old DC-3 with tin seats down its sides. I remember nothing of the course, where I was disguised to everyone's dismay as a Major in the British army, except the time off. In one such leisure period, having broken a lens of my old St-Malo spectacles, I took them to an Egyptian oculist who (as already recorded) revealed that those sold to me by the nefarious French optician were made of plain bottle glass. While making payment for my new pair to his secretary, I fell instantly in love with her in the half-dark. That night I composed a letter in French and paid the lift man a modest sum to deliver it to her. The following evening I brushed my hair carefully and went to the proposed rendezvous in an upmarket restaurant. She arrived fifteen minutes late, chewing a piece of Spearmint and accompanied by an unbelievably stout *'cousine'*. It transpired that, in addition to being just fifteen and of Turkish-Italian parentage, my lady love was much less attractive in full light. Her fat *'cousine'* was a pale blonde Circassian but none the more romantic for that, and as she rolled up the steps of the restaurant I christened her 'The Circassian Chalk Circle'. We sat down to dinner, my lady love extracting her Spearmint with a queer little hissing noise and depositing it on the tablecloth under the gaze of the head waiter. After they had both eaten solemnly the most expensive items on the menu, we set off for a concert of Beethoven piano sonatas, for which of course I had booked only two tickets. On the way, the light in the streets being less revealing, I began to feel a little better, when suddenly my love said, *'Eh bien, bonsoir!'* and disappeared into a house. The *cousine* explained that her father was very strict and never allowed her out after 9 p.m. I entered the concert hall (for what else could I do?) with the Circassian Circle on my arm and noticed to my dismay several fellow students from my training course sitting quite close. *'Moi, j'adore la musique,'* sighed the Circassian, whereupon she spread herself into her seat and fell asleep. Never again, I vowed to myself, would I write letters in French to the secretaries of Egyptian oculists. The only other disillusioning experience I recall from my time off was watching an American Colonel peeing down the lift shaft of my hotel.

The course concluded with a TAB injection. This was followed by indulging in ten days' 'enforced rest', the charming term used in a notice in the training centre as statutory after that then ghastly injection. My 'enforced rest' began with three memorable days with Ian Spalding (my contemporary at Sedbergh and Oxford), whose letters had long been keeping me alive. He and his battalion of jovial Sikhs chanced to be in nearby Palestine at this time. Of the many stories he entranced me with I must limit myself to one. This was of a man named H. Paul, who lived in Galashiels, where Ian had been brought up. One night this near-namesake of mine was woken by a handful of pebbles thrown up at his bedroom window. He opened the window and peered out. 'Is that Paul?' said a voice. 'It is,' he answered. 'Well,' said the voice, 'did ye ever get an answer to that long letter ye wrote to the Galatians?'

One evening Ian took me to a drinks party given by his Sikh officers. The talk was all in incomprehensible Urdu until one of them, Mohindar Singh, turned to me and said in a kind of English, 'King George, him nutting. General Montgomery, him nutting. De Colonel, him nutting. Spalding Sahib, him EVERYTING.' Mohindar Singh featured in a letter Ian wrote to me some months later from Italy (the Allies having started their advance there), describing the landing of his Sikh battalion in Sicily in July 1943. 'Your friend Mohindar Singh excelled himself on the Sicilian beaches, striding up and down in a pair of milk-white trousers and fending off the bombs with a stout ashplant.' His letter was largely about the visit I had paid him in Palestine, and I quote (apologetically) one of its passages. 'It was a wonderful three days, better than anything else in the war. It wasn't the "restoration of delight", but it was as if delight had sent her messenger before her to prepare her ways.' Alas, that delight was never, for Ian, to be restored. His next letter to me (it was from Monte Cassino) ended, 'Italy looks very beautiful just now: but divided into Fields-of-Fire.' It was the last letter he wrote, for in one of those fields-of-fire he was caught and killed. The war, as far as I was concerned, could do nothing worse.

It was of course months before I came to know of his death, and then only because three letters of mine to him were returned, with an explanatory note attached, from something that allowed itself to be called the 'Dead Letter Office'. I must not go on about him, but Greig Barr, hearing from me of Ian's death, wrote a sentence about him that I value. 'He had a lightning awareness (far keener than anyone I have ever known) of what lies below the surface. He did not need to be told the truth: he could talk nonsense but he *knew* the truth.'

In one of the many marvellous letter he sent me during the war (which I have kept) he wrote this:

I am not one of those who hold that the steam engine has killed Romance. The steam engine is a great kindler of finer passions. The only onomatopoeic line I ever wrote in my life was composed on the instant in an express train five miles south of Tebay. It went:

Chasing past them, posting on
To Babylon, to Babylon.

It was meant to sound like a 4-6-4 approaching Tebay. It does. And again:

> The nicest girl I ever saw
> Was passing sideways through the door
> At the other end of the corridor.

He was an only child and wars have a habit of marking out only-children for destruction – two other friends of mine among them. To their number we feared for many weeks that cousin Bill Monteith had been added. He was known to have been shot down in his fighter plane over Tobruk, which Rommel recaptured from us in June 1942, and taken prisoner to Rome. As the Allied forces pushed up Italy from the south, the Italians (but not of course the Germans) gave up the struggle and opened their prison gates. Most of the British servicemen so released managed to make their way through the German lines till they reached the advancing Allies. Bill evidently waited for the advancing Allies to reach *him*, taking refuge with Italian peasants who bravely concealed him from the Germans until they finally withdrew. But he had of course no means of communication with Aunt Moolie (his mother) or anyone else before the Germans disappeared. Bill paid yearly visits after the war to the Italian peasant family who had concealed him.

Returning to my 'enforced rest', I spent the remainder of it in modest lodgings in Jerusalem, drawing chimney pots from my bedroom window and exploring the Holy City. Both were disillusioning. The guardian of the Garden of Gethsemane wore a peaked cap round which were inscribed in letters of gold 'CHAMPION SPARKING PLUGS', and he extracted, like all the doorkeepers in the House of the Lord, an exorbitant fee for letting one in.

I was back at Gharian in time for the transfer of the Group to the intense heat of the flatlands below, near Castel Benito as Tripoli airport was then called. It had been the intention that we should guard an Italian prisoner-of-war camp there, but it was just then that Benito (Mussolini) and his armed forces retired hurt. The resulting celebrations took the form in our case of all-night poker and the consumption of A. Buchanan's Scotch whisky – made, I learnt later, not by a Scotsman of that name but by Abu Khanan, an ingenious Egyptian. Normally I preferred what I regarded as more cultural ways of passing so many stifling evenings. That night, though, I joined in and, perhaps because of a more cautious approach to Abu Khanan than my fellow officers, I had by 4 a.m. skinned them of £3 12s 6d (a big sum). I then slipped shamelessly away to my bed with my ill-gotten gains before I could lose them again.

Not, I hope, for that reason my Adjutancy was finally terminated by HHD after two and a half years. Maybe my release was intended as a birthday present, for on that very day HHD drew my attention to the date, which proved to be 23 September (my birthday). The question arose at breakfast as to how old I was. The matter was referred to the Quartermaster, who was thought to have a head for figures. He came up with one that was simply laughed out of court. My own opinion was that I had certainly passed nineteen, but HHD rejected this as 'a typical schoolboy exaggeration'.

I was to take command of No. 5 Company, camped 200 yards away up the wadi, but this was delayed by Area HQ appointing me Prosecuting Officer at the trial of an RAF Lance Corporal for having assaulted an officer on parade. He was pleading insanity. The Defending Officer produced the evidence of two witnesses to support the plea of mental imbalance:

1) On two occasions the Accused had been seen climbing to the top of a wireless aerial where he pretended he was a machine-gun.
2) On receiving his copy of the preliminary Summary of Evidence, he had promptly adopted the Squatting Position, shat in his mess-tin, and wiped himself with the Summary of Evidence.

As Prosecuting Officer I rose in reply and (according to one of my undelivered letters to Ian Spalding) spoke as follows:

Sir, I myself, not twice but on several occasions remember having climbed up wireless aerials and pretended I was a machine-gun. I have also climbed up the mast of SS *Stratheden* and pretended I was an albatross. I have even climbed up Pope's Tower at Stanton Harcourt and pretended I was Pope. All these enterprises I found exhilarating and no one has ever suspected *me* of mental imbalance. (Murmurings in Court.) As for the second instance of the prisoner's so-called insanity, I can only state, as the Officer who wrote the Summary of Evidence, that the purpose he is alleged to have put it to seems to me fully compatible with a normal and healthy mind.

The accused was duly convicted. My description of the earlier part of the trial was certainly factual. But in the account I gave of my speech it is possible that I was embroidering slightly on the truth.

I had hardly taken over 5 Company before I was summoned to the head-quarters of 12 Division SDF and told by the Brigadier who commanded it that I was to go forthwith on a staff course in Palestine preparatory to appointment as Brigade Major, the top staff job in the division! ('No similar appointment', I recalled Winston Churchill saying of someone else, 'since the Emperor Caligula made his horse a consul.') It wasn't actually a real Division but consisted of six Sudanese battalions and ancillary troops under a Brigadier with a brigade-size headquarters.

While I was packing my bags, a new role – so a letter from Cakemuir reported – was about to be filled by my indefatigable mother. She had been designated by the Women's Services of Scotland to 'address an audience of Prime Ministers [*sic*] in Randolph Crescent, Edinburgh'. This stimulated me to envisage in reply what would come of it; and since most references to my parents in these memoirs are to D, I will reproduce my prophecy about M, so that her signal qualities may also be given tribute. (She did in fact receive an MBE for her war services.)

> She will probably find herself transferred, wearing the rank of Major General in the ATS, from Randolph Crescent to Downing St, bicycling thither every morning from Cakemuir once she has cooked the breakfast, scrubbed the floor, weeded the garden, rolled the tennis courts, answered the mail, and written letters to each of her sons (putting them for good measure in the wrong envelopes). As she bicycles before dawn down the Great North Road, she will be composing lyrics on the wives of Cabinet Ministers, committing them to paper with one hand while she turns Scotch Corner with the other. Picking herself nonchalantly out of the ditch, she will pedal on to Pontefract preparing a lecture on 'Stockings I have Darned' for delivery at Nottingham to the Society for the Protection of Old Etonians. Breakfasting as the sun rises over Peterborough Cathedral on a dry oatcake previously secreted in her bosom, she will remember that she has forgotten to tell D where she left the gardener's ticket for the Pantomime. Swinging therefore with redoubled velocity into Grantham she will telephone Ford 25, obtaining military priority as a Major General and turning the heel of a pair of gloves for the Forces in Malay while the call is being put through. Looking at her watch as she remounts she will observe with horror that she is only 25 minutes ahead of schedule instead of her customary 40. Forgetting the awful warnings she lavished on her sons about the dangers of doing so, she will grasp the door handle of a passing Jeep and whizz behind it into Golders Green. Having duly thanked the American driver, she will drop off at Hyde Park Corner to buy her lunch at a convenient ironmonger's; and as the clock strikes 8 she will be tying the wheel of her bicycle to the lamppost outside No. 10. Running up the steps while fumbling for the key, she will dispose of her lunch to a hungry-looking newspaper boy. Having dusted down the Cabinet room, changed the blotting paper, and paid the servants their next month's wages, she will dash off a dozen Memoranda including a talk on Knots and Splices for the First Lord of the Admiralty. Everything will then be ready for members of the Cabinet, to whom her first question will be, 'Are you all quite sure your stockings are dry', and without waiting for the poor old chaps to expostulate she will add, 'In any case off you go and change them.'
>
> And this will go on every day of the year until she is 110 like Great Aunt Margaret, or her youngest son gets leave home, whichever (as they say in military correspondence) is the sooner.

Most of the inwardnesses in the above will by now be lost, but I have left it unchanged because she deserves a tribute. 'I know', one of her wartime letters to me said, 'how infinitely unimportant is anything I can do, and how infinitely important it is that I should do it.'

Back to my own infinitely unimportant role in Libya. The very night before I left 2 MMG Group for Palestine I came nearer death than at any time during the war. For I was woken at midnight by the Bash Shawish (Company Sergeant-Major) to be told that the wadi in which we were encamped had come down in a colossal flash flood and swept everything away. (My own tent stood on slightly higher ground.) While he was giving me his breathless report, in stumbled my British Sergeant-fitter, who had suffered an even ruder awakening. For hearing a noise, he had stretched out a hand from his campbed, and what should it encounter but his big black boots, followed by his bottle of whisky, floating past him into oblivion on the crest of a rising flood. I struggled up. It was a memorable sight in the moonlight – a sheet of chocolate-coloured water with only the tips of wireless aerials and van-mounted machine guns poking out of it, and my brave soldiers plunging in in their nightshirts to rescue any useful-looking chattels they could see floating past. On the far bank of the torrent I detected the Commander of the adjoining Company, which was also submerged, calling out to me disconsolately like Lord Allan's daughter. I waved cheerfully and returned to comfort my Sergeant-fitter, who was wandering about, with his pyjamas rolled up to his thighs, searching desperately in the shallows for his boots and his bottle. His fellow British NCO, however, I found sitting on his half-submerged bed, drinking (for there will always be an England) a mug of tea. By dawn the flash flood had passed on, but it was a night to remember – and all the more enjoyable for me since I left in mid-morning for Palestine without having to help clear up the mess. But I waved goodbye with a lump in my throat and a blank cheque from HHD in my pocket 'to buy a more reliable watch'.

No letters from the staff school at Sarafand have survived, and I remember little of the training I received, apart from a lecture by the great Glubb Pasha – an engaging little figure with a lump on his chin, but then enormously important as commander of Jordan's forces* – on the lifestyle of the Jordanian Bedou, and another by myself on 'Superstitions in the Sudan', a subject of questionable value to Staff Officers destined to supervise the destruction of Hitler.

For me the most valuable aspect of the course was that David Burnett – an architect, botanist, archaeologist, watercolourist and musical know-all – was also on it. He became one of my closest friends and taught me most of what I know in many of those fields. In the week's 'enforced rest' at half-term, he and I decided to go to Petra. We crossed the River Jordan without trouble, reached Amman and hunted for some way of getting farther. Glubb Pasha, at whose office we bravely called, was out. We then tried the railways, since the old Damascus-to-Mecca railway was still theoretically operable as

---

* In 1956 he was sacked by the young King Hussein, who, now that Jordan was an independent kingdom, doubtless felt impelled to demonstrate to other Arab leaders his rejection of British supervision.

far as Maan, not far from Petra. We were generously offered the use of one of those quaint machines on which engineers inspecting or repairing railway lines propelled themselves along them by agitating a huge croquet hoop on a pivot. We tried it out but concluded that our leave was too short. Then we heard that two lorries carrying sugar were just setting off for Maan (the first since the rains), and we hitched lifts on top of the sugar sacks. There was nothing recognisable as a road and halfway to Maan our leading lorry got stuck knee deep in the wet mud. Without hesitation, and demonstrating something engaging about the Arab mind, the second lorry simply accelerated furiously and drove straight into us from behind, pushing us right out of the mud but getting totally stuck in it itself with its front end bashed in. It may well still be there today. We pushed on in the survivor and reached Maan, which was unprecedentedly under 3 inches of snow, at nightfall. In the morning we got another chance lift to Wadi Mousa, where the police lent us horses for the few miles to Petra. The nights we spent there were the high spot of my war, dossing down in a cave with the 'rose-red city' below us in virgin snow, while David played *Eine Kleine Nachtmusik* on his recorder – the only sound apart from distant goat-bells to disturb the silence. No one now can hope to see it, as we did, blanketed in snow and empty, instead of steaming with tourists and disfigured with hotels.

After the course I spent (or intended to spend) ten days in Beirut improving my Arabic at the feet of the Professor of Psychology at the American University, there being no one else willing to offer me this service. Professor Fouad Najjar tried for a day or two, but his habit of constantly trumpeting his mucus and cracking his finger joints was so off-putting that I stole away to visit Baalbek instead. The direct route over the mountains was blocked with snow, so I had to make my way up the coast and across to Homs, where I thumbed a lift down to Baalbek on the back of a lorry carrying turnips. On the way the driver stopped to relieve himself. There was a thunderstorm going on, and just as he pointed out to me, away down below us, Krak des Chevaliers (the finest castle in the world, T. E. Lawrence called it), a thin shaft of sunlight pierced the black clouds and landed smack on Krak. I was so moved that I sat on a Roman milestone and composed an ode in French (a language in which I was even less skilled then than now). I still have the text to prove it. Twenty years later, when I was in the Embassy at Beirut, I took my family to show them the view of the castle where I had composed it. The long and the short of it is that, although the image is still as clearly engraved on my heart as Calais was on the dying Queen Mary's, no such view exists. There is no road from which one can look *down* on Krak. (There was no question of mistaken identity, for by this time I knew quite well every Crusader castle in the Levant.) So there it is – the only 'spiritual' experience of my life.

Baalbek itself was almost equally magical. Having arrived after dark, I opened the window in my hostelry bedroom in the morning, and there were the famous ruins right in front of me in unexpected sunlight and 6 inches of untouched snow. I drew furiously and of course broke into verse. It was not the decadent floridity of the Roman temple buildings which gripped me so much as the sheer vigour with which, up in these frozen hills on the frontiers of the known world, men had chiselled out these monuments, piling stones as big as cottages one on another, in honour of Jupiter and Bacchus, who were already names to laugh at.

On my way back to Cairo I shared a train compartment with a South African Captain who was writing short stories. Among his books littering the seats was a French anthology which fell open for me at a poem (by a Dumas) which I instantly copied into my own. I still have it by heart. I have never seen it elsewhere in print and would gladly reproduce the whole of it but will limit myself to three of its verses:

> *J'ai longtemps laissé ma pensée*
> *Flotter sur l'aile du désir;*
> *Mais ce soir je veux resaissir*
> *Toute mon âme dispersée.*
>
> *Les parfums, les couleurs, les roses*
> *Ont trop souvent su me charmer.*
> *Si j'allais oublier d'aimer*
> *Pour avoir aimé trop de choses!*
>
> *Aussi je veux m'examiner*
> *Dans la paix de cette heure tendre,*
> *Puisqu'il faut savoir se reprendre*
> *Avant de pouvoir se donner.*

It still moves me: '*Si j'allais oublier d'aimer, / Pour avoir aimé trop de choses*' (What if I were to forget how to love, by having loved too many things).

Another memorable francophone experience on this journey was meeting in a transit camp in Cyrenaica a small French priest who had spent seventeen lonely years in the Cameroon, and perhaps for that reason talked to me non-stop for two days about his eccentric convictions. Among these he declared that the easiest way to win the war was to send black troops against the German trenches, armed not with rifles and bayonets but stark naked with assegais and knobkerries. '*Et alors, coupe coupe*' (and he demonstrated with a porridge spoon) '*et les Boches* would run screaming for mercy.'

He presented me on my departure with a *Nouveau Testament*, inscribing its flyleaf with his private coat of arms, in which the Holy Ghost was descending on the Sacré Coeur in an aeroplane ('*Faut être moderne, vous savez*'). I could not quite share the general opinion in the transit camp that he was, in the ordinary sense, off his rocker.

CHAPTER 10

Kaimakam in Tripolitania

THE night of my arrival at HQ 12 Division SDF in February 1944 as Brigade Major coincided with a visit from the GOC Sudan (General Platt) and the top doctor in the territory. The latter, Corkhill by name, had spent many years collecting material for a book on snakes. Sitting next to me at dinner, he privily showed me the manuscript. One passage in it I memorised carefully: 'If you are bitten by the common *Gomfalopax* [or some such snake] kill it and turn it over on its back. If its scales run in lines across its belly, don't worry, it's not poisonous. If they don't, don't worry, it's fatal.'

So there I was, disguised no longer as a mere Bimbashi but wearing the insignia of a Kaimakam and the title of Bey, with a bogus full Colonel's crown and two stars on my shoulder. A short distance from the comfortable Italian farmhouse requisitioned as our mess, the Divisional HQ occupied the barracks some miles east of Tripoli at Tadjura (which the Americans bombed in 1986 in the belief that their enemy Qaddhafi was hiding there). Brigadier Gifford was a massive and tolerant character who also (sometimes) laughed at my jokes. We spent much time bathing in the Mediterranean, on whose beaches we dug up turtles' eggs, heartlessly – but not very successfully – playing ping-pong with them on the mess dinner table.

But I had a more engrossing pastime. This was to cruise around with two like-minded colleagues collecting Mesolithic flint implements from all over the desert, which we then 'classified'. The most interesting were the small hooked ones that we found in a metre-deep deposit of snail shells, obviously designed for extracting the snails. By November 1944 we had produced a learned article on our collection and sent it with a selection of our trophies to the great Dorothy Garrod at Cambridge. She replied enthusiastically and said she had sent it on to the even greater prehistorian, the Abbé Breuil, in France. We awaited his reaction breathlessly for six months and learnt on enquiring from Professor Garrod that the Abbé never received the parcel. So my incipient fame as a Stone Age expert was knocked on the head, presumably by a German fighter pilot.

As Brigade Major I did, to be sure, engage in some sort of military activity. Indeed, I once had to organise a 'divisional' exercise for all six battalions. This too ended ingloriously, for I ventured out to umpire its execution wearing my steel helmet instead of my more comfortable Bombay Bowler for the only time I remember ever doing so – and collapsed almost immediately with sunstroke. I recovered two days later just in time for the solemn post-mortem gathering of the senior (non-SDF) officers I had recruited as fellow umpires – a motley collection of flotsam and jetsam left behind by the 8th Army. The Brigadier asked them whether they had observed any irregularities in the exercise. Up got a coastal gunner, pale eyed from gazing for months into an empty sea, and said, 'About those irregularities, Brigadier, I ought to report that I noticed a Sudanese Corporal opening a tin of bully-beef with his teeth.' In a single sentence he made the whole Brigade exercise worthwhile.

The only other military exercise I was called upon to mount was due to Cairo Radio broadcasting its first severe attack on Zionism. The result was that the Arab peasants in Tripolitania set upon the Jewish peasants – with whom they had lived in complete amity for 1,200 years and who formed a third of the population – and burnt their synagogues and pushed their old women into wells. It was our job to go and enforce the peace under the nauseated leadership of the Brigade Major.

I did of course engage in that courageous venture to reconnoitre a negotiable route to the western Sudan across the middle of Africa (of which I recorded one disconnected incident on p. 52). Off we set in two jeeps, a signals van and three petrol lorries across 600 miles of what was marked sonorously on French maps as VASTES ETENDUES DEPOURVUES D'EAU (vast expanses deprived of water). We did not in fact get much farther than the Brach oasis in the Fezzan. For on top of a lonely sand dune 20 miles beyond it my jeep suddenly caught fire. Flames shot out from under the bonnet. We leapt out and threw sand all over it with our hats in the faint hope of extinguishing the conflagration. To our great surprise we did so before the flames had reached the petrol tank. The problem was what to do now. I could see no future either in pushing on to Sebkha, the oasis capital of the Fezzan, in our other jeep and the signals van (both already overloaded) or in going back to Brach, where we had left our petrol lorries. We had already burst all but two of our twenty spare lorry tyres on the sharp flints of the desert. Brooding on this conundrum I climbed into the seat of my still-smoking jeep and, from force of habit, I suppose, absent-mindedly pressed the self-starter. What should happen but that the jeep leapt quite normally into life. So after a casual look under the bonnet to see whether there seemed enough bits and pieces left there to make locomotion possible, we decided to push on to Sebkha. Our reception there by the French *méharistes* (camel-riders) who occupied it – all 'ologists of one sort or another posted with French logic to pursue their 'ologies in the Fezzan as army officers – left nothing to be desired. But proceeding any farther across Africa was out of the question. Back we went to Brach, met up with our petrol lorries and set off apprehensively on the long journey home. We chose at random a quite different 'route' in the hope of avoiding flinty

9 Tagiura village in Tripolitania sketched by GBP in 1943,
when Kaimakam in HQ.

terrain and not bursting all our remaining tyres. It was a rash decision, for
we found our advance blocked by a mountain range made of huge cannon
balls of black basalt, up which we had to lift each wheel of each vehicle
inch by inch for most of a day. By the time we had repeated this procedure
down the other side we were on decent sand again. Two days later we hit the
Mediterranean at the spectacular old Roman port of Leptis Magna and slept
on its ancient quay after celebrating our survival boisterously. The Brigadier
was not overly impressed by my report when we reached Tripoli, and GHQ
decided against trying to send soldiers home to the Sudan on leave through
the middle of Africa.

Then two alarming things happened. The first was a decision in GHQ
Cairo to send a Sudanese brigade to join the Allied forces in Burma fighting
the Japanese. In order to facilitate intercommunication with them, we were
instructed to teach our soldiers all the familiar Arabic words of command (and
the parts of the machine gun) in English. We spent days trying to get them
to substitute 'body-locking-nut-securing-pin' for the equally unpronounceable
Arabic version I had learnt in Abyssinia, and to persuade at least enough of
each company to respond to the strange command 'By the right, in column
of threes, quick march' in a manner not wholly chaotic.

The other development, doubtless a consequence of the first, was a visit from the GOC Middle East in Cairo to satisfy himself of our battle-worthiness. In this he was somewhat misled by attending some field exercises improvised by me. In the course of them, the General said to his ADC interpreter, 'Tell that Corporal there that the enemy has just advanced under cover down that hill and is about to cross the gap in the wall over there. What would he do?' The interpreter, an ingenious fellow who later rose high in the Sudan Political Service, held a rapid conversation in Arabic with the Ombashi concerned and turned to the General saying, 'The Corporal says he would instantly mount his machine gun behind that bush and, when the enemy reached the gap, open rapid fire.' What the Corporal had actually said, as I knew, was, 'I would run back to the officers' mess and tell the Bimbashi.' But the General was so impressed that he recommended to Brigadier Gifford the instant promotion of the Corporal to Sergeant.

Fortunately the Burma decision was later cancelled and we were all able to relax. It may be that the General's favourable impression of the SDF had been damaged by two incidents at dinner in the mess. By an odd tactical indiscretion my friend Henry Richards, the Divisional MO, of whom it was known that a single gin would put him to sleep, had been placed immediately across the table from the GOC. In the middle of the soup course, as could easily have been predicted since he had had more than one gin, Henry fell asleep, his spectacles resting gently on the mulligatawny. The General and the rest of us affected not to notice. Ten minutes later, when we were eating the pudding and discussing native education, Henry woke up. Perhaps a trifle abashed, he took refuge in his pipe, which he lit, blinking through the soup on his spectacles. And then suddenly, 'You're all wrong, General,' he said, 'you forget the only reason anybody ever does *anything*.' There was a short pause, pregnant if ever a pause was. During it Henry considerately laid aside his pipe, as if realising that it was incorrect to be smoking during the sweet course, and took a mouthful of his soup, by now quite cold and full of moths. 'Money!' said Henry. 'Money!' And he proceeded to light his pipe a second time, the smoke licking our Pèche Melbas. 'I don't entirely agree,' said the General nobly. 'Surely you would agree that the Sudan government's education policy has other motives?' But whether or not Henry would have agreed we were never to know, for he was already asleep again, his head on his chest and his pipe half submerged in his soup, like a bombed and burnt-out supply ship, down at the stern and smoking as she sinks. As if this were not enough, we all rose when dinner was over and, in accordance with long-standing custom in the Sudan, wandered off into the garden to spend pennies. 'No slit trenches ahead, I hope, Brigadier?' called out the General with a laugh. 'No, rather not,' said the Brigadier. A moment later a loud imprecation and a dull thud broke the stillness. Senior officers clustered round and there in the bottom of a forgotten slit trench lay the GOC.

Not long after, and more importantly for me at any rate, we had a visit from the Governor General of the Sudan, Sir Hubert Huddleston (my former formidable host in Erkowit), accompanied by the head of the Political Service, Sir Douglas Newbold. In accordance with the programme I had had to arrange, we set off to visit a battalion some 10 miles away – the Sudanese motorbicycle outriders ahead, the Governor General and Brigadier Gifford in the leading car, Sir Douglas Newbold and myself following behind. En route I was deeply engaged in conversation with Sir Douglas, having fallen instantly under his spell. As we neared a vital turn-off, it occurred to me that I had omitted to tell the outriders where we were going; and they would undoubtedly go straight ahead, oblivious to things like destinations. The only recourse was to catch them up. My driver accordingly accelerated vigorously, and we were almost abreast of the Governor General when I decided to put my head through the sun roof of our car and scream at the outriders. The only result was that my service cap blew off. Regardless of such minor disasters, there was nothing for it but to accelerate even faster. A matter of yards before the turn-off I caught up with the outriders and the whole convoy slithered to a halt. I then had to march over and explain things to the Governor General, saluting him (improperly) without my hat, which had to be recovered from the bushes several hundred yards back.

The only participant who had enjoyed the drama was Sir Douglas. It seemed to make him even more kindly disposed to me, and before we reached our destination he invited me to join the Political Service – not simply when the war ended but more or less straight away. This was most flattering, but I had the presence of mind to explain that my ambitions lay in archaeology. 'No problem,' said Newbold. 'When the present Sudan government archaeologist retires in a few years, the job will be open to you if you still feel that way.' Then, since archaeological exploration was one of his own wide interests, he recited to me his favourite piece of French poetry (now inscribed on the wall of our downstairs loo):

> *Avec ses quatre dromadaires*
> *Don Pedro d'Alfaroubeira*
> *Courut le monde et l'admira.*
> *Il fit ce que je voudrais faire*
> *Si j'avais quatre dromadaires.*

I was quite won over by this marvellous man. I did to be sure bore Bill Monteith and other friends by writing to them for advice. Bill, who had himself joined the Sudan Political Service just before the war, simply told me to pull my finger out and get on with it. 'But don't forget', he added, 'that the Englishman who spends his life in the East returns changed himself but leaves the East exactly as he found it.' I didn't believe him then, though maybe I do now. But I knew already that my future lay in the Sudan.

Unexpectedly, indeed incomprehensibly, I was sent about now on a course for junior unit commanders at Benevento in southern Italy, travelling for a second time by air and on my twenty-seventh birthday. Flying was still an exciting experience for me and naturally I burst into rhyme. 'Birthday over Naples Bay' began rather well:

> Dawn. At the young sun's shepherding
> Web-footed shadows flock from the grey sea
> And clamber up the valleys ...

I was proud enough to send brother Ian a copy of it in reply to a poem he had written himself (the only one on record). He was now a 'Phantom' in France, landing by glider behind the German lines. Scrap, incidentally, having taken part in the invasion of Italy with the Lovat Scouts, was now billeted in Florence in the Via dei Bardi, the smart street where Angelina Nannarone di Santa Vittoria, my old Italian teacher, lived. He was not billeted on *her* but on the equally euphonious Aleramo Scarampi, of whom more anon.

Knowing that David Burnett was on the staff of 8th Army HQ at Siena, I arranged at the end of the course to meet him in Rome (having looked up a hotel guide) at the Albergo Mussolini in the Via Vittoria. I hitched a lift to Rome and waited two hours at the rendezvous. No David. Rather surprisingly I found it was possible to ring 8th Army HQ from a public telephone box, and there on the end of the line was an exasperated Captain Burnett, who had also waited for an hour at the Albergo Mussolini in the Via Vittoria, and gone back to Siena in a huff. It transpired that there were two (perhaps more) Via Vittorias in Rome with Albergo Mussolinis in them, so we fixed a less ambiguous rendezvous, met up and spent two splendid days exploring the city and drawing pictures of it.

By the time I returned to our backwater in Tripoli, the Allied invasion of France was in full swing (D-Day had been 6 June 1944). A letter from D awaited me, urging me (for he was a collector of medals) to obtain for him the medal struck by Mussolini for his expected capture of Egypt and reputedly distributed in advance. In my search for any sign of it, I called on the 'Intendente' (Italian administrative boss) of Tripoli, whom the British had continued to employ, and asked him whether he knew how I could find one. His reply was peculiarly Italian. 'There can be no such medal, for if there were, I would certainly have issued myself with one.' Rumours of its existence, however, continued; but it was only fifty years later (much too late for D) that I received a photograph of it from King Farouk's nephew, Hussein Shereen, Jenny's acquaintance in Alexandria. It proved to have been struck in the summer of 1942 in anticipation of Mussolini's triumphant entry into Cairo. But if it *was* distributed in advance of that non-event, my Intendente had slipped up.

There was also a letter from M in her familiar handwriting, which remained unchanged from age eight to eighty. A lady working in M's office in Edinburgh and dealing with children's nurseries had in her charge one small boy who stank so badly that she had sent him home with a note to his mother asking her to wash him. She received the following reply: 'Dear Miss, you sent Harry home because he smeld. He only smeld the same as his father did, and I sleep with him for 20 years and he soots me very well, so you will have to make him soot you to. You must be some old made wot doesn't know the smell of a man.'

Months of impatient boredom followed in our backwater. All sorts of diversions were devised to keep the troops happy. To quote just one of those I described in letters home, we were accorded a visit from Johnny Reegan, described as 'the only English cowboy'. He was an enchanting cockney but skilled enough at riding horses to have given a performance even in Texas, where (he told me) devotion to our monarchy was much greater than in Britain. Placards had been strung across the streets of Texas, of one of which he showed me a photograph.

> 'Positively appearing
> Johnny Reegan
> The only English cowboy
> Born in Windsor
> KNOWS KING GEORGE.

While he was with us, he went hunting with one of our Nuba battalions, using their bare hands – hoping to improve their diet of bully-beef. They came back with eight hares, a partridge and a cat, all of which were popped into the pot. The cowboy was so delighted that he decided to cancel all his upmarket engagements and go off to the Sudan instead, to entertain nobody but Sudanese soldiers.

I had to go off to the Sudan myself, to attend some conference of military brass hats. More importantly I would take the opportunity to see Sir Douglas Newbold, accept his invitation to join the Political Service and sign on the dotted line. On arrival in Khartoum I knocked on the door of Robin Hodgkin, with whom I had arranged to lodge, and found him gloomily writing a commissioned obituary for *The Times* – on Sir Douglas Newbold. The great man was terminally ill from overwork and died two days later. So I never saw him.

Two or three years later, when the government archaeologist's job became vacant, I wrote to the Civil Secretary's Office and drew attention to Sir Douglas's assurance to me in 1944 that the job would be mine for the asking. They replied that there was no record of this on the files and that they felt obliged to appoint a fully trained archaeologist. Quite right too, but sad for me.

Back in Tripoli a recrudescence of my old Kufra head pains led at last to their diagnosis as sinusitis. It was decided to bore my frontal sinuses. When

I reached the front of the queue and a medico advanced on me brandishing a bare bodkin, Kaimakam Balfour Paul Bey ignominiously fainted in front of a lot of Sudanese other ranks. If the sight of a bare bodkin knocked me unconscious, could I, I wondered, ever have gone over the top to face a German bayonet?

On 18 May 1945 the war in Europe ended. As part of our own celebrations it fell to me to buy in the *suq* no fewer than 120 sheep for the Brigade and to watch the Sudanese ecstatically skinning them. The technique consisted of making a small hole in the sheep's hind leg and blowing powerfully through it to separate the pelt from the flesh. The pelt could then be drawn off like a football jersey.

The war against Japan, of course, was not yet ended (by the apocalyptic horror of the atomic bomb); and it was reported from Cakemuir that Ian, having survived his 'Phantom' operations and a terrifying action on D-Day, was now threatened with a posting to the Far East. This was humbling news for me, as I waited in my backwater for my number to come up for 'pythoning'– the term used for repatriation and demobilisation, priority being based on the number of years one had been overseas. My own turn was delayed by my carelessly misstating the date of my departure in 1941 from Liverpool in SS *Stratheden*, thereby causing the War Office to inform me that my pythoning was 'indefinitely postponed'. When they finally relented, it was again postponed for some reason, and it was not till January 1946 that I waved goodbye to Libya.

Journeying home to peace proved quite as testing as journeying abroad to war. After some days being sick in a boat, I and those with me were piled into a German train with all its windows broken to travel from Toulon to Dieppe in the coldest winter since Good King Wenceslas looked out. Brigadier Gifford's car, which he kept in Dorset and had kindly offered me as a means of getting up to Scotland, was buried in snow, deep and crisp and even. From London I telephoned Cakemuir but the lines were all down. A train took me to Edinburgh. The telephone lines were still out. A bus dropped me (the main road having been snowploughed) at the turn-off to Tynehead, nearly two miles from Cakemuir. I struggled through the snowdrifts carrying my kitbag under one arm and a bag of Mesolithic flints under the other; and my heart was pounding for more than emotional reasons when I rang the doorbell of the home I had not seen for six years.

There was no response and no sign of life. I tramped up to the gardener's cottage to be told that my parents had given up the struggle when the snow became serious and had decamped to Edinburgh. I dossed down for the night and then trudged back to the road-end through the melting snow. I hitched a lift to Edinburgh, rang (successfully) Uncle Mouse in Murrayfield and was told that M and D were on their way back to Cakemuir! So I bused out a second time, and there at the turn-off was the old Alvis. My father's first remark as

I went to greet him was, 'Glad to see you've got the Eighth Army ribbon on your battledress.' I could not, however, produce Mussolini's medal for the conquest of Egypt. Ten minutes later, there was M on the doorstep …

I had foreseen a spiritual glow on 'home returning from a foreign strand', imagining that the rows of turnips, smell of leaf mould, grating of cartwheels and the red faces of ploughmen with drips on the end of their noses would fill me with ecstasy, or at least a sonnet or two. But apart from the gladness of being restored to my parents, the effect of gazing out of the window at the sodden landscape did not retain its charm for long. I was shortly admitted to the Officers' Home in Belgrave Crescent, Edinburgh, to have my tonsils out. The hospital tedium was relieved only by Lionel Smith (Robin Hodgkin's stepfather, and till lately Rector of Edinburgh Academy after years as the first Director of Education in Iraq after the First World War). He was a friend of D's and looked in with piles of books: T. E. Lawrence's *Letters*, Burton's *Pilgrimage to Mecca*, Hogarth's *Penetration of Arabia*, etc., which helped to shore up my wavering enthusiasm for spending the rest of my life in a bit of the Arab world. (Douglas Newbold had warned me that the average expectation of life in the Sudan Political, 'taking into account all those who had died of drink, been speared by their cooks, or been bitten to death by rats', was fifty-four. And here I was, at twenty-seven, with exactly half my expected lifespan already over.) Lionel Smith also buoyed me up by relating how the Ottoman Sultan had sent Louis XIV (was it?) a giraffe, the first seen in western Europe. To get it from Marseilles to Paris they had had to work out a special route with no bridges over it so that the giraffe wouldn't bump its head; and this route could still be traced today from the village inns called Le Café de la Girafe in memory of its passage.

At the end of May I set sail for the Sudan. D at least was proud to have so 'imperialist' a son. I wished I was leaving M in better shape. She had aged much in the six years of the war, had become rather deaf and was gradually to become much deafer and to lose her hair and her memory. But she remained cheerful and sprightly and enjoyed relating how her wig kept blowing off on the windy Dean Bridge. She lived on for another seventeen years.

Sudan Political Service

CHAPTER II

The Blue Nile

THIS chapter and the next describe my activities for nine years as a Sudan administrator. They tend to concentrate (as did my chapters on the war) on the odder aspects, but there are plenty of published accounts of the serious features of the Anglo-Egyptian Condominium to satisfy anyone interested. In case its curious history has been forgotten, however, the following is a brief outline.

In 1881 the Sudanese fundamentalist Mohammed Ahmed began a revolt both against a century of Egyptian misrule and to promote his belief in his mission to restore the purity of Islam. He soon declared himself the 'Mahdi' (the one sent by God) and attracted widespread support in the northern Sudan. By 1884 he had achieved crushing military successes over Egyptian garrisons and their British patrons. In March 1884 the decision to evacuate all Egyptian garrisons was reluctantly accepted by the powerless Khedive* in Cairo. General Charles Gordon was sent to Khartoum to engineer ways and means, but before long he was besieged there by Mahdist forces. Prime Minister Gladstone continued to oppose British military involvement but was finally obliged to yield to public demands for the rescue of Gordon. The attempted rescue party was just too late, for in January 1885 the Mahdists captured Khartoum and killed Gordon. The Mahdi himself died soon after, but his successor, the Khalifa Abdullahi, went from strength to strength. Britain decided in March 1886 that in the interests of the wretched Sudanese he must be overthrown by military means. The determined Lord Kitchener was given responsibility for organising an Anglo-Egyptian invasion. (The parallel with the Anglo-American invasion of Saddam Hussein's Iraq in 2003 may be thought striking but cannot be pushed very far.) It was not till November 1898 that his forces managed to reach Omdurman, where superior firepower enabled them to massacre 11,000 Mahdists. The Khalifa himself escaped to Kordofan but was killed two months later. Agreement with the Khedive for joint Anglo-Egyptian government of his reconquered Sudan was signed in January 1899. Britain saw to it that Egyptians played only a minimal part in

---

* The Khedive was the nominal ruler of Egypt and the Sudan on behalf of the Ottoman government in Istanbul, which had little interest in those countries.

the administration; and after 1924, when serious Egyptian-inspired troubles occurred in Khartoum, this minimal part was reduced still further. The Condominium was thereafter called by the wags the 'Condominimum'.

My experiences on disembarking at Port Said and heading for this Condominimum were well up (or down) to standard. I paid an Egyptian doctor a little over the fee for the statutory rabies injection in order to obtain the necessary certificate without the injection. Next, I found that my lift-van (huge crate) of household goods and gods was not among the cargo disembarked. Accepting this as par for the course, I put my one tin trunk of clothing on to a train for Cairo, which I realised, as I neared the city, was not the train I had put myself on. This left me with only my night stopper (a modest sponge bag); and in my panic at the thought of arriving in the Sudan with nothing but that, I leapt off the train when it reached Cairo, leaving my sponge bag too, if you can believe it, to disappear before I remembered it. So there I was, in Cairo, with nothing but the clothes I stood up in and a wallet containing a few pound notes and a phoney rabies certificate.

The kindly manager of the hotel I found my way to was content to accept an IOU for my food and lodging. He also suggested my going to the lost property office in Cairo station, just on the off-chance. I queued up there behind a string of old Egyptian ladies carrying hens upside down and told the official my sad story. He instantly produced my sponge bag, neatly sealed with a lead seal and with a list of the contents attached. This would not, I felt, have happened at King's Cross. But of my trunk (and of course my lift-van) there was no sign.

I reached Khartoum still clutching, like Arnold's Scholar Gypsy, my imperishable sponge bag, and was ushered into the presence of Newbold's successor as Civil Secretary, Sir James Robertson (once a second-row forward in the XV at Merchiston Castle, the school in Edinburgh where brother Ian was now teaching). He instructed me to go straight on to Wad Medani, the Blue Nile Province capital. This seemed a trifle callous as I had no uniform and not even time to buy some clean undies. My train reached Wad Medani at the witching hour of 0015. No one met me (maybe a message had gone astray), so I figured the best thing to do was to find my way to the District Commissioner's house. There was one taxi at the station but its battery was flat, so I had to push it most of the way, stalling as it did at every corner. I was delivered eventually to the door of the Assistant DC, John Grover. In the pitch dark I banged at it nervously. No response. I banged several more times; and then, from the flat roof of the adjoining house, came a severe voice from a silhouetted figure with a shotgun, evidently suspecting burglary. 'What's going on?' it shouted, in Arabic. It turned out to belong to Denis Vidler, the Province Headquarters DC, who was later to become my immediate boss, close friend and father of my first godchild. But it had been an unnerving introduction to service in the Sudan.

In the morning Denis took me, still of course in my only grey bags, sports jacket and tie, to see the Governor. He posted me to learn my trade in the Medani District itself and to lodge, since no house was available, with John Grover. He had captained the Oxford University cricket XI, so it was perhaps as well that the tie I was wearing was that of the Oxford Authentics Cricket Club. Grover was kind in his butch way (his own expression) but threw me in at the deep end to deal with 'petitioners'. For three piastres anyone in the district with a grievance could get a licensed scribe to indite it on a special form in Arabic. I could understand little enough of their writing, but that didn't seem to matter. My first petitioner was a lady complaining that her husband intended to divorce her on the grounds that she couldn't look after their baby. 'Look, by God,' she shouted, and, advancing on my desk, extracted half her bosom and squirted a jet of milk all over it. I hardly knew, so ignorant was I of the facts of life, that this was humanly possible. In any case I didn't quite see what I could usefully do about her case; but fortunately she was dragged away by the Police Sergeant.

I was very soon indoctrinated into other facts of life – such as the behaviour of the stereotypical British exile on his day off. For I felt it incumbent on me to attend the ritual beer-drinking in the British Club before lunch on Friday – approaching the club through the fruit trees where my cousin, James Moncrieff Paul, an earlier member of the Service, had been electrocuted ten years before when he tried to pull a prisoner off a lethal wire he had severed when pruning them. The club bar was largely occupied by a civil engineer with an enormous eagle owl perched on his bare forearm. Apart from nipping small bloodstained pieces out of it (its owner being too far gone to notice), the eagle-owl occasionally turned its head through 360 degrees without visible discomfort, and finally decided to flap its wings. As these had a span of about 6 feet, they knocked many of the bottles and glasses off the counter. Some brave man then dragged it and its owner away, much as the Police Sergeant had done with my milky petitioner.

My next professional obligation was to buy a horse and even to ride it. When originally signing on for the Political Service, I had had to complete a form on which one of the questions was 'STANDARD OF HORSEMANSHIP?'. I had written with commendable honesty 'Precarious'; but in the decadent post-war days this was evidently not judged a bar to admission.

A few days later the Blue Nile came down in a record flood and most of lower Wad Medani was submerged in water overnight. We spent all that day filling sandbags and wading around to distribute them – quite uselessly. The following morning John Grover and I commandeered a boat and rowed ourselves to the office down the main street. We were presented on arrival with a small fish by the office messenger boy, who was sitting on its window sill fishing.

No doubt out of filial loyalty – and on my horse too – I visited the local scout troop. Tying up outside their door, I was enchanted to read the Fire Orders posted up on it, in English. This is what the typescript said: 'When a fire breaks out or similar motion falls, agitation is bound to ensue by means of terrorists and loaters. In this case the squad may be turned out to disperse the mob and overwhelm the Police.' I naturally posted the text home to the County Commissioner, Midlothian. 'Loaters' sounded lovely; and as for 'overwhelming the Police', Baden-Powell must have turned in his grave.

Towards the end of October I was listening, as was my wont in order to improve my Arabic, to the 7 a.m. news on Cairo radio and heard that the Egyptian Prime Minister, Sidki Pasha, had signed an agreement in London with Mr Bevin, our Foreign Secretary, and had announced on his return to Cairo that it had been 'definitely agreed that Egypt and the Sudan were to be re-united under one Crown'. I told John Grover. He told the DC. The DC told the Governor. The Governor telephoned Khartoum. Khartoum no doubt called London, and the details of the Sidki–Bevin agreement filtered back. It seemed to all of us (wrongly in fact) that Bevin had sold the Sudan and the Political Service down the river.*

But at least my reputation as an Arabist received a boost. So did the political effervescence of the Wad Medani townsfolk. Street demonstrations, mostly pro-Egyptian but good humoured enough, were not unusual even before this. I had indeed joined in one of them at the back of the procession. Those in front of me were shouting 'Ya'eesh Wadi al-Nil' (Long live the unity of the Nile Valley), but the rest of the rent-a-crowd, uncertain of the precise purpose for which they had been hired, were screaming with equal fervour, 'Ya'eesh Nadi al-Nil', which was the name of the local football club.

But now, following the Sidki–Bevin agreement, demonstrations became more serious. I went round calling on prominent merchants, most of whom proved to be pro-Egyptian too (perhaps for safety's sake). So it was a relief when I reached the shop of one who was notoriously pro-British. After inveighing against the folly of educating children who as a result spent their days lounging in coffee shops and spreading sedition, this merchant asked me whether I would like to see the telegram he had just sent to both Sidki Pasha and the British Prime Minister. They proved to be identical and read, 'Kindly note that we want neither the Egyptian Crown nor the British Empire. We speak on behalf of the whole Sudanese nation, Signed … ' The following night the town was lit up to celebrate the return of a local member of the Sudanese delegation that had been in Cairo lobbying for the unity of the Nile Valley and the removal of the British from the Sudan. Several hundred people carried him shoulder high through the streets. It was, as John Grover

---

* The Sidki–Bevin protocol on the Sudan and the differing interpretations placed upon it are fully described in my book *The End of Empire in the Middle East* (Cambridge, 1991/1994), pp. 24–9.

and I agreed, reassuring to know that we had the country wholeheartedly behind us.

I heard later of a demonstration at this time in the District of Gedaref, immediately to our east. It was a huge District with an English DC and three assistant DCs; and the demonstrators had paraded through the town shouting '*Yasqut al-Ingeleez!*' (Down with the English!). The three assistant DCs, who were all Scots, joined in the march, slightly altering the cry to '*Yasqut al-Ingeleezi!*' (Down with the Englishman!), and the whole demonstration roared with laughter at this brilliant joke. It was indeed one of the most engaging qualities of the Sudanese that, whatever verbal abuse was directed at the British or Britain's policy, it was never personalised, and even our leading opponents always remained in personal terms friendly. Anyway, we simply got on with our normal work.

I was sent up-river to inspect Sennar, a sort of sub-district of Wad Medani. (This was where the huge Sennar Dam had been constructed just after the First World War to irrigate the increasing concession area of the Sudan Plantations Syndicate.) I don't remember doing much inspection, apart from having to assess everybody's millet crop for the 10 per cent *Ushur* tax. This had to be done on camelback, so I had little spare attention for the millet. Fortunately I was accompanied by the old mamour (administrative assistant), Abdulla Karib, who cavalierly assessed everybody's crop in a flash, while entertaining me with long funny stories in Arabic about the Egyptians, acting the parts as we camelled along. Many of them were political parables to illustrate his antipathy to Egypt. His version of 'Moses in the Bulrushes' was especially hilarious from start to finish; but I have space only to reproduce the last page of my recording of it:

When Moses was about four, he started showing signs of being too clever by half, and Pharaoh told his harem to get him put down, like all the other foreign babies he had already slaughtered because of a Fiki's warning that one of them would grow up and assassinate him. After a fearful argument with his women, Pharaoh agreed to give the boy a chance as follows. They would get a tea tray and put on it a lump of charcoal, so, and a lump of dates, so. Then the boy would be called in and told to help himself. If he started in on the red charcoal, he was obviously of low mental calibre and no danger to the state. If he chose the duller-looking dates, he was clearly too clever for his age and should be killed off accordingly. So they call for a tea tray, put the charcoal and the dates on it, like so, and like so, and call in Moses. At the critical moment down flies Gabriel, who is one of Allah's *murasilas* [office messengers]. Fortunately Gabriel makes himself invisible and when he puts his hand over the dates so that Moses can't see them, nobody suspects anything fishy, and Moses is told to help himself. Seeing no alternative, he helps himself to the charcoal, pops it into his mouth, burns his tongue horribly, and lets out a flow of the most dreadful language imaginable. Pharaoh, seeing how stupid the child is to eat charcoal when there are dates on offer, laughs a huge laugh and lets Moses off. And later Moses grows up and kills Pharaoh just as the Fiki had warned.

I was so enthralled by this Bible story that I'd never heard before that I had forgotten it was intended by old Abdulla Karib as a contemporary parable. So, when asked whether I had seen the point, I had to get him to explain. 'The Sudan', he said, 'is like the boy Moses. The dates represent the delicious prospect of independence; the burning charcoal corresponds to continued British rule. If the Sudan is greedy and chooses independence, it'll get put down by the Egyptian King, whereas if it takes the charcoal, that may be less tasty to the palate but at least the Sudan will be allowed to stay alive and grow up.'

Meditating on the profundities of this parable, I began to wonder who was going to take the part of Gabriel. Not Mr Bevin, surely, who was hardly of a build to descend from the sky as an angel. I also found myself wondering whom the Sudan, when it grew up, would kill off in the interests of independence. It seemed wisest not to press the parable too far. In any case Abdulla Karib was already launched on his next story:

> You know my son, Muhammed. Well, when he was a boy, he was very partial to tinned peaches. Sometimes I would bring out a tin and open it at the top and we would polish it off together. When it was empty, he would seize me by the knee and say, 'Now, Papa, open it at the bottom too and we'll see if we can get some more peaches out.' The boy Muhammed is like the Sudanese. We open the tin at the top, which is the British, and when it's empty, we think we'll get some more peaches by opening it again at the bottom, which is King Farouk.

All this time, of course, what Karib was supposed to be explaining to me was how to assess *Ushur*. His technique, he said, was simply to add 2½ per cent to the previous assessment of each man's crop. This struck me as a bit summary, quite apart from the problem of working out 2½ per cent of what it was last time. But no one, Karib assured me, ever complained. His technique was to stand me in good stead four years later in western Darfur, when I was required to assess for the information of the United Nations the increase in all crop production over the previous year – single-handed, in an area the size of Scotland. 'Total area under pumpkins', and so on. I simply adopted Karib's formula, and again no one questioned the result, either in Khartoum or in the United Nations.

That night I was taken by the Sennar rest-house cook to hunt for crocodiles in the lake below the Sennar Dam. He put me in a boat and armed me with a torch and an axe, explaining that crocodiles were fascinated by torch beams and that, when a croc came alongside the boat in response, all I had to do was to hit it very hard on the snout with my axe. He would then cast a rope-noose round it, pull the beast ashore and sell its skin in the *suq*. The bit about crocodiles coming alongside when I shone the torch at them proved absolutely correct, but I felt alarmingly unequal to the rest of my task. So I took over the oars and he bagged a crocodile or two.

Another day I got myself driven out to Jebel Moya, a great prehistoric site excavated twenty years before by Dr Wellcome, founder of the Wellcome Trust and an amateur archaeologist. He had never got around to publishing his excavations, being I suppose too busy inventing cures for cancer; but years later I read the fat volume someone eventually produced from Wellcome's notes. It describes *inter alia* how Wellcome had invented aerial photography as an aid to archaeology. He did this by flying kites with expensive cameras attached and then pulling a long string to take what he hoped would be revealing vertical snaps. Endless cameras crashed to the ground, but he was enormously rich.

Jebel Moya revived my own antiquarian enthusiasms, and when I was back in Wad Medani, having already ceased spending Fridays in the club bar, I went off to excavate some mounds at Umm Sunut, 10 miles upstream: improper amateurism but thrilling, for I came up with beautiful black burnished bowls with raised fluting curling up from the base. I still don't know what culture they belonged to, or whether Umm Sunut has since been properly excavated.*

I did, to be sure, do some more serious work, learning in the process the workings of the Sudan Plantations Syndicate, the biggest agricultural cooperative in the world, whose headquarters were near Wad Medani. It was also known as the Gezira Cotton Scheme – the Gezira being the land between the Blue and White Niles over which the huge scheme extended. Each Sudanese participant was allotted a standard plot on which to plant cotton (and some smaller crops for food). The sale of cotton was the source of the Sudan's main revenue from abroad. The British cotton inspectors, each supervising his own 'block', impressed me much – though I never felt quite at home with some of them. The version of John Masefield's famous poem 'Cargoes' that I composed in their honour (so to speak) began as follows:

> Sweaty Block Inspector with gin-soaked armpits
> Trotting through the cotton on an old brown mare
> With a cargo of horse-whips,
> Whisky flasks, monocles,
> Polo sticks, poker-dice, and lotion for the hair.

(The whole version was printed in *Sudan Verse* in 1968.)

---

* I later wrote 'Early Cultures on the Northern Blue Nile', *Sudan Notes and Records*, vol. XXXIII, part 2, 1952, pp. 202–15.

My only serious setback at this time was a septic coccyx, the consequence of bumping for hours across cracked cotton-soil on the back of someone's lorry. The resulting operation – two, in fact, since the surgeon made a bosh of the first one – was excruciating. But this ill wind did blow me some good. For I was due to take my law exams in a month and was in hospital long enough not only to read some of the tedious 'required books' but even to learn by heart five chapters, selected at random, of the weighty *Sudan Government Ordinances*. This worked like a dream, for three of the five turned out to be the subject of questions in the exam. As a result (though my understanding of law was minimal) I received such splendid marks that I was appointed a First Class Magistrate overnight, empowered to sentence murderers to death.

The offenders I was required to try in my new magisterial capacity were fortunately not subject to the death penalty. The first was a man charged with pouring a bowl of boiling porridge over his mother-in-law. He pleaded guilty, with enthusiasm. The next offender was less easily dealt with. He was charged with throwing the police officer's telephone out of the window. For some minutes the accused sat on the floor of my court, urinating composedly and humming in a gentle baritone. He appeared completely oblivious not only to the dignity of the court but to its very existence. So I rose to my feet, feeling very wise and magisterial, bent over him and asked him his name in an encouraging manner. He looked up and, by way of reply, directed a gobbet of spittle at my head, straddling the target. I sentenced him to be sent to the Fiki (medicine man) at Managil 50 miles away, whose principal cure for lunacy was said to be the cat-o'-nine-tails. A sordid triumph.

I have related all these trivialities which took place in my first year as a Sudan administrator to illustrate something of the diversity of that now long-obsolete job. I aim to be more selective over my remaining eight years. But I stick to the view already expressed in the Introduction that the 'Trivial makes the world safe for the Sublime'.

As an illustration of that dictum I will reproduce a page from a letter written three years later as DC Hassaheissa (northern Gezira) to Kenneth Smith, my old friend in Magdalen College, who was now Deputy Governor of the Gambia:

The District has just been invaded by a band of (?hypnotic) *Fellata* – Nigerians who cross the continent to pick cotton. Twenty miles upstream from here a tall black-haired *Fellati* with a quaint deformity of the toes recently took two pound notes and a gold brooch from an old woman, giving her in exchange seven pound notes and an even larger gold brooch. She woke in the morning to find they had all turned overnight into pieces of ordinary paper, the brooch being distinguished from the rest only by a marigold done in orange chalk. A few days later in a different area a *Fellati* with the same deformity of the toes, but short and with white hair, was arrested for turning pieces of toilet paper into (ephemeral) pound notes at a shilling a time. Meanwhile in a third village a *Fellati*, about whose toes nothing has yet been reported, has been seen knocking showers of dollars out of the wall by tapping it with his finger-ring, and is also reported to have made an agreement with a merchant for a small consideration to turn five cigarette packets of sand into solid gold. The packets had been filled and put into the merchant's safe. The metamorphosis was to complete itself in three days. On the second of them the *Fellati* had disappeared. The only conjuror the Police *have* arrested (No. 2 of those described) is languishing in gaol, untried because we can't find anything in the Penal Code to charge him with.

I gaily related all this to some well-educated Sudanese who came to supper with me. They listened respectfully and then one of them solemnly said, 'There is nothing peculiar about such things, sir. It's all a question of *baraka* [grace]. Some *baraka* comes from the Devil, some from God. In Kamlin [a town 30 miles north of Hassaheissa] you may visit the headmaster of a school of Islamic jurisprudence who, if he has nothing ready to offer you as a welcome, will conjure a pumpkin or a box of chocolates out of the empty air. He does not consider this a miraculous gift, just a domestic convenience.'

My next leave home was marked by two initiatives. First, Lawrence Bussell, a doctor friend from the war, asked me to accompany him in his family's beautiful Victorian caravan from Uxbridge, where he was living in it, to Hull. Our precise destination was a village called Swine, where his sister, whose turn had come round for having the caravan for a year, was married to the vicar. Lawrence had bought for the journey a huge Suffolk Punch ('Lady') to pull the caravan up the green lanes of England (today doubtless all tarmac). It was as well that East Anglia is flattish since the caravan had no brake, only an iron 'slipper' which had to be inserted under a back wheel when going too fast downhill. Food rationing was still the order of the day. Lawrence had no ration book but that didn't seem to matter in East Anglia, for at the end of each day's travel farmers gave us without hesitation half a dozen eggs, lots of butter and a field for the Suffolk Punch. Twice we fell in with camps of genuine Romany-speaking gypsies, with whom we ate *hotchiwitchies* (hedgehogs) and exchanged a bagful of Woolworths clothes pegs for an equal bagful of the lovely ones they carved with their penknives. They thought the exchange absurdly generous on our part.

The diary we jointly kept came to light forty years later when Lawrence, then living near us in Devon, produced it. It is full of quaint incidents, but I have space only for one that took place as we neared our destination:

The Brigadier who owns south-east Yorkshire had agreed in advance to let us have a permanent site for the caravan at Swine. But at the last moment he cancelled his consent on the grounds that the District Council, of which he is Chairman, has passed a by-law prohibiting caravans throughout the whole area. We were enraged beyond measure and determined to singe his beard in his Elizabethan Mansion at Burton Constable. So we rumbled up his half-mile drive through parks and fishponds, drew up outside its splendiferous porch, and tied Lady's halter round the provocatively naked statue of Eros that stood there. This was watched through the windows by a goggling assemblage of the crème-de-la-crème of south-east Yorkshire who were there for a Sherry Party. We marched up the marble steps and rang a peal on the doorbell. The Brigadier himself came rushing out and thwarted our intention of giving him a piece of our mind by giving us a piece of his. So we unhitched Lady from Eros, leaving him with a nice pile of horse-droppings, and drove off shouting encouragement to Lady in Romany (or something like it). We had certainly done the Brigadier an unintended service by 'making' his Sherry Party for him.

My other initiative on leave was to take part in the excavation, in pouring rain, of an Iron Age fort on top of the Cheviots run by Peggy Piggott, the pretty young wife of Professor Stuart Piggott of Edinburgh University. Everyone adored her. I saw much of her during her subsequent difficult life – difficult since she had to divorce the Professor, and more difficult still when she fell in love, while writing the *Standard Guide to the Antiquities of Sicily*, with a psychotic Sicilian and married him. Two years later, when they were living in Bath, he became so unhinged that he had to be strapped to his bed and cared for night and day by Peggy for six months. One morning, when she had nearly died of the strain, he suddenly said, 'I'm going back to Sicily', forced his way instantly up, went, and was never heard of again. Peggy became Curator of the Devizes Museum, where in her old age she housed and cared for the penniless scholar A. W. Lawrence (T. E.'s brilliant but modest elder brother). In 1991 I took Jenny to call on her in her house in Devizes and to meet this great man. There was nobody in. Two days later we discovered why, when we opened *The Times* and there was A. W. Lawrence's obituary. He had died an hour or two before we had knocked on Peggy's door.

Back in the Sudan I was posted to take charge of Rufa'a, a sub-district of the Northern Gezira on the desert side of the Blue Nile. I was proud to be on my own, though the landscape was as desolate and featureless as anything in the whole country. The redeeming benefit was Mohammed Ahmed Abu Sinn, who shortly replaced his father as Nazir (paramount Sheikh) of the Shukria, the dominant tribe in the area. He was short, fat, and blackish, with most of a degree in medicine and an enchanting laugh. He became a special friend for life, staying with us in several places (his fine life ending in 1990 when I wrote his obituary for *The Times*).

Crocodiles were a nuisance in Rufa'a and I was expected to slay them from a boat – not with a torch and an axe as in Sennar, but with a police rifle: not an easy task when the Nile was rough. I was never confidently credited with one, though not far from where one croc escaped a man was found dead with a bullet in his head. I persuaded myself that it couldn't have been fired by me and that there was therefore no need to charge myself with culpable homicide.

I was now detailed to go up to Khartoum and take the minutes at the first meeting of the Governor General's Advisory Council for the Northern Sudan, a large body of handpicked greybeards. It was of course all in Arabic, and mine was still pretty basic. My minutes (in English) were, one might say, approximate. But they were evidently elegant enough for, when I read over to one greybeard my record of a speech of his, translating it back into Arabic, his comment was, 'Did I really say something as good as that? The glory to God!' I was lodged meanwhile with the Khartoum DC, whose house adjoined the Khartoum Zoo. Most of the zoo's animals were uncaged and allowed to wander at will. Sleeping in the open under my mosquito net I was woken one morning, not by my host's tea-bearer, but by a huge head pushing through the net. It turned out to be that of a giant eland.

The north end of Rufa'a District was controlled by a family of unscrupulous holy men who caused me much trouble. One of their constant complaints concerned an immemorial boundary dispute with a tribe in the adjoining District of Khartoum North, so I went to visit its DC with the suggestion that we should make a joint effort to settle it. He gave me some stark advice. 'What a young chap like you needs to understand', he said, 'is that these tribes *live* off their boundary disputes. They would never forgive us if we settled them.' The DC concerned was Jake Seamer, who five years later became a housemaster at Marlborough. There he made his mark by the advice he gave to another young chap. The boy had gone to him seeking a theological explanation of the Trinity. 'Well,' said Jake, 'it's like cricket. Three stumps, but if one of them is knocked down, the bails are off and you're out.'

I will record only two other incidents from my time in Rufa'a. First, I developed an extraordinary affliction on the soles of my feet. They were suddenly covered with huge yellow blisters and couldn't be stood on. There being no doctor in Rufa'a I had recourse, on the advice of my cook, to a character known as *Kura al-Kelb* (Dog's Leg), who had been one of Kitchener's camel boys fifty years earlier and now practised medicine on the strength of it. He covered my feet with a sort of spinach and told me to lie motionless on my sofa for two days, by which time the blisters would have vanished. I did as I was told. As work had to go on, dignitaries, policemen, petitioners, etc., filed into my house, slipping off their shoes as they approached holy ground, and were confronted round the corner by a pair of spinach-covered legs pointing at them like a pair of camouflaged trench mortars. When the two days were up, I dismantled the camouflage and found that the only change in my feet was that my toes had gone quite hollow and went in and out when squeezed, like those celluloid ducks one used to play with in the bath. My cook urged me to call in Dog's Leg for a further consultation; but I preferred to leave things to time as a less whimsical healer, and in due course my toes filled out again and the blisters filled in.

My cook was the anti-hero of the second and much more alarming incident. This occurred during a visit by the Governor General, his wife, his ADC and others. Sir Robert Howe, markedly different from his predecessor, General Sir Hubert Huddleston, proved a small, unpretentious citizen with a friendly smile. After they had attended a huge tribal gathering of the Shukria, I had to give this distinguished party lunch in my wretched bungalow. In case it should be needed, I had had the seat in its only loo hastily repainted twenty-four hours before. Lunch, designed by my cook, began unimaginatively with the distribution of slices of watermelon. Plates were in due course removed, and after an interminable wait, in came my cook with the second course. This proved to be more slices of watermelon. The fried goat and pumpkin which followed was something of a relief, at least to me. But while we were attacking it the Governor General expressed a desire to visit the loo. Another interminable wait followed. Eventually his ADC went to see whether he was having difficulty pulling back the rusty bolt on the loo door. It proved far worse, for he had stuck to the newly painted seat and was having difficulty in removing the paint from his posterior. I don't remember what the pudding was. Probably watermelon ... Altogether I did not feel that my prospects of promotion had been greatly advanced. And I almost gave up knitting the blue pullover for my cook that I had been working on for over a year. Nevertheless promotion unexpectedly came. For just before going on leave I was told that on my return I was to replace Denis Vidler as DC Northern Gezira.

It was at this time, May 1948, that I heard that Cakemuir had been sold off and that M and D were moving into a top flat in Belgrave Crescent, Edinburgh, a few yards from the officers' home where I had said goodbye to my tonsils. I remember little of my leave but the view of Edinburgh from the windows of their new flat across 'The waters of Leith, the waters of Leith,/ Whaur the lassies gang doon tae wash their teeth'. (Who on earth wrote that felicitous couplet? I think it must have been Topaz McGonagall.)

Back in the Sudan I took with me from Rufa'a to Hassaheissa the imperishable memory of two noises. One was Mohammed Ahmed Abu Sinn's laugh, the other was the equally magical sound made during their long migration by the *Rahoo* (the Abyssinian crested crane) flying up the river in endless huge Vs from Siberia to the tropics. Their cry still echoes in my head today. Moreover they tasted like turkey and had been a welcome substitute for the daily goat and pumpkin.

Hassaheissa, where Northern Gezira District was centred, was not everyone's idea of fun. But apart from two bouts of malaria, I enjoyed the job – to the point that, after two years in it, when I was being told by the Province Governor (Bill Luce) in his office in Wad Medani that I was to be transferred to Darfur, I took a quick improper look at the papers on his desk when he was momentarily out of the room. The top one was a letter he was sending to the Governor of Darfur. It said, 'The only thing I know to Balfour Paul's discredit is that he wants to stay in Hassaheissa.'

The work in the relative sophistication of the Gezira differed considerably from what I had been doing on the other, much less developed, side of the Nile. It involved, for instance, encouraging democracy and discouraging female circumcision. My addresses on the latter to my four Local Government Councils were a severe tax on my knowledge of Arabic, let along my knowledge of the female anatomy. But as usual it was my spare-time activities which I remember most vividly – such as discovering and excavating ancient burials at Goz Kabbaro (not at all the same as those of Umm Sunut) on the raised patches of sand inland that broke here and there the monotony of the muddy cotton-soil. The skeletons I dug up were surrounded by pots and querns and were wearing ostrich eggshell necklaces and stone lip-plugs.

My archaeological leanings were pushed still further by a chance visit from the great O. G. S. Crawford, who invented the Ordnance Survey of England, founded and edited *Antiquity*, and was now engaged on a volume about the Fung Kingdom of Sennar. I took him to my favourite riverain site of Arbagy, where I had been collecting bits of old Fung tobacco pipes, carved in stone and decorated, lying among ceramic sherds (some of these prehistoric, some of them twentieth-century). Arbagy was also where a silver coin had been found, issued by the Emperor Maximilian when recruiting a company of Sudanese soldiers for the invasion of Mexico in 1840!

My enthusiasm for archaeology had indeed become such that I planned, when I went on my next leave, to embark on a B.Litt. at Oxford and resign from the Sudan Political Service. In the event I embarked on matrimony instead (and was relieved that the SPS had not already struck me off their lists). My marriage came about this way: some of the pottery I had been excavating was wheel-turned, but the potter's wheel had not been in use in the Sudan for 1,500 years, and I decided to reintroduce it! So when I was home in Edinburgh I visited the Portobello Potteries. One of the girls employed to decorate its stoneware pots was Marnie Ogilvy. I had not seen her since those dreadful Scottish dancing classes at Winton twenty-five years before, when she was three. She seemed much nicer now.

Our courtship was brief, with just two months of my leave remaining, and we were married in Haddington Church. William Clark arranged with David Astor, owner of the *Observer*, of which William was now Deputy Editor, for us to spend our brief honeymoon in the Astor shooting lodge in the northern half of Jura (off the west coast of Scotland), where no one else lived except George Orwell (of *Animal Farm*, etc.). This was especially pleasing to Marnie, since she had once been walking with her friend Bromwen Pulsford round Islay and had gone to the Islay post office to ask how to get across to Jura, the next island up. The postmistress's lilting reply was, 'It's a willd place, Joora.

There's nobody'ld be wanting to go *there*.' But supposing someone did want to? As before she simply repeated the chant, 'It's a willd place, Joora. There's nobody'ld be wanting to go *there*.' So they never made it.

For our honeymoon I borrowed D's old Standard Vanguard and very nearly failed to bring it back. For on the evening before we were booked on the ferry, I was driving back from a fishing expedition – and in those unharvested lochs one caught two trout at every cast – and when I excitedly drew Marnie's attention to the sensational sunset I overturned the car in the ditch. We walked back to the shooting lodge and asked the housekeeper whether there was anywhere on Jura we could hire a tractor. She shook her head but said she would see whether anything could be done in the morning. We went to bed in trepidation. The ferry was at 9 a.m. As dawn broke we were woken by a rumbling noise, looked out of the window, and there was the housekeeper, still in her nightie and white stocking-cap, calmly driving a tractor with my father's car tied on behind, upright and magically undamaged.

We reached Hassaheissa without further mishap, but not for long. I had acquired a second horse and we set off on a ride. Marnie, so I believed, was a better rider than me, but her horse threw her almost at once. She had clearly done something awful to the top of her spine, and it was with great difficulty that we got her to the railway station on an improvised stretcher. Medani Hospital sent her in short order to Khartoum, where she spent two months in hospital, mending slowly, and was then allowed home. It was not lonely for her while I worked, as we had endless guests coming to visit the Gezira Cotton Scheme. We also had the eccentric Harry Oulton in the District, settling landownership in the far north-west for a planned extension of the scheme. We were breakfasting one morning when a young Sudanese panted up the drive with a piece of paper in a cleft stick, with which Harry had dispatched him on foot some 25 miles the previous evening. His urgent message consisted of the opening sentence of the German version of the Flopsy Bunnies: '*Es waren einmal vier kleine Kaninchen, sie heissten Flopsy, Mopsy, Topsy und Cottontail.*' Harry then went – not before time, we judged – on leave, and bought for £150, across a bar in the Isle of Wight, a small aeroplane, made (I learnt later) of Venetian blinds stuck together with Secotine. Mysteriously he received permission to fly back to the Sudan in it. On the way he landed at Tobruk and in so doing smashed the wooden 'skid' that took the place in his machine of the third wheel. An RAF carpenter in the Tobruk garrison could find nothing more suitable to replace it with than the curved end of a hockey stick. So equipped, Harry flew on, but had to make a forced landing on an island in the Nile, where he was arrested for entering Egypt without permission. That was the end of the aeroplane.

'Town Rides' were a feature of the traditional early-morning disciplines of Empire. Once a week the whole District Staff, one behind the other on horseback, would process through the streets (of Hassaheissa in my case) to check that householders were observing the proprieties. If one householder had failed to clean his street frontage, I would shout over my shoulder to my Sudanese Assistant to tell the man or woman to get down to it. My Assistant would shout over *his* shoulder to the Mamour behind him. The Mamour would shout over his to the Police Sergeant, who in turn would shout to the policeman at the back of the procession. By this time the offender, if not the offence, was probably beyond identification. But the policeman would arrest *someone*, and the administration of Empire would proceed. Whatever the defects of this system, the streets of Sudanese towns were a good deal cleaner than those of London (even the London of those days).

Another curious feature of the system, in this case the judicial one, was that the DC had to deal with offenders tried initially in the 'native courts' and passed up to him if the nature of the offence carried a penalty beyond the native court powers. The oddity was that the native courts applied unwritten customary law, whereas the DC applied the codified Sudan penal code. The two systems differed, especially on the taking of evidence on oath. Under the penal code we automatically put witnesses for both prosecution and defence on oath before hearing their evidence. This was regarded – very rightly in my view – as improper under customary law, since it meant that one side or the other (and possibly both) would be swearing a false oath. Under customary law no oaths were taken before all the evidence had been heard. The court then decided which lot were most likely to be lying, and the other side was then given the right of demanding an oath from the suspected liars. The oath could be demanded either on the Koran or on something even more likely to frighten them, such as the tomb of a local holy man. Those faced with this requirement would then either bow and withdraw their evidence or face the consequences of swearing falsely. In one case, I recall, the oath was demanded on the tomb of an especially holy man, 90 miles from Hassaheissa on the other side of the river; and the two parties were sent off there accordingly under police escort. I was told that one of the lot required to swear took the oath and fell dead on the spot. Nobody was surprised. Customary law seemed to me much more likely to ascertain the truth than the system I had to apply in my own court.

One Friday in summer, when I was unnaturally working in my office on my day off, my Police Officer, Nur ed-Din, blew in, wearing nothing at all but a short khaki shirt and waving a telegram he had just sent to the Province Governor. It read: 'A Happy Christmas to you and all your staff except Khalifa Mahjoub'. Khalifa Mahjoub was head of the Province Police and therefore Nur ed-Din's boss. But knowing Khalifa, I absolutely concurred with the sentiments in Nur's telegram – even though it was August, so that Christmas wishes were a bit premature. To my relief he was not sacked. His eccentricities proved no bar to his appointment, after independence, as a minister in successive governments, and he was still in the Cabinet when I went to the Sudan in 1978 and visited him in his house in Khartoum North surrounded by innumerable children. While he was describing their individual talents, a large lady heavily wrapped up came in. Nur proudly announced in his rather special English, 'And this here is my fertile wife.'

In February 1951 Marnie flew home to have a baby, due at the end of March. I was of course on tenterhooks, and when on 4 April I was rung up in my office by my cook to say that a telegram for me had been delivered to my house, I ran the half-mile there in under half a minute. My cook, equally excited, handed me the telegram at the door. It said, 'Tell Izz ed-Din to send Monthly Report immediate. Surveys, Medani.'

As if to compensate for this anti-climax, that afternoon the stacked cotton bales (thousands of them, the whole year's crop) in the ginneries 150 yards from my house went up in flames. Long after midnight I described the scene in a letter to Marnie:

> Already a quarter of the Sudan's total revenue for the year has been lost. Fire Brigades from as far away as Khartoum and elsewhere were soon on the spot. Meanwhile thousands of people milled around, including hundreds of police, 2000 locals, and 50 British troops – the latter doing everything in disciplined fashion, tremendously impressive in the smoky chaos. For hour after hour we rolled the huge sacks away from the flames, rolled and rolled till our tongues stuck to our mouths and our eyes were bloodshot with smoke and burning cotton-dust. A strong Haboob was blowing and sparks leapt 150 ft at a time. The only bulldozer in the area had been at work 12 hours so far, driven by a young man from Lancashire, imperturbable in the furnace and with a cigarette permanently between his lips. 'You're playing cricket on Friday', he shouted at me, letting his clutch in and roaring forward once more into the flames. Ali, my driver, received a blast from a 4" hose straight in the eye and I saw him being carried away. Hamed, my Police Officer, had had nothing to drink till midnight when I put him under arrest and dragged him to my house. Ali Hassan, my Assistant DC, observed (so he told me, when the worst was over) a bevy of Hassaheissa prostitutes desperately rolling sacks with the rest of us and moaning, 'All our business ruined!' My house has been full of people of all colours all night, bathing their eyes, swilling a bottle, and racing back into the fray.

It was the worst economic disaster the Sudan had ever experienced. But at least it took my mind off the Edinburgh Infirmary. A week later the right telegram arrived. My first child's birth was straightforward, but not the immediate aftermath. Babies delivered in Marnie's public ward were taken away and laid in rows on a long table outside. The first time Marnie's was brought to her to suckle she noticed with dismay that the label round its neck bore the nauseating name 'Sprote'. She swapped it for another, which seems to have been the right one.

After a bout of malaria I was given a week's leave and went all the way to Rashad in the Nuba mountains, where Bill Monteith was the DC. He had mentioned in a letter that he had recently asked a group of Nuba (who are non-Arab) where their ancestors had come from, and they had answered, 'Our ancestors were dropped here by flying Tebeldi trees.' So it would have been absurd for me not to go. The Nuba proved as bubbly as their mountains. Their Tebeldi (i.e. baobab) trees, which were new to me, were often 12 yards around the base, many of them used for storing water in; but I didn't see any of them flying or dropping babies.

Home leave (and the sight of Ann, my first child) arrived. The prospect of always having to sponge house room off relatives persuaded us to find a cottage of our own. So I set off, still in D's Standard Vanguard, to look for one in south-west Scotland. All those advertised proved wholly undesirable residences. Driving back along the Solway I passed Cardoness Castle (which was too big and in ruins) and there, round the corner, was just what I wanted. The trouble was that it wasn't for sale. But just for fun I found the lane that led to it, rang the doorbell and told the owner that I wanted to buy it, and that if he should ever think of selling, here was my address. A fortnight later I received a telegram from him offering it to me for the colossal sum of £6,500 – he clearly knew a sucker when he saw one. I took Marnie down to see it. She was equally enchanted. During the three weeks we lodged in the village (Gatehouse-of-Fleet) I finally brought to birth my long-gestated play, *The Lights Are Always Orange*. I sent it at William Clark's suggestion to the *Observer* theatre critic, J. C. Trewin. He wrote back, 'I think this is a genuinely unusual play, uncommonly dramatic and miles away from the routine stuff. I should try it first on one of the major Repertory Theatres, which would smooth its way for the future.' He recommended Denis Carey at the Bristol Old Vic. I was naturally over the moon and saw myself becoming Britain's leading playwright. Not so, alas, did Denis Carey. After six months' silence he sent it back as 'rather wooden'. The Birmingham Rep, then run by Sir D. Hall, was equally unimpressed, and I lost heart. I have just read it again after fifty years and rather liked it. It is based on the Vandal invasion of North Africa in AD 429, a colonial problem for the Romans. It is consequently a bit old fashioned, but there is at least a central Angry Young Man and a Kitchen Sink (and St Augustine to boot).

A more immediate problem was how to bring £6,500 into the world. This would have been for me a very difficult birth without the assistance of two midwives (my father and my brother Ian). We had Little Boreland (Wee B) duly surveyed, but on the day we moved into our dream house I put my foot through a rotting plank in the hall floor. I called in the village builder. He sniffed around and to my dismay proceeded to cut a hole in the adjoining sitting-room floor. He pushed his head through the hole and came up with a broad smile. 'It's the finest case of dry rot ah've ever seen in ma whole life.' We had to have the woodwork in the whole house stripped and replaced. (Indeed, we had to do so again the following year, but by then it was insured by Rentokil.)

When our leave was over we leased the house to a refugee German architect who had just married a startling young beauty in even more startling circumstances. He had been on a walking tour of the Pennines when a blonde girl galloping by on a black horse paused to ask the best way to the Scottish border, explaining that she was riding from Land's End to John o' Groats for the fun of it. Having touched his cap and given her precise instructions, he had caught a bus to the border crossing he had recommended. He had stationed himself there, and in due course along came the black horse and the blonde rider. He saluted and gave her advice on the next stage of her route. He then made his way to the top of the Beef Tub pass and again waited. Sure enough, up the pass he saw the black horse coming, and when it drew level he greeted the rider and asked her to marry him. She did. But alas it didn't last, and before we went to Little Boreland on our next leave she had run away, leaving the house in a horrid mess. Wolfie, as he was called, had gone off to find her, but never did. We had to find new tenants.

CHAPTER 12

Darfur

MY transfer to Darfur took place on my return from leave. On reaching the Province capital, Fasher, I was taken straight off by the Governor, Bill Henderson, who sang Scottish folk songs at the top of his voice as we bumped along to attend a vast tribal gathering in its southern District, Nyala. I was wearing a pair of riding boots I had borrowed from a friend in Medani, so tight that I was obliged to sleep in them at night. But what I remember even more vividly is the short melody played all day long by a Fur musician on an ibex horn. (It still runs through my head every day.) I could see already that I was going to enjoy Darfur.

The job of Resident Dar Masalit (Geneina) was unique in the Service, since one was not a plenipotentiary DC but the Adviser to the Masalit Sultan, whose kingdom had been incorporated (more or less) into the Condominium in 1916. That was when we overthrew Ali Dinar, the tough tyrant of Darfur, whose suzerainty the Masalit had never wholly accepted. The old Masalati Sultan, who died just before my arrival, had been notorious for always donning, when receiving British visitors, an RAF pilot's helmet and goggles (Geneina had been an air force staging post in the war). The eldest son, now Sultan, resembled his father. The younger one didn't: he was the only Masalati who had visited England, returning with a dinner jacket and a Harrods dinner service as symbols of Westernisation. I liked them both and played much hilarious polo with them and my mounted police – the only form of equitation at which a horse and I have ever remotely felt conjoined as one animal.

I wrote monthly 'Letters from Geneina' for the *Sudan Star*, which brought me a modest remuneration and served as the basis of my first article for *Blackwoods*, 'The Very Rich Hours of the Sultan of Geneina'.* (The horrors suffered fifty years later by the Masalit and other non-Arab tribes at the hands of the Janjaweed supported by the Sudan government were much in the world news in 2004. The unspeakable behaviour of the Janjaweed was officially defined by the American Secretary of State as genocide.)

Lying on the west side of the African watershed, Dar Masalit is better

---

* *Blackwoods*, after publishing several pieces of mine in subsequent years, sadly closed down in the 1980s after being much read by the British for 150 years.

watered than the rest of northern Sudan and grew more. Trekking round his kingdom and supping with me under the stars, the Sultan was stung one evening on the thigh by a scorpion. Recalling my own scorpion drama at Wadi Halfa I was naturally alarmed. But Abo Abdulrahman simply told his retainers to go and fetch some leaves of the tobacco plant (which was widely cultivated, for chewing). None happened to grow in the vicinity, so he stretched out a hand for my tin of Balkan Sobranie pipe tobacco, rubbed some on to his sting and went on unconcernedly with his soup.

Pain did not seem to worry the Masalit. Our only doctor was an Egyptian Copt, who had spent thirteen years qualifying in Glasgow, marrying in the process his landlady's daughter in the Great Western Road. No other job in the world was offered him but that of Medical Officer, Geneina. One evening he came to my house looking as white as an Egyptian can. He told me that one of his hospital patients, whose thatched house had caught fire when he was in a drunken sleep and had collapsed on top of him, had had to have his arm crudely amputated. The following afternoon the man had got up and walked away from the hospital, waving his bloodstained stump. The poor MO said he couldn't face doctoring people like this and wanted a transfer. He was in fact a sad figure. His Glaswegian wife had accompanied him out as far as Wadi Halfa, but stepping out of the aeroplane while it was being refuelled there she had taken one look at the steaming desert and flown straight back to Glasgow.

Western Darfur boasted a wide range of fauna – especially lions, which did much damage and had to be shot when possible. I was taken out one day to shoot one in a nearby village, it being taken for granted that I was a skilled marksman. There was the lion, sitting in front of a clump of bushes. I fired (a police rifle) and the beast leapt into the air and rolled over into the bushes. 'A hit! A veritable hit!' cried the spectators. There was indeed no sign of it moving and it must obviously be dead. I walked forward to view the corpse, and just as I reached the bushes there was a sudden roar and a very live lion leapt straight over my head and (fortunately) made off. I lost my reputation as a marksman but at least I had not also lost my life.

Crocodiles also abounded in the south in deep water channels – a geological oddity since these 'creeks' are not connected with any river, as they must once have been for crocodiles to thrive there. One day on trek I was eating my bully-beef sandwiches on the edge of one such water channel when I suddenly observed, immediately opposite me on the other side and about 10 feet away, the wide-open jaws of a huge motionless croc, the rest of which was hidden in the long grass. In and out of its jaws fluttered a small blue-and-gold kingfisher. This went on for a minute or two until the kingfisher, presumably noticing my presence, flew off. At this I saw and heard the crocodile clack its jaws shut. Whether it had been awaiting the right moment to snap and eat the kingfisher, or whether the bird had simply been cleaning its teeth for it, I do not know. Either way the beast looked visibly mortified.

There were also snakes galore. I heard that during the war an officer of the air force transit station in Geneina had gone for his tennis racket which hung with others on the mess wall, and found to his surprise that there were more rackets than usual hanging from the row of coat hooks. Three of them turned out on closer inspection to be snakes, curled up. I was not troubled much by snakes myself, although on one occasion I had to kill a cobra in our bathroom. But another cobra once did me a signal service. This was when a Sudanese Financial Inspector came to examine my District accounts. On arrival he was driven from the airstrip to the rest house and was about to walk up its steps when he saw a cobra poised on the top step in the rectangular posture of the species, eyeing him. He leapt back into the car and reached the airstrip just in time to catch the Sudan Airways Dove which he had arrived on, and returned to safety without further ado – to the great relief of my accountant and myself.

More attractive but no use for discouraging unwelcome visitors were the giraffes. The Sultan had a private herd of them in the bush west of the town. They were wonderful animals to watch floating through the landscape at treetop height – even more graceful than the Masalati girls whom I could also watch in the same area, submerging themselves in its large shallow ponds to collect the bulbs of water lilies, which replaced potatoes in the local diet. The girls always tricked out their coiffures with a water-lily flower, which stayed fixed there even when they were under water.

Marnie and I occasionally exchanged visits with the French Chef de District at Adré across the Chad frontier. The French system of colonial administration was curiously different from ours. For although they scooped up the cream (of which Chad produced little) and sent them to the Sorbonne to be turned into 'black Frenchmen', they treated the rest without visible sympathy. It is true they saw to it that the village elementary schools followed the same syllabus as those in metropolitan France. In the one we dropped into without warning, the little boys were duly singing the 'Marseillaise' and repeating the standard history lesson: '*Nous, les Gaullois, sommes descendus des Visigoths*'. But the French did not seem to muck in, as we liked to do, with the *non-évolués*. Nor did many trouble to learn the local language, though the formidable Chef de Région at Abéché, who supervised the three frontier Districts adjoining mine, was fluent in the local Arabic. He was not a lovable character. 'Maillaux, Pierre,' he barked with a fierce handshake when I first met him, giving his surname first in the official French manner. But he did see something of the surreal oddity of colonialism, as I had to admit when attending a vast tribal gathering at Abéché in honour of some visiting Parisian dignitary. I was walking with Maillaux behind the latter through the serried ranks of half-naked citizenry, whose job was to applaud the distinguished visitor. They didn't – until, after some fierce gesticulation from Maillaux, a thin cheer was vouchsafed. '*Vous voyez, Monsieur Balfour,*' he growled, '*la claque spontanée.*' I was much impressed with the ceremonial fan-dance laid on during the following march-past, for this was a very ancient ritual at the courts of African chiefs. In Darfur it survived only at the remote and tiny court of Sultan Dosa at Tini, where I saw it again later, in the top left-hand corner of the Province. But even Sultan Dosa was caught up in the pursuit of modernity, for the possession of a lorry (or *noory* in the local lingo) was becoming a status symbol for chiefs, and he therefore had a *noory* parked outside his mud house at Tini. It had no tyres, but that was immaterial since its symbolic importance did not require it to be mobile. (Twenty years later things had moved on, for I met Sultan Dosa's youngest son studying medicine at Baghdad University.)

The Chef de District at Adré came once with his wife to spend a night with us. Our house had a proper bath, theirs didn't; and when it was time to change for dinner, I took them along with some pride to enjoy the promised luxury, having had extra quantities of hot water prepared by the usual process of putting full 4-gallon petrol tins in the sun. Alas, the white enamel interior of the visitors' bath proved to be black, being totally covered in earwigs half an inch deep. So the Chabardès returned unwashed in the morning to their dependable French *douche*. In a sense they got their own back, for on Christmas Eve there arrived a truck from Adré with a present in the shape of a huge wild boar. At some hazard we managed to push it into a stable. The boar and I then sat down to consider what to do next. The boar reached a conclusion first, for by the time I woke in the morning he had battered down the stable door and (so I was to hear) cantered the 25 miles back to Adré. Unappeased, M. Chabardès sent him back again on another truck. There seemed no alternative but to have him slaughtered by a posse of fearless police. We served him up to every non-Islamic guest for weeks, until (for freezers had not yet been invented) this was no longer feasible. Great chunks had to be buried under my frangipani tree.

The trial of murderers, a privilege reserved for the Resident, took up a lot of my time. One of these was a lad who was deaf and dumb, but clearly guilty. My court had no option but to sentence anyone convicted of murder to be hanged; and informing this unfortunate by manual communication was a hideous task. Fortunately the Governor General almost always exercised his right of clemency and did so on this occasion.

But most of my time was spent visiting the heterogeneous tribes and listening to their insoluble problems. Happily this nomadic life enabled me to pursue my antiquarian interests. The *Short History of Darfur* which I eventually compiled and illustrated is still, I am told, on sale in Khartoum Museum. The ancient practice of local chieftains of building for themselves dry-stone or brick palaces on the tops of hills, chopped flat at enormous labour to provide a raised plinth, was one feature of the past that intrigued me. I discovered and drew quite a number of previously unrecorded ones.

But some other ancient traditions in Darfur may be of more general interest. For instance I once asked the shartai (head sheikh) of the Kaura pass, which divided Dar Masalit from its eastern neighbours, how his 80-foot stone-lined well had stayed firm for several hundred years. 'Easy,' he said. 'We just collected the horns of cows and goats and banged them into the gaps between the stones in the well shaft. The damp air caused them to sprout roots which spread round the stones and fixed them for ever.' On my expressing scepticism, he pushed his hand through the grass wall of his hut where his bath water ran out and brought it back clutching a cow's horn. It had sprouted precisely the tough sort of roots he had described. I next asked the shartai how the huge burnt bricks (13 by 10 by 3½ inches) used in some of the old palaces had been made as hard as iron so that they 'pinged' when you tapped them with a fingernail. 'We just dipped them in gravy,' he said. Again I expressed scepticism. 'But yes,' he insisted, 'any Sultan preparing to build a palace would hold a gigantic feast involving the slaughter of dozens of cattle, large and small. When these were being roasted, the gravies were caught and poured into big clay tubs into which the bricks were plunged. This made them hard as stone and they would never decay.' (I have since learnt that gravy, i.e. blood, makes an excellent glue and is used for that purpose in sundry crafts. So that story of the shartai's is plausible enough.)

The *dambaris* (locust wizards) also intrigued me. The dodge by which these itinerant magicians lined their pockets by protecting villages from invasions of locusts – redirecting them as a rule into the next parish – formed one of the subjects of my 'Very Rich Hours of the Sultan of Geneina'. Equally queer was the mystique attached to blacksmiths – a race apart in this region of Africa. 'Never marry your daughter', ran a local proverb, 'to a donkey or a blacksmith.' I used to watch blacksmiths producing iron out of local ore in tall mud kilns, 3 feet in diameter, four men blowing into holes round the bottom with bull-skin bellows for twenty-four hours without a break, sing-ing at the tops of their voices (when not gulping home-made maize beer) to keep themselves awake. One product of theirs was spearheads, of which there were many models. Each had its curious name: the 'No-Way-Back' (with ugly flanges pointing backwards and forwards), the 'Princess's Navel' (a nomenclature less easily explained), and so on. It was also no doubt the blacksmiths who were responsible for rendering arrowheads fatally poisonous by dipping them, I was told, in donkey's urine.

Beliefs were also widespread in the gift enjoyed by certain people of turning themselves for nefarious purposes into crocodiles or lions or hyenas. My Sultan's head judge, a saintly but supremely entertaining West African, gave me unrebuttable examples from his own experience. Others were openly recorded in the registers of local court books that it was my job to check, the term used in the 'charge' column being simply '*Bordubordu*' (the word used for this practice in the local lingo). Across the frontier in Adré I was told how a lion, which had been causing trouble carrying off young women and so on, had eventually been shot dead by the police in broad daylight; and when the populace converged on its corpse, it had already turned back into the sinister sheikh of a next-door tribe, with a bullet in his head. Many similar instances of *Borbudordu* were related to me.

I must limit myself to recording two other incidents during my time in Geneina, both related to attempts to meet a French vet to discuss diseased animals crossing the frontier. The appointed rendezvous was a well-known tree in a stretch of otherwise treeless wilderness north of Adré. No French vet turned up on my first attempt, but under the tree sat an engagingly scruffy character who told me he was of the So tribe. Now the So, who lived round Lake Chad away to the west, were famous in the past for being enormously tall and for being buried upright in huge pottery coffins. So I was interested to meet one. 'Is it true', I asked him, 'that your ancestors were very, very tall?' 'My ancestors', he replied, 'were so tall that they could shake hands across Lake Chad *without leaning forward*'. When I went a second time to meet the French vet, there sure enough was a European sitting under the appointed tree. So I dismounted and addressed him in my best French. 'What on earth are you talking to me in French for, Glen?' came the rejoinder. The man turned out to be Michael Barbour, a geographer at London University, whom I had met in England. He explained that he was walking across the continent from west to east, for fun. It seemed an odd place to meet a casual English acquaintance, under the only tree in a central African wilderness. (The French vet never turned up at all.)

My transfer to Kutum District, in northern Darfur, drew near. There was one thing I very much wanted to do before I left Geneina, but it took a long time to arrange and when I finally fixed it, I had only four days left before I was booked to fly home on leave. My object was to see (in order to incorporate it in an article I was writing for the journal *Kush*) an old Sultan's palace in the French district of Goz Beida, 80 miles south of Adré. The Chef de District there, M. Moutte, whom I had never met, had taken so long to reply to a suggestion of a visit from me that the rains had by now started. There was no road, only a barely discernible track. By the time I had got halfway down it, it was raining cats and dogs. The whole area became a lake, the track now wholly invisible beneath it. If we went off it, we would be stuck for days at best. Off it we went, into the wide ditch, and there we were. Wading 50 miles back to Geneina in drenching rain held few attractions. Missing the Sultan's palace at Goz Beida would be a minor inconvenience, but missing the weekly flight from Geneina to Khartoum and my connection from there to England would be a major one. None of my small party had any suggestions other than to refer the matter to Allah.

That may have been a better idea than I thought, for within a short time half-naked figures could be seen wading towards us from several ostensibly empty directions. Quite soon there were some sixteen faces looking, without expression, at our half-submerged vehicle lying at right angles to the direction we had been going. If between us we could bodily lift it back on to the invisible track, there would be just a chance of crawling on, either west towards Goz Beida or east back towards Geneina. Accordingly the whole lot of us bent our heads up to or over the nostrils in the muddy water to grasp the chassis. Our first exploratory heave was totally ineffective, but then heave-ho! and my van was lifted up into the air with shouts of triumph and dumped on the track, facing (Allah having so chosen) west. With two men walking ahead to feel with their toes where the track went, we crawled on. The floods began to subside a little and by midnight we reached our destination, which was fortunately on higher ground. We must have looked a strange collection, mud coloured from head to foot, when M. Moutte, rudely awoken, came out and peered at us with a paraffin lamp.

I knew from the Chabardès at Adré that Moutte was an offbeat loner, interested only in shooting beautiful animals. Their antlers projected from every wall in his loveless bungalow. I remembered the warning Mme Chabardès had given me of the primitive savagery in which Moutte lived, where they had once visited him. I didn't much care for Mme Chabardès. The conversation had gone as follows:

MME CH.: *Moutte, vous savez, est célibataire, et les indigènes là-bas n'ont jamais vu une femme. Mais jamais! Or, ils m'ont regardé et …*
ME: *Et qu'est-ce qu'ils ont dit?*
(Tableau – as they say – and the subject was changed.)

The sun was back in its place in the morning. I just had time to visit the erstwhile Sultan's palace. The present one proved to be still living in it, and he instantly had his retainers put on for me a display of the immemorial ostrich-feather fan-dance. The thunderclouds blew up again and we set off apprehensively on the return journey. The track was now visible most of the way, the thunderclouds veered off to the south, and we somehow reached Geneina by nightfall.

The Anglo-Egyptian Agreement on the disposal of the Sudan had been signed in March, and British wives in the Sudan had been made to go home before the political situation could become risky. So Marnie was already in Wee B. I should have gone straight home to join her but she urged me to accept a surprise invitation from Peter Shinnie, the government archaeologist, to join him for a fortnight on a big dig at Paphos in Cyprus, where Aphrodite had been wafted ashore.

On arrival in Nicosia I took a bus to Paphos in the far south-west. Or thought I did. But as my Greek bore no resemblance to the modern demotic, the bus delivered me to Famagusta in the extreme *east*. During the hour's wander before I found another bus that an English-speaker assured me was going at least some of the way to Paphos, an enjoyable thing happened.

Near the big mosque in Famagusta a Turk was sitting on the ground selling luscious-looking plums. That in itself was welcome, but better still he was wrapping them in pages he tore from a book bearing the intriguing title of *The Ocean of the English Language Spanned from Shore to Shore*, by Z. Praxinos. What was left of it consisted of 'A thousand synonyms for Death, culled from Shakespeare, Bible, and American Armed Forces', followed by 'Five hundred synonyms for Responsibility'. I bought all the plums and with them the remaining parts of the book. It was a riveting read and gave birth much later to a poem included in my published collection *A Kind of Kindness*.

The bus I boarded with my baggage (including a bow and poisoned arrows from Geneina) was packed with sheep and female Cypriots. Even without the sheep there was no empty seat, but I was offered the lap of the only male passenger, who turned out to be a grocer from my old Blue Nile habitat, Wad Medani. After an hour or two we stopped at a village post office. Our driver, after posting a bundle of mail, went round the outside of the bus collecting coins from the outstretched hands of the passengers through the windows and pushed the money so collected through another slot in the post-office pillar box. I said to my Greek grocer that it seemed a bit odd financing the postal service by this casual levy, and he replied, 'The money is for a saint. That is St George's slot.' Five minutes later – St George's goodwill notwithstanding – we tragically ran over and killed a small child. At this my fellow passengers all leapt off the bus and disappeared. I saw the Greek grocer clambering on to the back of a chance motorbike. 'What's happening?' I shouted. 'You're wait-ing for the police,' he said, and waved goodbye. The police eventually came, and after much questioning we (the bus, the driver and me) were allowed to proceed. At Limassol I had to change buses and was enchanted to find that my new one, a small covered-in lorry, was carrying a complete *sagiya* (water wheel) exactly like those on the Nile. Its buckets and chains were looped sinuously in among the seats like an archaic sea monster.

At sunset we reached Kouklia, just short of Paphos, where the dig was taking place. The thirty diggers were lodged in a roofless Crusader castle overlooking the beach where Aphrodite was said to have been wafted ashore on her conch. Our diet was limited (in my memory) to bread, lettuce and garlic three times a day. After a few days of strenuous work (5 a.m. to 3 p.m.) I was hungry enough to overcome my inherited disapproval of garlic and slip a few corms into my mouth when no one was looking. After a week I was swallowing them in handfuls like everyone else.

Peter Shinnie's group was allotted the area of the Temple of Aphrodite itself. In a week we had gone down 6 uneventful feet. Then we came on a rectangle of marble bearing an inscription in Greek. We carried it back in triumph to the director, Bruce Mitford. He looked surprised, disappeared for a moment and returned with a (1904 I think) excavation report in which there was a photograph of the same inscribed marble slab. It had simply been put back where it came from and in fifty years had been submerged under 6 feet of wind-blown soil. We were sensibly moved out of this recalcitrant site to an area outside the temple. After a few days working through dispiriting strata of old boots and shoes we struck a handsome (early Greek) mosaic floor representing Aphrodite. We glued it professionally on to a backing, moved it away and dug on down. Well below where the mosaic had been we came on a group of Byzantine coins, dating from a thousand years *later* than the mosaic – which was absurd. The director revealed that our mosaic too had been published long ago by a female Greek archaeologist, who had evidently relocated it where we had found it, beside what had then been the village cobbler's shop. Our group seemed fated, and it aggravated our resentment that other groups were finding treasures just below the surface all over the place.

I bicycled off for solace to Aphrodite's beach, hoping she would not let me down a third time but would emerge from the foam on her conch. She was nowhere to be seen, so (my diary records)

> I decided to impersonate her. Throwing off my clothes I leapt in and waited for something conch-like to carry me ashore feeling divinely amiable, bronzed, and salty. When I was thigh-deep in the steeply shelving shingle I was knocked for six by a monstrous billow, my feet were sucked away in the opposite direction, and I came to, gasping for breath, upside down on the floor of the Mediterranean. Fuddled though I was, my Homeric training stood me in good stead. I stumbled ashore, dripping and naked, and looked eagerly around for Nausicaa who ought, as I recalled from Book VI of the Odyssey, to be playing rounders on the beach with her classmates. She would then carry me off on a prancing chariot, introduce me to her wealthy father, and render me unconscious of the wickedness of bigamy with an amphora of Chateauneuf-du-Pape.* Alas, Nausicaa wasn't there either.

I flew home shortly after to the more dependable environment of Wee B. Perhaps I should insert that I did have one enjoyable bathe in Cyprus to look back on. We were taken by Bruce Mitford to call on his friend, the Bishop of Limassol. This was the future Archbishop Makarios, who was later to make the front pages of the world press as the first President of independent Cyprus. While we waited for him to appear we all plunged into the sea for a swim. Down came Makarios in full canonicals, threw them off, and plunged in to join us. It was difficult to imagine the Archbishop of Canterbury joining in a fun bathe, naked, at Margate. If he did, he would probably have been exiled, as Makarios later was, to the Seychelles.

And so, after home leave, to Kutum. It was both the biggest district in

---

* Chateauneuf-du-Pape was the only wine my father drank (and that just on special occasions).

the Sudan and the least 'developed'. When Wilfred Thesiger was Assistant DC there just before the war, the houses built for the two of them by Guy Moore, who was the DC there for decades, had no glass in their windows since (so Thesiger told me later) Moore considered the idea 'sissy'. Fortunately for sissies like me, glass had been inserted after the war and the bitter winds got in only elsewhere.

The fractious tribes 100 miles to the north-west were Zaghawa, who lived by camel stealing. The Beni Hussein in the forested hills to their south seldom emerged from them and lived inoffensively in round stone huts countersunk into the ground with only their conical thatch showing. I once looked in at one of their few and remote village schools and found the children standing up in turn to recite facts about Britain's railway system. I thus learnt from the Beni Hussein that the night express from London to Edinburgh took 7 hours 58 minutes, and that the diameter of the Mersey railway tunnel was 8.3 metres.

In the far north-east of Kutum an even more intriguing tribe with a King lived round the vast volcanic crater of Meidob with a permanent lake at the bottom: the only place in the world where I have watched hundreds of camels, some of them drinking, some copulating in their unexcitable way, and some giving birth – all at the same time. There were other different tribes in other places, and between them all they kept me almost continually in orbit.

Even more to my enjoyment the mountainous area near Kutum itself had on its summits the biggest ruined ancient 'cities' in Darfur. These were a struggle to reach, tearing my way through the infamous *kitir* bushes which no shirt survived. The most difficult of access, then almost unexamined, was Jebel Uri. The easiest and best known was Ain Farah, which had a permanent batheable stream beside it. The rocks overlooking this stream were peopled by large monkeys that would sit and watch us splashing around. 'You can't', remarked my adorable club-footed servant Da'oud, 'tell which is them and which is us.' My drawings and plans of these and other ruined 'palaces' can be seen in my *Short History of Darfur*. Altogether it was a wonderful job, and my notebooks were filled with the tribal oddities and infamies I collected on my constant treks.

My notebooks record that I had been reading much French and Italian as well as English. I think one could elaborate quite a metaphysic about the effect on the three races of their words for the Almighty and what rhymes with them – the Anglo-Saxon 'God' with its Calvinistical rhymes (sod, clod, rod and, of course, odd); the French *'Dieu'* (*bleu, feu, cieux,* fine empyrean rhymes); while the Italian *'Dio'* rhymes with practically everything. God has certainly presented the English rhyming poet – and perhaps non-poets too – with a problem.

A contrast of a different kind – between the British, the French and the Americans – had just been brought to my notice in a review by Ian Fleming of Sir John Hunt's book on his epoch-making ascent of Mount Everest. 'It is amusing', he writes,

> to speculate on what sort of book this would have been if Everest had been climbed by the French or the Americans instead of the British. The French would have indulged in flights of fancy, often expressed in rhetorical questions of the most unanswerable kind: '*A quoi pensait-elle, cette géante inviolée, en regardant l'approche si lente de cette chétive compagnie de nains?*' The Americans would have bothered about their bowels. In their attempts to tell an immortal story worthily, both would have been more exclamatory, more dramatic, more intimate.

I wish I could write like that.

My Zaghawa (not being Arab) were not much given to courtesy: the Genigergera, one of their sub-tribes, least of all. When any of them did turn up at meetings arranged for me to listen to their complaints, generally directed at their tribal head, the shartai, this is the sort of complaint I was faced with: 'Me follow that shartai? My grandfather, shartai struck him on the navel with a sword. My father, shartai slaughtered him across the throat. Me, he put my right eye out' (and he hastily closes his right eye and screws it up). 'I not want him. *Dutt!*' (*Dutt*, the Zaghawa emphatic negative, with which almost all their statements ended, is strictly untranslatable. The Russian *nyet* is, I suppose, the nearest European equivalent.)

In February 1954 Marnie went home to have her second child (Alison) in the Edinburgh Infirmary, born on 5 May and this time without that confusion over name tags.

As a break from keeping the Genigergera and others in something like order I arranged to go off on a week's camel trip into the uninhabited Gizzu area away up in the far north. This was beyond the dried-up Wadi Howar, which had once flowed into the Nile and was reported to be full of archaeological interest. Gizzu, meaning a good feed, referred to the annual exodus up there of Kutum camel-owners (or their slaves) in the dry season when, magically, the desert burst out from the dew-fall into a carpet of small low-growing herbs which the camels scooped up with their tongues and a peculiar swishing noise. I had the necessary camels, etc., all arranged with the King of the Meidob; but owing to the political ferment in the Nile Valley, orders came through at the last moment that DCs must stay at their base. Not that the Meidob or anyone else in Darfur were showing the least sign of fermentation. Surprisingly, however, summer leave home was not cancelled. Instructions simply said, 'Work on the assumption that this leave will be your last' – for the Sudanisation of British jobs was getting under way. More surprisingly still, families were allowed back when leave was over for the last few months of the Condominium.

Since elections to the Sudan's first parliament were to be held in October by

10 Arriving back at starting point in north-west Darfur from Ennedi exploration.
GBP with Ann and Alison in boxes on either side of his camel.

universal suffrage, much of my last few months in Kutum was spent explaining what elections meant. In largely illiterate areas like mine candidates were to be represented by pictures of animals, since it was assumed that voters could at least distinguish between, say, an elephant and a camel. Even so, it wasn't straightforward. When I asked a group of Meidobis which candidate (or the relevant animal) they would vote for, their reply was, 'The King hasn't told us yet.' In the case of the Zaghawa, I felt, it would be counter-productive of a shartai to express his preference – unless he told them to vote for the man he *didn't* want elected, so that his own (undisclosed) choice would come romping home.

The date for my own post to be Sudanised was fixed for the end of November 1954. Meanwhile I planned that, when the day came, I would set off with Marnie and the two children to explore by camel the Ennedi foothills – the Tibesti massif's eastward extension, which lay on the other side of the Sudan's frontiers with both Libya and the French District of 'Tibesti, Ennedi, Borgou'. If the *western* extension of Tibesti was full of prehistoric rock paintings as had recently been discovered, I didn't see why the Ennedi side shouldn't be so too; and I hoped there would also be lots of neolithic pottery lying around to support my belief in prehistoric links between Tibesti and the Nile.

Three prerequisites were put in hand. First, I had a sort of howdah with boxes on either side constructed by a carpenter, in which Ann (aged three) and Alison (six months) could travel after a practice or two. Second, I arranged with the Zaghawi shartai I liked most to prepare eight good camels for us near the frontier. Third, I sought to obtain a guide from the French Commandant (it was a military responsibility) of Tibesti, Ennedi, Borgou; and I cooked up telegraphically a meeting with him in advance on the frontier. He proved when I met him to be an agreeably eccentric bachelor, whom I found lying on a rope bed reading the matrimonial advertisements in a French magazine. '"*Quarante ans: paraît moins,*"' he read out to me. '*Elles disent toujours ça.*' Then he offered to exchange a whole crate of his champagne for a bottle of my Scotch. Whisky, he said, was an essential for a man who, having survived the Korean War, had been sent to run single handed an area half the size of France. In it he and his Tibbu clerk, he said, were the only people who could read and write. Thus if, for instance, he had to send, when in Ennedi, some instructions to the tribal head in Borgou 200 miles west, he had to dictate them to his clerk, who then travelled to Borgou, read out the instruction to the sheikh, wrote down the sheikh's reply, and travelled back the 200 miles to Ennedi to deliver it. More importantly for me, he promised to arrange for a Guraani man called Ordugu, who was said to know the uninhabited area I planned to explore, to meet me on a certain day at the last known water-hole on the way north towards it.

On my last night in Kutum a large party was staged for me, at which I gave an emotional address in Arabic. I loved the Sudanese and only wish that fate had decreed for them not the sad misgovernment they now suffer but something more like the future I forecast so optimistically in that farewell speech.

So off we went, driven to the frontier crossing at Bahai, where the camels were to be waiting, by Bobbie Raikes, the Province hydrologist, whose job was not being Sudanised yet; and he nobly agreed to come all the way up from Fasher and collect us again at Bahai exactly four weeks later. The account of the expedition published in *Blackwoods* (issue 1690 of August 1956) does not lend itself to extracts, and anyone interested can read it there. Here I will recount only one dramatic incident that justified by itself the whole adventure and will add another that does not feature in my published account:

Incident 1. Having left my wife and children at the last known waterhole I eventually come across Ordugu four days after I had despaired of doing so. While we rode on north together I naturally asked him about rock paintings. He assured me that he had wandered about this now virtually uninhabited area during much of his earlier life, had slept in dozens of its caves, and had never seen paintings on the walls of any of them. This was depressing but (just in case) I broke away from him and whipped my camel over to one of the many scooped-out *inselbergen* (rocky outcrops) in the vicinity. And there on its walls were paintings galore – spearmen with shields and vacant circular heads like old-fashioned petrol pumps, masked men with bows and arrows, ochre cows. Ordugu, when I called him over, was dumbfounded. He had slept, he said, several times in this very cave and had never noticed the paintings. What dumbfounded him most were the men with bows and arrows. He did not know what they were for, and the Guraani language had no word for them. The presence of his Guraani ancestors in North Africa before they pushed down here is recorded by Herodotus in the fifth century BC (assuming they are his '*Garamantes*'*), so these bow-and-arrow men must have been painted well back into prehistory. From then on I found cave paintings everywhere – girls dancing in line, cows chequered like crossword puzzles, giraffes, a lion or two – and the fun was fast and furious.

Incident 2. Another morning when Ordugu and I were trotting along side by side he pulled out of his pocket a small grubby roll of homespun, unwrapped it and passed over to me (if you can believe it) a passport photograph of Wilfred Thesiger. It transpired that Ordugu had been the man who guided Thesiger across Africa from Darfur to Algiers in 1938, his first great journey (apart from those in Ethiopia). Thesiger's powers of endurance on camelback were far beyond even Ordugu's, who was so impressed that he had carefully kept the small picture in his pocket ever since, as a talisman.

On our ultimate return to Bao, Bobbie Raikes duly arrived to collect us. One final dispensation on the long drive back to Fasher crowned the whole

---

* My identification of the Guraan with the Garamantes is not shared by current experts, who locate the latter away in the Fezzan. But when their once powerful state collapsed after the Arab conquest of North Africa, they must have scattered elsewhere.

Ennedi adventure. We had stopped for the first night with Shartai Tijani to thank him for his camels. I told him of my rock-painting discoveries and he said there was a big picture of cows, though not in colour, on a rock face a few miles south of where we were sitting. I had searched for cave drawings for two years in northern Darfur and had never heard of what the shartai was now revealing. So in the morning off we drove to look.

And there on a perpendicular rock face were full-sized cows, drawn by percussion and not in coloured ochre. And what was more, some of them had long horns pointing forwards and downwards, just as Herodotus described the cows of the Garamantes, which had therefore, he says, to graze in reverse. These prehistoric cow pictures had been splashed over the ages with flour and water. What was more, some of the mixture was still wet. Women had evidently been praying there for fertility for some three thousand years.*

On that note I must say goodbye to the Sudan. The fourteen years I had spent with its engaging people had contributed much to my emergence as (I hope) a genuine adult. It would be twenty-four years before I visited the Sudan again for one last time, in the improbable guise of a business consultant.

---

* I wrote this up for the *Journal of the Royal Anthropological Society* with illustrations: *JRAS*, vol. 86, part 1 (1956).

Diplomacy

CHAPTER 13

New Pastures (FCO and Chile)

WE flew from Khartoum to Jerusalem on 21 December 1954 in order for me to join Kathleen Kenyon on her fifth season's dig at Jericho. We lodged over Christmas in the Anglican cathedral hostel. And then disaster struck. On Christmas Eve Marnie went to Bethlehem for the midnight service in the birthplace of Christ. She returned feeling unwell, with flu-like aches and pains. In the morning the Bishop's wife, a trained nurse, looked at her and had her rushed to the Augusta Victoria Hospital suspecting polio. Her suspicions were confirmed (and the infection traced back to the waterhole in Ennedi). She was soon almost totally paralysed and could hardly breathe. All I can face recording here is a remark made to me by the American matron in the hospital. 'She's a real peach, your wife. Half an hour ago she whispered to me "Lipstick." I got it from her bag and put some on. She wanted to look her best, you see, for what may be the last time you'll see her.'

There was no iron lung in Jordan. The only hope was to get her to the Hadassa Hospital in Israel. But how? Jordan and Israel were actively at war. Firing across the no man's land on either side of the Mandelbaum Gate (which was of course closed) was fairly regular. The British Consul couldn't help to get it opened. At the last moment the Armenian doctor in charge of the Augusta Victoria remembered that he had been at school with the Israeli Director of Immigration and somehow got in touch with him under the counter. In a matter of minutes Marnie was put in an Arab ambulance which took her (and me) to the Mandelbaum Gate. There she was carried on a stretcher across no man's land to where an Israeli ambulance was waiting. I waved a helpless goodbye.

For two or three weeks I had no means of knowing whether Marnie was still alive. Then (since the shooting had died down) permission was somehow obtained for me to go through the Mandelbaum Gate on foot to the Hadassa Hospital. I found her in a bed in a corridor (for the hospital was over-full), still largely paralysed but alive and smiling; and thanks to the iron lung she was able to breathe without much difficulty. The Jewish doctors and nurses were admirable – though I was amazed to learn that on the Jewish Sabbath they had to smuggle Muslim women in to do the cleaning and other basic tasks. I was allowed to cross over and see her once a week, and since it was quite a long walk I soon hired a bicycle. But I found that bicycling through the Orthodox quarter on the Jewish Sabbath (i.e. on Saturday, that being my authorised day) exposed me to angry expostulations and occasional volleys of stones from young Jews with ringlets. So I reverted to going on foot.

Meanwhile I was otherwise confined (with the children) by the Jordanian authorities to the hostel on the unconvincing grounds that polio was non-existent in Jordan and we might infect the population. After a month of this confinement I decided to ignore the prohibition and took the children all round Arab Jerusalem. I even went down one day to Jericho (my joining the dig had of course been out of the question), and Kathleen Kenyon showed me around her impressive discoveries. None of these was in fact as remarkable as that of the (third) Lady Mortimer Wheeler, who was busy on underground Bronze Age burial chambers near by and who took me to see the only one that had not been broken into and pirated over the centuries. She had found it still sealed with a plaster door, in which she had bored a small hole which she then peered through. And there was a complete burial, grave goods and all, undamaged by four thousand years of time thanks to the gases that rise underground in the Jordan Valley and stifle all microbic life. The wooden bed on which the occupant was lying began disintegrating when attacked by fresh air with microbes in it. But none of the experts could explain why the bed had only three legs – until King Haakon of Norway (or was it King Gustav of Sweden?), an amateur archaeologist, came by. All his own ancestors, he said, had slept on three-legged beds since that was the only way to get a decent night's sleep on bumpy ground. The burial and its reconstructed bed are now in the Amman Museum.

On my way back from Lady Wheeler's tomb I became separated from her and wandered over to the edge of the village where noisy celebrations (with drums) were going on. Peering over the heads of the celebrants, what should I see but Lady Wheeler, naked from the waist up, dancing in the centre with a red hankie in her hand. When she finally broke off amid applause, she explained to me, 'I collect drum beats, and this was a new one to me.' I never met her again but was privileged to become quite a friend of the great Kathleen Kenyon. She stayed with me once in Amman in the 1970s and, her business being archaeological, I took her to call on Crown Prince Hassan, who was interested in Jordan's past. Being, like so many female archaeologists, unconcerned with conventional proprieties, she sat opposite him with her knees wide apart and her loose pink bloomers alarmingly open to inspection. The Crown Prince gave me a quick but unmistakable wink. (In my retirement Kathleen Kenyon, by now a dame, sucked me into the Council of the Jerusalem Institute of Archaeology and then, as Chairman, into the new Amman one.)

After two months Marnie was judged sufficiently out of danger to be flown to England on a stretcher, and I was allowed to take the children through the Mandelbaum Gate to accompany her. Rather movingly the nurses in the hospital hired a bus and came down to Lydda airport to see her off. On our arrival in England she was whisked off to the Radcliffe in Oxford and later to the Headington Hospital, where there was a swimming pool. Into this she was lowered daily for the next few months from a sort of crane to exercise such limbs as were coming back to life.

The Hendersons (Bill Henderson has figured in Chapter 12 above as my Governor in Darfur) were now living in Oxford's Park Town and nobly put me and the children up while I set about looking for gainful employment. This was an experience then new to me. The Second World War had saved me from experiencing it earlier – though even if the war had not supervened, it may be that the cushioned upbringing and classy education enjoyed by people like me would have saved me from unemployment. (How different life is for the young today!) Various jobs were in fact offered to me, including (thanks to Greig Barr, now its sub-Rector) the Bursarship of Exeter College, Oxford. I would, I felt, have proved a poor hand at managing the College's sundry estates and counting its teaspoons. Nor was I much attracted to any administrative jobs in the shrinking colonies after years in the less constricted service of the Sudan. Fisons interviewed me for a job selling fertiliser and wisely turned me down. There were a few openings in archaeology but I was simply not qualified for any of them.

Then suddenly the Sudan Re-employment Agency wrote suggesting I should apply for the one remaining vacancy out of the seven that the Foreign Office had been persuaded to make available to ex-Sudan officials. By a singular stroke of luck, though I was not aware of it at the time, the only other applicants were an irrigation engineer with no obvious qualifications and a province judge (a middle-weight boxing champion who had once knocked out a Sudanese postmaster with a straight left through the postal *guichet*). He told me, when we met for the interview, that he had no intention of accepting the job if offered and had applied only under pressure from his wife, a Spanish *contessa*, who rather fancied life in a British Embassy.

I heard nothing for three weeks of suspense. During them, since I imagined that the experience would give me new insights into the Eternal Verities, I took up an offer from my old Magdalen friend Keith Joseph to spend a weekend in All Souls College in his empty rooms. To my dismay the conversation at dinner between its distinguished inmates centred on which horse was most likely to win the 3.30 at Newmarket; and the nearest they got to the Eternal Verities was a heated argument on whether the French for Jesus should or should not be pronounced with the final 's' silent. On neither question could I contribute usefully – not that anyone invited me to.

Eventually I was informed by the Foreign Office that the vacancy was mine. When I reported for duty in Whitehall, the Head of Personnel greeted me with unexpected bonhomie and said, 'Would you like to know why we chose *you?'* I said I would be more than interested. 'Well,' he said, 'the fact is that at the two interview boards [he had sat on both] everyone rather liked the tie you were wearing.'

I might insert here that when the original batch of ex-Sudanis were being interviewed, they all (by arrangement) asked whether the intention of the Foreign Office was that the six to be selected would all be dumped, as Arabic speakers, in the Persian Gulf (the Arab side of it) to release the genuine diplomats for proper jobs elsewhere. 'Certainly not!' they were told. 'We will be taking them purely on merit.' Within two years five of the six were in the Persian Gulf; and by the time I was posted there myself in 1964, the Political Resident, the five Political Agents and for good measure the Consul-General in Muscat were all ex-members of the Sudan Political.

At first, however, I was slotted into the department dealing with the Communist countries to learn the trade, and pretty quaint it seemed. *Carlton-Browne of the FO*, the hilarious film take-off of that institution, which filled the cinemas for years, was not (or so it seems in retrospect) nearly as funny as the real thing. Like any worthwhile body, of course, the Foreign Office managed to be both absolutely serious and absolutely hilarious, and kept the two qualities more or less in balance. But the process of learning the trade was more than serious. Every morning on my table in the depressing sort of 'maid's bedroom' at the top of the building, which I shared with two others, was dumped a pile of papers about Poland and Czechoslovakia. Each paper was inside its own numbered 'jacket', on which minutes had to be inserted. All jackets started in the 'Third Rooms', where the appropriate junior 'Secretary' had to decide what to do with them. Unless it was a document I could happily mark 'Put away' on the grounds that it appeared valueless, I was required to insert a learned minute and recommendation and send the jacket upwards or sideways in the hierarchy until someone sufficiently high up decided what action should be taken. The jacket then returned to me to take it. This might involve drafting a 'submission' to a minister, which then went up the hierarchy being hacked about as it went until, beautifully typed on blue paper, it reached its ministerial destination. One of the first submissions I had to draft resulted from a proposal by our Ambassador in Warsaw that an Anglo-Polish Extradition Agreement should be drawn up. (I had to find out first what 'extradition' *meant*.) Another sort of problem, particularly for a 'third room' Secretary who had, like me, no knowledge of the countries he was dealing with, was that draft replies to Parliamentary Questions, cleared at appropriate levels on the way up, *had* to reach the minister concerned within forty-eight hours. Critics of the FO would be edified to know that every kind of incoming communication had to be dealt with in a standard fixed time. Letters from the public had to be answered within a week. (An admirable discipline that would seem to have lapsed.)

It was all very nightmarish for a beginner; and there was rarely anyone free to consult. I once discussed our system with someone in the Italian Embassy whom I had to visit. He expressed amazement and told me that in *his* service documents went to the top first and worked their way downwards, so that 'Third Rooms' simply carried out instructions and were never required to show initiative. That conversation, incidentally, occurred years later when I was seeking to extract confidential information from successively the French, the Japanese and the Italian Embassies. The experience was entertaining. The Frenchman kept me waiting for half an hour and then told me to put my questions in writing and they would be considered. The Japanese gave me an expensive lunch at Pruniers but nothing else. The Italian took me straight to the Embassy's secret archive room, unlocked it and said, 'Make yourself at home!'

I had, of course, to find somewhere to live and a nanny to look after Ann and Alison. London was too expensive and I rented a cottage at Farnham. This meant two hours' travel from door to door each way, six days a week. (The five-day week hadn't then been invented.)

This manner of life struck me as pretty disagreeable and I explored the possibility of resigning from the FO. Here I will relate only the interview I had for a job with MI6. The unaccommodating interviewer sat me in a chair facing the sun, which streamed into my eyes through the window behind him so that I couldn't even see him. 'The job', he said, 'will require you to work in the hinterland of Aden and penetrate our security targets.' I just summoned up enough *nous* to ask him what the security targets *were*. 'Ah,' he said, 'that's what we don't know. That's what you'll have to find out for yourself.' I decided against this bizarre appointment – and just as well in the light of future developments in the Aden Protectorate, for in 1967 the British were driven out of Aden in humiliating circumstances, quite a number of their office-bearers having been assassinated. So it is fortunate I hadn't become one, or I might not be writing these reminiscences.

While I slogged on in the FO, Kenneth Smith happened to come home on leave from Aden where he was the Governor's Director of Personnel. I told him of the MI6 interview. He shamefacedly explained that some weeks earlier the Governor had decided to secure an Intelligence Officer and Kenneth had told him that the right man for the job was one Balfour Paul, who had just left the Sudan. Kenneth now made up for this wickedness, however, by insisting that I found somewhere to live nearer the FO than Farnham; and that Sunday he drove me to London to inspect all the modest houses for sale within striking distance of Whitehall. The only one we saw where he said he would be prepared to visit us was the half-built 20 Essex Villas, which was rising from a wartime bomb-hole on Campden Hill. Of course, I hadn't the money to buy it without borrowing. Mortgages for home-buyers were by no means the norm in those days; and it was only the fifth of the building societies I ventured into that judged me a safe enough risk for a loan of £8,500.

We moved in, occupying the ground floor and basement while the builders, who were months behind schedule, constructed the second floor above our heads. Marnie had by now left hospital on crutches and was delighted with the half-built house.

The only episode I will record of our time there is this. I sometimes spent the FO lunch break walking – with rolled umbrella and bowler hat, of course – round St James's Park with Jock Duncan (one of the earlier Sudan recruits in the FO), eating our sandwiches and boiled eggs and stowing the eggshells under our bowlers since there were never any litter bins. Jock was an enthusiastic composer of light music, and one day he told me he had just won a competition advertised in the *Sunday Pictorial* for a theme tune for a new production of *Three Men in a Boat*. The advertisers had offered him £500 down for the copyright; but being a Dundee man he calculated that he might do even better elsewhere by waiting. (He never succeeded.) Anyway, he asked me to draft a lyric to match his tune, since he was 'no good at words'. This was the origin of *Sunlight on Water*, a musical comedy based on the goings-on at 20 Essex Villas. When (to jump ahead) it was finished, Jock waited outside his door in Argyle Road, past which bicycled every morning the leading man in the then rave musical *Salad Days*. Eventually Jock managed to stop him and thrust our *magnum opus* into his hands. The man thrust it back, telling him the proper thing to do was to take it to Boosey & Hawkes. He did, but lamentably *Sunlight on Water* was not snapped up by the West End. Jock was shortly posted to New York, from where he wrote to me saying he had offered it to a leading Broadway agent whose considered judgement was that the dialogue (my immortal words!) 'needed pepping up'. 'If', wrote Jock, his Dundee origins still showing through, 'I get this done here, will you accept 20% of the profits instead of a half-share?' I told him that if he got it pro-duced on Broadway, he could keep *all* the profits. But Broadway too missed its chance. Every time I met Jock in later years he would play the songs over to me with mutual nostalgia.

Keith Joseph – now a baronet, MP, alderman of the City, and Fellow of All Souls, as well as owning Bovis and another huge building firm – had meanwhile met (at a tea party with the Chief Rabbi) a pretty Guggenheim girl, Hellen, on a visit from New York, and married her. On our next home leave they established the habit of dining with Marnie and me once a month to discuss a set book. At one such Friday supper in their house, when a Greek tragedy was the menu, Keith excused himself at 10 p.m. saying he had work to do. Hellen explained that he had just been appointed Secretary of State for Wales – a principality into which he had never set foot – and felt he must bone up on it before paying his first visit to Cardiff the following Monday. He had therefore borrowed from the London Library every book that mentioned Wales and was now upstairs reading them. She told us afterwards that he had sat in his chair without moving or going to bed from 10 p.m. on that Friday until the train left Paddington on Monday morning. By then, being a fast reader with total recall, he knew far more about Wales than all the burghers of Cardiff put together. The latter, who had been properly outraged at the appointment of such an outsider, were of course sharpening their knives in anticipation, and (as any Gentile could have foreseen) were even more outraged when they discovered that he knew far more about their country than they did.

There was another unexpected outcome of our friendship with the Josephs. Hellen had quickly decided that she too, like so many Jews, must make her mark in her adopted country and took up sculpture in bronze. Within a few months she won the top award in the London Salon of Sculpture. By the time we were home again on leave she had run out of models for her heads and persuaded me to sit for her. Her subjects, she assured me, didn't have to have handsome or interesting faces, and it would mean only two or three sessions of an hour or so. In fact it involved my sitting in her studio for six whole afternoons, motionless and forbidden to open my mouth, while she examined my features at close range with hideous scrupulosity, breaking the silence only to mutter, 'Nothing straight anywhere.' A few weeks after this ordeal ended, a friend of mine rang me up to tell me, between bouts of hysterical laughter, that she had just attended the opening of a new exhibition of London sculptors. On entering it she had passed first a head of Winston Churchill, then one of J. F. Kennedy, and then one of *me*! Indeed, she sent me the catalogue, and there was my head gracing the cover. Nothing straight anywhere.

Work in Northern Department of the FO had its brighter moments. One day I was instructed to 'represent the Foreign Secretary' at an athletics competition between Britain and Czechoslovakia, at which the famous Zatopek, who had just beaten the world record for the mile by running it in less than a minute or something, was performing. At the ensuing reception in the Czech Embassy I arrived so late that there were only a few people still there, leaning against pillars with glasses of slivowitz (plum brandy) in their hands. I followed their example. Suddenly in rushed a cluster of local schoolchildren clamouring for Zatopek's autograph. He had long since left, but seeing an athletic-looking figure leaning against a column, they approached me and said, 'Mr Zatopek, isn't it?' I offered no denial, tossed off my slivowitz and signed a string of autograph books, Zatopek ... Zatopek ... Zatopek.

I seemed therefore to be getting the hang of diplomacy. A more impressive illustration of that technique, given me by my boss, followed. On some BBC programme a harmless reference had been made to the 'Polish Ambassador's trousers'. The Pole (a Communist of course in those days) was enraged by such discourtesy, and came round to protest to the head of Northern Department, Tom Brimelow. As the Polish desk officer I was called in to attend. Brimelow's pacifying approaches made no progress until he said, 'But surely,

Ambassador, you haven't forgotten what Karl Marx says on page 380 of *Das Kapital*?' and proceeded to recite it to him in the original from memory. The Ambassador, who was clearly unfamiliar not only with the German language but also with the works of Karl Marx, was flummoxed. What bearing page 380 had on his trousers I have no idea. But he shook hands and withdrew. Game, set and match to Brimelow.

Brimelow, I should add, was later to become the top man in the Foreign Service. As such he nobly attended a dinner given for me by the Jordanian Ambassador when I was appointed to Amman in 1971. Sitting next to Brimelow, I told him of my admiration for his triumphant handling of the case of the Polish Ambassador's trousers fifteen years before. He couldn't even remember the occasion and declared that, although he had probably once read *Das Kapital*, he certainly never had bits of it by heart in any language. Such are the qualities of the top achiever! (He became a Labour Lord in the Upper House.)

Shortly after the trousers incident, the first popular outburst in Poland against Soviet Communist oppression occurred at the Poznan International Trade Fair. One of the British exhibitors looked in on his return and told me how, when the shooting started at the fair, a Polish exhibitor had rushed over to the British pavilion, seized a Union Jack and wrapped himself in it, explaining that our flag was the best protection against a bullet. In those days Britain was evidently still Great!

The last and far more significant incident I will recall of my stint in the Foreign Office occurred when the Hungary desk officer was on leave and I was acting for her. On 21 October 1956, as I recorded in my diary:

> The people of Budapest are storming the streets, shouting for freedom and Nagy [the Hungarian boss of whom they were hoping much]. All Nagy has done is to appeal to the occupying Soviet forces to 'restore order'. It looks as if the FO will decide ('on balance') that the best hope for the ultimate liberation of Eastern Europe lies in a hands-off policy of gradualism in dealing with Moscow.

In the light of what happened thirty-odd years later (Gorbachev and all that) it looks as if the FO pundits may have deserved more credit than I gave them in 1956. But of course what ditched any prospect of the West intervening in Hungary was the Anglo-French lunacy of invading Suez in secret collusion with Israel that very week. In the resulting furore the plight of the wretched Hungarians didn't stand a chance.

The Suez folly was certainly a more disastrous episode than anything else that overtook Britain during my diplomatic life. It destroyed for ever Britain's standing in the Middle East. I did not have the guts to resign from the FO as one or two others did – and as did William Clark from his job as Prime Minister Eden's Public Relations Secretary. There was of course some public support for Eden, but more from simpler folk who favoured 'having a bang at the Wogs' than from the middle classes (Tory or not), or indeed from the top Generals when they were let into the secret plot of invading Egypt. For what it is worth, I noted in my diary how one morning of that dreadful week when I was going up in the ramshackle lift in the FO I heard one very senior official whisper to another, 'Great relief in Number Ten this morning.' 'Oh, why?' 'Because they have been told of one junior official in the Ministry of Pensions who supports the government.'

I was still under training in the FO when I made my debut as an after-dinner speaker – that 'last infirmity of noble minds'. A body consisting of all pre-war entrants into the Sudan Political and calling itself the Fallen Angels (a reference to the popular description of members of that service as 'cock-angels') had started having annual dinners. My old boss, Denis Vidler, ran it and I was invited as guest speaker. My speech was apparently judged entertaining. I suppose it was this which set me on the slippery slope, for making after-dinner speeches became a habit – especially on Burns Nicht (celebrated all over the world by thousands of those who wish they were Scots).

My two-year training being over in 1958, I was posted to Chile, and off we went by sea through the Panama Canal. (There was then no airline service between England and Chile.) It proved a peaceful and agreeable country, the only one in Latin America that had never (then) had a revolution. I was the Embassy's Information Officer – a luxury of which embassies worldwide were later deprived as an economy, but at this period the Information Officer in Santiago was assisted by a local Englishman and two full-time Chileans and was required to be the Embassy's eyes and ears and in constant touch with the media. More enjoyably the Head of Chancery was Nicko Henderson, who went on to be Private Secretary to the Foreign Secretary and successively Ambassador in Bonn, Paris and Washington (a unique achievement). He was a singularly laid-back and entertaining colleague and we remained in touch for years until he moved out of my humbler sphere. Thereafter I met him only on two occasions. The first was when we were both 'kissing hands' with the Queen. For these rituals, performed when one was going somewhere as Ambassador, one had to be in morning dress; and characteristically Nicko, having mislaid his waistcoat, arrived at Buckingham Palace without one, his red braces showing. The Queen's Gentleman-in-waiting lent him his own. The result was grotesque, since he was short and stout while Nicko was tall and thin. But Nicko (so the Gent. told me) appeared quite unaware of his bizarre appearance – though the Queen wasn't.

The other occasion we met was when Nicko was Ambassador in Paris – and his clothes, like his French, were so awful that he went down (so a French duke told me!) an absolute treat. Jenny and I were driving home from Tunis on my retirement and got Nicko to invite us to lunch in his ritzy residence. I mention this only because Nicko told me he had recently read my valedictory dispatch from Tunis and was using two of its 'funny stories' in speeches he had to make. One of them had related a memorable malapropism by the leader of the Tunisian Women's Rights Movement at a gathering hosted in our house by Jenny. 'So, my friends,' the lady had declared in her peroration, 'this bad treatment of women is a spectre that still haunts Tunisian society. It is high time we circumcised this ghost.' The other story of mine that Nicko had used emerged from the visit Princess Margaret paid us in Tunisia and will be related when we get there.

In Santiago too we had a royal visit. This was from Princess Marina of Kent and her ravishing twenty-year-old daughter, Alexandra. I still wear the cufflinks Marina gave me – a routine issue not connected with the curious service I happened to render her. She and the Chilean President, Alessandri, apparently hit it off well and a silly rumour got around that they were having an 'affair'. The British tabloids, in particular the *Daily Mirror*, were all agog. I chanced to be the only person in the Embassy when a cipher telegram arrived from the FO demanding instant action to suppress the calumny. The *Mirror* was the only tabloid with a correspondent in Santiago, a Chilean Marxist called Claudio Veliz, whom I had sedulously cultivated, even climbing mountains with him. I whizzed round to his house and found him fingering a cable from the owner/editor of the *Mirror*, the notorious Cecil King, requiring him to pursue this highly marketable story. I told Claudio it was rubbish. 'You are my friend,' he said, 'and if you promise me on your honour that it's nonsense, I will take your word for it.' I promised, took him straight round to the telegraph office and stood by him while he sent a cable to Cecil King (whom he knew personally) consisting of the two words 'Kill it'. And it was killed. One of the things I have done for England! In those happy days slurs on the sexual behaviour of members of the royal family were unheard of.

Marina and her daughter did, however, enjoy freedom of an unusual kind on their 'day of rest'. Nicko Henderson extracted them from the company of our new fussy Ambassador, appropriately called Pink, and took them up the Andes in two borrowed Chilean army jeeps. The one the royals were in broke down halfway up. Nicko, who was ahead in the other one, didn't notice. As it was summer and no skiers were around on this otherwise unused track, the Princesses sat for some time, vainly expecting Nicko to come back to look for them. By chance a lorry came up carrying manure for the garden of the (seasonally empty) ski resort. The Princesses climbed on the back of it and continued up the mountain with their toes in the manure. They eventually found Nicko waiting nonchalantly at the top of the mountains (13,000 feet) and had the time of their lives dashing around in bare feet and frying eggs on a Primus. Unfortunately they forgot that the Ambassador was giving a dinner for them at 7.30. I was among the waiting guests as the hours passed. The tension could be cut with a butter knife, not least since the Ambassador was known to consider himself overdue for a knighthood, and losing two of Britain's top Princesses in the Andes was unlikely to help his reputation. Eventually at 10 p.m. the royal party arrived (without Alexandra, who had gone dancing with the Chilean army). Marina, with a brief apology, skipped upstairs to change. The Ambassador, his frenzy not abated, turned to the Princess's ADC and blurted, 'I remember hearing that her late husband, the Duke, was always late for everything.' 'I'll just run upstairs,' said the ADC, 'and tell her what you have said' – and he did. The atmosphere at dinner was distinctly frosty. The Ambassador's name, incidentally, did not appear in the next birthday honours. But Nicko became a frequent guest of the Duchess in London.

But my most engaging memory of Nicko was when, having been offered the use of her huge house in the south by the grande dame of Chilean society, he took me there for a weekend, instructing me to teach him three minor arts – chess, fly-fishing and horsemanship. The climax of the third of these vain exercises was this. Soon after we set off into the forest, and unobserved by me, Nicko fell off. When I saw his horse gallop past me riderless, I cantered back to see whether Nicko was still alive. What I saw was Nicko hobbling towards the marble steps of the great house. At the top of the steps stood the butler, dignified and motionless, bearing in his hands a large silver tray. On the tray sat a small roll of Elastoplast.

Another bizarre and unnerving incident overtook me in the Santiago Museum. The directress, a German refugee called Lipschitz, had offered to show me round on a Sunday when the museum was shut to the public. Her guided tour ended in front of a glass case in which sat a fifteenth-century Inca prince aged eight. He had apparently been sacrificed, in accordance with an Inca ritual, in the farthest corner of the Inca Empire, on top of the permanently snow-covered Chilean Andes, and had been found there by some Chilean skiers five hundred years later still deep frozen and therefore intact, in his full princely regalia with his toys around him. They had carried him down 15,000 feet and lodged him in a fridge before he could thaw, and he was now Madame Lipschitz's prize exhibit. In silence she now opened his glass icebox, drew him gently out, and held him lovingly in her arms for a long minute, stroking his forehead – the child she had never had herself. Not a word broke the silence. It was an eerie experience to witness. There was, I should add, no sign of her 'child' having suffered a violent death. He is thought to have been put to sleep with a drug and to have woken up dead. Even now the fingers of this *Momia del Cerro* (Mummy of the Mountains) were as pudgy as they had been five hundred years ago. Two other such sacrificed Inca princelings have since then been found in other corners of the Inca Empire.

Our neighbours across the street in Santiago were the Director of the Chilean National Ballet and his wife, herself a dancer. Heinz had been the leading performer in the German Ballet Jooss before the war and had been performing in Edinburgh (where Marnie had fallen in love with him at sight) when the war broke out. In order to avoid internment he and his wife had hastily disappeared to Chile, where they founded the Chilean Ballet. It was sensationally good; and when I was acting for the British Council man (on leave), I tried to get them invited to the Edinburgh Festival to perform Heinz's *Carmina Burana*. I failed, of course, but he and his wife became the most entertaining friends. They had a ten-year-old son who suffered from wetting the bed. Heinz, being an ingenious fellow, wired in an electrically operated bicycle bell to the boy's undersheet, designed to go off at the first drop of liquid. This worked splendidly but had an awkward side effect. Whenever he was in the streets and a passing bicyclist rang his bell, the boy automatically ran for cover, clutching his crotch.

Life was darkened when news arrived that summer of D's death. 'I suppose', I wrote in my diary, 'that the death of a man's father is the first thing that sets him thinking about his own.' A poor comment, but at least I added, 'What I admired (and envied) most about D was his obvious self-fulfilment. He took and gave in equal measure and saw nothing in his life to regret.' His funeral service, I heard, filled St Giles' Cathedral.

Chile had more painters to the square metre than Montmartre, and poets in almost equal density. These included the world-famous Pablo Neruda, whose first (discarded) wife we knew well. I still have a woodcut of hers that she gave us of a man riding through trees, unaware of faces peering out from them. It bears the untranslatable title *El Caballero sin inconvenientes* – an expression that might (but without the irony) have been applied to my father.

But it was another painter who became our closest friend. This was Nemesio Antunez, gentlest and loveliest of men, who ran the Chilean National Gallery. He and his pretty wife Inez introduced us to a Chilean poet and his Swedish wife Inga. Shortly afterwards the poet went off to Sweden to give poetry readings and came back with another Swedish blonde on his arm, expecting Inga to welcome her into a *ménage à trois*. Inga understandably walked out, but I cannot suppose it much lightened her misery that she was subsequently fallen in love with by *me*! This occurred when Marnie and I took her with us on a trip to Peru – including Machu Picchu, a romantic enough location. Oddly enough, on another trip we made to the Atacama Desert in northern Chile, we were accompanied by Nemesio, and Marnie fell in love with *him*. We both in due course recovered. Both trips were memorable in other ways too. Peru resulted in another article for *Blackwoods* (May 1960) entitled 'Beggar on a Golden Throne' (the description of Cuzco – once the capital of the Inca Empire – used by the splendid Inca guide we hired there).

The Atacama Desert was astonishing in a different way. 'It consists', as I wrote in a letter to David Burnett, 'of a series of dried-up salt-lakes, and its surface is not of soft and sweeping sand-dunes like the deserts I'm accustomed to, but is hard and crusty and looks like a choppy sea frozen while its back was turned.' This was where dozens of British made their fortunes in the nineteenth century, digging up its nitrate crust and selling it as the best fertiliser all round the world (70 per cent of the total at the end of the century) – until, as one might expect, a German (Fritz Haber) invented in 1909 a chemical substitute. The Atacama then reverted to empty desert – empty, that is, except for the abandoned settlements (*oficinas*) of the British nitrate miners. 'They haven't', I wrote, 'slowly buried themselves in sand as would happen in a proper desert. They just remain as they were, suspended in time. The wagons still queue at the pit-heads, the shop-signs still creak in the wind, and through the window of one manager's sitting room a friend of mine has seen a grand piano, hardly even dusty after a hundred years of silence.' I learnt that each *oficina* insisted on its British staff wearing in the evenings its own brand of tartan dinner jacket (maybe most of them were Scottish). As for the native workforce, the macabre landscape was dotted with tiny toy churches, 2 feet high, marking the spots where many of them died (drunk, allegedly) miles from anywhere. A lot of them still had little wreaths of faded paper roses hanging round their steeples.

A decade or two before Chilean nitrates established themselves, quite a number of Englishmen made a fortune from the droppings of seabirds on small islands off the coast of Peru. These deposits too, often as much as 100 feet thick, were sold all over the world as marvellous fertiliser. Indeed, Lord Tennyson allegedly composed a short poem about one of the English merchants who became enormously wealthy from guano. It runs:

> Mister Gibbs
> Made his dibs
> In foreign birds'
> Turds.

What put an end to the successful exploitation of guano was simply that consumption so outstripped production that the islands were progressively scraped bare.

Marnie could now drive with a metal stick operating the footbrake since her right leg remained inoperative. She had inevitably a bad crash at a crossroads, but by her standards this was only a minor mishap, and a few months later she managed to give birth to our third daughter, Cati. Nemesio became her godfather and organised a second (civil) christening in his wooden house. For this ceremony he had privily arranged with Violeta Parra – the wild Communist Andean folk singer, recorded by the BBC – to compose a song in Cati's honour and sing it over her cradle in Nemesio's huge candlelit room.

Nemesio, like all members of the Chilean intelligentsia, was a *soi-disant* Communist. This was the only way of opposing the somewhat uncultured right-wing government before Allende's revolution. I might add, rather proudly, that some two years later I was discussing with some top official in the lunch canteen of the FO the selection of Nicko Henderson as the Foreign

Secretary's right-hand man. The official told me that he had been picked out partly because of the Ambassador's dispatches from Santiago which Nicko had doubtless drafted. He mentioned one such dispatch – on Communism in Chile. It had in fact been written entirely by *me*.

I must limit myself to a few other memorabilia of our time in Chile. One was the visit my now lonely mother was persuaded to make. She came out in what she called a 'Flying Machine'. It was, I suppose, a risky venture, for by now her memory was largely gone and she never quite knew where she was. When the Flying Machine stopped in Buenos Aires, where she had to change flights, she got out, looked around and said to a group of people, 'Where is Glencairn?' By God's grace one of them was an Anglo-Chilean who knew me, and he brought her with him to Santiago. I think she loved her month's stay although, since her mind remained geared to Edinburgh, she could never understand why the sun always seemed to be shining in December (Chile's midsummer).

Another, but regular, visitor was Scrap's Anglo-Italian friend Alaramo Scarampi, on whom he had been billeted in Florence in 1944. I must now set out the melodramatic circumstances that had brought him and his family from Florence to Chile. Some years after the war ended, Alaramo had suffered anguish watching 'eleven million' German tourists passing his window in the Via dei Bardi; and in an access of despair he had got his small son to borrow a globe of the world from his school. He had then seized an old-fashioned hatpin from his wife's hat and pushed it through Florence on the borrowed globe to see where it came out on the opposite side of the world from eleven million German tourists. This proved to be the middle-south of Chile, and without further ado he bought passages for the family to Santiago. On arrival they hiked south, bought a patch of forest where the hatpin had come out, cut down as many trees as necessary, grew things, and were happily living there when we came to Chile. It was as well that the hatpin had not emerged 100 miles farther south for, as I discovered when I went fishing there, this was an area exclusively inhabited by descendants of German immigrants who had colonised a chunk of Chile in the 1870s. In a hundred years none had bothered to learn the language of their adoptive country. (Hitler, incidentally, was still popularly rumoured to be hiding away in the area concerned.)

A third visitor was a young Englishman, Richard Easton, whom I ran into at the British Council and who disclosed the following horrific experience. He and a fellow Cambridge undergraduate had set out to cross South America at its widest point – from Bahia in Brazil to Lima in Peru – in a Brazilian jeep. After some weeks, about halfway across, they found themselves in the dense jungle of the Matto Grosso. They were obliged to abandon the jeep and continue on foot, constructing rafts whenever they had to cross rivers. They met no one, but one day, when they were separately carrying their chattels from one river valley to another, Richard, coming back for a second load, found his mate lying dead on the ground with spears laid radially round his body. In this appalling situation there was nothing he could do but push on alone. Somehow or other he eventually reached Lima. He then hiked down to Santiago where I met him, and he came to stay with us and recover.

His story was to have an even more horrific ending. The following year he decided, incredibly, to do the crossing again with other Cambridge friends. This time it was he who was done to death by tribesmen in the Matto Grosso. When I heard of this, I wrote to his parents. One sentence in their reply especially moved me: 'He loved life: but if he had to die this was the way he would have chosen.'

But a strange mystery about Richard's story emerged recently. In November 2004 Jenny and I met the great explorer Robin Hanbury-Tenison, and I mentioned Richard Easton. Robin told me that he himself had been Richard's companion on that 1959 crossing and that so far from being speared to death in the Matto Grosso he had simply parted from Richard halfway across in order to get home for his own wedding. Robin confirmed that two years later Richard had set out to repeat the crossing with a mutual Cambridge friend (the now celebrated John Hemming) and had himself been done to death in the Matto Grosso, his body being found with spears and clubs around it. So how could Richard Easton have given me in Santiago that (apparently fictitious) account of the death of his companion in the same area on his previous (1959) crossing? There is a four-year gap (1957–60) in my notebooks, so I have no records to quote; but Richard's conversation with me in 1959 is fixed immutably in my memory. Was he, by some prophetic oddity, foreseeing what would happen to his own self two years later and attributing it (for plausibility's sake) to his companion in 1959 (which I now know was Robin)? There seems no rational explanation – unless my memory is totally haywire.

I cannot move on from Chile without recording two odd experiences in my official goings-on. Both occurred on visits I had to pay to Valparaiso, Chile's great port. On the first, I was sent down in the absence of my commercial colleague to report on a floating Japanese industrial exhibition. This was in the days when Japan had barely begun to challenge the West at its own industrial game. I sweated round the bowels of the huge ship, alarmingly impressed by the exhibits. When I emerged at last into the steaming air I was handed a glass of Japanese 'Scotch'. I tossed it down and realised that I couldn't tell the difference. It cost about 50p a bottle. If the Japs could make even Scotch whisky as good as ours and infinitely cheaper, the sun (I concluded) must be finally setting on the British Empire. Fortunately there was a sequel to this trauma. Thirteen years later in Baghdad an Iraqi doctor friend was going on a mission to Japan. I told him of my Valparaiso experience and asked him to get me a bottle of Japanese Scotch. I dined with him on his return. He produced the promised bottle. I took a nip and had a bad headache for two days. My doctor friend told me that the Japs themselves wouldn't touch the stuff and simply concocted it for export to the backward races of South East Asia. (By this time, however, the sun had already gone down over the British Empire.)

On my other visit to Valparaiso I was deputising for our Consul. A British rating had been left behind by a visiting British frigate, and having been found by the Chilean police fighting drunk had been lodged in the clink. My job was to attend his trial two days later. The judge spoke kindly to the accused, mentioning how much the Chileans had admired the British navy ever since Commander Cochrane had helped Chile gain its independence from Spain in 1819. He then asked the accused whether there was anything he wished to say in his defence. The accused, who appeared to be still under the influence, wobbled forward to the judge's desk, tapped it with his knuckles and said, 'Give me ten good men – I *take* your fucking country.' I was too appalled to wait and see what was done with him.

We left on transfer shortly after. At the airport, as the gangway was being removed for take-off, we saw Nemesio striding towards the plane on his long legs, carrying a canvas he had just completed as a present for Marnie.* It was a large semi-abstract of the Island of Chiloë, which, though 15 miles long, disappeared under the sea eighteen months later when the most savage earthquake in Chile's history altered its whole central coastline. The painting remains in the family.

---

* Nemesio remained in touch. Many years later, long after Marnie died, he lived for a time in London where the Director of the Royal College of Art lent him his own studio to paint in; and I was able to introduce him to Jenny. Alas, he died in Valparaiso in 1994.

CHAPTER 14

The Lebanon

BEFORE proceeding on my posting to francophone Lebanon I was sent to 'perfect my French' (as the French say) in Tours, lodging for two snowbound months with the pleasant family of what was then called a commercial traveller. Meanwhile I was being taught how to pronounce French diphthongs correctly by a linguist from Poitiers University.

It was during that winter (1960) that General de Gaulle, the President of France, made his first and most memorable television address to the nation. This was to announce his unexpected decision to give rebellious Algeria its independence. I watched the TV with my host and his family. It proved a curious revelation of the difference between the French and the British forms of patriotism, for when de Gaulle fired his bombshell, the whole family burst into tears. '*La gloire de la France*', they cried, had suffered an unbearable humiliation ... When the British Prime Minister announced his decision to withdraw from (let us say) Egypt five years earlier or Aden seven years later, did any British commercial traveller and his family burst into tears? More likely they opened another bottle or two of Bass and lit another fag.

Much more extraordinary was a lecture given to us by a professor of history from Poitiers, describing the unsuccessful flight to England of France's great rationalist philosopher Descartes, expelled from his country in the 1640s for his unorthodoxy. During the sea crossing a violent storm had blown up and the ship's captain ordered all passengers to throw their heavy baggage overboard. They all obeyed – except one man, who was reported to be sitting resolutely on his portmanteau below deck. The captain gave orders for the man and his portmanteau to be forcibly brought up. This was done but the man still refused to remove himself from it or even to say what was in it. The captain had it forced open. Out jumped a tiny homunculus which disappeared into the sea. The distraught Descartes (for it was he) declared that he had captured the homunculus when digging up a mandrake, under whose roots, as everyone knew, such little men live. The ship was eventually driven ashore near Amsterdam and Descartes was taken under arrest to be tried for disobeying the lawful order of a ship's captain. Our lecturer had himself discovered the whole bizarre story in the Amsterdam court records.

I have myself dug up many mandrakes since then, in the hope of meeting the famous challenge of John Donne (a contemporary of Descartes):

> Go and catch a falling star,
> Get with child a mandrake root.

But despite promising squeaks I have never chanced upon one with child.

In the light of what became of the Lebanon fifteen years after I went there, it may seem strange that in 1960 it was a politically dull little country where nothing ever happened. It made up for this by being the crossroads of the Middle East, where the gossip of the Arab world, and therefore the foreign journalists, converged. The Lebanon was also ravishingly beautiful, its mountains, valleys and sea coast all lavishly decorated with wild flowers and Roman temples, and even clumps of biblical cedar trees – those at least that had not been chopped down by the Australian infantry in the Great War to brew tea on.

I had not done more than six months as the Embassy's Information Officer before a kindly catastrophe overtook me. One of my Section's jobs was to produce every week an hour's English-language programme for Radio Liban. One day, in the middle of the regional Information Officers' annual conference, I was called to the telephone. The caller was the Lebanese Director-General of Information, in a state of electric indignation. He had just been deluged by phone calls from angry listeners to my English Hour protesting that today's programme had consisted of a discussion between three generations of Jews in Canada as to whether they should or should not join the Zionist bandwagon in Israel. (The *News Chronicle* correspondent's wife, who produced the English Hour for me, had incorporated, without bothering to listen to it herself, a recording distributed by London under some harmless-sounding title for use by all Middle East posts. Presumably London hadn't bothered to listen to it either.) I had to hurry round to the Ministry and eat very humble pie. But the happy upshot was that my Ambassador generously transferred me from Information to his Political Section (Chancery), which was more fun.

The Chancery job involved quite a lot of wining and dining with Lebanese politicians. In the course of this an incident occurred which I proudly record. At a large dinner party with a Lebanese MP a power cut took place and we were plunged into total darkness. This was about 11 p.m., by which time the Frenchified Lebanese had the habit, under the influence of alcohol, of switching from French to talking their own language. I found myself in a group of them and ventured to contribute some Arabic sentences to the conversation. Just then the lights came on again, and one of the party turned to me and said, 'Was that you speaking? I thought it was an Iraqi Bedou.' Rightly or wrongly I took this as the nearest to a compliment I have ever received for my Arabic.

In my four and a half years in Beirut I learnt a lot about the Levantine lifestyle but will only record a few oddities here. One morning during rush hour there seemed to be more than the usual horn-blowing outside Dr Yenikomshian's block of flats, of which we occupied the third floor. I looked out of the window. In the narrow street below (one-way traffic having not yet been introduced) opposing lines of vehicles had come to a total standstill facing each other. At the head of one line was a large truck, at the head of the other a taxi. The horn-blowing was deafening but purposeless. I waited to see what would happen. Eventually the taxi-driver got out and advanced on the truck-driver, who was simply sitting in his driving seat with his hand on his horn, reading a newspaper. A violent argument and probably a bout of fisticuffs looked inevitable. But what actually happened was that the taxi-driver just borrowed the truck-driver's newspaper, returned to his taxi and proceeded to read it. I had to hasten to the Embassy, on foot of course, and have no idea how the problem was ever solved.

Another illustration of the Lebanon's eccentric traffic practices occurred when we were driving back at midnight from watching the magnificent Margot Fonteyn and Nureyev dancing at Baalbek on the steps of the Temple of Bacchus. We had driven well off the road to eat our sandwiches and were peaceably doing so when a Lebanese driver crashed into our rear end. There was nothing for it but to wait, under Lebanese law, until our respective insurers' 'referees' could be summoned from Beirut. After two hours they came. Their joint conclusion was that I was 25 per cent to blame. I protested that my car had been 15 yards off the road, stationary and with its inside lights on. How could I have been to blame at all? 'Ah,' they said, 'but if you had not been there, it would not have happened.' Lebanese logic – impenetrable but incontrovertible.

Having mentioned our landlord, Dr Haik Yenikomshian, I will insert two tributes to the Armenians of the Levant. Dr Yeni, as he was called, was Professor of Internal Medicine at the American University of Beirut, and while we were there he retired in his seventies. I came upon him sitting in his garden in a deckchair under an almond tree with the *Collected Works of William Shakespeare* on one knee and the *Oxford English Dictionary* on the other. His English was curiously imperfect, and he explained that he had decided he must hurry along to master the whole of Shakespeare before it was too late. He was still engaged on the task when we left two years later.

During that time I arranged with some French and Lebanese friends to join them on a week's expedition to southern Turkey. We were to foregather at the famous Baron Hotel in Aleppo. Driving there (alone) to join them, I stopped to photograph one of Syria's enchanting 'beehive' villages of round thatched huts. In parking I snapped the half-shaft of my Ford Zephyr in the concrete roadside drain and had to abandon it. A Syrian from whom I thumbed a lift explained that there was no hope of my obtaining assistance from an Aleppo garage since a national holiday was about to start and everyone would be knocking off for three days. Then he added, 'But it's a Muslim holiday and the Armenians don't celebrate it. So you must find an Armenian taxi-driver to take you to the Armenian quarter and look for an Armenian repair shop.' I did just that, and ended up at dusk in the house of an Armenian blacksmith,

who said he would see what could be done and I should return at ten
o'clock in the morning. I did so. There in his yard was my car. His son had
hired an (Armenian?) winch and brought my car in. No one in Aleppo, he
had discovered, stocked Ford half-shafts, so he had started making one on
his rudimentary lathe. Thirty-six hours later he had miraculously done so,
mounted it, aligned the wheels, and my car was ready to drive away. In the
course of our conversations I mentioned that I lived in Beirut in the house
of an Armenian doctor, Yenikomshian. 'Haik Yenikomshian?' exclaimed the
blacksmith. 'The greatest man alive. He saved thousands of our lives during
the Turkish massacre of Armenians in 1915 and herded us all south into Syria.
I worship him.' And he refused all payment for two days' work, declaring that
he would never accept a penny from any friend of Dr Yenikomshian.

Twenty years later Jenny and I also broke down near Aleppo, on another
Muslim holiday, and searched for my Armenian blacksmith. Alas, he had died.
But we found another Armenian mechanic – too young to have experienced
the Cilician massacres – and this time I was allowed to pay. In the course of
my wanderings in the Middle East I often had occasion to wonder where the
Arab world would be without its Armenian minority.

Reverting to more strictly Lebanese peculiarities, I was woken one morning before dawn by a Lebanese employee of the Embassy who told me that
a coup d'état was going on and that I had better get up and see what was
afoot. I drove round the town and ran up against soldiers and armoured cars
everywhere. Apparently an obscure body known as the Parti Populaire Syrien,
or PPS, was attempting to overthrow the Lebanese government. I managed
to get to my Ambassador's house. Sir Moore Crosthwaite was somewhat
grumpy at my waking him at what was still an ungodly hour, but he struggled
out of bed and we made our way to the Embassy. The coup had by now
evidently failed. That afternoon the Minister of the Interior, Kemal Joumblatt,
announced that the attempted revolution had been engineered by the British
and that he had himself seen the British Ambassador at dawn on the roof of
the Embassy signalling to a British warship offshore … There was nothing
to be gained by our insisting that the British Ambassador had been asleep
till after the coup had been suppressed and that there was no British warship
nearer than Malta. A scapegoat was needed, and the British were still reputed
in those far-off days to be behind every Arab misadventure.

The Foreign Office still maintained, of course, its school at Shemlan in
the hills above Beirut, where we were teaching Arabic to all and sundry. The
students were mainly younger diplomats and businessmen but included an
occasional member of the Secret Services. This fact may well have become
known to the Egyptian press since some of the instructors were Egyptian; and
the illustrated Cairo magazine *Al-Musawwar* published an article attributing
wicked activities to the school. The article included a photograph showing the
'young spies' being taught to stalk through the woods at Shemlan carrying

secret messages. The students did indeed stalk through the woods at dusk, but what they carried were the Arabic word lists they were required to master overnight. As a result of the publicity given to the article, however, it became customary to refer jokily to Shemlan as our 'spy school'.

One of the words inexplicably taught to students was the Arabic for 'having six fingers on the right hand'. During my brief stint as Information Officer my Assistant, Patrick Wright (later to be head of the Foreign Office), burst excitedly into my office to tell me he had just been visited by the Imam of Tripoli and, if I would accept his word for it, there on his right hand were six fingers. Patrick sadly admitted that he had felt it inappropriate to show off his Arabic expertise by mentioning the subject to the Imam; but it had been a great moment in the life of an ex-student of Shemlan.

In Beirut there were four Boulos brothers, the exiled sons of a Protestant pastor of Haifa. All four, like so many Palestinians in exile, had got to the top of their respective trees. One was the best physician in Beirut, one was the best surgeon, a third was head of the American University Faculty of Music, and the eldest, who had no profession at all, had made himself the richest man in the country. As he was known to have a magnificent collection of Persian rugs, I made his acquaintance and learnt from him how his rise to riches had begun.

Fifteen years before, he had visited his younger brother studying medicine in Edinburgh. Taking tea at McVitties in Princes Street, they had been engaged in conversation by a stout Scotsman. The latter, hearing that Habib Boulos had no job, asked him whether he would like one. 'What would I have to do?' asked Habib warily. The Scotsman disclosed that he was the owner of Munrospun Knitwear and that, if Habib would care to be his Middle East representative, every time a Munrospun pullover was sold there he would receive a percentage commission. This sounded undemanding enough. Habib returned to Beirut and, though playing no part in promoting the product, kept receiving cheques from the firm every month. This, he said to himself, seems to be the way to make money without actually doing anything. So he obtained appointments from other British firms as their Middle East agent, and by the time I met him he had worked his way up to becoming the agent of De Havilland Aircraft. Three of the latter's famous Comets had just been bought by Middle East Airlines and Habib, without having lifted a finger, had received a percentage commission of (I think) £150,000 for each one.

When I was visiting his carpet collection in his seaside mansion just outside the city, he told me how he had effortlessly made a million in another even more ingenious way. Beirut had been in the throes of an enormous high-rise building boom. A municipal decree forbade builders to dump their excavated soil within the city limits. Habib's original villa lay just outside those limits and, as he was infuriated at the erection by some villainous man of a tall house that blocked his view of the sea, he offered all builders the opportunity (on a monopoly basis) of dumping their spoil on his land on payment to him of a shilling a load. They had jumped at this, and in six months Habib's plot of land extended 50 yards out into the sea beside his nefarious neighbour's villa. Habib then built himself with the proceeds of his monopoly deal the mansion he now occupied on the point of his new land, blocking the sea view of his defeated neighbour. 'Now look at this rug,' he went on with a cackle of laughter, unrolling a magnificent antique he had just bought in London for a king's ransom.

Another prominent citizen who revealed unexpected qualities was the Russian Orthodox Bishop of Tyre & Sidon. I was seated next to him at a lunch given for the visiting Archbishop of Canterbury by the Orthodox Archimandrite in Beirut, with whose Church as a whole Canterbury was seeking a closer understanding. Tyre & Sidon and I talked Arabic painlessly enough throughout the meal, but when we all rose to take our leave he turned to me and said (in Arabic), 'I do speak some English, you know.' I raised my eyebrows in suitable admiration, and the English he came out with was, 'I love you. Goodbye.' I could not help wondering when or how he had learnt the expression.

A different quirk of the Lebanese sense of humour was disclosed by the Embassy's splendid Oriental Counsellor, Maroun Arab. The circumstances were these. A monumental mason in Tripoli had come to me in the Embassy with a gift he wished to be sent to Buckingham Palace as a humble tribute to our great Queen. It was a Phoenician galley he had ingeniously carved out of soapstone. I was vexed when Buckingham Palace replied stuffily to my resulting letter that 'Her Majesty only accepts gifts from those with whom she is personally acquainted'. As a result of further correspondence I was informed that Her Majesty had agreed as a special concession to accept the soapstone galley, and I was thus able to assure the monumental mason that his gift would be displayed in the palace. (In fact it was sadly smashed on the way, though dispatched by confidential bag in a specially made box.) To my dismay the sculptor came back a month later with *another* gift for the Queen in the shape of a monumental birdbath, 3 feet high. I gave him such bogus assurances as I could. Round the rim of the birdbath was a Kufic inscription which I was unable to read, and I appealed to Counsellor Maroun Arab to translate it for me. He studied it and turned to me with a look of horror. 'You can't possibly send this to Her Majesty,' he declared. 'What it says is, "Madam, your husband is deceiving you."' I hope he was teasing me, but in any case there was no way I could send a stone birdbath to Buckingham Palace. I don't remember what we did with it.

Four years later I was given another demonstration of the homage paid in those days by the outside world to the royal family. I was then in Bahrain, where a local citizen of Pakistani origin, Khudadad Khan, was in the habit of composing unforgettable odes in honour of the Queen's birthday. Those of 1967 and 1968 came my way and I reproduce the second of them here.

On the occasion of HER MOST EXCELLENT MAJESTY'S *Happy*
BIRTHDAY.
The 22nd of April 1968

Here are some verses like last year's again
    To celebrate in the most beautiful way;
In the Sixteenth year of the Blessed Reign
    Your Most Excellent Majesty's Happy Birthday.

These are like fragrant pretty flowers
    Selected with great care and pain;
To be scattered in beautiful showers
    On the way of Your Majesty's train.

I would have very much liked to be
    In Old Merry England proper and meet;
To be there and with my own eyes see
    And lay the flowers under Your Majesty's feet.

But being far away on this Auspicious day
    In a small Island called Bahrain;
I am sending these flowers all this way
    By a fast International Aeroplane ...

The flowers in the gardens do all thrive
    On the gardener's sweat and the soil;
But the words of a poem can only arrive
    From the poet's soul by racking toil.

I pray to GOD with my most humble mien
    WHO every body's prayers always HEARS;
That Queen Elizabeth Second May Reign
    Many many long and prosperous years.

And May Your Majesty's Family Royal
    From the very youngest and the old;
And all the Staff, loving and loyal
    Remain all healthy and true as gold.

Your Majesty's servant is getting very old
    His Battery of energies are nearly cold;
One of these days Your Majesty may be told
    That Your Majesty's poet is laid in the mould.

BAHRAIN   Your Most Excellent Majesty's
16-4-1968   Most humble and Abject slave.
                 Khudadad Khan

I learnt recently that Khudadad died in 1993. Were he still alive today he might have found difficulty in renewing the hope in his penultimate stanza that all members of the 'Family Royal' would remain 'true as gold'.

While on the subject of literature I enjoyed collecting misuses of English in foreign publications and showed an amusing misprint in Beirut's English paper, the *Daily Star*, to my colleague, Alan Munro. Alan came back with the following headline in the *Daily Star*, which had appeared when I was on leave, in connection with a secret session of the Arab League Council at Shtaura in the ante-Lebanon:

ARAB LEAGUE MEETS IN PRIVY.

Not, of course, a misprint: just a misunderstanding of one of the finer points in the English language.

I cannot stop myself quoting here two instances of foreigners using English a bit off-beam, which I added to my collection. The first is the notice put on the dressing table in each bedroom of a hotel in Basle (sent to me from there by Peggy Piggott):

THE LITTLE SISTERS OF CHARITY FAVOUR NO RELIGION
AND HARBOUR ALL DISEASES.

The other I owe to Peter Lunn, the head spy in the Embassy. He had been having lunch, rather imaginatively, with his Soviet opposite number. The conversation had turned, even more oddly, on the reactions of the famous American evangelist Billy Graham on coming across, during a walk in Hyde Park, a boy and girl ostentatiously necking in the dirty grass. The Soviet spy, whose first foreign language was obviously French but who spoke to Peter in English, had advanced to Peter the following patriotic comment: 'In Moscow the herb is so fresh you may lie on it in a chemise alone and stay pure.'

But I will close these extracts from my collection with what we must hope was a straightforward misprint in the *Saigon Daily Post*. This recorded a visiting English lecturer on Hobbes quoting to his audience that philosopher's famous dictum thus: 'The life of man is solitary, poor, nasty, british, and short.'

Reverting to life in the Lebanon, various British visitors contributed to my entertainment. I have already mentioned watching Margot Fonteyn dancing with the Royal Ballet at Baalbek. After one of the five successive performances we went to, the Ambassador gave a huge party for the visitors by moonlight in the Temple of Zeus. I bravely went up to Margot. 'You won't remember', I said, 'having lunch four years ago in Kensington with Feefa Adam,* at which I was privileged to sit next to you.' 'I certainly do remember,' replied Margot.

---

* Feefa Adam, an old friend of the Ogilvies, had been Ambassador in Panama and had attended Margot's wedding there to her Panamanian husband; and he had nobly invited Marnie and me to meet them.

'You answered all my questions about the habits of camels.' Like other great people Margot had the gift of making you feel, however insignificant you might be, that you were the one person in the world she most wanted to talk to. I had another experience of this when I sat next to Freya Stark, the great Arabian travel writer, at a Beirut lunch party. Fortunately I was on her left, which was the only direction she ever conversed in. This was because of the large hat she always wore at a rakish angle to conceal the absence of hair on the right side of her head, which had been torn out in her youth in an accident with a machine. Though much less ravishing than Margot, she too had that gift – though I can't remember what she can have got me to talk about. She already knew about camels.

Another rewarding British acquaintance was John Carswell, who taught painting, rather avant-garde, in the American University (and later became Sotheby's expert on Oriental art). He had an enchanting two-roomed cottage in Junieh Bay, north of Beirut, on the edge of the water. The first thing that confronted the visitor on entering his cottage was a medium-sized elephant: or rather, the half that could fit into his small sitting room. The rear half was in his bedroom, the wall between having been neatly carved out round the elephant's middle. He explained that he had found the elephant on a rubbish dump in the university, having been thrown out by the biology department, and had privily salvaged it. Its only defect was that some of the stitching down its tummy had come loose; and one day he had pushed a hand inside and drawn out of the straw stuffing a French newspaper published in Paris during the German siege of 1870. So the pachyderm was now in its post-humous nineties.

One of the teachers of English at the same university was Professor Christopher Scaife, whose conversation was a constant delight. I only mention him here, however, because of a chance meeting twenty years later in London. He had retired from Beirut long since to grow olives in Umbria; and he turned up unexpectedly in London. Recognising me across the street, his first words shouted from there were, 'Hallo there! Did you ever hear about the weekend De Musset and George Sand spent together in Rouen? No? Well, their hotelier was so proud of having such distinguished guests that he begged them to enter their names and professions in his visitors' book. De Musset hesitated over his profession and murmured, *"Si je n'étais pas dans la ville de Lamartine, je me signerais "poète".* George Sand, who was of course a woman (reputedly of an accommodating kind) but used a male *nom de plume* to get her writings published, then took the pen and, gazing wistfully at the ceiling, said, *"Et moi, si je n'étais pas dans la ville de Jeanne d'Arc, je me signerais "vierge".'*

It was about this time that my old Sudanese friend Sheikh Muhammed Ahmed Abu Sinn paid us one of his welcome visits. Michael Scott, Marnie's brother-in-law and my own exact contemporary, having been born at the same moment of 23 September 1917, also visited us that year. He was then

11 Sudanese notable Muhammed Ahmed Abu Sinn, staying with the BPs in
Beirut in 1962, holding Cati.

a marvellous raconteur, and I will record two of his reminiscences (neither
of which figured in his obituary in the *Daily Telegraph* in January 1992 describing him as 'a remarkable polymath, scholar, mystic, writer, orientalist,

and traveller'). He had lost his right eye in the war rescuing a fellow soldier from a minefield in Suffolk, and told us how at the top of an escalator in Piccadilly Circus underground station his glass eye had dropped out and he had had the surreal experience of watching with his other eye his glass one bouncing down the escalator till it disappeared in the works at the bottom. (He wore thereafter a black patch.)

The other of his reminiscences was even more bizarre. Just after the war he was setting off from London to spend a weekend with friends in the country and was awaiting a train during the rush hour at Paddington station. A man standing in front of him on the packed platform appeared to be fingering something on his chest under his large greatcoat. Michael edged inquisitively forward and asked him what he was doing. 'I'm waiting', was the reply, 'to find out where there is an empty compartment when the train comes in. My gold pendulum will tell me.' When the train arrived, the man was able to position himself precisely by the door of an empty compartment. Michael got in and sat beside him. In the course of conversation the man said, 'Why don't you come and spend the night at my house and we'll see if you have the same diviner's gift?' So Michael changed his plans and did. After supper the man placed on the table three photographs of British soldiers in uniform and said, 'Take my pendulum and tell me whether these soldiers are alive or dead.' Michael balanced the pendulum over the first photograph and it swung uncontrollably from left to right. 'I suppose this one is alive,' said Michael. 'You're right. Try the next one.' This time the pendulum remained motionless. 'Is he dead?' said Michael. 'Yes, try the third.' Over the third photograph the pendulum wobbled uncertainly. Michael was nonplussed. 'Surely you can guess,' said his host. 'This man is reported missing, captured or killed.' So Michael bought himself a gold pendulum and never looked back, using it mostly to discover water in various deserts.

I had a strange experience myself when I went for a week's leave from Beirut to dig at Little Petra or Beidha (4 miles north of Petra itself) with Diana Kirkbride, one of that astonishing breed of tough female archaeologists to which Kathleen Kenyon (see p. 156) belonged. The only way to get there was by borrowing a horse from the police at Wadi Mousa. It was August and the heat was appalling. My Bedou guide kept me alive by knocking prickly pear fruit down with his stick, rolling them on the ground under his leather sandal, whipping off the loosened spines and skin with his knife, and holding up to me on its point these life-giving delicacies – all done in six seconds. But by the time we reached Little Petra we were out of the prickly pear area and my tongue was as dry and congealed as a dead parrot's. I couldn't articulate at all – but there was Diana striding up and down a steep sandbank in a temperature of 117 degrees and a thick tweed skirt. She took me to her tent to recover. By the table was a bowl of water with a yellow-and-black rim round it. On closer inspection I realised that the yellow-and-black rim consisted of closely wedged hornets. 'Don't worry,' said Diana. 'Hornets are quite friendly as long as you give them a drink.' After a week's work excavating the craftsmen's houses in her sixth-millennium BC settlement (then declared to be the oldest walled town in the world, but overtaken since), I set off on foot for Petra to seek a lift back to Wadi Mousa. This is where the strange experience occurred. Darkness was falling and in those rocky valleys I lost my sense of direction. Eventually I saw a light and made my way towards it. It proved to come from an isolated Bedou tent. Its unfriendly occupant declared that because of the war with Israel foreigners were not allowed to nose around in the area and he was obliged to cut my throat. I naturally thought he was joking, but he proceeded to take his arm-knife out of its sheath. In the tense exchanges that followed I mentioned desperately that I was a harmless archaeologist and had been working for a week with the well-known English lady Diana Kirkbride. 'The Sitt Diana!' he exclaimed. '*Wallahi*, any friend of *hers* must be all right.' He laid down his knife, and I spent the night in his tent talking agreeably of the Sitt Diana. He had himself worked for her some years before, and at dawn he guided me to Petra.

Some years later the magic of Diana's name again served me in good stead. I had gone from Amman to see the Roman city of Jerash for a day or two, and since I could find no householders in the nearby village willing to let me sleep on their property, I drove through an entry into the site itself which bore a NO ADMITTANCE notice. I was just unrolling my bedding behind a convenient Roman wall when a burly figure appeared and ordered me out. So I simply said (on the off-chance), 'But I am a friend of the Sitt Diana Kirkbride,' whereupon he bowed and said, 'Then make yourself at home.' So I lay down on my bedding roll and a minute or two later he returned with three eggs and a big smile.

But back to Beirut again. That summer Marnie had her fourth child, which turned out to our surprised relief to be a boy, Jamie. But less happy things occurred as winter approached. My mother died and I flew home for her burial in Crichton churchyard (see p. 32). Then Marnie tripped over one of her crutches and smashed her bad leg in several places.

Before we leave Beirut I must give an account of the only occasion in my life when I have attracted the attention of the British media – namely the Kim Philby affair. For part of what follows I am indebted to the impressively scrupulous study of Philby's life by Patrick Seale and Maureen McConville, *Philby: The Long Road to Moscow* (Hamish Hamilton, 1973). Philby wrote his own version earlier in Moscow entitled, when published in London in 1968, *My Silent War*.

When I took up my post as the Embassy's First Secretary (Information) in the autumn of 1959 I was aware that the Americans had entertained suspicions about Philby in connection with the disappearance to Moscow of Maclean and Burgess in 1951 (see below), but as he had been declared innocent by our Foreign Secretary in the Commons in 1955 there was no reason for me to treat him with caution – particularly since he soon struck me as the best-informed and most communicative journalist around, in his capacity as a correspondent of the *Observer* and *The Economist*. I was impressed to discover that he dictated his pieces for them to his current wife Eleanor straight out of his head – in my presence on one occasion – and never even read them through. Eleanor simply went off without further ado and cabled them to their destinations. He became a close friend, infinitely entertaining – and indeed helpful. For instance, following the Lebanese minister's allegation that the attempted coup by the PPS (see above, p. 174) had been engineered by the British Embassy, Kim assembled a number of Lebanese journalists in his flat in my presence and assured them categorically that the minister had been inventing. Our two families often went off together at weekends to picnic in remote places. When his remarkable father St John Philby – the prolific writer on Arabia, protégé of King Ibn Saud and convert to Islam – was visiting Beirut in the summer of 1960, Kim took me to lunch with him. The conversation was, I fear, scrappy and inconsequential. The old man died elsewhere a few weeks later, was brought to be buried in Beirut and was described by Kim on his tombstone as 'The Greatest of Arabian Travellers'. I never fathomed Kim's relations with his father. He clearly admired (and perhaps adopted) St John's lifelong determination to pursue his personal convictions regardless of criticism, and he once showed me with pride the manuscript of St John's last (unpublished) book on Arabia. It was exquisitely drafted in small neat handwriting without a single correction – as if he, like Kim, did not need to read his work through to check its precision. But I had the impression that they did not in fact get on all that well.

I should now explain the circumstances (though they were unknown to me at the time) that had brought Kim to Beirut as a journalist. He had been awarded the OBE for his outstanding intelligence work in the war, and since then he had held several key posts abroad before being sent to Washington in 1949 to head the counter-espionage team attached to our Embassy, working closely with the CIA and the FBI. That same year the CIA began to suspect that a Soviet agent, located probably in the British Embassy, was leaking secrets to the Russians. They could not identify who it was. There were a number of possibilities. These included Philby, though they knew he was highly regarded in his own service for his professionalism and integrity.

Then in 1951 the notorious disappearance to Moscow of Donald Maclean and Guy Burgess caused severe shock. Maclean, after some years in the Embassy in Washington and a nervous breakdown, had recently become head of American Department in the Foreign Office. Burgess, a member of Philby's counter-espionage team in Washington, had made himself intensely disliked by the Americans for his disreputable behaviour in society. Both Burgess and Maclean had become politically suspect, and it was thought on both sides of the Atlantic that someone must have tipped them off in the nick of time to escape while they could – the 'Third Man' syndrome. It was not forgotten by the CIA that Philby had been providing Burgess with accommodation in his flat, and this understandably strengthened their misgivings about him. Could he be the Soviet agent they had been seeking for eighteen months to identify? The CIA conveyed their suspicions to the SIS in London, but such investigations as were carried out there produced no evidence to damage his good name. The CIA, however, pursued its own investigations relentlessly, and early that summer its Director wrote a stiff letter to the head of the SIS, Sir Stewart Menzies, declaring that the CIA/FBI would not countenance further dealings with Philby and demanding his removal from America. After further rapid and no doubt heated Anglo-American exchanges Kim was called home to face interrogation by Sir Stewart himself. Disarmingly he tendered his resignation straight away 'to spare his superiors from embarrassment', while insisting on his total innocence. If only in the interests of relations with America, acceptance of his resignation was judged necessary. So he was laid off.

Left without employment he had to struggle for the next few years in various modest jobs to earn enough to support his then wife Aileen (who died in 1957) and his sundry children. There were plenty of his ex-colleagues who thought he had been unfairly treated as a scapegoat. But doubts about his past were entertained in some quarters in London, and eventually Marcus Lipton, MP, who had been carrying out extensive private investigations, raised his unfavourable conclusions in the Commons. This was when, on 7 November 1955, Foreign Secretary Macmillan in response declared himself fully satisfied that Philby was guiltless. Philby followed this up by giving a masterly and persuasive press conference himself, and Lipton was obliged to withdraw his charges. Sir Stewart himself, however, had misgivings, and there could be no question of reappointing him. Sir Dick White, who had been head of MI5 and was now transferred to succeed Menzies, had even sharper misgivings.

The following year, 1956, there was a new development initiated by those who felt sorry for him. With prompting from the Foreign Office and from the influential David Astor (of the *Observer* family), the editors of the *Observer* and *The Economist* gave him a job as their correspondent on Middle East affairs, based in Beirut. And that was what he was doing when I went to Beirut in 1959. My friendly association with him, as described above, proceeded happily over the next three years. One wet night (23 January 1963) Kim and his wife Eleanor were coming to a dinner party in my flat. Eleanor arrived and said that Kim had phoned to say that he was held up but would be along a little later. He never came.

What had just happened (though I was only allowed to learn the facts – or some of them – later) was the following. The counter-espionage experts in London had finally caught up with Kim's Soviet allegiance and his involvement as the Third Man in the disappearance of Maclean and Burgess. Nicholas Elliot, an old colleague of Kim's who had recently completed a four-year stint as the head intelligence sleuth in our Beirut Embassy, was sent out to confront him with the damning evidence, but with authority – since Kim had, it seems, been a double agent in Beirut under deep cover – to offer him immunity from prosecution if he came quietly to London and told the SIS all he knew about its Soviet counterpart and his dealings with them. He evidently undertook to do so and was allowed by Elliot to go home for the night – the night, that is, of my dinner party.

He had, as we were to learn, been picked up by a Soviet ship waiting for him in Beirut harbour. His whereabouts, however, remained unknown for quite some time, but when the news of his presence in Moscow finally became public knowledge, there was hell to pay. The Anglo-Saxon press converged on Beirut. My association with Kim was quickly picked up. I was instructed by the Ambassador to say nothing.

To add to the extensive coverage given to Kim's disappearance by the British press the well-known journalist Clare Hollingworth drafted a detailed article for the *Guardian,* which was not in fact published. Writing about the occasion in her memoirs (published in London in 1990, entitled *Front Line*), she says that the *Guardian* editor suppressed it for fear of prosecution by HMG for libel because of the clearance given to Philby by Foreign Secretary Macmillan (way back in 1955). This sounds at best curious. The account given to me by my Ambassador was that the article included an insinuation that I had had homosexual relations with Philby and that it was the risk of prosecution for libel by me (not by HMG) that had caused its suppression. This would mean that the article had been submitted to the Foreign Office for clearance, which also sounds curious. Anyway, whichever account (if either) is true, the article was not published and I never saw its text. In April, however, the *Guardian* did publish a much-revised article by her. It is a clever and suggestive piece that makes much of Kim's early association with Communists but is careful not to declare her conviction that he was the Third Man. It makes no mention of me. (The original version had – so she states in her memoirs – given my name as the host at the party on 23 January, but it twice described me absurdly as 'the British chargé d'affaires' – not an important error but hardly one suggesting the concern for accuracy to be expected of so prominent a journalist.) Shortly after this her revised article appeared in the New York journal *Newsweek*, stating explicitly that Kim was indeed the Third Man, and HMG was obliged to admit that Philby was thought to have gone to Moscow. So the basic facts were thus finally out.

In the aftermath of that fateful night of 23 January I was instructed to keep a close watch on Eleanor. She appeared to be totally unaware of her husband's double nature. (Seale and McConville are themselves convinced that she was a political innocent who simply loved him, as did sundry other women.) Presumably for purposes of a SIS debriefing, a flight to London was booked for her and Kim's twelve-year-old son, Harry, whom Kim adored. Apparently on instructions, clandestine or not, from Kim, she sought to alter the booking to one that involved changing planes in Soviet-controlled Prague, where Kim would meet them and take them to Moscow. On this occasion our spies (who knew of this, presumably from cipher intercepts in London) upstaged Kim's Soviet contacts in Beirut by marking a certain wall with a misleading sign which would lead them to act too late. Eleanor was put firmly on the direct London flight, and Kim had a long and unproductive wait at Prague airport.

In September 1963, however, she did manage to fly to Moscow to join him.* From there she wrote to friends in Beirut, an American couple named Fistere, whom I knew. They showed me the letter, in which she described what life was like in Moscow, 'queueing in the snow for bread' and so on. But what interested me more was the postscript in Kim's unmistakable handwriting. It consisted of this one sentence: 'If you only knew what hell it is when your personal affections clash with your political convictions.'

Despite that postscript he published in *Pravda* a list of the British spies in the Middle East, with my name at the top! He knew well enough that this was nonsense. If he meant it as a joke, knowing that our spies would pick it up and tell me (as they did), it was a singularly bad one.

So there we are. Philby was the most remarkable and successful Soviet agent in British history. Perhaps his most astonishing achievement during his years as a leading figure in Britain's own espionage fraternity was to be widely expected to reach its absolute top. It would indeed have been a bizarre situation if the head of Britain's secret anti-Soviet organisation had been at the same time a top figure in the Soviet anti-British one. That prospect, however, may have been cast in question during his time in Washington by his weakness for the bottle. There are many doubtless true stories of his dreadful behaviour when drunk. I can only say that in the three years when I was often in his company in Beirut (a period during which, as we now know, he was under severe mental stress and might well have taken refuge in alcohol), I never once saw him drunk. He may of course have contrived to be sober in the presence of an Embassy First Secretary in the expectation that I would convey a favourable account of him to my Ambassador. Deceiving me in this or other ways would have caused no difficulty to so practised an operator.

One reason for the stress he must have been suffering at this time was the arrest in Beirut of another notorious Soviet agent in the person of George Blake, and his receiving in London the longest sentence for spying under the law, totalling forty-two years. His arrest had taken place in 1961 when

---

* She did not stick Moscow for long. She returned to the USA in 1965, published a book, *Kim Philby: The Spy I Loved*, and died in 1968.

he was studying Arabic at Shemlan (see above). He had been whisked away to London and no doubt stringently questioned. What Kim couldn't know was whether he had revealed the facts about his (Kim's) own duplicity. Kim's apprehensions, already acute for other reasons, such as the defection to the West of a senior Soviet spy, must have been extreme.

It is of some relevance to insert the following about Blake's young wife, who was with him in Shemlan. When Blake's fate was being sealed (but not made public) in London, the wife of a colleague of mine in the Embassy was sent up to Shemlan to apprise her of the appalling facts. The two girls had been close friends at school and ever since. Mrs Blake convinced the Embassy girl that she was simply *unable* to accept that the man she loved, with whom she had spent seven blissful years, had been an active Soviet agent throughout. If this declaration of ignorance was genuine, Blake's achievement in concealing the truth from her is as remarkable as Kim's with Eleanor.

The story that circulated about Blake's subsequent escape from Wormwood Scrubs has a certain entertainment value and deserves mention too. In the form it reached me, he is said to have constructed a radio transmitter from his prison bed springs, contacted on it an accomplice outside, leapt over the high prison wall, and got away in his friend's waiting car. It sounds too rich to be true, even for a top spy, but he certainly escaped and was never recaptured. Moscow is of course where he went.

A last word about Philby. He was an unforgivable traitor to his country, responsible among much else for the assassination by his Soviet associates of many brave men. All that I can say is that in the half of him that I knew (the deceitful half, of course) he was a most enjoyable friend. The great Graham Greene, who had been his close colleague in intelligence, spoke sympathetically of him even after he defected. The conclusion reached at the end of their book by Seale and McConville is that he did what he did in the conviction that Communism was right and that in his eyes its dictates had to be obeyed on moral, as well as political, grounds. After his death in 1988 his last (Russian) wife Rufina paid repeated visits to Britain without revealing her identity. Eventually she agreed to be interviewed by a journalist. In the resulting article in the *Observer* of 8 June 2003 she is quoted as saying 'My Kim betrayed Britain but taught me to love it well.'

And there I leave him. The whole episode had for me one curious aftermath. Six years after Kim's defection, I was fishing for trout in a loch near Moniaive with Hamish Blair-Cunynghame, the most distinguished of my oldest friends and then head of the Royal Bank of Scotland. As we idly cast our flies, he mentioned that he had just had a letter from the FO Security Department asking whether he had any reason to doubt my political reliability. I suppose it says something for the security people that six years after the Philby business they were still questioning anyone of moment who was traced as knowing me, in the hope of establishing whether I was a crypto-

Communist and even a 'Fifth Man'. I read in the press some years later that they did locate the real 'Fifth Man', living peacefully in France. I do not recall whether he was taken to court, but this development may at least have put an end to any further investigations of myself. The 'Fourth Man', as is well known, was the notorious Anthony Blunt, keeper of the Queen's pictures, etc. He came out to Beirut in December 1962 telling the British Ambassador, with whom he stayed, that he wanted to search the northern end of the Lebanese mountains for a rare frog orchid, and in due course he told the Ambassador that he had found one. In 2004 a man studying Blunt rang me up and told me that his researches had led him to suspect that his real reason in coming to Beirut was to warn Philby that the SIS were catching up with him. If that is so, the British Ambassador and the frog orchid must just have been used as a front.

In the summer of 1964 the prospect of transfer to Dubai in the Persian Gulf, though it meant promotion to Counsellor, filled me with gloom. To cheer myself up I decided to buy a Caucasian rug. Nalbandian, one of the local (Armenian) dealers, persuaded me to buy not one but three. When I had handed over my fat cheque, he asked whether I would care to know where he bought most of his stock. I said I would. 'In London, of course. I go there regularly to examine the bundles arriving from Russia and Persia. I leave the rubbish in London, and bring the good ones out here to sell to people like you for twice what I paid for them.'

This was the beginning of a slippery slope down which I slid with my cheque book. The final bump occurred four years later when I walked past the Persian Carpet Gallery in Brompton Road. In its window was displayed a ravishing big Shirvan *saph* (multiple prayer rug), due to be auctioned with others the following morning. Fortunately I couldn't be there since I was due at lunch in Oxford with the great Albert Hourani, at whose feet I was then studying at St Antony's. At that moment a Foreign Office friend came out of the shop and said, 'Hallo! I trust you're coming to this gorgeous auction tomorrow.' I explained why I couldn't. He then said, 'Excuse me a moment,' disappeared into the shop, where I saw him making a phone call, came out and announced, 'I've told Albert Hourani you're ill in London and can't make his lunch.' I was appalled but could hardly ring Albert myself and tell him that my friend was lying. So I stayed the night with this deceitful acquaintance and went to the auction. When the beautiful *saph* came up the bidding petered out at an absurdly low figure, so I couldn't help putting in a bid. Only one higher bid followed, so I put in another. So did the other man. The adrenalin took over, and the two of us went on and on and on … and ON. I was quite out of control and was bidding sums well beyond my possible maximum. Suddenly the other man stopped and the *saph* was knocked down to me. All the hard-faced dealers in the hall came up and patted me on the back. 'You've saved this rug for England,' they said. I looked mystified. 'Didn't you know who you were bidding against? He's the richest rug-collector in Brazil, a multi-millionaire, which is why we all knew it was a waste of time competing. And you outbid even *him!*' I have never disclosed to anyone else the gigantic sum I somehow paid.

CHAPTER 15

Dubai

THE seven small Arab sheikhdoms at the lower end of the Persian Gulf were known for over a century as the 'Trucial States' because their rulers signed under British duress a series of truces between 1830 and 1843 designed to end mutual hostilities at sea (and 'piracy'). Britain's maritime supervision was reinforced in 1892 by the 'Exclusive Agreements', which explicitly prohibited them from having dealings with any outside power other than Britain. These agreements were also imposed seriatim on Bahrain, Kuwait and finally, in 1916, on Qatar. Control of this *mare nostrum* was exercised by a 'Resident' at Bushire (away up, somewhat oddly, on the Persian side of the Gulf), appointed by, and answerable to, the British Government of India. This remained the case until the transfer of the Resident in 1946 to Bahrain, where he was placed under Foreign Office control. The British authorities had always preferred to keep the precise status of the sheikhdoms undefined, describing them to the outside world simply as 'States in special relations with Britain'; and it was only in 1949 that they were accorded the title of 'British Protected States'. This itself was a vague enough term, for the protection assured under the old agreements was only maritime. The term was no doubt chosen to distinguish them from 'Protectorates', in which Britain assumed responsibilities inland. (In formal terms nothing much changed until Britain's withdrawal from the Gulf in 1971, when Kuwait, Bahrain and Qatar became independent members of the world community, as did the seven from Abu Dhabi eastwards, which became collectively the United Arab Emirates. When I was posted there in 1964 these revolutionary changes were, of course, still to come.)

The Dubai I went to bore little resemblance to the oil-rich city of today. Apart from its huge commercial buildings and port at Jebel Ali it hosts international competitions in every known sport, and its ruling family owns most of the world's fastest racehorses. But in 1964 it was a sleepy little town snaking down its long creek full of dhows. Its only architectural merit was the cluster of wind-towers in the Persian quarter. The wind-tower, the predecessor of air conditioning, was divided vertically into four quadrants, and any movement of air outside was sucked down whichever quadrant it might be moving towards. Dubai's source of external income was from smuggling goods (imported quite legally by Dubai itself) into the barely administered southern coasts of Iran, which was hungry for them. (There was one other and more ingenious source of revenue which I shall describe later.)

The job of Britain's Political Agent there – and under those old Exclusive Agreements no non-British diplomats were allowed anywhere in the Gulf – was to advise the rulers of the six small Trucial States from Dubai to Fujeirah on the 'proper' government of their sheikhdoms. (The seventh Trucial State, Abu Dhabi, having found oil, had by now been awarded a Political Agent of its own.) In the previous century 'advice' could be rendered effective by dispatching a British gunboat, no longer an option now. But unlike one's predecessors one at least had air conditioners, an office and a clerk. No longer did the Political Agent compose his manuscript dispatches sitting under a palm tree in the stifling heat, shifting his writing hand from pool to pool of sweat.

I suspect I was the last British diplomat to issue a 'Freedom Certificate' to a runaway slave. The recipient, who had run into the agency compound and clutched the flagpole, saying she had run away from her cruel master in southern Iran and crossed the Gulf, must have heard from someone that the representative of the Queen of England could give her a paper guaranteeing freedom. On looking into things we found a bundle of old 'Freedom Certificates', dug them out and dusted them down. I signed and handed one to the lady, who went off proudly waving it. I don't know whether it worked.

In 1964 Dubai was not, in FO terminology, a 'car-owning post', for the good reason that there were then no roads that ordinary cars could make use of. The Agency itself, however, was provided with a number of Land Rovers to bump around from sheikhdom to sheikhdom. In that connection the best story I fell heir to related how, some years before, Sir Rupert Hay, the Political Resident in Bahrain, had shipped his saloon car down to Dubai for a tour of the Trucial States and was bouncing along the bumpy terrain in it. He was wearing, of course, as he did for formal visits, full uniform. This included, in summer, a white helmet with its pickelhaube spike on top.* At one particularly vicious bump he was thrown upwards so violently that the spike went right through the roof of the car and stuck there, with the result that he was suspended by his chinstrap in midair, being rapidly throttled. His ADC leapt out, clambered up on to the roof and unscrewed the spike just in time to save his boss's life. (*Si non e vero, e ben trovato.*)

I too suffered from having to wear full uniform on certain occasions. The winter model was of gold-braided blue serge, with a sword in a sword-belt, and a Napoleonic hat. And this was what I had to wear when calling on an American Rear Admiral in his visiting frigate offshore. I could never remember whether the hat should be worn Napoleon-fashion with the horns projecting sideways over the ears, or pointing fore and aft. On this occasion I made the wrong choice, and as I stumbled up the frigate's gangplank towards the Marine

---

* Mine still hangs in the kitchen at Uppincott along with Jenny's hat collection.

band marshalled to pipe me on board on their silly little pipes, the pipers evidently thought me funny. Thrown off balance by seeing them nudging each other, I tripped over my dangling sword and fell flat on my face halfway up the gangplank. Even the Admiral failed to keep a straight face; and such are the rules on American warships that he couldn't even offer me a stiff whisky to restore my morale.

One of the oddities of the post – peculiar to Dubai, indeed unique in the whole service – was that the Political Agent had, for some lost reason, a bagpiper on his staff: a Pakistani bagpiper admittedly, and not a very good one at that. I was the last Political Agent to have a private bagpiper, for the wicked Welshman who succeeded me had him struck off the strength. But throughout my two years in Dubai he marched up and down outside the windows of my tin-roofed bungalow at dusk, making conversation impossible inside; and he accompanied me everywhere on trek. As to that, I cherish one special memory. The Deputy Political Resident in Bahrain had come on a visit and I took him over the mountains and down the appalling bumps of the Wadi Ham to camp near Khor Fakkan on the Indian Ocean. Its curving beach, one of the most beautiful in the world, looked gorgeous when we reached it as the sun sank. Tents were erected along with a whole marquee for us to eat and drink in. We were busy doing just that when a totally unprecedented tempest descended. Vast breakers thrashed in from the sea, and from the rain-swept hills immediately inland flood-water raced down upon us from behind. Our individual tents were quickly blown out to sea; and in the flashes of lightning I could see the Deputy PR gallantly clutching the centre pole of the marquee in his vain determination to save it (and the crates of booze it contained) from suffering the same fate. It was no use, and we all just made good our escape in a lorry. We took refuge in the house of a kindly schoolmaster in the nearby village. The storm had blown itself out by dawn and we drove back to where our camp had been. There was no sign of any tentage, the beach was washed as smooth as a billiard table, and there along the now quiet water's edge was marching my bagpiper playing a Highland lament.

Apart from the smuggling trade already mentioned, Dubai's only source of foreign revenue, ever since pearl fishing in the Gulf had been ruined by Japan's invention of cultured pearls, was the export of gold to India. This curious phenomenon deserves a whole paragraph, since history of that kind can never be repeated. Indeed, it came to an end when Dubai discovered oil soon after I left. The practice depended on the grotesque fact that, while the Indian rupee was the currency of the Gulf States as well as of India, the rupee coin (as distinct from the rupee note) was worth twice as much in the Gulf as its value in India. The import into India of gold, which Indians love, was prohibited by Indian law. So what the ingenious citizens of Dubai did was as follows. They imported into Dubai, quite legally, aeroplane loads of gold ingots from London, loaded them into 'launches' (dhows with fast engines) and sailed them out towards India, stopping just short of its 3-mile territorial waters and therefore outside the Indian navy's legal area of operations. There, under cover of night, the ingots were transferred to small Indian fishing boats and, if they were not intercepted by the Indian navy, rowed ashore. Once landed, the 'fishermen' smuggled them up country, where the thirst for gold was strongest, and sold them for rupee notes. The notes were taken to banks (in Bombay as a rule) and exchanged at par for rupee coins. The coins were then privily rowed out in sacks in the same fishing boats to the same launches waiting just outside territorial waters. The launches took the sacks back to Dubai where the coins, as explained above, could be converted into twice as many rupee notes. Half of these notes were then converted into sterling for the purchase in London of another planeload of gold ingots. Each successful launch trip thus meant 100 per cent profit, apart from modest expenses, to the 'shareholders' in the business. These included every man-jack in the town from the ruler downwards. Such was the 'honour among thieves' that loads of ingots could safely be left overnight piled up on Dubai airstrip unguarded. The ingots, incidentally, were conveniently packed in London into waistcoats with numerous narrow pockets into which they fitted, thus simplifying the concealment of their porterage on arrival in India.

The Indian government naturally sought to prevent this ludicrous racket and stationed a so-called Trade Agent in Dubai, whose function was to keep his eyes fixed on Dubai creek and notify Bombay whenever a suspicious-looking launch sailed off. The Indian navy was then alerted and occasionally made a catch inside (and sometimes no doubt a little outside) the 3-mile limit of its lawful operations. Why the Indians could not prevent the rupee coin having twice its proper value in the Gulf I could never understand. What they were eventually obliged to do (this was soon after I left Dubai) was to withdraw their whole currency from the Gulf, leaving the rulers to invent currencies of their own.

But while the earlier practice continued I was myself used as an unconscious pawn in the game. A dhow-owner invited me to accompany him on a pearl-fishing expedition. The opportunity delighted me as this ancient art was now rarely practised. Throughout the day our pearlers dived, wearing little but the traditional turtleshell nose-clamp and holding between the big and the second toe of one foot the knot at the end of the rope to signal when they wanted pulling up. I watched them propelling themselves round the seabed with one arm and clutching with the other the loose rope-basket to pop the oysters into. The rest of us spent the day knifing the captured oysters open. As I recall, the day's work produced only three tiny pearls. Towards sundown we set off back to shore. My host, however, landed me 15 miles north of Dubai, where, he informed me, he had positioned a Land Rover to take me home. I presumed this was a kindly arrangement to save my time. But as he said his goodbyes he gaily explained that his dhow was heading for India and under the deck that I had been opening oysters on was £75,000 worth of gold. The pearl-fishing invitation had simply been a dodge to convince the keen-eyed Indian trade agent that this particular dhow, since it had the British Political Agent on board, was obviously innocent.

Dhows of all sorts were of course always lining Dubai's creek and were a source of fascination to a landlubber like myself. I liked their type-names – the *baghala*, the *boom*, the *sambook*, the *jalboot*, and others less pronounceable – and I spent happy afternoons nosing about in them. Nosing is the right verb, for one popular cargo was sacks of smelly sharks' fins destined for Japan, where, apparently, they are, or were, highly valued as an aphrodisiac. The crew must have suffered abominably before they reached their destination.

One other nautical expedition I enjoyed immensely. We were invited by the local manager of the Grey Mackenzie trading firm to join a party in his company launch going right out of the Gulf round the Musandam Peninsula and along the Arab shores of the Indian Ocean. We spent one day tied up, near the mouth of the Gulf, in the famous and well-hidden Elphinstone Creek, which had been used by the Royal Navy as a hidey-hole in several wars and bore on its vertical rock faces huge and rather moving graffiti in commemoration. When we had rounded the Musandam Peninsula the Indian Ocean came magically alive with phosphorescence until our boat seemed to float in gold. By this time we could gaze up at the mountainous hide-outs of the Shihooh, a strange, unvisitable tribe living there in considerable numbers, speaking a fossilised form of medieval Persian, owing allegiance to no one, and surviving (it was said) on a diet of wild honey and anything they could grow on rare patches of soil among the barren rocks. Martin Buckmaster, the Gulf Frontiers Officer, tried about this time to climb up and make their acquaintance but retreated under a hail of bullets.

The Shihooh gave me too an unnerving experience. They had gone to war with the ruler of Ras al-Khaimah, whose subjects, they alleged, were trying to colonise the edges of their tribal territory. A company of the Trucial Oman Scouts – the British-led force set up in 1950 to help the rulers keep order – was dispatched to deal with things, and when I arrived on the scene I watched with admiration the British Company Commander walking forward to invite the Shihooh to parley with me while bullets spattered the ground around him from the sangars the Shihooh were manning on the crags above. (The ruler of Ras al-Khaimah himself preferred to observe events through binoculars from the roof of his distant palace.) The parley eventually took place in a small cave, my Native Affairs Officer, Ali Boustani, who spoke every language including even Shihoohi, acting as interpreter. The Shihooh all shouted at the tops of their voices, especially those who couldn't squeeze into the cave and totally blocked the entrance so that no air could squeeze in either. After two hours of this, just as I was passing out from asphyxiation, Ali Boustani miraculously got them to agree to choose three spokesmen while all the rest would climb back up the mountains to their sangars. I was thus enabled to crawl out of the cave for a breather and watch them climbing up one behind the other and shouting an incomprehensible cry which meant, so Ali Boustani told me, that they were very angry. We then crawled back into the cave with the three spokesmen. After a further noisy half-hour some sort of armistice was agreed and I made good my escape, leaving the Trucial Oman Scouts to enforce it. I do not recall the terms of this Pyrrhic victory. I then drove to Ras al-Khaimah town to report to the ruler. Walking up the sloping tunnel that gave access to his palace, I rounded a corner and came face to face with His Highness on his hunkers peeing down the tunnel towards me.

Life in the Trucial States was not all as diverting and diverse as the preceding paragraphs might suggest. There was a lot of sweaty routine activity, but anyone interested can consult *The End of Empire in the Middle East*, Chapter 4. My non-routine activities, though not all cakes and ale, are what I record here, and I may as well add a few more.

The search for oil was what occupied most of the rulers' minds. Shakhbut in Abu Dhabi had already struck the jackpot and expectations in my own six poorer sheikhdoms were intense. One day the American company (Continental Oil) with the Dubai concession announced that they had 'found' at a site away inland. Great excitement. Continental flew the ruler and me out in one of their aeroplanes to witness the 'spudding-in', surrounded by a goggling crowd of locals. Down the bore shaft went the 1,000-foot tube to bring up the first specimen of 'black gold' in Dubai. Up it came again, bearing alas not oil but boiling-hot salt water, exploding in all directions. One American oilman was badly scalded. The disappointment was unspeakable. I was flown back to Dubai by a silent pilot. When we landed, he drove the plane without stopping straight into its hangar (though the entrance was barely a foot wider than the plane's wing span), jumped out with a golf club and walked off with a nod to practise his No. 3 iron shots on the airstrip. The disastrous spudding-in was not, I suppose, as breath-stopping for him as it had been for me.

My next inland expedition was more rewarding. Freddie de Butts, the Commander of the Trucial Oman Scouts (who died in 2005), invited me and my family to accompany him into the Liwa sand-sea in the area of the undefined Saudi–Abu Dhabi frontier. Its dunes are, I believe, the highest in the world. De Butts had mysteriously acquired two American Power-wagons to negotiate them. No other vehicles, not even Land Rovers, could. When faced by less serious sand dunes on the way, the only thing to do was to accelerate furiously, hoping, when (and if) one reached the top of the dune, that it was one of the convex kind enabling one's truck to slither safely down the far side. If it was one of the *concave* kind, the likelihood was that the truck would turn head over heels in the empty air. We eventually reached without disaster one of the tiny Liwa oases, inhabited at this time of year

12 Sheikh Rashid bin Sa'id al Maktoum, ruler of Dubai, with Political Agent
GBP in 1965.

only by a few resident palm trees. Even the Power-wagons wouldn't attempt
the colossal dunes enclosing the oasis – 500 feet high and angled at 44 degrees
or whatever is the maximum angle soft sand allows. They could be climbed
only on foot, but the labour was well worthwhile. The game was to carry up
with one a tin tea tray on which one then tobogganed furiously down again,
making a tremendous booming noise like thunder (presumably due to the
friction of the sand away down underneath). We spent hours doing this and
slept it off under the friendly stars. We met no Bedou anywhere; and what
good this expensive week – expensive, that is, to HMG – did in the context
of Britain's responsibilities in the Gulf would be difficult to identify. But it
was supremely good fun.

A visit from Prince Philip, the Duke of Edinburgh, was not such good fun.
I had been instructed at the last moment that he did not wish to be greeted
on arrival by a lot of people, such as the wives of the British community (who
had all been busy looking out hats and gloves). I took action accordingly. When
the Duke appeared out of his plane at Sharjah airport, he looked round and
muttered to my dismay, 'There don't seem to be many people here.' There
were only the Commanders of the Trucial Oman Scouts and the air force,
myself and the ruler of Sharjah (to whom, in the course of his stop-off for
drinks, he was less than courteous). I was not sorry when he flew on.

Of all my six rulers, Sheikh Rashid of Dubai was the one I most enjoyed.
His nose went through about three right angles, the slapping noise of the
slippers he always wore was unforgettable, and his jerky Arabic was not easy

to penetrate. He once asked me how much of it I understood. 'Oh, about thirty per cent,' I said boastfully. 'Mmm,' he replied, 'Craikk, now [James Craig, my predecessor, was the best Arabist in the service], he understood about forty per cent. But never mind,' he added, 'it's not what I say that matters, but what I *don't* say.' Rashid was enormously energetic, flopping off every morning in his slippers to inspect the projects he kept launching in the town with the proceeds of smuggling and the gold trade. The frequent sheikhly supper parties he gave for visiting dignitaries were often memorable – one in particular. This was in honour of a British trade mission led by a lord whose name I forget. The procedure at all such parties was that the first sixty or so sat down at the pi-shaped table and scooped up the piled food with their fingers. When anyone had had enough, he simply got up and left, and someone lower down the pecking order came in and took his place. The man eating next to Lord X got up and went away and was replaced by one of the ruler's falconers, who deposited his hawk on the table between himself and Lord X. I saw the lord shrink in his chair. Sheikh Rashid, giving me a distinct wink, gestured to the falconer, who responded by picking the hawk off the table and relocating it on his right shoulder, very close to His Lordship's left ear ... The ruler rose and conducted his guest out for coffee.

I had trouble myself on a different sheikhly occasion when I had engineered an invitation to lunch in Buraimi with Sheikh Zayed (the future ruler), who governed inland Abu Dhabi on behalf of his elder brother, Shakhbut. I duly arrived at 1 p.m. at his *mejlis** after a four-hour drive from Dubai. We chatted away till 1.30. No sign of lunch. Two p.m. came ... 2.30 ... and still no food. Realising that he must have forgotten his invitation, I rose and took my leave. I had driven only a few hundred yards when a retainer caught me up in a jeep. 'Sheikh Zayed', he said (presumably someone had reminded him of his invitation), 'suggests you might care for some lunch in the town restaurant.' He led me to it, the only two-storey building in the arc of mud buildings that was then the Buraimi market. At the top of its rickety stairs I found a closed door on either side and opened the one on the right. There was the restaurateur, asleep on his rope bed. He struggled up and took me through the other door where there was a sort of card table and two chairs. 'Lunch will be ready immediately,' he said in Arabic. He came back twenty minutes later, not, as I had hoped, with the usual piled-up savoury *mansaf* of rice, meat and vegetables, but with a fried egg, two sausages, a slice of bacon and a bottle of tomato ketchup. 'Where', I asked him in Arabic, 'did you learn this excellent British cuisine?' His reply was in English: 'Fourteen years in Cardiff in the merchant navy.'

When I visited Buraimi twenty-five years later it had become a university

---

* The building, of whatever kind, used by sheikhs for giving audiences or holding gatherings.

city of high-rise blocks, hideous Lebanese villas and posh European food delivered by air and served in smart restaurants by waiters with napkins over their forearms. On that occasion I was accompanying Professor Shaban from Exeter University to visit the Buraimi University; and as we sped in a limousine along the new two-lane motorway from Abu Dhabi I said to him, 'There don't seem to be any camels around.' 'No,' said the professor, 'the Bedouin have long since tethered them all on the motorway to collect the insurance.' He may have been exaggerating a bit, for the following year, when I was sent out to Abu Dhabi to try to extract money from Sheikh Zayed for Exeter University, I discovered on my arrival, by glancing at the local daily, that His Highness would be out that day attending a camel race-meeting. So there were still *some* around. But the prizes for the camel-race winners, I noticed, were Pontiac limousines.

The other Trucial ruler I most enjoyed was Sheikh Mohammad al Sharqi of Fujeirah, the tiniest of the sheikhdoms, occupying a patch of desert on the Indian Ocean. For some reason I engineered an invitation for him to visit England. He came to enquire about the arrangements but seemed interested only in the number of 'Guns' he would get on arrival as a head of state. I knew from *Foreign Service Instructions* on state visits that he was entitled only to *one*. (The Political Resident, incidentally, when visiting any sheikhdom whose ruler had been presented with a ceremonial piece of artillery, was entitled to eleven.) But as I was reluctant to disappoint him and wouldn't myself be present when he went, I asked him how many Guns he would like. His answer was 'A hundred and forty-four'. 'My goodness,' I said. 'Why a hundred and forty-four?' 'Because that was the number of shells fired by the Royal Navy at my father's fort in 1907. You can still see many of them in its walls.' Off he went to England, but I rather doubt that he even got his entitlement of one Gun. Today, alongside the crumbling remains of his father's mud fort, stands a huge Hilton hotel. Fudge, as he was called, never found oil but exploited hundreds of European tourists instead – or rather his son Hamad now does, as he himself died in 1974.

But they were not all as harmlessly entertaining as Fudge. The two Qasimi ones, of Sharjah and Ras al-Khaimah (both confusingly named Saqr), were, though entertaining enough, restlessly anti-imperialist. The Sharjah one, a poet of some repute with whom I had enjoyed many arguments, had been going farther in early 1966 than was acceptable in publicising his anti-imperialism. Since we had no constitutional power to depose a ruler, the only way to get rid of him was to obtain a written request from all the leading members of his family for his replacement. Fortunately he was widely disliked, partly because he spent much of his small income on whisky; and the necessary document was furtively secured. I was then instructed to invite him to the Agency, present him with the evidence of his family's dissatisfaction, and (if he didn't go quietly) take him under arrest to a waiting RAF aircraft to be flown in disgrace to Bahrain. Two days before this was to take place I collapsed with an unidentified fever (attributed to overwork!) and was flown there myself on a stretcher to be hospitalised. The deputy PR had to fly down to Dubai and conduct this exercise in 'indirect rule' on my behalf. Sheikh Saqr went in exile to Cairo, but slipped back a few years later when the imperialists had left the Gulf, and assassinated the cousin who had succeeded him. He was caught in the act and imprisoned by the President of the new United Emirates, Sheikh Zayed, in an underground hole in Buraimi.

Soon after I returned from this collapse the Arab League, under the direction of the charismatically anti-imperialist President Nasser, set about trying to detach the Trucial Rulers from their residual allegiance to Britain with promises of cash. The League's deputy head descended on Dubai (we had a curious dinner together) and successfully persuaded one or two of the penniless rulers led by Sheikh Saqr of Ras al-Khaimah to declare that they would have no further truck with the British. Indeed, Saqr dispatched his armed retainers to man the sand dunes at the borders of Ras al-Khaimah and prevent any approach to his sheikhdom by us. Shortly a cipher message from Bahrain informed me that an aeroplane carrying Egyptian engineers was on its illegal way to initiate projects with the Arab League's promised £5 million and must be prevented from landing. I didn't quite see how I could stop it but, having discovered its call sign, I whizzed out to the Dubai airport control tower to get one of its (Arab) traffic controllers to forbid it to land. The control tower proved to be ominously deserted. There were five mysterious microphone things round its walls, so I shouted the call sign into the nearest of them. There was no acknowledgement. I shouted even louder into all the other four with no better result. I drove back to the Agency to await developments. Fortunately a phone call from Bahrain disclosed that the Arab League aircraft, having been buzzed by the RAF, had been diverted and would not now be coming.

I left Dubai for leave and transfer a few days later. The Political Resident, Bill Luce, the last of the great imperial proconsuls, flew down and restored the faltering allegiance of the disaffected rulers. In this he was assisted by Prime Minister Harold Wilson, who had just overruled the negative attitude of his Cabinet and personally ordered the grant of £2 million (better than nothing) to the Trucial States Council of Rulers.

But before I leave Dubai, the visits there of two prominent Englishmen are worth recording. One was Jeremy Thorpe, then leader of the Liberal Party – a function less rewarding than that of financial adviser to the ruler of Dubai, which mysteriously he also held. His visit was memorable for his disclosure at a dinner party in my house that he had the gift of levitation. This he demonstrated by lifting the 20-stone Scottish manager of the Bank of Dubai on one finger! It seemed a pity that a politician with such magical gifts had no chance of becoming Prime Minister.

The other visitor was Reggie Maudling, who had been Chancellor of the Exchequer until Labour ousted the Tory government in 1964. He said he would like a swim, though it was winter and the Gulf waters were rough. I drove him to an empty bay and in we went. After gallantly doing my breaststroke for about two minutes, I paused to check that my guest was OK. I was a bit alarmed that I couldn't see him anywhere, until a gap appeared in the big waves. After another five minutes I thought it time to make for the shore, and this time he was emphatically nowhere to be seen. I grew seriously alarmed, since it does a man's career no good to go drowning Chancellors of the Exchequer, even those out of office. There must have been another three minutes of frenzy before he suddenly popped up right beside me – and explained that his passion in life was to swim under water holding his breath for up to seven minutes. I mumbled that I wished he had told me this at the start.

The only other people, as far as I know, who can do the same thing are the Nilotic Shilluk in the Sudan. Twenty years before this, in my Brigade Major days, I had organised a brigade swimming gala in the pool that had belonged to the erstwhile Italian Governor of Tripolitania. One of the competitions involved diving for plates. One or two British competitors went in first and came up to much applause with eight or nine of the twenty-six plates in the pool. Then a Sudanese entrant dived in and seven minutes later came up with every single one. He proved to be a Shilluk (the only one in the Brigade). The British competitors thought it very unfair, and no more of them deigned to compete.

CHAPTER 16

Bahrain and St Antony's

THE post of Deputy Political Resident in Bahrain, to which I was now un-expectedly elevated, made me number two to the great Bill Luce, the boss of the five Political Agents in the Gulf and the Consul-General in Muscat. It meant a step-up, but it was mostly an office job and might have been boring but for two people who became lifelong friends.

Tony Parsons, the Political Agent in Bahrain itself, was marvellous company. We spent many afternoons in the oleander-fringed tank in his garden doing our breaststroke up and down while we discussed Dylan Thomas's poetry. During the two years we both spent in Bahrain he chose to fill small gaps in his general knowledge, first by learning Anglo-Saxon and second by examining the credentials of Christianity. For the latter he read, evidently for the first time, the New Testament, and I recall him saying, 'Actually, there's some quite good stuff in it.' Ornithology was one of his passions. I was ringing him one morning on some 'high policy' matter when I heard him put his receiver down. I waited on mine for at least a minute, feeling a bit undervalued. Then his voice came through again. 'Temmink's stint,' it said. 'Outside the window, on the seashore. Never seen one in my life before.' Birdwatching is a stupendous compulsion. He always had binoculars on his desk – though whether he maintained this practice when he became Britain's Permanent Representative at the UN in 1979, or when he sat in No. 10 Downing Street in 1983 as Prime Minister Thatcher's personal adviser on foreign affairs, I do not know.

Tony's wife Sheila, though not everyone's cup of tea, was almost as clever and entertaining as him; and on the rare occasions she put pen to paper the result was memorable. I have kept a letter she wrote to Marnie when they were posted to New York for the first time, in 1968. In it she wrote:

> Nothing is as I thought it would be. Instead of feeling hemmed in by the huge buildings, there is a great sense of space from the long straight streets going on for ever. The skyscrapers are lovely. Like everything else they twist and struggle to get higher than their neighbours. But they do so with dignity and their goal is the sky. There are no hidden surprises round gentle corners as in most cities. It's all geometric shapes and sharp angles, except for the wonderful arching bridges suspended from the sky, and the curves of niggers in hats leaning against things.

13 Marnie with her four children, Ann, Alison, Cati and Jamie in Bahrain, 1967.

What wouldn't I give to be able to write anything as good as that last sentence (though I wouldn't have used the word 'niggers')?

It says something for Mrs Thatcher that when she chose Tony for the (new) job of personal adviser she knew he had always voted Labour. They seldom, he told me, agreed about anything during the long sessions they were closeted together. On one occasion the following memorable exchange took place:

> MRS T: Thank heavens, Tony, I'm not a member of *your* class.
> TONY: May I ask, Prime Minister, what class you're putting me in?
> MRS T: Upper-middle-class intellectuals. They see everyone else's point of view and have *none* of their own.

Tony had, of course, plenty of strong views, as she must have learnt. But he admitted that she had the quickest brain he had ever encountered and, less expectedly, that her femininity was riveting.

On his final retirement I pushed Tony both into buying a house in Devon's

Ashburton (as our neighbours) and into accepting a modest Research Fellowship at Exeter University (as my colleague). His premature death in August 1996 was an irreparable loss to thousands – as irreparable as had been to Tony himself and Sheila the much more premature deaths of their two gifted sons.

The other blessing in Bahrain was Major David Goddard. David and I came together because he was the army representative on the Gulf Intelligence Committee which it was my job to chair. I don't remember our weekly meetings producing much intelligence, but David's membership produced much fun. The army was clearly not the natural ambience for an eccentric of such uninhibited individualism; and it was no surprise to me that he abandoned it (just before I left Bahrain) in favour of setting up on the creek in Exeter a museum of the world's working boats. Despite my lifelong preference for dry land, I became a founding member. (After twenty years as a tremendous tourist attraction it was closed down for absurd reasons by the misguided City Council and dispersed elsewhere.) My only other contribution to his maritime museum was to send him in 1970 from Baghdad two Tigris *guffas* (6-foot-diameter coracles), which were the principal river craft on the Euphrates and the Tigris until well into the twentieth century. I watched them being made for me, by feel alone, by a blind girl 20 miles south of Baghdad. She deftly twisted their frames from pliant pomegranate branches and coated their basketwork undercarriages with hot pitch. Before I found a means of dispatching them to Exeter, the Embassy staff and I used to have races in them in the Tigris. It is no easy matter propelling a round coracle against the current with a sort of tennis racquet; and our efforts no doubt reassured the crowds of Iraqis leaning over the huge Baghdad bridge to watch us that the British were no more than harmless buffoons.

Two other experiences in Bahrain deserve recording. Both occurred when I found myself acting as Political Resident during the two-month gap between the retirement of Bill Luce and the arrival of his successor, Stuart Crawford.

First, Sheikh Zayed of Abu Dhabi called on me at the suggestion of the Foreign Office, where he had just paid a visit. He asked for assistance in removing from the rulership of Abu Dhabi his notoriously awkward elder brother Shakhbut. Bill Luce had long wanted his removal but the family had not previously had the courage to request our intervention and (as explained in the case of Sharjah, p. 198) we were constitutionally debarred from ousting a ruler without a written request from his family. None of Shakhbut's predecessors had died peacefully in their beds, and he would have reacted fiercely if he had got wind of a petition from the family for his removal. So plans had to be made in complete secrecy.

When all was ready I flew to Abu Dhabi, ostensibly to pay a routine call on Shakhbut. Two companies of the Trucial Oman Scouts (the TOS) were privily positioned overnight on 'training manoeuvres', sufficiently near the

14 Sheikh Shakhbut's palace in Abu Dhabi in 1966.

palace to intervene forcibly if needed. I spent the flight from Bahrain reading
Alice in Wonderland, which seemed appropriate, particularly the passage in 'The
Walrus and the Carpenter' which runs:

> The eldest oyster winked his eye
> And shook his heavy head,
> Meaning to say he did not choose
> To leave the oyster bed.

For that was exactly how, as I expected, the interview worked out. In the
small upstairs room of his mud-walled palace Shakhbut grew white with
anger when I told him that his family wanted him out. He growled inaudibly
to a summoned servant, and shortly I could see his fifty palace guards carrying ammunition boxes up the stairs to man the castellated walls. My object
had been to persuade Shakhbut to step down with dignity. A TOS guard of
honour would be fallen in outside the palace to present arms on his way to
a special plane waiting on the airstrip. He would have none of it, and after
fifty minutes I was glad to be able to make my escape unscathed. I spent
the afternoon trying various dodges to get him to accept defeat. His brother,
Sheikh Zayed, not only rejected my suggestion that he should enter the palace
and parley with his brother, but would not even venture to speak to him on
the telephone (on the one line that had not been carefully cut). The TOS
finally closed in all round the palace, shouting at the armed retainers to come
out and lay down their muskets. Group after group nervously emerged, and

eventually word came that Shakhbut would do so too. The guard of honour did its stuff, and off he was flown to Bahrain. On my own return there the following day I was summoned by its ruler, who had been gravely upset on learning what had happened to his friend Shakhbut. (Every Gulf ruler tended to be close friends with the next ruler but one, the intermediate ruler being traditionally the opponent of both.)

Shakhbut came to rest for a while in a huge empty hotel in Muhammerah in south-west Iran, where his now jobless Private Secretary Bill Clark (also ex-Sudan Political) went to visit him. Bill was devoted to Shakhbut but hugely entertaining about him. His account of the visit was superb. He was allotted one of the vacant luxury suites in the hotel, all unswept, and found that the only way to expel his bath water was to scrunch away with his big toe at the cockroaches blocking the plug-hole. Every afternoon crowds of penniless Persians would assemble under Shakhbut's balcony eager for largesse. Shakhbut would emerge and solemnly throw them handfuls of dirhams (the equivalent of the 'bawbees' or halfpennies which in my childhood the wealthy Scots comic Sir Harry Lauder used to distribute from *his* balcony in the North British Hotel in Edinburgh, and which were treasured for ever).

Shakhbut was allowed to return home some years later when Sheikh Zayed had established his own rule, and he seemed to bear no one, not even the British, any grudges. To be honest, I rather admired his attitude to money. It is a moot point whether the citizens of Abu Dhabi are happier today, burdened with the fabulous oil wealth released by Zayed, than they had been under the press of poverty on which Shakhbut had insisted. The fourteenth-century Ibn Khaldun has a famous passage describing how the acquisition of wealth destroys a tribe's vigour and its powers of survival. I should add that the only largesse Bill Clark ever received from Shakhbut as his Private Secretary was a pair of slippers. The idea of paying him his salary never occurred to Shakhbut, and Bill Clark would never have dreamt of asking for it.

Shakhbut died in November 1994, lamented, I suspect, by many others as well as by me.

The second memorable experience that fell to me as Acting Political Resident relates to the Gulf's other notorious autocrat, Sayed Saieed, the Sultan of Muscat. The RAF flew me to his hideout in Salalah away down in the country's farthest corner to discuss various minor matters. (I really just wanted to meet the formidable old dinosaur.) On climbing out of the aircraft, I was told by a messenger that the Sultan desired me to lodge in the palace, a grim-looking mud fort on the seashore, and I soon found myself locked up in its guest wing. Smoking was forbidden there. Bill Luce, a chain-smoker, had told me how he was once staying in it, waiting interminably for an audience, and had become so desperate for a cigarette that he broke the strict rule. He then flushed the loo on the butt-end to conceal his misdemeanour. What he didn't realise was where the loo ran out; and five minutes later the Sultan's big black major-domo walked in, carrying the butt-end on a bodkin, shook his head severely at the Political Resident, and walked silently out again ... I too found it exasperating to be locked up for hours in the guest rooms (though they were handsomely furnished with 'Canalettos' and copies of *Playboy*) and towards dusk I stole down the servants' stairs – that door being unlocked – for a breather on the beach. Groups of white-clad Dhofaris were squatting not far off and I walked along through hundreds of hermit-crab houses to one such group for a chat. Unexpectedly a venerable figure addressed me in English, saying he was the headmaster of the Salalah Choir School. I was much impressed that Western culture had evidently been allowed to penetrate this remote corner of Arabia, but it finally became apparent that what his school taught the young was not to sing in harmony but to make coir mats (out of palm fibre).

In the morning I was ushered into the Sultan's study. The old despot dealt magisterially (but with an engaging twinkle) with the points I had come to raise. In one case, concerning rent for the RAF airfield near Salalah, he said, 'But have you forgotten the letter your Secretary of State for India, Leo Amery it must have been, sent me in 1945, April I think it was?' Whereupon he swung round to the shelves behind his desk where he kept the state archives, flipped through them and pushed over to me a letter from Amery, written twenty years before, which I had never heard of and which totally destroyed my argument. He had had no warning of what I had come to discuss and he evidently had all his state papers by heart. He trounced me in a different way when I raised a final matter. This was whether he was agreeable to changing the rule of the road in his kingdom from left to right. The Trucial States rulers had all done this and were understandably anxious that Muscat should do so too, since lorries came and went across their long common frontier. They had asked me to draw his attention to the fact that they had written several letters to him on the subject but had received no reply. 'I do remember', said the Sultan, who spoke very good English, 'receiving letters from the whippersnappers over there. But I see no reason to change my practice. If one of their truck-drivers meets one of mine coming towards him on the same side of the road, it is up to the Trucial States driver to take avoiding action.' I used all the arguments I could think of to persuade him, but to no avail. My final one was that Muscat and Britain were by now almost the only countries in the world where cars still drove on the left. In Britain, I said, we were conscious of the disadvantage to our economy, but our road system was so elaborate that to change the rule would cost us untold billions. So we were obliged to go on manufacturing cars with the steering wheel on the wrong side to export them abroad. It was all very regrettable. 'Ah,' said the Sultan, 'but *my* net export of motor cars is very small.' Obviously I looked crestfallen at my failure to win the argument. His Highness then leant forward, patted me on the knee and with a knowing smile said, 'Never mind, Mr Balfour Paul. When *you* change, *I'll* change.'

Sayed Saieed may have been a tyrannical ogre, but when four years later his son Qaboos threw him out in a palace revolution (with covert British assistance), I couldn't help feeling a twinge of regret. There were, and still are, plenty of tyrants around in the world but few, I expect, with such an engaging sense of humour.

There is much that can be said against the autocracy of the 'whipper-snapper' rulers in the Gulf itself. No one would have forecast, when we withdrew our protection in 1971, that thirty years later the 'sheikhly system' would still be in place there. Even when I was in Bahrain (1966–68) its ruling family, the Al Khalifa, faced a good deal of local pressure for democratic change. Sheikh Eissa, the ruler, regarded his subjects with genuine affection but expressed little sympathy towards those who showed political discontent or even anti-British animus. In 1967, when the six-day Arab–Israeli War broke out and the 'Big Lie' gained currency (that British aircraft had taken part in the Israeli destruction of the Egyptian air force), a screaming mob gathered round the British Agency, evidently determined to climb in and sack it. When this looked imminent, Tony Parsons, watching from his office window, observed a car pushing through the crowd. Out of it stepped the tiny ruler, who climbed on its bonnet and shouted at the mob to go home and not be silly. And they all went, without a further word.

I now learnt that I was to exchange jobs with a certain Ewart Biggs, the head of the department of the FO whose main job was sifting intelligence and collaborating with our spies in MI5. But the exchange was cancelled since Ewart Biggs ingeniously pleaded that his small daughter suffered from 'sand asthma' and couldn't be taken to Bahrain. (It was to do him little good, for when he was sent to Dublin as Ambassador, he was tragically blown up by the IRA and killed.) I was replaced by someone else, and since they had no other job for me I was given a year's sabbatical in the Middle East Centre at St Antony's College, Oxford, as a Supernumerary Fellow.

To St Antony's I went in September 1968. I felt a good deal more Supernumerary than Fellow, but two genuine fellows did their best to make me feel at home. One of these was Elizabeth Monroe, author of *Britain's Moment in the Middle East* (London, 1963) and other admirable studies, including a full-length biography of St John Philby. She had rung me up in advance in Bahrain and arranged a house, schools and even a daily help for us. The other was the centre's director, Albert Hourani, a supreme scholar. He supervised my production of an article on the history of Syria since the breach with Egypt and had it published in *Middle Eastern Studies.** Fifteen years later he persuaded me to write *The End of Empire in the Middle East*.

---

* Vol. 6, 1970, under the nom de plume Martin Seymour.

The changes that had come over Oxford students since I had been one struck me forcibly. The Teddy boy period I could just remember. That was when the 'lower classes' took the mickey out of the rich by clothing themselves with Edwardian flamboyance. But now the young in England, including those at Oxford, had swung to the opposite extreme, their trousers tattered and patched like the clothes of Mahdist dervishes. But if they lacked decorum, they struck me as rather nicer and more open than my own Oxford generation. The same is probably true of the jeans generation that took over the world thereafter and shows no signs of dying out.

What I enjoyed as much as anything at St Antony's was the weather. I had not spent a winter in England for twenty-eight years; and watching English rain sluicing down over the arabesques of leafless trees filled me with delight. But a more momentous happening that winter was the first landing on the moon. Brother Ian was staying with us at the time and he and the family sat up all night watching it on television and, in Ian's case, photographing the great moment on the screen. To my shame I had gone to bed, to be sure of a clear head to get on with my 'work' in the morning. Today nobody would bother to sit up all night to watch the landing of a spaceship on some remote planet, but in 1968 the landing on the moon was a revolutionary excitement.

During the year I set about learning Persian in the vague hope that this might enable me to escape from continuous service in the Arab world. In May I went to London to take, confidently, the FO intermediate exam in that language. Arriving at the examination centre two minutes late, I made my way to the room indicated to me at the reception desk. There was no one there save one candidate and a stern-looking female addressing a dictation to him. I sat inoffensively down and listened pen in hand, but concluded that I had come to the wrong room and that this one was for the examination in Serbo-Croat or something. But after ten minutes' acute embarrassment I realised that what the lady was dictating *was* Persian, even if not pronounced the way my young Persian tutor at Oxford had taught me. All I could do was to scribble something resembling the last few lines of the *dictée*. I was scarcely more successful in coping with the other parts of the exam – oral conversation and an essay. I received as a result the lowest mark, so I was informed, ever awarded in a FO language exam – 8 per cent. So there was nothing for it but to remain in my Arab rut. (The examiner, incidentally, turned out to be the Hon. Ann Lambton, a famous scholar on Persia, and when I met her some years later we had a hilarious conversation about my performance.)

The blow was softened a week later when the FO personnel department rang to tell me that I was to go to Iraq as Ambassador. You could have knocked me down with a feather. Elizabeth Monroe's comment when I disclosed the news to her was, 'How clever of the Foreign Office to send someone to Iraq who doesn't *look* like an Ambassador!' I certainly never looked like one, but whether the FO was being clever is open to doubt. In my own view British

Ambassadors needed to look the part – at least in those days when Britain still mattered greatly in the world.

Before we left Oxford one of our visitors was Bill Henderson, my only Province Governor in the Sudan with whom I had felt wholly at home. He brought us a whole crate of whisky and a string of characteristic reminiscences, two of which I entered in my scrapbook. One of them recalled an incident he had witnessed in Sir Douglas Newbold's office in Khartoum in wartime 1941. A Free French army officer had come up in something of a rage from Port Sudan where his request for permission to land troops from his passing ship for a few days' rest had been inexplicably refused by the Political Service Commissioner, named Springfield. In his (almost) perfect English he had exploded to the great Sir Douglas, 'That Mr Springfield, he is a veritable busybody. He has a finger in every tart.'

When the conversation turned to the eternal verities, I introduced Bill to Larkin's 'Church Going'. He was entranced. Its last verse about a church the poet visited was something he had been in travail with for years. (Haven't we all?)

> A serious house on serious earth it is,
> In whose blent air all our compulsions meet,
> Are recognized, and robed as destinies.
> And that much never can be obsolete,
> Since someone will forever be surprising
> A hunger in himself to be more serious,
> And gravitating with it to this ground,
> Which, he once heard, was proper to grow wise in,
> If only that so many dead lie round.

That verse is one that has buzzed in my head for thirty odd years.

One great man I came to know at Oxford was Sir Reader Bullard. The son of a railwayman at (I think) Stirling, he had filled many difficult diplomatic posts with distinction, was as obviously 'good' as anyone I ever met, and now lived in his eighties in a tiny house near St Antony's, where he was regarded with a veneration not usually entertained for ex-diplomats. When he heard of my posting to Iraq, an old post of his own, he took me under his wing; and after my arrival in Baghdad he wrote me splendid letters full of encouragement and quiet humour. But the lunch he gave me and a retired Regius Professor of Mathematics at Cambridge in a modest fish restaurant in Walton Street started a remarkable saga. The Cambridge professor told us over the fish and chips a strange story of a young Indian bank clerk in Madras, from whom he had received a twenty-page letter consisting of mathematical hieroglyphs with his name at the bottom. Judging the young man to be either a genius or a lunatic, the professor had brought him to Cambridge, where it became clear that he was no lunatic. But within a few months he collapsed with TB and was removed to hospital in London on Denmark Hill. As an act of kindness, the professor had gone one day from Cambridge by train to visit him. To make conversation he said, 'I came in a taxi from Liverpool Street. Rather a dull number – 1,729.' '*Dull* number?' murmured the dying young genius. 'But 1,729 is the smallest number that can be represented as the sum of two cubes in two different ways.' I soon forgot what the professor told us were the two cubes and worked it out only laboriously long after: $10^3 + 9^3$ or $12^3 + 1^3 = 1,729$.

There were several reasons why that story stayed with me. The first is that two years later I went up from Baghdad with Cocky Hahn, the General Manager of the Iraq Petroleum Company, to visit the company's operations in Kirkuk, then run by a Palestinian Iraqi, Hilma Samarra. Learning that our host had mathematical leanings, I recounted to him, at the lunch party he gave us, the professor's story. When I had finished, the man said, 'Yes, you've got the facts more or less right.' 'What d'you mean?' I said. 'How do you know that?' 'Because,' he replied, 'I was the Regius Professor's other genius pupil.'

The second reason the story stayed with me is that ten years later, when I was working in the Public Record Office, I went from my lodgings in central London to visit my daughter Ann in Ealing. It was late at night, and the Tube I travelled in was empty long before Ealing. Having nothing to read, I picked up a tattered copy of *Computer Science* or some such periodical lying on the floor. What should it contain as its leading article but the same story of the young Indian with TB and Professor X's taxi number.

Incidentally, that lunch at Kirkuk produced two other memorable moments. I was seated opposite Iraq's 'Minister for Kurdish Affairs', Sami Abdulrahman, a Kurd for whom the Baathist government had invented this non-job in an attempt to curb Kurdish discontent. This was a year or more after Kurdish rebels had shelled the Kirkuk oil installations with a 3-inch mortar. Referring to that occasion, Cocky Hahn, who had been in Kirkuk at the time, said to the minister, 'How on earth did those rebels fail to hit these huge installations?' 'Well,' said the minister, 'it wasn't the installations they were aiming at. I ought to know, because the rebel who carried the mortar twenty miles and fired it was *me*!' (General astonishment.) 'Then what *were* you aiming at?' asked Cocky. 'You!' said the minister. Hilarity ensued. (They certainly were/are an entertaining, if difficult, people, the Kurds.)

And then, to illustrate why he had been Professor X's 'other genius pupil' at Cambridge, the Manager observed, in the disarmingly un-British manner of gifted Arabs, 'All the boys born in my village in Palestine were geniuses. We put it down to something in the water in the village well.' He went on to relate how, as a teenager in 1937, during the Palestinian revolt against the Zionists and British policy, he had been sitting one day on a tree trunk in the village street reading an English book, when British troops invaded the village looking for Palestinian 'terrorists'. The Platoon Commander had stormed up to him and snatched the presumably subversive book from his hands. It lay open at the page bearing the famous sentence ''Tis a mad world, my masters'. The officer took a look, silently handed the book back to him and with a courteous smile went off to continue his duty. 'That incident', the Manager said, laughing, 'explains why, despite everything, I have always liked the British.'*

* Soon after I left Iraq this splendid man was thrown into prison by Saddam Hussein on the ludicrous charge of disloyalty to his adoptive country.

Experiences as Ambassador

CHAPTER 17

Iraq

IRAQ is a vast and rather drab country, relieved by the Kurdish mountains in the north, the Shatt al-Arab in the south (where the Garden of Eden is improbably claimed to have lain), countless fine archaeological sites, and what was a splendid National Museum until it was looted and vandalised in the tragic events of 2003. Baghdad itself was in 1969 a gigantic village enlivened by many non-Baathist Iraqis whom I came to know – lively, imaginative people. The Iraqi doctors alone formed an enthusiastic chamber orchestra. There were extraordinarily large numbers of serious painters. An engineer friend who wrote 'concrete poetry' offered, when I expressed ignorance of that art, to send me 'a lorry load'. And so on.

Of Iraq's painters one I should mention was Lorna, the English wife of Iraq's leading establishment artist, who went off his head in later life and tried to slice her up with a carving knife. She told me how she had decided two or three years before to record the whole townscape of old Baghdad. In the course of this enterprise she had recently been painting the old Jewish quarter with its beautiful projecting *mashrabiyas*. Having not quite finished, she went back the following morning to complete it. Overnight the whole street had been bulldozed to the ground by the Baathist authorities. Her painting, completed from memory, which I bought from her, hangs in our home, and the Jewish brass doorknocker that I picked up in the rubble is now on our front door.

It was of course exciting to be the head of an Embassy – the biggest I ever headed – and to live in the huge house that the British oil company had once built for its boss, with its vast garden and lawns large enough to accommodate three croquet grounds as well as a 'tame' mongoose. The latter was tethered to a palm tree and used by my cook to catch rats in the kitchen area on a long string. As for the lawns, I was a keen enough diplomat to enjoy staging ambassadorial croquet parties – knocking my Soviet colleague's ball almost into the Tigris.

The Soviet minister (number two in the Embassy and doubtless its head KGB spy) became quite a close friend. He had learnt enough English to enable him, he told me, to read 'every English novel published up to 1910' – not, he explained, for enjoyment but 'to increase my documentation'. He was known as 'Cauliflower-ear' and told me why. Being a Siberian and living as a young man at below-zero temperatures, he was *carrying* his girlfriend home through the snow from a university dance and couldn't release a hand to rub his left ear and keep the blood circulating in it. His ear was consequently frostbitten and had never recovered.

But much my favourite colleague was the Belgian, Marcel Dupret. Belgium being America's Protecting Power, he had taken over the US Embassy building, from which the Americans had been expelled two years before. In it (Embassies being extraterritorial sanctuaries) an Iraqi opposition leader had taken refuge. After looking after him for months and refusing to surrender him, Marcel devised a plan. He staged a noisy party in the Embassy one night, and at 1 a.m., having concealed the Iraqi in the boot of his car, he drove it himself out of the gates, singing at the top of his voice. The Iraqi security men stationed there to ensure that the wanted man didn't escape assumed that the driver was just another drunken European diplomat and let the car through without examining it. Marcel then drove 600 miles non-stop to the border with Kuwait, where, by alleging that he was on an official visit to the Kuwait government, he was again waved through – and the wanted man was free. Marcel was later transferred to Morocco; and at a garden party in the Sultan's palace rebels broke in waving Kalashnikovs and appeared to intend shooting. Marcel walked forward alone to parley with them and was shot dead.

One great benefit of being posted to Iraq was that my wanderings around it enabled me to examine a lot of ancient famous sites – Babylon, Ur, Nineveh, Ctesiphon, Hatra, etc. Since then many of them have been desecrated by looters or by the American military in the course of the Anglo-American invasion.

Before I went to Iraq, Elizabeth Monroe at St Antony's had asked me to collect for its Middle East Centre any early family records I could trace. A pair of elderly English gents, Lynch by name, in neat white duck suits and identical white moustaches, who still lived in Baghdad, came as fashion required to call on the new British Ambassador. Had they, I asked, any old family papers of historical interest? One of the two told me that an ancestor of his had set up in Baghdad in 1841 a local trading company, and then in 1861 a 'Tigris & Euphrates Steam Navigation Company', buying up for the purpose any old East India Company steamboats still operating in the area. The company, managed throughout by members of the Lynch family, had struggled on till the end of the Second World War and had then gone into liquidation. He then told me that he had been planning to write a history of the company and had asked his aged aunt in Baghdad to lend him the family papers that she had in her custody, but (he added sadly) the old lady confessed that she had burnt the whole lot to heat her bath water.

Much more exciting is an earlier episode in steam navigation in Iraq which I learnt about. In 1835 Francis F. Chesney, then a captain in the British army but already an experienced explorer and surveyor of the Levant and Meso-potamia, sought to validate his conviction that the Euphrates river was a better and quicker route to India than the existing long journey round the Cape of Good Hope. With determined backing from the novelist Thomas Love Peacock, then an official of East India House in London, and aided also by encouragement from King William IV, Chesney had designed the construction of two iron steamboats by Lairds of Liverpool – almost the first steamboats ever built of iron. He then conveyed them out in pieces to Suedia on the coast of Syria. His staggeringly dramatic account of the rest of the story figures in his *Narrative of the Euphrates Expedition,* published years later in 1868, which I read avidly. It describes how his party, which included Henry Lynch of the Indian navy as second-in-command, mounted the iron plates and boilers on flat-bottomed boats with wheels and sails attached and, with the help of eighty buffaloes and a hundred men, dragged them over miles of vile tracks to the headwaters of the Euphrates at Bir. (The lighter wooden parts were mounted on camels.) The two steamboats were eventually put together at Bir, were named *Euphrates* and *Tigris,* and were launched into the river with the intention of steaming the 1,000 miles down to Basra and establishing the route as a commercial enterprise. They had not got very far before a violent storm broke out, so violent that *Tigris* was instantly and irretrievably sunk in the mud under 30 feet of water, drowning twenty of the twenty-seven people on board. Chesney himself (I quote from memory) was hurled by the waves through the air on to the far bank, landing in a thorn tree, and was saved from death only because one of its long sharp spikes struck the Bible in his waistcoat pocket and got no further. Something that could only have happened to a Victorian!* After a moving appeal by Chesney the survivors pushed on in *Euphrates* alone. Despite more savage setbacks, and although the plague was rife in Baghdad and other towns, they reached Basra in June 1836, but the project was abandoned two months later on orders from London.

One memorable resident of Baghdad whom I got to know was a French Dominican priest, Jean Frey, author of three volumes on pre-Islamic Iraq. His Iraqi followers, who numbered about twenty, once said to him, 'It's all very well for *you*. You can always get out.' He thereupon renounced his French nationality, so that he never *could* get out. But what I most remember him for is a conversation we had one evening about the famous pre-Islamic palace at Ctesiphon (east of Baghdad), built about AD 250 by the Sassanians as the capital of their Persian Empire, until they were overthrown by the Muslim

---

* After writing the above I located in 2002 in St Antony's College one of the very rare copies of Chesney's *Narrative* and went there to read it again and check my recollections of reading it thirty years before. To my dismay the incident of the thorn tree and the waistcoat Bible was not there. But I could not have invented anything so splendid.

Arabs in the seventh century. The phenomenal open arch of the ruined palace still stands. No one, I said, seemed to know how such an arch could have been constructed by the Sassanians. Jean Frey replied by quoting a line from a Syriac poet of the fifth century in Iraq about a camel. Describing its adorable hoofs, the poet had said, 'They are smooth and rounded like the arches of bridges built by Greeks.' In Sassanian times, Frey explained, 'Greeks' meant non-Arab people from Antioch, and the Sassanian rulers must have recruited engineers from Antioch to build their Ctesiphon palace.

But the man who contributed most to my entertainment in Baghdad was Cocky Hahn. South African in origin, he had been a South African diplomat in Washington but disliked apartheid so strongly that he resigned and became a British subject. He was now General Manager of the Iraq Petroleum Company and was constantly in my office (for we were his cipher channel) dispatching unsuccessful arguments to IPC headquarters in London for a more concessionary policy towards Iraq. He was 'retired' in consequence. We shared many interests, and years later Jenny and I often visited him and his unusual collection of rare objects in his medieval monastery in Dorset. His premature death there in 1989 was a great sadness.

A character of a more peculiar interest was an old Englishman living in Basra. I should have met him when I went to acquaint myself with the British community there, totalling five, but he failed to turn up at the resulting lunch party because (I learnt) he had no teeth and no money to buy any, and therefore felt he could not lunch with an Ambassador. When I did later meet him it transpired that he had been a gunner in the invading British army from India in 1915; and when General Townsend's force surrendered to the Turks at Kut al-Amara he had been one of the few who survived their frightful march as prisoners of about 1,000 miles to Ankara. After the war he had returned to Iraq and married an Iraqi girl in Basra, where he had lived in abject poverty ever since. A year after I met him I heard that he was being expelled from the country, aged eighty-odd, as a suspected spy. He had no relations in England and nowhere to go. I had him to stay with me in Baghdad while I pleaded with the Minister of the Interior to cancel the absurd expulsion order (one of my few successes with the Baathist authorities). While he was our guest he told me a mass of marvellous stories about his early life in Iraq. Here is one of them.

On the advance up-river towards Kut in 1915 his unit had been inspected by a visiting General from India. The General had required my friend's seven-man gun team to demonstrate their firing drill. On the order FIRE! one of the seven had instantly knelt on the ground with his right arm curled above his head. 'Why on earth are you doing *that?*' snapped the General. ''Cos I've always done it, sir,' was the reply. It transpired that the battery had been issued some months earlier with trucks to pull its guns in place of the traditional mules. Previously it had been number seven's job, when the gun was fired, to put his arm over the mule's neck to stop it taking fright and bolting – and here he was, still going through the old drill routine without the mule.

That lunch in Basra took place in the imposing house still owned by Gellatly Hankey & Co., the British firm that had dominated foreign trade in the area for years until expelled by the Baathists three years before. The firm still had one British official there to pursue a mass of (retrospective) shipping correspondence. The official concerned showed me an enchanting curiosity. In an old file cupboard he had discovered the company's laundry accounts of 1901, when there were six resident British members of staff. The accounts revealed that their laundry had been regularly dispatched in wicker baskets across the river and up-country in Persia to meet the nearest railway, and on it to the Edgware Road in London. After laundering it had been scrupulously repacked (with tissue paper, lavender and all) and returned by the same route, the whole turn-around being completed in three weeks. I thought the company's laundry arrangements so entertaining that on my return to Baghdad I regaled some of my colleagues with the story. The Polish Ambassador said he didn't consider it unusual. 'Until the recent world war,' he declared, 'we Polish officers in Warsaw always sent our laundry to London. It was the only way to get our evening boiled shirts properly ironed.'

Of Iraq's physical attractions I picked out at the start of this chapter the mountains of Kurdistan, the Shatt al-Arab marshes and the National Museum. Here are some comments on each of the three.

The mountainous Kurdish area up north is as different from the Arab flatlands as Kurds are from Arabs, and singularly beautiful. There was only one short period in my time when the iron curtain imposed by Saddam Hussein to prevent outsiders visiting the rebellious Kurds was briefly lifted. In the course of it (August 1971) I took the family there during the harvest when the cropped grain heaped on village threshing-floors was being threshed by remarkable mule-drawn sledges looking rather like large Atco lawnmowers. The villages themselves, of low stone-built flat-roofed cottages, were barely distinguishable from the stepped and slatey rocks that formed their footing and their backing. I also received an invitation from the famous Kurdish leader, Mustafa Barzani, to take my family to spend the New Year weekend as his guests in his remote hideaway, virtually unapproachable by wheeled transport, where he knew himself safe from the attentions of the Iraqi army. Two days before we were due to set off, Marnie collapsed with her terminal illness (see below). So I never met Barzani, the last almost undisputed leader of Iraq's persecuted Kurds. He died in 1974. His son Masoud thereafter led that half of the fractious Kurds known as the PUK against the rival Talabani group, the KDP.

The Shatt al-Arab consisted of a huge area of water forming the estuary of the Tigris and Euphrates in which the 'Marsh Arabs', with whom Wilfred Thesiger spent seven years, lived on islands of compacted reeds. Round and

15 Reed-built *mejlis* of a sheikh of the Marsh Arabs in southern Iraq on a visit by BP family in 1969.

about these islands they punted themselves in high-prowed canoes called *taradas* amid water buffaloes and masses of black-and-white kingfishers and waterfowl. I took the family down to the area by train, booking our tickets at Baghdad station at an office that bore the jolly superscription TOP CLASS BOOKING OFFICE. It was a memorable visit, punting incompetently around in a *tarada* and taking coffee with one of the head sheikhs in his marvellous *mejlis*. This resembled in size and design the nave of a Norman cathedral but was constructed entirely of reeds. Saddam Hussein, during and after his war with Iran in the 1980s, drained – for declaredly strategic reasons – much of the Marsh Arabs' area and killed or drove out in their thousands its suffering inhabitants. If the marshlands are successfully restored, how many of its old inhabitants will return to them? Or will most of them in the interim have become landlubbers like the rest of us?

The National Museum, where I spent many days off, was the site of a distinctly uncanny experience. A visiting German archaeologist, who had in the past dug sundry Sumerian and Babylonian sites, offered one Friday (when the museum was officially closed) to show me round the principal exhibits. In due course we reached the famous Royal Burial of Ur. In front of the bier bearing the richly apparelled Prince and Princess lay the skeletons of the horsemen and horses that had been pulling their chariot to the place of burial; and round the bier knelt the skeletons of the maidservants buried with their royal employers – one of them still visibly adjusting her right earring as if she had arrived a minute or two late for her own funeral. I asked the German professor how he thought the multiple burials surrounding the royal pair were to be explained, for there was no sign that the lives of the maid-servants and horsemen had been forcibly ended. Had they been drugged asleep so that, once buried, they woke up dead? 'Well,' said the professor, 'I was once digging a site on the east of the Tigris when one of my Iraqi labourers came and asked me if I could get a doctor to cure his paralysed small son, whom he took me to see lying motionless on his rope bed. I managed to get two German doctors to come. After their examination both said there was nothing medical science could do for the child. Then something unbelievable happened. The boy's mother, having heard that the foreign doctors could do nothing, came to where the boy was lying, dropped on her knees, shuffled slowly round the bed, and ended beside her paralysed son in an attitude of prayer. After a minute or so, the boy rose from the bed and walked about, miraculously cured. His mother never stirred. She was dead. I saw all this', the professor continued, 'with my own eyes. All I could presume was that she had voluntarily surrendered her own life and conferred it, so to speak, on her adored son. In subsequent years, I questioned many medical experts but none had any better explanation to offer. I am convinced', he concluded, 'that the handmaidens of the royal couple at Ur, whom they worshipped as divine, made the same voluntary surrender of their lives as an act of devotion.' The professor stood silently beside me for some time, looking meditatively down on this scene of mysterious self-sacrifice manifested 4,000 years ago.

Would the handmaidens of Saddam Hussein, I wondered, when by good fortune he died or was otherwise got rid of, behave in the same way? I thought that unlikely. And when in 2004 he was finally disposed of (if he really has been) there was no sign of such domestic devotion – though it soon became apparent that plenty of Iraqis would prefer to continue being ruthlessly tyran-nised by Saddam than be governed by invading Americans. Before I set down my own first-hand impressions of that remarkable thug, it may be helpful to summarise the complicated and gruesome story of the rise of Baathism, and eventually of Saddam Hussein himself, to power in Iraq.

Back in October 1959 a group of young revolutionaries led by the then un-known Saddam made a botched attempt to assassinate President Abdulkerim Qassem. For this Saddam was sentenced to death – *in absentia*, for he had fled to Syria. There he was noticed and patronised by the founder of Baathism, Michel Aflaq. During the short-lived union of Syria and Egypt (1959–61) Saddam and other refugees were sent from Damascus to Cairo 'to complete their education'. When Syria broke with Egypt Nasser's Egyptian authorities naturally kept a close watch on their activities. (The CIA too is alleged to have shown an interest in them as potentially useful pawns in their game against Qassem and his Communist supporters, and even to have provided Saddam with a safe flat.) In 1963, when Qassem was successfully assassinated, the leader of the plot was the Baathist Colonel Ahmed Bakr; but since the plotters had not all been Baathists they allowed the non-Baathist Abdulsalam Aref to assume the Presidency, with Bakr as his Prime Minister. Saddam returned from Cairo only after the Qassem assassination, meeting up with Aflaq in Damascus on his way. Saddam now planned to assassinate President Aref, but his plan misfired and he was imprisoned. After twenty months in gaol he escaped into hiding. When Aref died in a helicopter crash in 1966 he was replaced as President by his brother, Abdulrahman. Three months later the focus shifted to Syria, where the left wing of the Baath ousted Aflaq from his command of the movement. He took refuge in Baghdad, becoming the 'spiritual' leader of the rival Baathists of Iraq. President Aref was pushed out in another Baathist coup in which Saddam played a minor role as a gunman in bogus army uniform. Bakr became President and Chairman of the party's Command Council. Saddam received no immediate appointment but was shortly given (since no one else wanted it) the job of running the unpopular security apparatus, and so efficient was he that Bakr soon made him effectively his right-hand man. Not long after my arrival Saddam set about removing possible obstacles to his own advancement, and in May 1971 he got his first cousin and rival Vice-President, Hardan al Takriti (the only top Baathist from whom I ever got any help), assassinated in Kuwait. Bakr remained officially president for another eight years. Only once during this period did he seek to exert his primacy by announcing his plan for the union of Iraq and Syria – a plan popular with the public but not with Saddam, who had plans of his own for the future of Iraq. He cleverly upstaged Bakr on this issue and privately demanded his resignation. When Bakr duly announced his resignation in July 1979 Saddam paid him fulsome praise in speeches, but once he had assumed the Presidency he proceeded to execute hundreds of suspected opponents in the party, alleging that they had been wickedly trying to drive a wedge between Bakr and himself. Saddam brooked no opposition thereafter from any direction.

These latter developments still lay in the future so far as I was concerned. My own impressions of Saddam during my time in Iraq are based largely on the two private sessions I was able to secure with him. The first of these was the more dramatic, and is described on the first page of these memoirs. Certainly he became an utterly bestial dictator, but, when he was starting out at least, his powers of argument were skilful enough to wrap *me* round his little finger.

My most gruesome experience of Saddam's brutality occurred late in 1970. I record it mainly because of its almost more dispiriting aftermath. We knew from our 'secret sources' – as evidently did Saddam from his – that an Iranian-sponsored coup against him and his Baathists was being planned for a certain date. On the evening concerned I was at a dinner party in the Belgian (American) Embassy. At about 11 p.m. the Iranian Ambassador, who was one of the guests, was called to the telephone and vanished. We never saw him again. What had happened was the following. Saddam, working as often late at night in the Government Palace, waited until the conspirators entered it and had crept, thinking they were unobserved, to within a few yards of his room. His hidden guards then pounced on them. Under torture they produced the names of some seventy fellow conspirators who, whether guilty or not, were instantly rounded up and shot without trial. Their corpses were then loaded on to lorries and kicked out at the doors of their homes with shouts to the occupants of 'Take your dog!'. I was so nauseated when I learnt of this behaviour that I couldn't speak to a Baathist for several days. During them I paid an under-the-counter call on the leader of the secret opposition, a pleasant, democratic individual not involved in the Iranian plot. I told him of my anti-Baathist nausea, and (here comes the 'dispiriting aftermath') this was his reaction: 'What are you complaining of? If *we* had been in power, we would have done exactly the same thing.'

None of the above frightfulness, however, was of the same order for me personally as the ghastly spongiform encephalitis that overcame Marnie at the end of 1970. I will draw a veil over its details. I flew with her to London, where she died in March 1971, by which time I had returned to Baghdad. It seemed harsh that she should have been fated, during the twenty years of our marriage, first to be thrown from a horse and severely damage her spine, then to contract polio, and finally to be smitten with a rare fatal affliction. Such cumulative hardships seem to be the way of the world. Sometimes they even bear down on whole families. I feel ashamed to have suffered so few physical hardships myself (as yet).

For the rest of my time in Baghdad I did not move around much. Then something distinctly bizarre happened. On 31 November 1971 I had returned in the small hours from the usual 'Burns Nicht' celebrations. From force of habit I switched on at 7 a.m. the BBC World Service news on my bedside radio. The first item announced that the British Ambassador in Baghdad was being expelled by the Iraqi government. This was news to me. I got up, went to the Embassy and rang the Ministry of Foreign Affairs over and over again. No one there was prepared to speak to me. So eventually I went round and dumped myself in the Protocol Department until someone in authority would tell me what was going on. I sat between two amiable protocol officials on the sofa making conversation for three-quarters of an hour. Then the bizarre happened. The hands of the clock on the wall opposite our sofa had, as everyone knew, stood motionless at 11.20 ever since the Iraqi royal family had been slaughtered in the revolution of 1958. Suddenly the three of us heard and saw the minute hand lurch inexplicably forward to 11.21. We turned to each other in wide-eyed amazement. At that moment the door under the clock opened and a messenger announced that the head of the Political Department would receive Mr Balfour Paul. (As I never entered the ministry again I do not know whether the clock has ever moved any farther forward, or if its sudden agitation after thirteen static years was simply a macabre coincidence.)

The head of the Political Department informed me amicably over coffee that his government had decided to sever relations with Britain because we had failed to stop the Shah of Iran seizing the Tunb and Abu Mousa islands (near the mouth of the Gulf) from their Sharjah and Ras al-Khaimah owners. (The Shah had carefully staged the seizure twenty-four hours before our defence commitments were formally terminated.) I must, said the official, remove my whole Embassy within ten days. He also thanked me with a disarming smile for having presented him, a few weeks before, with a book on the history of the Gulf written by my Counsellor, Donald Hawley. Without it, he said, he could not have drafted the expulsion order that he handed me, since he had not previously known even the whereabouts of the disputed islands. After much shredding and burning of secret documents, a Comet collected all of us and our baggage. Two days before we left a young Iraqi engineer friend sent me by hand of the Dutch Ambassadress an album he had put together of photographs of Baghdad in 1917 (when Britain first occupied it in the First World War).

A month after our expulsion, when I was having some leave in my cottage in Dumfriesshire, I was rung by the FO and asked whether I would chair an international conference on the conservation of seals. I thought they meant Sumerian and Babylonian cylinder seals, which I had been studying in the Baghdad Museum. Only after agreeing enthusiastically did I discover that the seals the conference would be studying were the Antarctic ones with flippers; and about *them*, having spent my life in the deserts of Arabia, I knew precisely nothing. I was assured that this didn't matter; the British delegation were experts and would help me out. In fact the fortnight's argument in the Vauxhall Conference Centre in about eight different languages was rather fun. At 2 a.m. on the last night (2 February 1972) we all signed an international convention aimed (fruitlessly, I suspect) at protecting the poor beasts. Champagne was brought in, and the head of the Soviet delegation proposed the chairman's health, dubbing me 'Lord Privy Seal'.

He also invited me to lunch two days later in the Soviet Embassy – the first such display of mateyness, I learnt, since the expulsion of 105 Soviet spies the previous September. Towards the end of this lunch my host, Counsellor Kotlyan (himself doubtless a Soviet spy), told me after copious consumption of vodka the following enchanting story about the Hungarians declaring war on the USA in (I think) 1943. Not very certain of the protocol, the Hungarians had sent a fairly junior official round to the State Department in Washington. He was received at equivalent rank, and this, according to Kotlyan, was the conversation that ensued:

HUNGARIAN: I have come to inform you that my government is declaring war on *your* government.

AMERICAN: Oh, yes? Who did you say you represented?

HUNGARIAN: Hungary. The Kingdom of Hungary.

AMERICAN: The Kingdom of Hungary? So you have a King?

HUNGARIAN: Well, no; we have a Regent. Horthy, Admiral Horthy.

AMERICAN: Oh, you're a naval power, then?

HUNGARIAN: No. Actually we do not have any sea.

AMERICAN: But you have claims against the USA?

HUNGARIAN: No, we have no claims against the USA.

AMERICAN: Then you have claims against our ally, Britain?

HUNGARIAN: No, we have no claims against Britain.

AMERICAN: Then it's our other allies, the Russians, you have claims against?

HUNGARIAN: No, we have always had very good relations with the Russians.

AMERICAN: Then what do you want to declare war for? Who *do* you have claims against?

HUNGARIAN: We have claims against Romania.

AMERICAN: Against Romania? Then why don't you declare war against the Romanians?

HUNGARIAN: We can't. They're our allies.

If the Communist Russians were all like Counsellor Kotlyan, I felt, we should get along with them much better. (It was twenty years later that thanks to Gorbachev Russian Communism collapsed.)

When that seal conference finally broke up, I would gladly have declared war against the Italians. The brand-new Italian Fiat I had bought two days before conked out in the middle of Vauxhall Bridge and I had to push it across the Thames single handed in pouring rain at 2.30 a.m. The AA found the distributor clogged, to their amazement, with bits of copper wire.

CHAPTER 18

Jordan

IT WAS Tony Parsons as Under-Secretary for the Middle East who (so he told me) persuaded the Foreign Secretary, Douglas Home, that the right man to get alongside the Hashemites in Jordan was none of those whose names had been submitted to him, but Balfour Paul! The Queen had little option but to approve, as she had done when I was sent to Iraq. 'Kissing hands' followed in Buckingham Palace. One doesn't actually kiss them, but talking to her at close quarters and alone, I was struck by her unexpected beauty and by her easy conversational manner. Indeed, she almost laughed at my jokes. I certainly laughed at hers.

By the end of July 1972 I was installed in Amman, having handed my credentials to King Hussein. It was a friendly post, though apart from the children's holidays somewhat lonely for a widower bouncing about in a big house with a mass of servants and a Social Secretary. I will record only two memorable incidents before I ceased to be lonely (in September 1974).

In June 1973 I accompanied King Hussein on a week's visit to London. He called (with me) on Prime Minister Edward Heath in No. 10 – for tea at the impossible hour of 3.30 p.m. The King started a trifle tactlessly by saying of President Assad of Syria, 'A reasonable man but he suffers from having to carry his party with him.' (This remark might have been even less tactful if he had been calling on one or other of our subsequent Prime Ministers.) He then droned away earnestly on Jordan's problems and I noticed that Mr Heath's eyes had narrowed until they were positively shut. What, I asked myself, does an Ambassador do when his Prime Minister falls asleep giving tea to a visiting Head of State? Cough loudly? Kick his ankles under the tea table? I glanced at King Hussein. He gave me a royal wink. A few moments later, to my relief, Mr Heath opened his eyes and conversation rambled on till the King took his leave. The security arrangements were formidable, for the King was still exposed to much Arab hostility following his crackdown on the 1970 attempt of Palestinians, driven out of their own country by Israel, to replace his regime with one of their own. As he drove away from No. 10 with car-loads of security men fore and aft, Mr Heath made up a bit for the humourless shortcomings of his hospitality by whispering to me, 'It's the poor buggers in the cars all round him that I'm sorry for: it's them that'll get shot.' Fortunately no shootings occurred.

The other incident was more dramatic. In October 1973 Presidents Sadat and Assad (of Egypt and Syria), who three days before had met up with King Hussein in Cairo and accepted his proposals for a peaceful compromise with Israel, suddenly declared war on Israel without even warning the King. (This was the third Arab–Israeli war.) Sitting with him in his cement bunker overlooking the Jordan Valley as the Egyptians and Syrians launched their attacks, I was moved to see the King wiping tears from his eyes over the deceitful treatment he had received from the two Presidents. Maybe they did not trust him, but his position was indeed intolerable. If he too declared war, the Israeli air force would destroy what was left of his Kingdom in a matter of minutes. If he didn't he would be branded as a traitor by all Arabs. It looked as if a pro-Arab gesture *had* to be made.

The following night the King, Crown Prince Hassan, Prime Minister Rufa'i, the US Ambassador (Dean Brown), and myself were assembled in conclave to discuss an idea from my Embassy by which Jordan, if it entered the war, might be spared destruction by Israel. Agreement on this plan had just been reached when the phone rang in the next room: evidently a long-distance call, as we could hear the Prime Minister shouting his head off. Shortly, he looked round the door with a white face and whispered, 'It's Idi Amin [the nutcase dictator of Uganda]. He insists on flying here tonight to see His Majesty.' Instant pandemonium ensued (as recorded in my diary when I returned to my house).

KING HUSSEIN (snatching his military beret and making for the exit): I'm off to visit the Brigade I'm sending to Syria.

PRINCE HASSAN (also making for the door): And I'm off to inspect the ... the Jordan Valley Development Commission.

DEAN BROWN You'll never find it in the dark. I can't even find it in daylight (a neat jibe at the Crown Prince's pet organisation).

KING and CROWN PRINCE (together): Prime Minister, it's up to you. *You* must meet him.

PRIME MINISTER But the airport's blacked out. I won't even be able to see a black man in the dark.

KING You'll recognise him by his teeth.

PM But what am I to *do* with him?

KING Put him in a hotel. Give him a briefing ...

PRINCE HASSAN ... and a medal.

KING: And tell him the King won't be back till he's gone.

Hilarious applause all round – and this in the middle of a conclave solemnly examining the faint possibility of saving the Hashemite Kingdom from obliteration.

In the event the dodge (which involved negotiating a sort of compromise between Golda Meir, the Prime Minister of Israel, and King Hussein) proved viable, and in the morning the King announced on the local radio the dispatch of his crack Armoured Brigade to 'do its duty' on the Syrian front. Dean Brown told me of a conversation he had had with the head of the Royal Diwan, Adnan al-Awdeh (a special friend of mine), just after the King's announcement:

ADNAN Isn't it marvellous?

DEAN BROWN *What's* marvellous?

ADNAN The Arabic language. To be able to say such ludicrous things in such ravishingly beautiful prose.

King Hussein, whom I liked enormously, had great skill in English too. The foreign press shortly converged on Amman in an attempt to learn *something* of what was going on in the war, since the authorities in Cairo, Damascus and Tel Aviv would tell them nothing. I urged the King, despite his natural reluctance, to give a press conference: anything that enabled the hungry journalists to file a story would redound to his credit. After the resulting conference, a group of British pressmen called at my office. 'He's tremendous,' they said. 'And what did he tell you?' 'Well, nothing really. But it sounded splendid.'

The King's brother, Crown Prince Hassan, also impressed me much, but for different reasons. While the King was a pragmatist, Hassan was a theoretician. I once called on him in his bedroom when he was in bed with a fever. A dozen books on economic theory littered the bed. He read them all. Unfortunately the two brothers did not see eye to eye, and when the King was dying in 2003 he arranged for his eldest son (by his British wife) rather than the Crown Prince to succeed him. Hassan remains an effective public speaker with a worldwide reputation.

Since the end of 1972 my activities had been hampered by the day-long attentions of the Alsatian dog that the Foreign Office had sent out from London to protect me from being kidnapped by Palestinian extremists. Druid, as I christened him, was described as the scion of a long line of Cruft's champions. He arrived on the doorstep of my house in a crate marked VICIOUS THIS SIDE UP (and therefore not delayed by Customs) two days before Christmas, just as the British community assembled all dolled up for my Christmas party. He was accompanied by the Pet Library's *Guide to German Shepherd Dogs*, dedicated by its author Miss M. Pickup to 'All those beloveds who have gone on Ahead where Separation is Unknown'. She declared that a 'mere' three hours training per day will 'make' an Alsatian but that this 'making' has to be completed in its first six months. Druid proved to be seven months old on arrival and distinctly 'unmade'. The vicissitudes of life in his company were too grotesque to recount in full. I will give two simple examples. My instructions from London were that he had to sleep in my bedroom; and on one dramatic evening, by the time I returned from some National Day reception, he had located in my chest of drawers, and consumed, a year's supply of vitamin tablets. This inspired him to lay a paper-chase of foam-rubber mattressing all round the room and to masticate half the top cover of my bed on which, after recovering from a bout of nausea on the carpet, he remained comfortably ensconced till my return, relieving himself on it at intervals. On another occasion he jumped up on to the mahogany dining table that was set for a grand dinner party, scattering the cutlery, chewing up the napkins and leaving permanent teeth marks in more than one silver napkin ring. I might add that, since good Muslims will not touch dog-shit, one of my less agreeable tasks was the daily carrying of a bucket all round the house to collect Druid's droppings.

After the 1973 war, the Foreign Office decided that Druid was not protection enough, and requested that the Jordanian authorities provide me with a bodyguard of four armed policeman to accompany me everywhere. They were a slapstick quartet and much funnier than Druid. They carried their guns in pieces in canvas bags, and any kidnappers that showed up would have done their job long before my protectors had assembled their weaponry. On one occasion, as they got out of my car, one of them emptied the pieces in his bag all over the pavement at the feet of the passers-by.

The imposition of these bodyguards took place when Jenny Scott came out as my Social Secretary, and they and Druid must have complicated her life almost as much as they did mine. Fortunately the Foreign Office accepted my plea that I might dispose of Druid to a member of the British Embassy in Tel Aviv who liked Alsatians. After Druid had gone I wrote a spoof dispatch on this 'security experiment' to the Secretary of State, copying it to the Ambassador in Outer Mongolia. I learnt later that my dispatch featured (ironically I hope) in the syllabus of Foreign Office security courses for some years.

There is a long gap in my diary and the next significant entry is dated 4 July 1974. I had got back from the celebrations of Independence Day in the American Embassy and once more listened with Jenny to my record of *The Magic Flute*. Maybe the Queen of the Night's great aria sent Jenny a bit out of her mind, for the next thing that happened was that she said she would marry me.

She flew home to tell her parents of this grotesque decision. They took it on the chin, to the point of sending me a current press cartoon. It pictured an elderly man saying to his prospective son-in-law, 'If you can keep her in the manner to which she's accustomed, for God's sake tell me how you do it!' I was conscious simply of sharing the emotion expressed in comparable circumstances by Laurie Lee:

> Now as the almond burns its smoking wick
> > Dropping small flames to light the candled grass,
> Now as my low blood scales its second chance,
> > If ever world were blessed, now it is.

16 Glencairn and Jenny at their marriage in Devon, September 1974.

We were married in the church at Brixton, Jenny's home near Plymouth, on 21 September 1974.

There can be few more enchanting places for a honeymoon than Istanbul (at least as Istanbul was in 1974). Despite its dominating minarets it has not lost all sense of the civilisations that preceded the Ottoman Turks – none of them arguably more to be admired than the achievements of the Ottomans themselves, whatever their defects. And there were no defects at all in the large antiquated empty hotel we lodged in. From it we looked down on the

Bosphorus loud with the whooping of ships' funnels and the swish of pigeons in the sun. The ancient city itself is an endless delight. As for the Turks, they seemed to share with the Egyptians the ability to make fun of themselves. The manager of the Turkish car-hire company we patronised advised us strongly against renting a car of Turkish manufacture, explaining that they were constructed not of metal but of vegetable material, so that when they broke down they were quickly eaten up by goats and donkeys. Whatever car it was that we did hire took us safely down the Aegean coast.

On the Residence doorstep on returning from our honeymoon we were faced by an alarming wedding present from the Melhuishes (my Counsellor and his wife). For this they had chosen – without, I think, positive malice – a hive of bees. Fortunately Jordanian bees are very gentle, and over the months we were able to extract lots of honey painlessly. Matters were very different when we took the hive (without the bees) to my subsequent post in Tunisia, for the black Tunisian bees that took over are the most vicious in the world. Two-thirds of the team of Romanian bee experts sent by the UN to teach the Tunisians the art of bee-keeping had gone off home in high dudgeon, but the team's heroic leader, Mr Popa, proved happy to help us. When he came to harvest our honey crop he dressed up (for the first time in his life, he told us) in full protective kit, advising me to watch the process from a safe distance of 50 yards. He eventually came over with pounds of honey but with a dozen angry bees inside his head-net and his huge leather gauntlets bristling all over with bee-stings like a hedgehog. He had, he assured me, worked for so many years with bees that not even a hundred Tunisian bee-stings worried him.

Diplomatic life is, for wives, a sequence of trivialities and was not Jenny's scene. But there was plenty to laugh at and, in off-time, plenty to see. Throughout our time in Jordan we spent as many nights as we could in unfrequented corners of the country sleeping out among rocks said to conceal snakes and scorpions and drawing pictures. Neither Jenny nor her parents (who came on a visit) can have been disappointed by the night we camped under the echoing sealing-wax crags of Wadi Rum, made famous by T. E. Lawrence in *The Seven Pillars of Wisdom*. They sent our voices back to us unchanged two whole seconds later. No fewer than three meteors chose that night to blaze through the million stars above us as we lay in the soft red sand. Less instantly enjoyable, however, was the climax to our snorkelling venture next day in the coral banks at Aqaba, when we poked at a strange sea-beast with spiky feelers. It reacted by darting at us. Fortunately it missed. We discovered on returning to our hotel that it was the rare 'Chicken-fish' whose lethal sting allows only twenty minutes to reach a hospital and an injection of life-saving serum.

Only a few other features of our time in Jordan can be squeezed in. The first does me no credit at all. I had taken Jenny in our Peugeot round sundry

17 Ambassador GBP and Jenny meeting King Hussein and the visiting Shah
of Persia (and their wives) in the palace in Amman, 1975.

Crusader castles in Syria, ending up at dusk in Damascus where we bought
for £20 a big chest inlaid with mother-of-pearl. We tied it, precariously, on
to the rackless roof of our Peugeot with string and set off at midnight for
Amman. It had been a long day and both of us were tired, so we coxed and
boxed at the wheel. I had taken over near Jerash and very soon fell asleep.
The car veered across the road, mounted the ground-level end of a crash
barrier immediately overlooking a precipice, and came to a halt on top of it,
wobbling perilously over the edge of the cliff, its guts torn out by the crash
barrier's successive projections. We suffered no damage ourselves, but what to
do next? Should Jenny stay alone in the car at 1 a.m. while I (with luck) hitched
a lift to seek rescue in Amman? Or should *she* hitch a lift while I guarded the
car (and the mother-of-pearl chest, which miraculously was still balanced on
the roof)? In the event, *she* hitched a lift in a car full of shrouded Arab men.
They couldn't have been more courteous and took her to rouse the sleeping
Ramsay Melhuish by throwing stones at his bedroom window. Loyally he
turned out – at 2.30 a.m. – and drove her back in his station wagon 30 miles
or so to rescue the Damascus chest, our other baggage and me. Our poor old
Peugeot, for all I know, may still be wobbling on the crash barrier.

The week we later spent at Mystras and in the Mani Peninsula of Greece
(having won tickets there in a charity raffle) gave me the chance of admiring
much Byzantine art; but spending the last day in the National Museum in

Athens restored my preference for the arts of Classical Greece. Nothing surely can touch the graceful humanity of Hellenic art – before the decline into Hellenistic self-conscious decorativeness, let alone the subsequent decline into the nervous piety of the Byzantines.

Now that Jenny could act as my chaperone, I was at last able to pay a call on King Hussein's widowed mother, Queen Zein, in the modest palace she occupied a hundred yards from my Residence. The conversation was in French, and to jolly it along I mentioned that, like her, I had a daughter at Benenden school, whose headmistress, the formidable Miss Clarke, had put me firmly in my place during the one discussion I had had with her. 'Ah,' said Queen Zein with a twinkle in her eye, 'I too once had trouble with Miss Clarke.' I expressed surprise. 'But yes,' explained the Queen, 'I had rung her up to say I was flying to England to take my daughter Basma out to supper. "I'm sorry, Your Majesty," said Miss Clarke, "but Basma has already had this term's quota of nights out, and I must say no." "But I haven't seen Basma for months and I am flying two thousand miles to see her." "I fear", said Miss Clarke, "that I cannot make an exception." Baffled and amazed,' Queen Zein went on, 'I rang the Jordanian Ambassador in London and asked him to intervene on my behalf with the Foreign Office. The Ambassador said that my best plan was to appeal to my fellow Queen, Elizabeth, who had also had a daughter at Benenden. So I rang Buckingham Palace. Queen Elizabeth expressed sympathy but said she had never succeeded in exercising any influence over Miss Clarke and suggested that I try the Archbishop of Canterbury. I rang the Archbishop. Two days later I was informed that permission had been granted for me to take my daughter out to supper. '*L'Angleterre,*' she concluded, turning her palms and her eyes to heaven with a smile, '*l'Angleterre, la voilà!*'

Another memorable visit was the one we paid with the US Ambassador and his family to Medayin Saleh, Saudi Arabia's little-visited version of Jordan's Petra. The expedition started badly, for on reaching the Saudi frontier Jenny and I, plus my two youngest children, had to drive most of the 450 miles back to Amman to retrieve our passports, which I had forgotten to collect from the manager of the hotel we had all lodged in at Kerak. In our subsequent non-stop attempt to catch up with the well-organised Americans we ran out of petrol in the middle of nowhere in Saudi Arabia, and our lives were saved only by the chance passage in our empty area of a Saudi Prince in three limousines with petrol to spare. Having eventually caught up with our friends at Tabuk, we all drove on. As we neared our distant objective a colossal rainstorm – unprecedented in a Saudi May – reduced the track to liquid mud, in which we stuck for a long wet night. We reached Medayin Saleh with difficulty the next day, and may well be the only foreigners in history to have seen its Petra-like tombs reflected in a huge lake of rainwater. The ill-fated Damascus-to-Medina railway, incidentally, ran – until Lawrence of Arabia stopped it running in 1916 – through this complex of tombs; and

18 Cricket match against King Hussein's XI. GBP bowling to General Zaid
bin Shakir. The King at the bowler's end.

the pretty little Turkish railway station of red-tiled brick was now the only
solid structure in the area built since the second century AD.

Ma'aloula in south-west Syria was an experience of a different kind. Three
thousand feet up on its ridge of sandstone molars, it is the biggest of three
small villages whose Catholic inhabitants still speak Aramaic, the language
of Christ. The villagers' pale blue houses with woggly balustrades climb on
top of each other up the steep cliffside towards the monastery. Both times
Jenny and I went there the one remaining monk in its monastery put us up
and fed us on what he grew in the monastery garden.

The visit to Amman of the Shah of Iran and his wife, for which King
Hussein gave a party, will remain the only occasion on which Jenny and I have
shaken hands with two heads of state, now dead, and their spouses. Another
royal occasion was the Embassy's cricket match against King Hussein's XI.
I had to put myself on to bowl when the King was at the wicket. He had
absolutely no skill with the bat, so it was vital that only long hops on the leg
were bowled at him, since there was always a chance that he might connect
with one.

After four and a half years in Jordan the Foreign Office accepted my plea
to spend the last two years of my service in the North African Maghreb, the
only part of the Arab world of which I knew nothing, and in September 1975
we prepared for our move to Tunisia.

I was sorry to say goodbye to King Hussein and sundry other Jordanians, notably Mamdouh Bisharat – the only Arab I have ever met who was equally at home in his ancestral farm on the Yarmouk and in a smart country house in England (where he would take the mickey out of the party by leaping into the breakfast room in white shorts, especially if it was raining, with cries of 'Who's for tennis?'). On his farm he milled his own flour in a conical Roman device of black basalt which had been worked for 1,500 years, bathed in a huge Roman swimming pool, and had his butter made by an old lady timelessly rotating milk in a sewn-up bull-skin (which might almost have been Roman too). The only unpleasantness Mamdouh had recently suffered was that the Israeli military, visible on the occupied Golan Heights across the river, occasionally fired shells at his house and had knocked down bits of its upper storey. They compounded this offence by later blowing up another farm of Mamdouh's in the Jordan Valley.

Perhaps the saddest aspect of our move for Jenny was leaving the disabled children in the Amman Rehabilitation Centre, to whom she had become something of an angel of light. I remember vividly the expression on the face of a twelve-year-old boy condemned to lie there for ever on his stomach, while Jenny showed him how to make pots with clay.

Rather than flying home for our leave we chose to drive. Our first stop was inauspicious. My intention was to show Jenny the basalt Roman township of Bosra Eski-Sham in southern Syria, whose present Arab inhabitants dry their cowpats for fuel on fluted columns carved in Roman Emperor Trajan's day. Standing on one such fallen column I was in full flow when I fell off and slipped a disc. While Jenny rushed off to fetch our car I lay on the ground, unable to move an inch and surrounded by citizens of Bosra who clearly took me for another European worse for drink. The painful journey to Damascus is best forgotten. Once there I lay on the kindly British Chargé d'Affaires' sitting-room carpet for four days while an enthusiastic Armenian showed Jenny all sorts of unexpected bits of old Damascus till I was fit to proceed.

We must be almost the last Europeans to have seen the architectural marvels of medieval Hama in the middle of Syria before some were knocked to pieces by President Assad's artillery in 1983, Hama's devout Muslim Brotherhood inhabitants having rebelled against his secular rule. Farther on, the Basilica of St Simeon Stylites kept us drawing it, photographing it and munching its luscious figs for days. I have never understood the attraction (or for that matter the godliness) of sitting on top of a column for years on end as an object of pilgrimage. St Simeon's column has melted down by now to a stump.

The famous underground churches and 'fairy chimneys' of Goremé (in eastern Turkey) were the next essential stop. There is something slightly Walt Disneyish about the whole place – an impression accentuated by the English-language guidebook provided by the Turks. For example, its passage

19 Jenny on St Simeon's shrunken pillar at Qala'at Sima'an in Syria, on the way home in 1976.

on the symbolism of animals in the church frescos includes this: 'BULL. Due to its snorting and potency, the bull comes in first rank in religion.'

The snorting and potency of the Force 10 gale that bulldozed into us two days later, however, when we were camping beneath the fifth-century basilica at Alahan, south of Konia, had nothing Walt Disneyish about it. I had just set my hair on fire in a candle flame when the gale came along and, though it put my hair out, almost blew our tent (and us) into the sky. It was as well that we had climbed the mountain up to the basilica that afternoon, as we wouldn't have had the energy to do so after that memorably sleepless night.

But of all our excitements on the way through Turkey nothing can compare with Termessos – the mountain city 20 miles north of Alanya and the only place in his conquest of the known world that Alexander the Great failed to capture. Why Termessos is not better known is a mystery, for it enjoys the finest site and sight imaginable – a complete 'Greek' city (theatre, agora, temples and all) built of huge blocks of granite on the topmost crag of a mountain range, its theatre on the riding edge at the summit. From it we looked down on the sparkling Mediterranean one way and the blue mountains of middle Turkey the other. All over its precipitous flanks, up which we could scarcely scramble through the scrub, stood at all angles dozens of gigantic sarcophagi with charming figures carved on them. Termessos may be little visited because of the wild and lawless wilderness it leaps up from. 'DANGER – NO CAMPING' said a large notice on an open patch at the foot of it; and certainly during the night we camped beside that notice we dared not light so much as a match, and we talked in whispers. Fortunately none of the bloodthirsty brigands said to inhabit the area showed up.

Baffa in western Anatolia also deserves a mention. We camped by its long freshwater lake mainly because of my long-cherished belief (based on reading it somewhere) that its fish swim up and down its east–west length from one end to the other in accordance with the tides in the distant Mediterranean with which it was connected in prehistory – the fish having retained the habit ever since, thanks to some piscine folk memory. I also understood that at the narrow neck in the lake's middle ingenious Turks could be seen leaning over with a butterfly net and scooping up the fish on their twice-daily passage through it. Alas, there were no Turks doing this, and, as Jenny dispiritingly observed, there has never been any real tide in the Mediterranean anyway.

We crossed the Bosphorus into Macedonia, paid a passing tribute to the unique pebble mosaics in the palace of Alexander the Great and his dad, and reached our next high point in the shape of Meteora. Meteora's early Orthodox monasteries perch magically on the tops of unscaleable pinnacles, described by soulless geologists as 'deltoidal cones', looking down on miniature villages in the plain below. I have no answer to the question posed in the first stanza of a poem this astonishing place inspired in me:

> O sky-high nests of monks where stone trees soar,
> Concrete the bridge, concrete the steps that now
> Domesticate your abstracts in the air.
> Earlier, winched by basket, the holy troubadour
> Sang at God's window bravely enough; but how,
> With no more purchase than a prayer,
> Did the first, the very first, get footing there?

Home, then, to 20 Essex Villas in Kensington. Among the family and friends we visited countrywide was Miss McD (see Chapter 3), not seen by me since 1936 and now living with her photograph albums in the house in Helmsley that Ian had quietly secured for her.

At the risk of name-dropping I will also pay tribute to the other ageing lady whom Jenny and I went on to visit near Helmsley. This was Lady Read, widow of the great Sir Herbert, living then in her cold stone grange at Stonegrave. She had been an affectionate patroness of Jenny's at York University and put us up for the night. Her favourite story about Sir Herbert told of how he had mounted a fierce campaign against the siting of an early-warning station or some such high-tech horror on his beloved North Yorks moors. His campaign to prevent this desecration was of no avail; and when it was built, Sir Herbert went to put a match to it or do something violent to manifest his anger. To his amazement he found it the most ravishing construction imaginable – three silver spheres beautifying the wild landscape beyond belief.

After supper Lady Read told us of another moving incident relating to her husband. She had just been leading us along the draughty corridors of the grange and into freezing rooms full of Sir Herbert's tremendous art collection, much of it given to him by distinguished artists as an act of homage – for he was the Onlie Begetter of a whole modernist movement. She told us how, shortly after Sir Herbert died, the famous Ben Nicholson (who surprised her by proving short, squat and pipe-smoking) had rung the grange doorbell. She showed him round, and when he left and she was closing the front door, he had half turned round and she saw that tears were streaming from his eyes.

She mentioned to us in a throw-away manner that with all those millions of pounds' worth of great paintings in her lonely house she always slept with a revolver under her pillow. Though old and able to walk only thanks to the two wooden stakes driven down her upper legs, she still went regularly all the way to Glasgow to play the viola in the city orchestra. Of such is the kingdom of heaven.

I took Jenny to meet my two brothers, both of them eccentric in their own ways. Ian, formally retired after forty years at Merchiston School but still employed for next to nothing as its odd-job man, was living in two tiny rooms in its disused sanatorium along with his collection of birds' feet, each neatly mounted on a slim rectangle of oak. (One of them, I was enchanted to notice, was labelled 'Domestic Hen'.) Scrap's eccentricity took a different form. During his twenty years on the island of Mull he had given up seeking an income from breeding mink and growing tulip bulbs; but there he was, in his torn old kilt, smoking (non-stop) and drinking (not far off it), supported by his adoring children and about the same number of cows. More eccentric still was an old man called Finlay whom he took me to visit since I had known him in the Persian Gulf as Supervisor of Lighthouses. He now lived in a cottage by the sea, where we found him burying plastic bags of peas in a peat-hag against the impending nuclear cataclysm. One other feature of Scrap's life on Mull deserves recording. He acquired an income of sorts (though he had never in his life, he told me, paid income tax) by buying up abandoned stone sheep-fanks, roofing them with corrugated tin, installing a fridge, and renting them out in summer to 'dentists from England'. When I was doing my sabbatical year at St Antony's my next door neighbour was a young American philosopher – the leading expert, I was told, on Wittgenstein's impenetrable works – and he asked me whether I knew anywhere in Scotland where he could take his wife and children for a cheap holiday. I told him of Scrap's sheep-fanks on Mull. He duly rented one and was reported later to have been so enchanted that he never came back.

CHAPTER 19

Tunisia

WE arrived in December 1975 in Tunis – the least inspiring job in the service but the most inspiring Residence to do it from.* It had been the summer palace of a top Tunisian miscreant, from whom the Bey who then ruled Tunis had confiscated it in 1856, presenting it on permanent loan to the British Consul-General. Though needlessly grand, it is cheaper for HMG to keep it on than to buy or rent something more modest. It stands in 20 acres of garden and was, as a Foreign Office inspector had recently minuted, the only ambassadorial residence in the world with a plough on its inventory. The head gardener spoke no understandable tongue but, according to a note left by my predecessor, 'would be a crook in any language'. We found he was lodging an acquaintance in our hen house for a fee, lighting it with a concealed lead from the kitchen; and we heartlessly replaced his lodger with hens and geese. Various kinds of acacia burst into golden blossom everywhere, concealing our private tennis court. Citrus fruits, pomegranates, quinces, etc., were there for the taking, and magnificent *Schinus* trees enhanced the view of the estate from our cosy back balcony. Beyond them, at the far end of the property, was a little tree-fringed water tank to swim in. This lay alongside the early Consul-General's personal railway station. When the Consul-General wished to cover the 12 miles to the city or the Bey's palace in comfort rather than by carriage with a cavalcade of horsemen, he would send a boy with a paraffin lamp, if it was dark, to stop the passing train in this private railway station, and it would wait until he deigned to mount it. Those were the days! By my time the railway line had been shifted elsewhere.

The house itself, however, has remained unchanged. Its public part was sumptuous. The walls of its huge reception room were covered, Topkapi-fashion, with hand-painted tiles and hung with royal portraits the size of ping-pong tables. They made the grand piano look quite small. The front of the house was approached up a curving jasmine-rich double stairway and then through arches carved in Moorish plasterwork. No wonder Field Marshal Alexander made his headquarters in it in the heady later days of the Second World War, accommodating Winston Churchill and others for a time.

---

* I wrote a short history of the house for *Country Life*, 3 May 1979, pp. 390–92.

I did not take enormously to the Tunisians. They seemed to combine in a dubiously sophisticated way the less attractive aspects of both the Arab and the French character. It is a common Tunisian boast that their country has been the meeting place and beneficiary of successive great civilisations for two thousand years – and a common non-Tunisian riposte that the many civilisations that have passed through have left no surviving trace. There were to be sure individuals whom we found tremendously engaging, though most of them were Tunisian only by circumstance or adoption. A Jewish photographer, Jacques Perez, became an entertaining friend. So did the Hungarian-born doctor-poet Lorand Gaspard, whose impenetrable French poetry won the equivalent in France of the T. S. Eliot Prize. He lived with the French ex-wife of President Bourguiba's Tunisian doctor. She too published poetry.

We also became attached to the gifted young artist (a genuine Tunisian) Fathi ben Zakour, whose abandonment by his attractive Canadian wife, soon after we left, reduced him to life in a mental home for some years. Among the pictures of his that we possess is a huge semi-abstract yellow-and-black falconer on horseback, which he sent from Tunis to Devon as a present for our daughter Finella when she was born.

The most impressive non-Tunisian residents, who became close friends, were the Baron Leo d'Erlanger and his American wife Edwina. He had fallen for her, when she was a *Vogue* model, simply by seeing her exquisite ankles through a ground-level slit from the cross-Channel boat he was in as she disembarked from another. He pursued her ankles for months with bathfuls of flowers until she finally capitulated in New York. They lived near Tunis in a sensational mansion in Sidi Bou Said. It was built using skilful artisans from Morocco by Leo's father, who wrote there his five standard volumes on Arab music. As the son of a wealthy banker Leo had been brought up in grandeur in what is now the French Embassy in London, where the world's most famous pianists had played duets for his father on two grand pianos in the drawing room. But now, in his seventies, he used as his bedroom a tiny attic room at the back of the great house with nothing in it but an iron bed and a wooden chair – presumably to erase his private shame over the indulgences he had enjoyed in his youth. He was amusingly open about his early unsaintliness. I remember him enjoying telling us how his mother had taken him as a young man to tea with a prominent old lady in London. During the visit he needed to blow his nose, and when he pulled his silk handkerchief from his breast pocket out fell all over the lady's rosewood tea table a dozen 'French letters'. He had the most exquisite manners of anyone I have ever met. Among the many great things he had quietly done as an adult was his involvement in, and financing of, the Bouncing Bomb (invented by watching a thrown golfball skipping over a stretch of water), which helped us to defeat the Germans in the Second World War. Edwina asked Jenny and me to write a biography of Leo, and we tape-recorded the pair, as well as interviewing

20 Jenny's drawing of the British Ambassador's Residence at La Marsa.

some of his distinguished friends in France, Switzerland and Britain, including the famous photographer Cecil Beaton and Barnes Wallis, who took the credit for inventing the Bouncing Bomb. But their son Rodolphe vetoed a biography that would include any indication of impropriety on his father's part, so we abandoned the project. Sadly Leo died a year after we left. *The Times* carried the long obituary I wrote.

Even more important, to Jenny especially, was Margareta Ternström, wife of the Swedish Ambassador – a splendid character, an imaginative painter and future godmother of our son.

Tunisia as a country has much to admire but as it has long since been handed over lock, stock and barrel to the tourist industry I will record only a few of its less familiar phenomena. Perhaps the one that engaged us most was a remarkable Berber potter, Juma bint Mohammed, who lived with her peasant husband on a prehistoric hill-top making use of some of its under-ground tombs. She was an independent self-made artist, beautiful as well, and wearing (even when working) full Berber costume held in place with the traditional six-inch silver fibulae on her breast.

Of Tunisia's other crafts the ones we relished most were those that had died out. The mosaics that Tunisia boasts are all Roman or early Christian, more sophisticated than those we had studied in Jordan and Syria – though my preference remains for those in Jordan's Mukhayyat Church, near the mountain from where Moses (for better or worse) viewed the Promised Land.

Most of the old silver jewellery, for which credit does go to Tunisia's

Muslims, had by now been boiled down for remaking to suit vulgar modern tastes; but we collected small pieces all over the place. The *Yid Fatima* (Hand of the Prophet's Daughter) which I acquired for Jenny has hung round her neck ever since, whenever she travels, as a protective talisman against calamity – which was indeed its traditional Islamic function. Rug-making was now practised only in Tunisian government factories, where young girls in rows earned a pittance, and had lost all originality. The weavings we did like were the blankets of sheep and goat hair, nicely urine stained, woven by country-women in northern Tunisia. A retired French army nurse, Henriette Tommy Martin, collected these blankets from them and sold them on their behalf. Henriette became a good friend, and a decade later we took our two children to stay with her in her medieval cottage in Normandy. Shortly afterwards she set off on a year's pilgrimage to Jerusalem on foot, pushing her necessities in a pram. Monasteries and nunneries in Europe, she told us (and she was a devout Catholic), shut their doors on her, but Turkish and Arab peasants always welcomed her in for the night and would take nothing in return except the drawings she did of their children.

We owed to Henriette our acquaintance with a rare human being, Fatma Sleimani. Fatma was a hunchbacked dwarf 3 feet high from El Oued in southern Algeria, who ran single handed not just the El Oued hospital but apparently everything else in the town, as well as her household of a dozen or more. She came to stay for a few days with Henriette, and on arrival in Tunis by bus was mugged by thugs and robbed of every penny. She couldn't even ring Henriette until a passing policeman gave her the cost of a local call. Henriette brought her to supper with us. Physically she barely came up to my waist; psychologically she was ten times my height. A year later we visited her remote desert township in Algeria, where she found space for us to sleep on the crowded roof of her family house. We were properly impressed by the way the whole town seemed to jump to her commands. She died, alas, still young, in the early 1990s, and should be making a sensational difference to the Islamic paradise.

In the craggy sub-deserts of Tunisia's Berber south we came upon things to remember. One strange activity we witnessed was the production of olive oil by four old Berber ladies at Chebika *by hand*. They were kneeling on the edge of a stone water channel in a remote gorge, using the passing water to help them squeeze oil, very slowly, out of pre-hammered olives into empty old tomato tins. All they would accept from us in exchange for a tinful – and it tasted excellent – was a few aspirins.

Some features of Princess Margaret's five-day state visit deserve recording. As a (fairly) devout monarchist I limit myself to instances when her good qualities were uppermost. (Her nightly alcohol consumption made her unattractively grumpy in the mornings.) I took her to see the excavations going on at Old Carthage, where the British team (one of thirteen international groups) was working on the intriguing 8-shaped 'Punic port'. Its leader, Henry Hurst, held up to the Princess the pottery figure of a mother and child, which they had just discovered underneath the Punic (i.e. Phoenician) level. The archaeological fraternity were all dumbfounded, since what could something clearly Byzantine be doing *below* a Punic structure? 'But it's not Byzantine,' said Princess Margaret. 'In Christian art the baby is always off-centre, and this one is in the middle of the mother's lap.' She proved to be dead right. Perhaps she should have been an art historian instead of just the Queen's sister.

We took her on the inescapable duty visit to the birthplace of the once great President Bourguiba at Monastir, accompanied by the Foreign Minister and Bourguiba's American-educated forty-five-year-old son, the only top Tunisian fluent in English. We were sitting, struggling for conversation, in the ghastly dolled-up room Bourguiba had been born in, when someone mentioned the recent 'Watergate' scandal. That was when the Democrat headquarters in Washington had been found bugged, to the embarrassment of President Nixon's Republicans. I remarked diplomatically that Nixon had declared those responsible for the outrage to have been some unidentified plumbers. 'That's right,' said Bourguiba junior, whose English was nearly (but not quite) perfect, 'the plumbers were the buggers.' Princess Margaret glanced momentarily at Jenny with a half-concealed smile. She was less restrained when we got home.

Then there was the vast drinks party for the British community we gave in her honour in our great hall. The Princess behaved splendidly, even when one of our male guests collapsed dead drunk at her feet and had to be carried out. Later, when she was eating scrambled eggs with us in our private quarters, I explained that the man concerned, Captain Bone, was a retired British army PT instructor who had married a Tunisian Jewess on the island of Djerba and had lived there happily with her for thirty years despite the fact that *he* spoke only English, and *she* only Arabic and Hebrew, so they could never talk to each other. 'Ah,' said Princess Margaret, whose separation from Lord Snowdon was soon to be made public, 'if only that had been the case with me and my husband, everything might have been all right.' There were other memorable moments in her visit, and I remain of the school that holds that the mythical fairy-story Princess reflects a genuine if irrational human craving.

We made several trips into Algeria. The reputation of the Algerians for xenophobia, no doubt a reflection of their hostility to French colonialism, struck us as exaggerated. We found many of them entertaining. When we first crossed into the country and were going through the laborious formalities, I approached the banker sitting near Customs and Immigration to obtain some local currency. The old man counted me out very slowly a large pile of small-value notes so worn and torn that I protested no merchant would accept them. 'But *I* will,' he said with a twinkle. 'You buy your vehicle insurance from me and then I put them all back in my safe.' Even the thieves who broke into our locked car two days later in the city of Constantine had a sense of humour of a kind. Not only was our car parked immediately outside both the Province Governor's offices and police headquarters but, having removed the suitcases containing all Jenny's and my clothes for a month, the thieves considerately left our passports and traveller's cheques on the back seat.

The Algerian landscape is magnificent and varied: red-roofed Berber villages twisting down impregnable riding edges from higher elephant-grey peaks; wild flowers in nameless profusion, including acres of blue larkspur in the desert where the nomads' tents were dyed red with pounded red rock from a nearby outcrop; other Bedouin tents in the snow-covered Atlas mountains, their unique weavings roped down to huge carved multi-purpose tent pegs; plenty of brave Roman remains, etc., etc. Of the desert in the far south I remember especially, in the middle of nowhere with flat sand stretching emptily as far as the eye could see, a warning notice on the side of the road which read CAMELS CROSSING. (The now familiar concept of virtual reality had not then been invented.)

I cannot write about Algeria without paying tribute to the young Algerian engineer Jenny met when she later visited Constantine with a visiting childhood friend. She and her friend went from hostelry to hostelry but there was no room in any inn. In the last one this young Algerian, who chanced to be there, said to them that the only thing to do was to drive down to Hippo Regius (as it was called when St Augustine was its Bishop) 30 miles away on the coast and hide for the night on the beach. It was, he said, forbidden on security grounds but it might prove safe. So down they drove under his guidance, and he bade them goodnight as they settled apprehensively into the sand. When they woke at dawn, there to their surprise on the sand dune behind them was the young engineer. He had sat there awake all night to protect them against malevolent passers-by.

On our third trip to Algeria we went with our French poet friends, Lorand and Jacqueline Gaspard, on a sudden determination to explore the famous rock paintings of Tassili in the far south. This involved catching a local aeroplane from Algiers to Djanet, the take-off base for Tassili. The taxi we had ordered failed to turn up, but a kindly Algerian businessman gave us a lift all the way to the airport. There we were informed that no aeroplane went nowadays to Djanet, whatever our tickets might imply. This happened to be the day after the presidential elections in Algeria, and it somewhat restored my morale, as we pushed through the crowd in search of a senior official with whom a protest might be lodged, to see over an avid reader's shoulder the headlines of an Algerian daily. I expected to see in large letters who had won the election, but the words of the main headline were: 'DECLIN DU FOOTBALL BRITANNIQUE'. (Maybe the fortunes of Tottenham Hotspur were of more interest to the Algerians than those of the candidates for the Presidency, since

21   The Tassili mountains in Algeria. Jibreel, their last and only inhabitant, with
our guide Kandoweess, squatting to right of photograph, 1977.

there was only one.) Then suddenly a man in a sort of uniform told us there
was an aeroplane going to Djanet, 'over there, just leaving'.

Looking down at the octopus-like arms of the sand dunes of the Sahara
was a delight; but that cannot be said of our *atterrissage* – down into a rocky
hollow past the crashed remains of a previous flight ... The only way we
could find of getting from the airstrip to Djanet village, where there was a
grass hotel, was on a lorry load of cement bags.

The Tassili mountains themselves soar suddenly out of the desert to 6,000
feet. When we had eventually climbed to the top and crawled into our bedding rolls we were colder than I have ever been in my life. This seemed odd
in the middle of the Sahara; but while our teeth chattered, we were at least
able to gaze out under the full moon at one of the now very rare thousand-
year-old Tarout trees, which are peculiar to this mountain range. This one
was especially sacred, used by the occasional passers-by as a left-luggage office.
Bundles left hanging from its huge branches enjoyed complete safety until (if
ever) their owners returned.

Led by our Touareg guide, whose indigo turban covered everything from
the shoulders up except his eyes, we wandered for five days through Tassili's
sensational picture galleries. Some of the exhibits date back five thousand
years. There are books in plenty for those interested, though they leave many
unanswered questions. How, for instance, did the wheeled chariots, quite often
represented, figure in the perspectives of these ancient artists, for nothing on

wheels could ever have got up here? One uncovenanted benison we enjoyed was meeting by chance the only man, Jibreel, now living on these remote pink mountains. He had nothing but his camel for company, two small tin teapots to keep him nourished and a moufflon horn to carry anything else in. 'Flour? Bread?' I queried, and he roared with laughter as if the idea were comical. (The poem I wrote about Jibreel features in my *A Kind of Kindness*.)

At the end of our week we were about to start the long downward climb to the desert when round a corner came another unexpected apparition. This was a group of twenty young pitch-black Africans. They asked us, politely in French, if this was the way to Libya. They then explained that they were walking to Libya in search of work from their homeland away down in Niger. We had to admit that we were 'strangers here ourselves', and all we could do to help them reach Libya was to point vaguely north-east. For their phenomenal journey they carried nothing except their shoes (in their hands, of course, like all desert walkers) and one big white bundle. This, we discovered, was an enormous long sheet in which they wrapped themselves together at night, hugging each other innocently for warmth. We gave them such food as we had and watched them walking on to where the streets were rumoured to be paved with gold. If they ever got to Libya, they would doubtless be expelled as illegal immigrants. And what then … ? Meeting those courageous young men made our own week's walk seem very small beer.

When we reached Djanet again towards sundown, Jenny and I climbed up its modest acropolis, which was covered with empty broken-down huts, to watch the sun setting over Tassili. Sitting on a pile of stones with our cameras, we were assailed by an armed policeman who rudely told us we had entered a secret military area where photography was forbidden and that he must confiscate our cameras. Our cameras were full of valuable snaps of rock paintings and we pleaded ignorance. 'You must have seen the notice over there,' he snapped, and reached out for our cameras. We said we hadn't seen the notice. 'Well, you'll see it now,' he said, and led us to do so. But there wasn't one. 'I'm sure there used to be one,' he muttered, and sloped off grumpily, without our cameras. It was, I suppose, a good try.

In the village, predictably enough, no one knew whether an aeroplane would be coming the following day (or any day), or where it would be going if it did. But it might, they told us, be worth making our way to the airstrip at dawn in the 'airport bus' to see whether anyone there knew. So at first light we climbed on to the familiar road-making lorry along with thirty other hopeful travellers whose tickets were in many cases for Tamenrasset, a destination in the opposite direction to ours. There was no news at the airstrip. Then, unexpectedly, a small aircraft appeared. The one and only airport official could not say where it would be going next but urged us all to weigh ourselves on the airport scales. Some did, some didn't, and we all rushed forward helter-skelter and climbed aboard (standing room only). As the door shut and the plane rumbled into motion, the pilot looked round from his cabin and announced, as if he had tossed a coin and it had come down heads, that he was heading for Algiers. A loud moan went up from those of our fellow passengers who had hoped it would come down tails, and who were now being flown 500 miles in the wrong direction.

We experienced a rather similar pantomime some months later at Aswan. Jenny had been paying a visit to our Egyptian friends, named Greiss, in Cairo and had heard of two cancellations on a Swan Company boat going up the Nile. I flew instantly to Cairo so that we could take them up. The trip was disrupted when we reached Karnak since violent bloodstained riots were taking place there to coincide with a state visit by President Tito of Yugoslavia and President Sadat of Egypt. Like other tourist boatloads anchored offshore, we were naturally not allowed to land, and our boats steamed on to Aswan. At dawn we all got ourselves to the airport there for the scheduled short flight up-river to the marvels of Abu Simbel with its cliff façades of huge carved pharaohs. Pandemonium developed when it was revealed that all available aircraft had been commandeered to take the two endangered Presidents and their huge retinues back to Cairo from Karnak. All we could do was wait, interminably. After an hour or two one small plane, capable of carrying about a third of the assembled tourists, hove into sight. The wretched airport staff tried fruitlessly to pick and choose but (as at Djanet) everyone surged forward, blue-rinse matrons from America elbowing small Japanese ruthlessly aside. Somehow everyone squeezed into the plane, ignoring the cries of the staff that it was impossibly overloaded. How on earth the pilot risked taking off I cannot imagine – presumably because no one had any baggage.

My final months as a diplomat followed. My four children came out for their last visit to an Embassy of their father's, Jenny staged an exhibition of her batik pictures in Fathi ben Zakour's gallery, and I wrote my final vale-dictory dispatch to the Foreign Secretary. I was not depressed to be leaving the job but sad to say goodbye to such a marvellous Residence and to a number of friends.

We decided to drive home through Sicily, Italy and France, and set sail for Palermo on our third wedding anniversary, 21 September 1977. Tunis had been an undistinguished end to my main career; but that, I noted in my diary, 'should simplify the transition from being a soap-opera Excellency to the realities of insignificance'; and I added to my diary, just before I fell asleep in the good ship *Sardegna*, my favourite lines from the French poet Apollinaire:

> Il est inutile de geindre
> Si l'on acquiert, comme il convient,
> Le sentiment de n'être rien.
> Mais j'ai mis longtemps pour l'atteindre.

Retirement Reversed

CHAPTER 20

Starting Again: Middle East Association and Academia

DRIVING through Sicily, Italy and France is a common enough experience and full of enchantments. I shall limit myself to recording a few of these, of a kind that might not happen to every traveller.

We had been told that the puppet theatres of Sicily still operated in Palermo and should not be missed, since they were not like any other puppet theatres in the world. So we sought one out. The 'theatre' consisted of a tiny shed. Outside its curtained entrance the mother of the puppeteers sat with her knitting to collect any entrance money – until the moment when the two puppeteers drove on their motorbike right through their mother's curtain to where the audience of fourteen sat expectantly on hard benches, and got down to business. The puppets, 4 feet in height, were invisibly operated by strings to pull and rods to push. The programme that night was declared to be '*El Re Ruggiero el gigante*', but the story didn't matter since apparently the performances were always about Christians triumphing over Muslims. This one, brilliantly done and funny, worked up to the slaughter by the hero of ten enemies in ten different ways, one of them being cut in half vertically to the applause of the audience. After the show was over we invited ourselves behind stage and were shown how it was all done. Each puppet, incidentally, weighed more than a stone. Puppet shows I have seen in England, for example at Little Angel, may be more sophisticated but are nothing like such fun. Anyone who goes to Palermo should seek out a puppet theatre, if any still survive.

In the middle of Sicily can be found the stupendous but seldom visited fourth-century Roman mosaics at Piazza Armerina, the liveliest and most imaginative of all those Jenny and I examined round the Mediterranean; here were slaves pushing ostriches up the gangplank of a ship, a children's circus race, women in bikinis, and so on.

There is so much genuinely worth seeing in Sicily that I would advise *against* visiting the Convento dei Capucini in Palermo. In its catacombs the mummified citizens, dating from towards the end of the nineteenth century, are propped in serried ranks to be visited on Sundays by tipping the custodian monks. Many of the grinning figures are still in their clothes, their facial skin still clinging to their cheekbones. The macabre practice of stacking the dead like this was still going on in the twentieth century. If the Sicilian public still approve of so revolting an exhibition no wonder the Mafia there can get away with murder.

The only other passage in my Sicilian diary that I will draw upon does the Sicilians, or at least a village just outside Taormina in the island's north-east corner, more credit. We had been encouraged by Elizabeth Monroe to descend on her friend Daphne, living in a fine house there. The house had been built around 1900 by her uncle, who had purchased a whole stretch of hilly landscape for £17 and had filled the house with his remarkable collection of objets d'art. In 1940, when Mussolini declared war on us, he had had to catch the last transport out of Sicily to escape internment, abandoning everything. When the war ended five years later and he was living in England, the villagers sent a plea to Britain's Foreign Secretary that the old man's return to Taormina was 'indispensable'. So he returned. He found his house in immaculate condition with all his treasured objects and furnishings exactly where he had left them when he fled in 1940. The devoted villagers had removed them all from his house and hidden them in their cellars for five years to save them from being looted by German soldiers. When they learnt that their plea for the old man's return was to succeed, they put them all back.

One of Daphne's many splendid stories of her life in Sicily concerned the Romanian archaeologist with whom she had worked near Taormina. He had found the curious local dialect easily understandable to a Romanian like himself, and he attributed this without hesitation to the fact that the Roman legionaries posted there two millennia previously were recruited in the lower Danube valley! From her balcony, where we sat entranced at sundown listening to her (as had done, we learnt, many distinguished admirers such as Bertrand Russell), we could look across at the smoking cone of Etna. In the garden of our Devon house is a chunk of the colourful lava which we carried down, still hot, from the lip of the crater the following day. (Etna erupted catastrophically not long after our visit.)

Southern Italy itself, which we then drove through, cannot present anything more horrific than Pompeii. I am still haunted by the staring eye-sockets of those mummified victims engulfed in boiling lava as they (and their pet dogs) ran vainly for safety in AD 79. Their wall frescos, incidentally, show that the Pompeian painters had mastered perspective long before anyone else.

Young men on motorbikes polluted the splendid Umbrian towns we stopped in next (including Spoleto, where Michael Adams lived for three years and wrote an excellent book on Umbria). On all the Umbrian hill-tops the Middle Ages push up proudly into the sunlight. But how the inhabitants of any of them found either the time or the vigour to keep on building or rebuilding so beautifully when they were constantly being attacked by their immediate neighbours (let alone by Germans, Popes or anyone else with soldiers to spare) is a mystery. All middle Italy provokes the disturbing question of whether great art flourishes only in cultures dangerously self-assured, intolerant and given to killing everybody on the next hill-top. How is it that a people who paid such homage to personality, who valued lifestyle above everything, valued life itself – or at least the life of other people – so little?

We wandered on through the magic of the Quattrocentro, etc. Despite the staggering achievements of the Renaissance we both shared a preference for the 'simplicities' of the Romanesque. Nothing man-made, however, could match the magic of the Lower Alps when we finally drove over them, freshly snow-covered and sparkling in the sun.

As for Paris, our stay in that incomparable capital vouchsafed two contrasting experiences of French hospitality. The first was the Hôtel du Dragon, a Left Bank hostelry recommended to us by Jacques Perez in Tunis. It turned out to be a low-class brothel. So either it had gone distinctly downmarket or else Jacques had, as often, been mischievously teasing us. They found, however, a decent enough room for us. The second experience was lunching with Gaston Palewski and his wife, the Duc de Talleyrand's daughter, in their magnificent eighteenth-century chateau 20 miles south of Paris. Leo d'Erlanger, a close friend of Palewski, had arranged for us to contact him for assistance in compiling our proposed biography of Leo. Hence the invitation to lunch. Madame la Duchesse was the archetypal French aristocrat, ravishingly beautiful at sixty, ostensibly frail and gentle, but firmly conscious of the rights and duties of the French nobility. We were by no means the only guests and certainly the least distinguished but were treated with impeccable courtesy. The whole occasion was a marked contrast to the Hôtel du Dragon. In some ways the Hôtel du Dragon was more fun.

Soon after returning to England I flew to Basle to interview another of Leo's friends. Switzerland is much too tidy to appeal to me, and what I remember most of my visit is reading in bed a comment by the historian Stewart Perowne on the annual Palio (horse race) in Siena, which Jenny and I had just missed. 'If', he remarks, 'anything is still left remarkable under the visited moon, here in Siena it is man himself.' A man who could think of 'visited' (instead of 'visiting', as in *Antony and Cleopatra*) writes the witty sort of English that is as far above me as the visited moon itself.

Back at 20 Essex Villas, I started the retirement job I had unexpectedly been offered with the Middle East Association in St James's, bearing the portentous title of Director General. At weekends Jenny and I scoured England for somewhere to settle until a chance conversation led us to Bradridge House, a Regency hunting lodge near Totnes in Devon.

Our (brief) beautiful friendship with Spike Milligan, of *The Goon Show* and other fame, deserves a mention. He had written to me in Tunis about his proposed visit to Tunisia's 'Mareth Line' with a soldier friend who had won a posthumous VC there in 1943 and who, being still very much alive, wanted to see just where this Milliganesque distinction had befallen him. The visit never came off but Spike invited us to supper in Soho on our return. Of the many inconsequential stories he poured out over the claret I will record only one of his Irish ones. Spike had arrived at some country hotel in Cork and the porter helping with his bags had called out, 'Follow me, sir, I'll be right behind you.' When Spike came to supper some weeks later at 20 Essex Villas he told us all the same stories over again. This could hardly go on for ever and our beautiful friendship petered out.

While we waited excitedly for the agents to complete our house deal for Bradridge and for Jenny to complete our expected baby (which happened in fact almost simultaneously) we attended meetings in London of the Poetry Society and of the British Rug and Textile Society. The latter's founder, Jenny Housego, had invited me on to its committee under the mistaken impression that I knew a lot about Oriental rugs. Jenny (my one) had become increasingly enthusiastic about both carpets and poetry – a combination that had aroused my own enthusiasm ever since reading Flecker's *Hassan* when I was at school. Thus:

CALIPH: What a man you are for poetry and carpets, Hassan of my heart! When you tread on a carpet you drop your eyes to earth to catch the pattern; and when you hear a poem you raise your eyes to heaven to catch the tune. Whoever saw a confectioner like this?

HASSAN: ... Dost thou not know what crowds gather to hear the epic of Antari sung in the streets at evening? I have seen cobblers weep and butchers bury their great faces in their hands.

CALIPH: Ah, if ever there shall arise a nation whose people have forgotten poetry or whose poets have forgotten the people, though they send their ships round Taprobane and their armies across the hills of Hindustan, though their city be greater than Babylon of old, though they mine a league into the earth or mount to the stars on wings, what of them?

HASSAN: They shall be a dark patch upon the world.

Romantic Georgian soda water no doubt, but it still moves me.

If meetings of the Poetry Society did not noticeably improve the poetry I wrote myself, a special reward at one of them was Douglas Dunn reading *his*. His poem 'The Concert' in his collection *Love or Nothing* (beginning 'The last piano in the world is about to be played') is full of marvellously comic images that became part of our private language.

On 10 July the world was enriched by the arrival of Finella. I had completed the cradle I was making for her out of old Sudan mahogany just twenty-four hours before it was needed. Michael Adams agreed to be her godfather.

I did nothing so creative in the Middle East Association. The job called for at least a working knowledge of business economics, and I had very little. But if I left no impression on the MEA, the three 'missions' I carried out on its behalf certainly left impressions on *me*. These were successively to Libya, Saudi Arabia and the Sudan.

Two incidents in Libya, where I accompanied Viscount Limerick, the chairman of the Council for Middle East Trade, delighted me. One occurred when our host the Ambassador took us at my request to the famous Karamanli mosque in Tripoli, which it had been impossible for me to get into during my time there in the war. We had of course to take our shoes off as Islamic proprieties require on entering; and to my dismay Lord Limerick said he would rather stay outside. Eventually we persuaded him to join us. He took his shoes off reluctantly, disclosing large, unaristocratic holes in the toes of his socks. I comforted him by pointing to the usual plebeian holes in mine.

The other enjoyable incident was this. We were denied access to President Qaddhafi himself (dictator of Libya since his 1969 revolution against the Senussi monarchy, and author of the notorious *Green Book* on the proper way to run a socialist Arab state) but were received by sundry ministers. They all seemed remarkably sensible, particularly the key Minister of Oil. 'Of course,' he declared, 'we're all terribly loyal to Qaddhafi. It's just a pity his *Green Book* is such rubbish.'

What I remember most from my mission to Saudi Arabia was the dinner party in Jiddah to which our Ambassador took me. Other guests were the President of Aramco (the huge oil company), the Chairman of the First City Bank of New York, and suchlike other top American tycoons. Our host was a Saudi businessman whose immigrant father had set the family up by attaching himself to King Ibn Saud as his personal doctor. Saudi Arabia, as everyone knows, forcibly prohibits and punishes the consumption of alcohol. But there is one law for ordinary people and another for the very rich; and I have never seen anywhere else such quantities of Scotch and bourbon as were consumed by the guests and by our Muslim host in this house. After dinner our host climbed on a box in a corner and addressed all those American tycoons on the way the world's finances should be managed. I watched them all goggling spellbound as they listened to this man who, so one of them privily observed to me, 'had only come down out of the trees a short time before'.

As for the Sudan, its condition thirty years after we had left it to its independence was desperately run-down and saddening. Most of my old friends were dead, and the young scarcely seemed to notice the squalor. I was cheered, however, in Wad Medani (my first post in 1946) when taken to breakfast in what had once been the British Club. A very old man sitting in the garden rose when I went in, came towards me and said, '*Sabah al-kheir* [good morning], Mr Balfour Paul.' I record the incident simply because, when he revealed his identity, I recognised him as a very successful merchant who had been old when I had had dealings with him thirty years before and who was totally illiterate. I think he had forgotten *nothing* in his ninety years. So much for the value of education! The next instructive experience was spending two days with the closest of my old Sudanese friends, Mohammad Ahmad Abu Sinn. He no longer ran the Rufa'a District as the paramount chief of the Shukria tribe, democracy having replaced him with a twenty-three-year-old 'administrator' from Khartoum, but the people still venerated him. He assembled in his courtyard one evening a mass of citizens who might have remembered my presence in 1947/48. What pleased me most in the ensuing conversation was the following. The news had just broken of the mass suicide of fifty American 'groupies' in Guyana; and while we were on the subject I asked the assembled Sudanese whether there was much suicide in their own (desperately impoverished) country. There was no response, until someone at the back said, 'I believe there was a woman who killed herself in 1924.'

Finally there was a morning in Khartoum when I was shown round its newly designed museum by the enthusiastic Nubian archaeologist in charge. His special treasures were the frescos from fifth-century Nubian churches. With delight he pointed to one where black, brown and whitish peasants were working together in a palm garden as equals, and to another where a white Virgin Mary was smiling arm in arm with a black princess. This splendid Muslim was smashed up in a car crash a year later.

Settling into Bradridge was an invigorating experience. I was in fact commuting by the week to the Middle East Association (there was a posh flat for me above the shop), leaving Jenny to cope with everything. It meant catching a hideously early train from Totnes on Monday mornings, Jenny struggling up to drive me to the station in her nightie. On one of these helter-skelter mornings I learnt one of the benefits of living in Devon. We reached Totnes station in a snowstorm to see the train just pulling out. Dashing across the footbridge I prevailed on the kindly stationmaster to stop the train and let me get on. Then, through the window and the falling snow, I caught sight of Jenny rushing over the footbridge in her white nightie waving my forgotten umbrella. The stationmaster, obviously enchanted by this unusual apparition, withdrew the whistle from his mouth until Jenny had pushed the umbrella through my window. Even the Consul-General in Tunis at his private railway station (see p. 240) could hardly have been more courteously treated.

Among those who came to stay at Bradridge was the painter Sheila Shewbridge, part owner and now guardian of Jenny's parrot. She was distinctly 'fey' but deserves tribute for the following reason. Living in Wimbledon, she had been properly revolted by the obscenity of the graffiti and drawings covering its much-used railway bridge. So every night in the small hours, when nobody was about, she took huge cans of paint and little by little erased the obscenities and painted in their place large pictures of rats dancing in a rats' ballroom. She took care never to be seen doing it, but as the days passed she began to find expensive tins of paint of the colours she was using deposited anonymously in the grass by the bridge. Some time after this huge labour of love was completed and there were jovial rats waltzing all over the bridge, the secret somehow leaked out and was written up as a lead story in the press.

We had a holiday in northern Spain in February 1979, and a curious experience in the village of Guadalupe. The latter's steep, cobbled and flowery streets converge upwards and are crowned by a glorious monastery whose Franciscan monks take in guests. They took us in and gave us trout for supper. Having supped on one, I thought at 2 a.m. that I was dying. Between vomits I groaned Jenny awake. Her nostrums for food poisoning were in our car outside the monastery, whose only gate was firmly locked. Jenny groped her way in pitch dark along the stone corridors in her nightie and banged on the Abbot's bedroom door – presenting him with the sort of apparition that Abbots (since *Carmina Burana*) must surely expect to be spared (or only dream about). But the good man opened up. A key was found for the huge monastery door, and my life was saved.

In October 1979, after two years in the Middle East Association, I decided to resign. There was the prospect of a job at Exeter University. A visit (with Jenny and Finella) to the unorthodox head of its Arab and Islamic Department proved fruitful. Professor Mohammad Shaban instantly attracted me. He was the only Egyptian in history to have married a girl from the Shetland Islands, and he added to his record of unorthodoxy by giving me a Research Fellowship in the Centre for Arab Gulf Studies, which he was in the process of setting up. The fact that he spent much of the next three months sitting in my room exchanging 'funny stories' is, oddly enough, no comment on his scholarship. For he was one of those who do not need sleep and his routine was to work at home all night and spend the day working (or talking) in his department. His wife Bessie told me they met only at drinks time, when Shaban would consume half a bottle of Scotch before sitting down to work till dawn. He had been a British subject for twelve years but remained 101 per cent Egyptian. The debt I owe him is enormous. His end was not uncharacteristic. He had to take endless pills to stave off sundry painful afflictions; and during a visit to his family in Egypt in 1994 he said to Bessie one evening, 'I can't stand taking all these pills any more.' So he threw them away then and there, rang up his friend the ruler of Sharjah to say goodbye, and was dead by the morning.

As Chairman of the Council of the Amman Institute of Archaeology I attended a conference on Jordan's past organised by Crown Prince Hassan in his old college (Christchurch) at Oxford. I mention it simply because of a sensational lecture, unlikely to find its way into print, by an old friend of mine from Beirut. This was the unorthodox Armenian archaeologist Kalayan, who, when I was in Beirut, was charged by the Lebanese government with the restoration single handed of thirty-two important Graeco-Roman sites in Lebanon. Two top British archaeologists sent out to see what he was doing found him to their horror sawing in half a fluted marble column at Tyre to facilitate (he explained) his task of reconstruction. By the time they had accompanied him round another dozen of his thirty-two sites they had reached the unexpected conclusion (so they told me) that he was, quite simply, a genius. So I thought his lecture at Oxford would be interesting. It was more than that. For he disclosed his absolute conviction, based on a degree in mathematics and a study of Vitruvius, that the harmonic proportions of all Greek and Roman temples are reducible to simple mathematical ratios, each classical god having his own formula, for example $\sqrt{12}/\sqrt{\pi}$ for Zeus. The correct proportions were known, he insisted, to all classical architects and priests, and no priest would serve in a temple wrongly proportioned for its god. Kalayan's personal history was as remarkable as his architectural convictions. During the Turkish massacre of Armenians in Cilicia in 1915 his father was slaughtered. His mother, allowed to survive only because she was a dressmaker employed by the wives of Turkish officers, escaped with her baby to Aleppo, got him schooled, and here he was, sixty years later, lecturing in Oxford University. Without persecution, one may ask, would the world's minority peoples produce such a disproportionate number of geniuses?

In December of the same year (1979) my last offspring, Hamish, made his impatient entry into the world a month ahead of schedule. The following year, thanks to Jenny's mother babysitting, we were able to fly off to New York to stay with Tony Parsons (then Our Man in the UN) and Sheila. The New World proved quite a shock to this ageing representative of the old one. Here are a few extracts from my diary:

> The point about this Land of the Free is that the visitor finds himself uncertain whether to love it or hate it, to open his arms in admiration or to recoil in distaste. The even odder point is that he may find himself doing both simultaneously. Americans are all things that the British are not, despite their widespread and apparently genuine pride in their Anglo-Saxon origins. You could of course argue that what makes them as a nation so different from us is their ethnic diversity. But that won't quite do, since these ethnic groups, so far from merging to produce a new identity, remain singularly isolated from each other. New York's Chinatown, Little Italy, Harlem, etc. are worlds apart from society's mainstream. Its Jews, though rich and powerful, are widely disliked (partly no doubt for that reason). Yet the pride in being American is deeply rooted and seems to be shared by each and every group. Or consider the physical structure of New York. The clutch of soaring skyscrapers in Manhattan is singularly beautiful, while Fifth Avenue and Madison Avenue for all their classy reputation are as undistinguished architecturally as Pimlico.

But New York's surprises pursued us everywhere. In Chinatown, where the Chinese lifestyle seems preserved intact and the shops are full of dried seahorses and black fungus, Jenny and I flopped into a Chinese teashop desperate for a cup of Chinese tea, and all that they could offer us was a Tetley's teabag. Perhaps the biggest of all New York's surprises (its stupendous museums cannot be called surprises) was SoHo, where we were taken by Margareta Ternstrom, whose husband was now number two in Sweden's UN delegation. SoHo is a substantial area near the river. It consists of rectilinear streets of joined-up six-storey warehouses built in the nineteenth century by successful manufacturers of exports and importers of hardware, but abandoned now that trade follows a different channel. These huge solid structures had been imaginatively converted into avant-garde art galleries and the like, their outsides painted brick-red, blue or ochre and laddered all over with old iron fire escapes wriggling down like fork lightning. One 'warehouse' we went into housed a spoof exhibition entitled 'The Archaeology of SoHo', the exhibits (displayed on upturned rubbish skips) consisting of tear-off beer-can openers, flattened fruit tins, old sparking plugs sprayed with gilt, etc., all bearing appropriate spoof labels, and ending up with a hilarious 'sales counter'. Altogether a tribute to Americans.

As for Tony Parsons and the UN, the best of many stories he told us was of the day he first exercised a British veto on a Security Council resolution. As he sat down again in some embarrassment, his Soviet colleague (who sat next to him) whispered: 'Don't worry, Tony. It's like adultery – rather shaming the first time but great fun when you get used to it.' Tony burst out laughing and was caught doing so by the world's TV cameras, thus jeopardising (he feared) the rest of his career. A debate we attended in the General Assembly seemed to confirm Sheila's description of it as the 'UN General Wastepaper-basket'.

I conclude these random reflections on New York by recording that Margareta Ternström was able, being herself a professional painter, to take us into the heart of Harlem to visit her black artist friends in their modest headquarters. They couldn't have been friendlier. The white–black confrontation throughout the US is, to be sure, visibly easing. (Not that we are much less racist, for different reasons, in England.)

Being shown round New York by Margareta, who clearly loved it, was bound to be stimulating. Washington, by contrast, proved flat and unlovable. The Mall itself is certainly an impressive stretch of the Higher Kulchur, custom-built and conscious of it, with the Capitol like a huge eggcup at one end and a meaningless great monolith at the other. Philadelphia, our next stop, is memorable mainly because our English hostess drove us out of its capitalist bravura westwards into the country of the conspicuously non-capitalist Amish. The Amish are not a mere bunch of groupies but 100,000 breakaway Quakers living a doggedly seventeenth-century life in a self-contained county. No cars, no electricity, no posh hotels – just wooden houses and barns and cornfields, between which in homespun clothing they move around in horse-drawn buggies. The men wear long beards when married, but moustaches are outlawed as smacking of militarism. So too are buttons. The only thing that struck me as faintly improper (apart from naming their capital town 'Intercourse') is that they all seemed to cultivate tobacco. Its use is forbidden to themselves but they are happy to exploit the moral weakness of the rest of America. The rest of America has, however, the moral strength to leave the Amish in peace.

We had travelled for hours and hours (New York, Washington, Philadelphia) in the comfortable trains used only by the few Americans who do not possess several large automobiles. Yet a glance at a map showed that all we had covered was the equivalent of one square centimetre of a sheet of A3. The sheer immensity of their country, quite apart from its power in the world, must, I felt then, be a source of pride to its citizens – though whether it is still a source of universal pride since the 'imperialist' invasion of Iraq in 2003 must be less certain. As for an ignorant, insular-minded visitor like me, well, I had swallowed with enjoyment the odd concoctions of one square centimetre but how would my digestion cope if faced with the spicey strangenesses of the whole A3?

CHAPTER 21

More Excursions and Occasional Alarms (Yemen, Dubai, Oman)

BACK in the cosiness of Devon, Finella and Hamish were growing. They had not yet reached the wonderfullest age for children, which as every parent knows is from six to ten – old enough to question intelligently but not yet intelligent enough to reject their parents' replies. They still trust them, or so parents like to believe. Disenchantment, when it comes, is doubtless inevitable and right but no less disturbing for both parties.

A series of family weddings took place. At Bradridge, Cati (now a nurse) married Malcolm Ramsay, a Scottish Presbyterian minister, and Ann, a museum curator, married Bedford archivist James Collett-White. We attended Scottish weddings of Scrap's daughters. Jamie Howard, the husband of his third daughter Philly, had just taken over the management of his parents' almost uninhabited island of Ulva, off the coast of Mull. One enchanting outcome occurred twelve years later when Finella sailed that way in the *Eye of the Wind* on the Tall Ships race, and Philly, having somehow heard of this, rowed out from Gometra – a small island next to Ulva – and shouted for Finella, whom she had not met since the day Finella had been her bridesmaid. The crew on deck, who knew her only as 'Froggy', shouted back that there was no one called Finella on the *Eye of the Wind*. Fortunately Finella overheard, ran up on deck and had a spirited conversation, *altissimo voce*, across the foaming deep with her enterprising cousin. Alison was later to marry Ray Edwards, a Welsh landscape architect, but at this time was studying the violin in Prague on a British Council bursary. When we paid her a visit we stayed with our Ambassador, an old friend. In his historic Residence on the citadel he lodged us in the very room where Mozart had composed several sonatas!

I learnt many new things at Bradridge. Christine Raikes, a very old lady living in a small part of an old mill-house in South Brent, was an especial friend of Jenny's. The pictures she painted of old toll-houses in Devon now hang in Dartington Hall. Riddled shortly after with cancer, she was dragged for the first time in her life to hospital, in Plymouth. Deep ray treatment there sent her almost blind, whereupon (being bored) she ran away from hospital and somehow found her way home. Jenny visited her there. She was lying on her cramped sofa bed, and she held up a large piece of paper on which she had scrawled something she had just heard on the radio she was clutching. It read, 'Life is too serious not to be taken lightly.' She was eventually moved to a hospice, where we found her on the day before she died drawing the different-shaped chimney pots that were all she could see from her bedroom window.

Another source of wisdom at Bradridge was the splendid stonemason (later given an award by the Prince of Wales) who did some jobs for us. He taught me to lay bricks and pavements and the philosophy that went with it, or with him. Meanwhile, Patricia Beer, then Writer in Residence at Exeter University, at whose feet I sat, was teaching me much about poetry. These two experiences produced a poem in Syllabics about the stonemason, which ends admiringly thus:

> Enough
> for this man that his skill had
> truth by the forelock. In his
> tough credo, whatever was
> indisputably valid
> was also good for a laugh.

Patricia was the most amusing conversationalist I have ever met, and she and her husband Damian became close friends. She died, alas, in 2003.

We had ideas of going to live in France for a year so that our children would pick up its heavenly language effortlessly. But all we did was to take them there repeatedly on holiday. ('Not *another* cathedral, Mummy?') I will record only my envy of a country so large that it is easy to get happily lost in it, and so full of marvellous objects that almost any village church contains dusty unregarded works of art that in Britain would be the centrepieces of city museums. On one such expedition we stayed at Retournac in the Auvergne with Dominic de Grünne, a polymath Belgian count met on a tour of the Yemen run by the travel company Serenissima. He had built himself a handsome house next door to his elder brother's bigger one. In the large 'garden' round his house he allowed, apart from wild roses, only teasels in which birds came to drink the dew collected in their bracts.

From very near Dominic's house Robert Louis Stevenson started out on his famous *Travels with a Donkey*. We hadn't time to follow in his donkey-steps; but on a later visit to southern France, Finella and Hamish ended a two-day *randonné* on horseback in the very village (St-Jean-de-Gard), and possibly in the very hostelry, where RLS finished *his* and where his donkey died.

Having just mentioned the Yemen I will say something of the four visits Jenny and I paid to that remarkable, and in those days almost unknown, country. North Yemen was in the early 1980s just beginning to admit foreigners in the wake of the revolution in 1964 that overthrew the xenophobe Imam. South Yemen, previously Britain's Aden Protectorate and by this time an independent Marxist state, was even less open to outsiders. I was eager to see something of the only Arab country I had never entered, and Jenny and I had been casting around for the cheapest way of contriving this, when one morning Professor Shaban came into my room and unexpectedly said, 'I'd like you to organise a symposium on the two Yemens. Would you be willing to go out and talk to the two governments?' Would I *not*? So off I went, and Jenny with me, in August 1982. Sana'a has since those days become a tourist mecca but it was then a revelation, and the medieval building in the old city where Rosalind Wade, my Social Secretary in Baghdad and now an archaeologist, lodged us was a splendid introduction. The top floors of such buildings are traditionally used by the owners for entertaining male friends and chewing *qat* (the slightly intoxicant leafage of a local shrub, chewed remorselessly by all male Yemenis). And beautiful they are – unevenly plastered walls and ceilings, coloured glass filling the top semicircles of the ogival windows, window panes of solid alabaster in the older houses, embroidered mattresses and cushions to recline on, and some sort of low table in the middle for hubble-bubbles, brass candlesticks, etc. Ibn Khaldun in the thirteenth century described Sana'a as the cleanest city in the Arab world. It was now the dirtiest. But no one minded the rubbish; nor did we, for there is so much above rubbish level to rivet the eye. The expert on Sana'a architecture, a Cambridge professor, told us that the city would soon be floating on its own sewage as that Western invention, the water closet, progressively replaces the faultless traditional system. Under the latter, excreta simply passed down a defined 'long drop' into a stone box at street level. The proceeds were collected in carts daily, dried in the sun outside the town, and then spread in the gardens scattered among the town's tall residential blocks to fertilise vegetables. These were then eaten by the residents, and the whole circular process began all over again. No way had apparently been discovered of disposing of Sana'a's modern sewage since the water table is too near the surface.

As for North Yemen as a whole – the only Arab country never to have been colonised, except briefly by the Ottoman Turks – it was good to find oneself among Arabs with no post-colonial hang-ups, content to chew their *qat*, stroll around with their curved daggers at their waists, and think themselves the finest people in the world.

In the swimming pool of a classy hotel in Sana'a that we gatecrashed we ran into, or swam into, John Hemming, then head of the Royal Geographical Society, Amazon explorer, expert on Inca architecture and much else besides. We teamed up with him and his wife Sukey to explore the north of the country by taxi. We drove down mountains as precipitous as Peru's Machu Picchu on the fine road just completed by thousands of suffering Chinese (and financed by China). Beside it we passed a number of unexpected small pagodas. Our taxi-driver explained that these had been constructed by the Chinese workforce to commemorate those of their fellow workers who had

22 Sana'a medina, Yemen.

been shot by concealed Yemeni tribesmen for presuming to drive a road through mountains that the tribes had kept the world out of for centuries. An oddity of a more engaging kind was revealed in a mountain village to which we had diverted on our way back. Climbing the vertical crag to what had once been an impregnable fort and was now the village gaol, Jenny and John were hallooed at by a prisoner looking down from his barred window, who invited them to come and have tea with him. On reaching the top they found their way into the prison, where the prisoner ceremoniously served them (along with the only visible warder, who also received an invitation) with mint tea in his cell – not the sort of experience likely to be enjoyed by those rambling near Princetown prison on Dartmoor.

A less agreeable incident took place when a Yemeni tried to break through the narrow window of the upstairs bedroom in a borrowed house in Sana'a where Jenny and Rosalind were sleeping. He was repulsed only by their poking a handy broomstick at him through the window. He tried again the following night, with the same result and hopefully with a broken leg from being broomsticked right off the top of his ladder. (This took place when I was down in Aden seeing anyone in its government or university who had obtained permission under the Anti-Fraternisation Law to speak to me.)

This first visit to Yemen sparked off Jenny's fascination with indigo. On her return to UK her mentor, the renowned dye-expert Susan Bosence, hearing from Jenny that the ancient indigo industry of Yemen was dying out, urged her to return (and obtained the necessary funding) and record it. She did so – and never looked back. It was to result in a PhD and book on *Indigo in the Arab World*, followed by a volume, *Indigo*, commissioned by the British Museum Press, on indigo throughout the whole world, which sold in thousands.

On one of our visits to Yemen, we wanted, as part of these indigo researches, to get to al-Beidha, a remote town in the south-east corner. The only way of getting there was in a *mushterika*, a shared taxi. These conveyances (almost all Peugeots) had to be full to the limit before they would set off. 'Full' meant three passengers in front, four in the back and several in the boot. So we had quite a wait in the village where the *mushterika* eventually set off from. A man in nothing but a loincloth and a dagger sitting by – indeed *on* – my right thigh turned to me after an hour or so of deafening general conversation with everyone else and said (in Arabic), 'That was a splendid affair at Heathrow last night – 25 million pounds of gold stolen without spilling a drop of blood!' (I hadn't, as he had, been listening to the BBC Arabic news on which this spectacular robbery had featured.) An hour or so later, when the taxi stopped in the middle of nowhere for everyone to have a pee and Jenny and I were doing so behind a convenient rock, the rough-looking tribesman in one of the front seats started doing rifle practice in our direction. He scored, fortunately, no direct hits, but it was an alarming experience. Finally, when we reached al-Beidha, we were emphatically told by a policeman that foreigners like us were not permitted to spend the night anywhere in the town because it wasn't safe for them. Our problem was solved only by the arrival on the scene of a more helpful policeman, who escorted us to the town gaol (a very substantial old Turkish fort) and put us in a cell three floors up, turning out the previous occupant in his shackles to make way for us, and then locking the door 'for our safety'. There was nothing in the cell but two iron bed frames and no form of sanitation. There were in fact basins at each corner of the central stairway but we couldn't get there, and in any case they were all blocked and running over. But there was a fine view of the old town from our window, and we were kindly let out by the gaoler in the morning. We made use of this free accommodation for two nights, and in daytime we suffered nothing worse then being stoned by children who had seen us obvious infidels entering the house of a Muslim citizen (actually a friendly indigo-dyer).

Another unusual, and in its own way more humbling, experience befell us on a bus journey from the dusty coast at Zabid (a marvellous relic of medieval architecture) back to Sana'a, 7,000 feet up. After half an hour or so we saw a man in a white *gallabiya* 100 yards ahead signalling to the driver to stop. He stopped, exchanged a few words with the shrouded figure, then took off his turban and carried it upside down round the bus, collecting in it small coins from all the passengers except Jenny and me. He then emptied the collection into the hands of the man on the road who, we now realised, was not a would-be passenger but a blind old man. Jenny and I were not invited to contribute since, as infidels, we were not required to give alms to the poor. We felt distinctly less 'superior' as the bus drove on.

I would not wish to give the impression that the Yemenis were unfriendly – quite the reverse. The first time we visited the Queen of Sheba's old capital at Marib in the far east of the country, close to the site of her famous dam, we were invited by the wife of an antiquities guardian to spend the night as her guests. On her cottage's flat roof there was just room for us to sleep alongside her most recent baby, which was cradled in a goatskin hung from two small tripods and ingeniously protected from the millions of mosquitoes. The mosquitoes were obliged to concentrate on Jenny and me – after we had been fed by our hostess with pancakes and honey.

Incidentally, 1,400 years after the Queen of Sheba's death her fame was still extensive even in the most far flung parts of the Middle East. In 1941 a Sudanese soldier in Abyssinia told me how the hoopoe got its crown. This happened, so he confidently declared, when the Queen of Sheba foregathered with King Solomon of the Jews in the desert midway between their capitals. The sun was at its hottest, so the Queen summoned all the hoopoes from far and wide to flutter above their heads in a solid cloud and shade them. For this service they were rewarded with crowns of golden feathers. I wonder how she would have rewarded the ruler of Abu Dhabi, whose crown is already gold, for financing the construction of a vast new dam a mile upstream from Marib. Jenny and I must have been among the last to walk around the still-visible layout of the area irrigated by the Queen's own amazing dam, built in the fifth century BC.

We were also among the last to witness indigo dyeing in Zabid. This had been going on there since the Queen of Sheba's day or earlier, and in 1964 there were still about 150 indigo factories in this town. Then came the 'modernising' revolution; and twenty years later there were only two left. On our third and last visit in the 1990s there was only one. On that occasion the young owner, who had become quite a friend, insisted on our sharing lunch on the cluttered floor of the workshop with him and his workers. The latter – including the two old men who sat on their hunkers all day and every day beating the dyed cloth with heavy great mallets to make it shiny – were indigo blue all over, especially their fingers. The food we all groped after from the common platter must, after ten minutes' finger-plunging, have absorbed a fair quantity of indigo too. Jenny and our two children (who were with us this time) had a troubled afternoon.

I cannot leave Yemen without relating what occurred the last time we left it. At Sana'a airport sundry other foreigners were gathered round the same check-in desk as Jenny and me, filling in the obligatory questionnaire. One of the questions to be answered (No. 13) was 'Reasons for leaving the Yemen?'. In some doubt about an appropriate sort of response, I looked over the shoulder of a burly American. His ballpoint had just dealt with that very question. His answer read 'State of the plumbing'. (What action the Yemeni authorities would take if answers to their questionnaire were ever examined can only be guessed.) A much more serious problem arose for me when I discovered that the Yemeni girl running the check-in desk had attached only four baggage receipts to my ticket, whereas we had handed in five pieces of baggage. I queued up again to draw her attention to this. 'The best thing you can do', she said, 'is to go and check that your five bags are all out there on the tarmac.' 'But how can I get there?' She thereupon pulled me through the gap where travellers place their baggage to be weighed, and I found myself whisked away on the conveyor belt round several corners and eventually out (on all fours) through the flap where the baggage disappears on its way to be dumped on the tarmac for waiting labourers to stack it appropriately. The latter showed no surprise at the emergence through the flap of this unusual piece of baggage and politely indicated where I should best look. I found our fifth bag safely ranged with the other four; but the only way of rejoining Jenny inside the departure hall was to reverse the process by which I had left it. This meant crawling on my hands and knees along the conveyor belt in the *opposite* direction – an exercise by no means as simple as going up a descending escalator in a London Tube station. With some damage to my hands and the knees of my trousers I managed to make it, emerging through the flap and doubling along the conveyor belt (against the traffic, of course) amid the raised eyebrows of the queues of other travellers. The girl at the desk gave me no more than a bland nod as I stepped ashore, and got on with her job as though the odd procedure she had imposed on me was a frequent feature of it.

The other visits I paid to the Arab world at the request of Professor Shaban were not nearly such fun, for I was sent to raise funds for Exeter University. In 1980 my task was to beg my old friend Sheikh Rashid of Dubai for a few thousand pounds to bring Gulf Arabs to Exeter to study. Sheikh Rashid showed no enthusiasm about higher education for Gulf commoners but expressed readiness to help over a decent bricks-and-mortar project if we needed cash for that sort of purpose. As it happened, the building of the new university library had been stopped at ground level by Mrs Thatcher's cuts in university expenditure, and the upshot was that Sheikh Rashid sent me a cheque for £750,000 to build all the rest. The consequence of this was that I was sent to get double that gigantic sum out of Sheikh Zayed of Abu Dhabi, who could in principle be relied upon to outdo his rival in Dubai in everything. My attempt was a laughable failure. After a fortnight's waiting in a dry and dreary 'hotel annex' in the Indian quarter (the Gulf Football Competition was taking place and all real hotels were full), I was given audience. A jolly exchange of reminiscences took place, at the end of which I requested the modest sum of £2 million. Sheikh Zayed told his heir apparent, Sheikh Abdulla, to fix me up, whereupon the pair of them disappeared through a private door at the back of the vast *mejlis*, leaving me alone with the powerless Head of Protocol. It took another fortnight to get a further audience, not even with Sheikh Abdulla but with the Court Chamberlain. A nought had evidently got mislaid in the instructions passed down the line, for the Court Chamberlain told me a cheque for £200,000 could be collected from the Lebanese clerk outside the door. The clerk concerned was an unattractive nark who, when handing over to Professor Shaban two years before a cheque for £10,000 from Sheikh Zayed, had demanded a PhD in exchange. He was given a proper flea in the ear and now saw an opportunity to avenge himself. So when I asked for the £200,000, he declared that it would reach me through the UAE Embassy in London. It never did, despite repeated reminders.

This at least served to undermine my reluctant reputation as a fund-raiser, which was finally exploded when I was sent to seek another £750,000 from Sheikh Rashid. By this time he was senile and may not even have recognised me. So I called privily on Mahdi Tajir (a Customs clerk in Dubai in my days there), who had been summoned back from his UAE ambassadorial post in London as the only person Rashid would trust to give him twice daily the spoonful of medicine prescribed. I had decided that Mahdi was the man to employ as an intermediary for my £750,000. When I called on him in his glitzy mansion and was working up to popping the question, he chanced to mention that during the previous week he had been visited by Sir Geoffrey Arthur (the final Political Resident in the Gulf). Geoffrey had explained that he was raising funds for an ophthalmic hospital in Arabia and thought that Mahdi might help secure a contribution from Sheikh Rashid. 'I asked Geoffrey', Mahdi went on, 'how much he was trying to get from Rashid; and when he gave me the figure of £750,000, I simply got out my cheque book and gave it him myself, that way being much less trouble.' Any determined fund-raiser would at this point have announced, 'How extraordinary! That's precisely the sum I tried to get from Sheikh Rashid this morning for Exeter University. So why not just get out your cheque book again?' But I simply couldn't bring myself to do it, and returned to Exeter empty handed. I have to admit that I found it highly distasteful begging money from erstwhile 'dependants' who had suddenly become infinitely richer than us old imperialists.

One final fund-raising expedition, much more dramatic than those above, remains to be described. Exeter University had been more or less promised half a million pounds by Sultan Qaboos of Oman. Since it kept on not arriving, it was decided that the Vice-Chancellor, the University Registrar, Professor Shaban and sundry minor figures including me should fly out to pursue the matter. The friendly ruler of Sharjah lent us his private aeroplane to get us as far as Sharjah (next door to Oman) and put all twelve of us up as guests in his marble Meridian Hotel. Actually there were thirteen of us, since Jenny (on the indigo trail) had flown out with us as a sort of stowaway. Our host spent the next few days trying to persuade his friend Sultan Qaboos to allow us to enter his country. (The necessary No Objection Certificates were in those days very hard to obtain.) Eventually permission was given for only five members of our party – the four top brass and me. Once again we smuggled Jenny on board the ruler's plane as a stowaway, Omani indigo being the object of her research. But the situation then got out of hand. On arrival in Muscat the five of us were received, not by the Sultan himself (who had disappeared on tour) but by his Minister of Finance; and in the course of our conversation with him about the £500,000 Professor Shaban became so angry with the minister that he rose to his feet and threatened him with his stick. In the ensuing mêlée we judged it wisest to withdraw at once in case we were arrested and to fly back on our waiting aircraft to Sharjah. But by now Jenny's whereabouts were unknown. She had neither money nor clothes with her since her baggage was with ours, and she knew no one in the whole country; but in our haste to escape we had to give her up as a lost cause!

Fortunately, as we learnt later, she managed to contact a British weaver, Gigi Crocker, whom she had never met but with whom she had corresponded. Gigi lived at the other end of the country but immediately drove 600 miles across the desert to meet Jenny in an oasis and accompany her round the mountains of Oman, where the growing of indigo, and dyeing with it, were rumoured still to survive. The two girls (who became firm friends) dossed down under acacia trees wherever they happened to be – not a thing that could be safely done in many countries – and duly recorded what was left of the Omani indigo industry. To abridge the rest of the story, she was eventually advised to call on a prominent Omani banker who, she was told, might advance her the cost of an airfare home. He immediately presented her with the price of an air ticket at his own expense. I should be surprised if the head of NatWest in London would treat a penniless Omani the same way.

Shortly before this I had got myself invited, again by posing as an expert, to conduct four Members of Parliament – two from each House – round Oman as guests of the Sultan. A helicopter was put at our disposal and we flew all over the place, greeting both the Sultan's soldiers (still at war with their South Yemeni neighbours) and his whales and sharks, peaceably basking in the crystal coastal shallows. But the only reason I mention the trip is this. When we were in Salala the Omani Brigadier commanding the troops in Dhofar told me how the previous week the great Wilfred Thesiger had sent to his Bedou friend Bin Kabina (who had crossed the Empty Quarter with him on his famous camel journeys in 1945–48) a message via the Brigadier's Signal Section proposing that they should get together at a certain well on the edge of the desert to talk of their memorable shared experiences. Bin Kabina's telegraphic reply through the same channel had simply said, '*You* provide helicopter and I come' – a suggestion so appalling to Thesiger, the greatest twentieth-century desert traveller, that it must surely have snapped a heartstring. Incidentally, a year or so later I took Jenny to see Wilfred in his

Tite Street flat in Chelsea on one of his rare visits to Britain to ask whether he would lend her some photographs of indigo-covered Arabians. He couldn't have been more gracious, inviting her to look through his serried volumes of superb photographs and make use of any she fancied. (I did not mention Bin Kabina.)

CHAPTER 22

Jaunts and Jollities (North Yemen, Peru, Egypt, South Yemen)

SERENISSIMA, an upmarket travel company, made something of a hit by taking its customers to off-beat corners of the world before a hundred other companies recognised that idea as a money-spinner. Serenissima had the further merit of taking on trust the qualifications of those who proposed themselves as lecturers, and it was by exploiting this opening that I got taken on in the 1980s to lead tours in four or five countries that I knew only indifferently.

It was the first company to take groups to North Yemen when that marvellous country began admitting foreigners. Michael Adams, designated as its first prospective tour leader and sent out to explore the possibilities, had an alarming experience. In Sana'a two taxis were secured to test the zigzag road that dropped 6,000 feet to Hodeida, the country's main port. Michael was invited to travel in the leading one, but preferred to share the second with his wife. Halfway down, the leading taxi went over a precipice at a hairpin bend, and Michael had the unenviable task of climbing down and hauling the driver's body up to the road.

Nothing similar happened when, on the basis of my one previous visit to Sana'a, I was employed by Serenissima as lecturer on their second tour. Serena Fass, the foundress of the firm, accompanied the party as manager, to suss me out; but my subsequent tours were even more fun since Jenny was appointed as manager on them all (though she had no qualifications for the job). There was always a mixed bag of customers. For instance, the second group I took to North Yemen included the Duke and Duchess of Bedford, the American owner of Heinz 57 Varieties, and an out-of-work garden labourer from Portsmouth. I took the trouble to enquire in advance about the Bedfords from the top man in the Foreign Office, who was another aristocrat. His comment was memorable. 'The Duke's a nice fellow,' he said, 'but the Duchess ... she comes across a bit strong.' (She fell downstairs on the eve of our departure and broke a leg, so the Duke came alone.) As for 'Heinz', he turned out to be not the stereotypical American tycoon 'with two-tone shoes and a roving eye' (a nice generalisation coined by Alistair Cooke, to which Jenny drew my attention) but a cultured character fascinated by Yemeni architecture.

But on other tours we were less lucky in the clientele. In South Yemen and the Hadhramut we were burdened with a fat slob who brought no clean undies with him for a three-week tour. We discovered this when we asked him to lend some to another stout client, the distinguished painter the late Derek Hill, whose luggage had got lost. The slob was also often disagreeably drunk. Indeed, on the airport bus at Aden carrying half our party (including Jenny) to the aircraft he started a bout of fisticuffs with an inoffensive compatriot. Jenny pushed forward to try to stop this unseemly punch-up and was impressed when a group of young Adeni men, horrified that an English lady should get involved in such male vulgarity, overpowered the tipsy slob on her behalf. Two unattractive couples on a tour we led to Peru in 1986 also stick in my mind, not for coming to blows but for their philistine behaviour when our coach took us to Sacsawayman, one of the marvels of the world some miles outside Cuzco. We had been travelling for some days at anything up to 13,000 feet and, to escape mountain sickness, the instructions were that no alcohol should be drunk. When the rest of us tripped off excitedly to explore Sacsawayman, these two couples stayed grumpily in the coach drinking Coca-Cola and reading out-of-date English newspapers. On our return they gave voice to a memorable protest. 'Never again', they declared, 'will we go on a tour *above the alcohol line.*'

But that Peruvian tour had splendid moments for *us*. At Lake Titicaca, for instance – the highest and biggest inland lake in the world – Jenny and I were standing on its bank one blissful evening when a reed canoe came paddling in our direction from some distant island. The three men in it, all in local costume, stopped knitting their fabulous woollen caps and stepped ashore. As they walked past us, one of them looked at Jenny and said in a sort of Spanish, 'I met you in London three years ago.' It transpired that he was a weaver who had been sent to represent Peruvian craftsmanship in an exhibition at the Commonwealth Institute, which Jenny had visited.

Another great moment in Peru was at Nazca, meeting the old German lady Maria Reiche, who had by then spent forty-five years studying the mysterious 'Nazca Lines' and still could not offer a satisfactory explanation. She was now nearly ninety and almost blind but told us she had every intention of continuing her researches – living, as she always had, in a ramshackle hut full of rats. She died in 1998. The Nazca Lines, I should explain, are gigantic outline drawings up to 400 yards long, scraped in the rough desert, of hummingbirds, monkeys, scorpions, etc., which can only be seen in perspective – and perhaps therefore can only have been designed – from half a kilometre up in the air. They are generally dated to several centuries BC, and who then could hover half a kilometre up in the air? *We* of course can fly over them, though in the rickety old Cessna made available to us tourists I felt too airsick to enjoy the amazing sight. Fortunately I was not seasick as well when we were taken in motorboats to the Ballesteros Islands to enjoy their gigantic congregation of sea lions. They sing what sounds very like Gregorian chant, and we watched the old bulls, the size of hippopotami, not exactly conducting the singing but slumped in rocky pews in this Ballesteros cathedral, scratching their noses. I repeat, scratching their noses.

But there are so many marvels in Peru; and as for Machu Picchu, see it and die. Things had sadly been made easier for tourists since Marnie and I went there in 1958 (see p. 166). In those days the only way to get there from Cuzco was in an antiquated bus fitted with iron wheels to run on an otherwise disused railway line; and as we plunged in it down the jungly Urubamba valley, large orchids that looked like hummingbirds tapped at the bus windows – unless they were hummingbirds that looked like orchids. But Machu Picchu as a whole remains romantic enough to survive, one hopes, the worst that the modern world can do by way of 'improvements'. So does Cuzco, that 'Beggar on a Golden Throne'.

A curious incident occurred when our 1986 tour was on the way from Cuzco to Machu Picchu, by a rather more modern train than in 1958, but of only one carriage. We had stopped at some small intermediate station, and after we set off again someone noticed that three Peruvian passengers had got left behind on its platform. Our engine driver, having been informed, stopped the train. He then sent the small boy who worked as his mate to climb the nearest telegraph pole, attach an instrument to the telegraph wire and send a message back in this enterprising way to the station 3 miles back to tell the missing passengers that the train would return to pick them up. We then shunted all the way back and collected them. None of the locals seemed to think the procedure odd.

The main protein in the traditional Inca diet was and is guinea pigs. Every Inca house has dozens running about (making it easy to feed unexpected guests). On our last night in Lima on that Serenissima tour guinea pig was an alternative main course at our posh restaurant dinner; and I felt it incumbent on me as leader of the group to order one. It proved, to everyone else's merriment, to consist of absolutely nothing but leathery skin stuck to the animal's skeleton. How the Inca with a guinea-pig base to their diet were robust enough to control an empire wider than the distance from London to Moscow is a mystery. Peru left me with plenty of other insoluble questions but I will mention only one.

How came it that the Inca with an elaborate and compelling religion of their own accepted a foreign religion imposed on them by their brutally 'unchristian' Spanish conquerors? The Inca remain a devoutly Catholic people, though they combine Catholicism with a lot of pre-Hispanic practices and superstitions. In Cuzco Cathedral you will find a huge painting of the Last Supper by an early Inca artist, in which the dish in front of Christ consists simply of a roasted guinea pig. Other religious paintings exhibited in Cuzco include a beautiful *black* Virgin Mary and another in which she is giving suck from one breast to her child and from the other to St Peter, aged about sixty. Nothing of course remotely irreverent was intended, any more than in other Inca religious paintings showing, for instance, the Archangel Gabriel with a musket over his shoulder, or St Jerome among whose saintly paraphernalia on a table at the mouth of his cave the painter has placed a smart toothbrush.

But enough of our Serenissima episodes. As a more enterprising venture we took our children out of school for a term in 1989 to Egypt and Yemen. The experiment began badly. When around midnight we reached the flat in Cairo provisionally booked for us by some acquaintance of our Egyptian botanist friend Lutfi Boulos, and had struggled up four long staircases with our four months' baggage as well as a sort of wooden coffin housing Finella's cello, the flat proved so awful and the landlady so repellent that we struggled down again. A kindly passing taxi-driver piled everything, and us, into or on to his cab and we set off to find a hostelry for what was left of the night. Every hostelry we tried was full. The taxi-driver thereupon offered to put us all up in his distant house as his guests. (Imagine a London taxi-driver doing the same for a visiting Arab family!) We tried one more hotel consisting of the fourth floor of a block in Zamalek. As the fifth floor was evidently a brothel it looked discouraging, but it (the fourth floor, that is) proved splendid. Two days later an Egyptian air force General, introduced to us by a friend in our Embassy, readily offered to rent us his flat, also in Zamalek. We could understand his readiness when we went there. But it had certain merits and we cleared up the mess and settled in.

Arrivals in Cairo are often hazardous. When Jenny and I went there from Tunis in 1976 no one was allowed to leave the airport as violent food riots were taking place and a curfew had been imposed. There were hundreds of stranded people sleeping in rows all over the airport corridors and the prospects looked dim. By chance we ran into a group of American aid workers who managed to persuade the police that they *must* be allowed into the city, to help the Egyptians. So Jenny and I disguised ourselves as American aid workers and slipped into their truck.

Cairo is an amazing city. Since my first visit in 1941 its population had risen from half a million to some 15 million (and is now probably several million more). How it ticks over at all, let alone in so good-humoured a fashion, passes comprehension. Somehow everyone seems to get food, and some at least of the rubbish gets collected in donkey-carts by the Zabbaleen. These, an ethnic group of Copts, dump it all on a hillside outside the city, living on the acres of garbage themselves and ingeniously breeding pigs on it. According to reports they do better financially than most other workers in Cairo. In our part of the city, built of large blocks of flats, there is a hollow square from roof to ground level in each block, and into this giant wastepaper basket householders on all floors tip their garbage. The Zabbaleen, who obviously need to look upwards when at work, clear it all out and stow it in their donkey-carts. The ones we got to know were friendly and smiling. 'Everyone in Cairo', said eight-year-old Hamish after a couple of days, 'is so nice and friendly that we'll have to be nicer too.' To balance this tribute, however, he asked us whether the Arabs 'not only write backwards but *think* backwards too'.

At this time my elder son Jamie was working in Upper Egypt for CARE on an agricultural project and we could get together now and then. We also saw something of CARE's headquarters in Cairo, awash with secretaries and computers. None of the staff seemed to visit the field projects which were, after all, their *raison d'être*. But I doubt whether the Egyptians thought this improper. They all seemed to regard the separation of management and workers as right and proper. The peasants working with Jamie – and they did work – bore, he said, no visible resentment at the behaviour of the Egyptian *effendis* to whom, under CARE's policy, Jamie would in due course hand over management of the project. These *effendis* stood around all day leaning against trees with cigarettes in their mouths, doing absolutely nothing. The peasants told Jamie that such educated people would lose face if they dirtied their hands. It was OK for *him* to dirty *his*, since he was one of those absurd foreigners, but it would be unseemly and unacceptable to the workforce if Egyptian managers dirtied theirs.

Finella and Hamish were favourably excited by everything else they saw in Egypt. We took them first to Siwa, the most westerly of Egypt's desert oases. Jenny had gone there two years earlier when she walked round the other distant oases, occasionally getting lifts from passing Arab lorry-drivers. ('But, Jenny,' said her friends on her return to England, 'lifts from Arab lorry-drivers in remote deserts? Wasn't that dreadfully dangerous?' 'The only dangerous part of my journey', Jenny replied, 'was from Gloucester Road to Heathrow by the Underground at midnight.') On her previous visit to Siwa she had been taken in a Land Rover by Clara Semple and her friend Hussein Shereen, King Farouk's sister's son, a sad but amusing character who has since stayed with us in Devon. On the present occasion we were lodging in Alexandria with the Semples in their British Council house, where Hussein brought his parents to tea with us. His mother, originally married to the Shah of Iran and divorced as unable to produce male children, had then married Ismail Shereen and disproved the Shah by giving birth to Hussein. She was still sensationally beautiful at eighty. As for Ismail Shereen himself, he related to me how he had been *Chef du Cabinet* to six successive royal cabinets before Nasser's republicans abolished the monarchy. It is a pity he could not risk writing *his* memoirs, and he has since died.

On the way to Siwa we stopped at El Alamein to visit the famous Second World War cemeteries. It was interesting to observe the different ways that combatant countries looked after theirs. The German one was a vast pile of neat stone masonry, kept locked. Others were open but indifferently cared for. The Commonwealth War Graves Commission is undoubtedly the one British institution that does its job better than any foreign counterparts. Among the endless rows of gravestones at Alamein I noticed with a pang a long string of Argyll and Sutherland Highlanders and reminded myself that 'There but for the grace of God … '. (In point of fact the credit goes less to the grace of God than to that confusion over names in 1941 at Geneifa; see p. 77). Those lying there – indeed, in the whole vast cemetery – were almost all in their early twenties, as I would have been.

Siwa was enchanting in a dozen ways, though much of its mud-built acropolis has melted into the peneplain since the remarkable travel writer Rosita Forbes got there in the 1920s, and though its oracle in the Temple of Ammon, famous for a thousand years, has long been silent. In the old, old days everyone consulted it, including Alexander the Great. No one knows what questions he asked or what answers it gave, but he was so taken with Siwa that he said he wanted to be buried there. Then off he went on the hippy trail to Kathmandu and died in Babylon on his way back – too far off for his wish to be carried out. The Temple of Ammon intrigued me for two other (semantic) reasons. It allegedly gave Ammonites their name because their coils resembled the ram's horns on the statue of the god. And it also gave its name to Ammonia for the almost more improbable reason that ammonia was first manufactured close to the temple from a distillation of camel dung. (For these unlikely derivations I am indebted to both Napoleon Bonaparte and Baedeker.)

Jenny managed to find in Siwa the house of the family she remembered from her previous visit, who manufactured olive oil by propelling a huge millstone round and round *manually* to crush the olives into sludge. The family had been doing this for five generations. Those supplying the olives received four-fifths of the oil produced, the remaining fifth being the operator's modest take. No wonder the present owner had a sideline, making ingenious rope-and-bamboo bird traps of a kind unchanged since Pharaonic times. Jenny had been intrigued by this invention on her previous visit. Since he hadn't one spare at the time, the old maker said he would have one ready for her on her 'next visit'. And as soon as we now entered his yard, two years later, he greeted her by saying, 'Madam, I have that bird trap waiting for you'! (It now hangs on our Devon wall.)

In north-west Egypt we visited the very early Coptic monasteries in the desert, which still had a monk or two looking after them. On the opposite side of Egypt we spent several days *inside* St Catherine's famous Greek Orthodox monastery in Sinai as guests of the monks. We were granted this privilege thanks to the intervention of Alex Rondos, whose American wife was giving cello lessons to Finella. Alex, born of Greek parents in Tanzania but later head boy at Cheltenham College, was now head of CRE, the biggest foreign charity in Egypt. Being himself Greek Orthodox as well as a dispenser of charitable funds, he had close relations with St Catherine's and had received the Abbot's agreement to our lodging there. It was a memorable three days. The site (nestling under Mount Sinai, which we climbed), the architecture and the superb array of icons are all vastly impressive, and such monks as we were able to meet were intelligent and obviously saintly people. The one who was put in charge of us, Brother George, was an English-speaking Greek. His engaging personality inspired another poem, 'Brother George's Confession', published in *A Kind of Kindness*. He had spent twenty years in the monastery but never felt qualified to apply for full monkhood, take the necessary vows and risk being pitchforked by devils off the ladder to heaven – the fate await-ing unsatisfactory monks shown in one of those splendid icons. Among his 'failings' was an irrepressible love of beautiful things – such as the silver *Yid Fatima* round Jenny's neck, acquired in Tunisia. He asked her to send him a similar one if she ever could – and she did. But whether it reached him and he was allowed to keep it we shall never know.

We all did pencil drawings at St Catherine's. The best was the one done by Hamish. Thereby hangs a bizarre tale. A year or two later his drawing, hanging in our kitchen, was seen by an East German scholar visiting Exeter whom Jenny had run into at a woad conference(!) at Erfurt. He, Müllerott, asked permission to reproduce it in a book he was writing about an old Prussian dynasty. He later sent us a copy of his book (in German, of course). I have struggled through it more than once in a vain effort to discover what Hamish's drawing of St Catherine's was doing in it. But for an eight-year-old to have a drawing published in a work of deadly German scholarship was quite a coup.

On our subsequent trip up-river we lodged on arrival at Karnak on the 'wrong' side of the Nile in a grotesquely cheap hostelry recommended by Clara Semple. Grandly named the Queen Hotel, it stands in a small village overlooking the impressive remains of the Pharaonic temple of Medinat Habu. Haq Ali, 'the amiable old scoundrel' (in Clara's words) who owned and ran the hotel single handed, was drunk every evening from 7 p.m. on, so the suppers he cooked for us at about 7.30 were at best unpredictable. He was back to normal for breakfast, serving it for us on the flat roof of the hostelry. From it we gazed down on the village women laying lumps of dough on flattened cowpats by the wall of the great temple for the sun to cook – and jolly good the resulting loaves tasted. Close by lies, or is said to lie, Ozymandias, King of Kings, seventeen feet long: but I could not detect Shelley's 'sneer of cold command' on his face. The fallen statue may in fact be of Rameses II and not Ozymandias (whoever he was) at all.

During our time as guests of Haq Ali (at £1 a day, all meals included), we did all the usual things on both sides of the river, and some less usual. The latter included riding over the stupendous mountains on donkeys to reach the Valley of the Kings and to examine on the way the little-visited tombs of top commoners. These proved almost more exciting than those of Tutankhamun, etc. But the main reason I have included Haq Ali in these pages is what followed. When we left him we hired a tatty old taxi to take us up the rough track on the same (west) bank of the Nile for three and a half hours to Aswan. When we finally arrived there no hotel would admit us unless we presented our passports, and I realised I must have left them in Haq Ali's drawer. (The only rule of hotel management that Haq Ali observed was that Guests should Deposit their Passports with the Manager.) Haq Ali's hostelry was not connected with anything as modern as the telephone, and was much too far away for me to go back late at night to recover them. Eventually one sympathetic hotelier suggested that we go and appeal for mercy to the Chief of the Province Police, who was known to work late. (It was now 11 p.m.) This seemed an unlikely gambit, but we found his offices and were unexpectedly ushered into his presence. There was the great man, seated at his desk studying editorials from *The Times* and the *Herald Tribune*. This unusual police activity resulted, so he explained in Arabic, from his passionate desire to learn English, and 'proper' English. After listening to my appeal for his urgent intervention with *any* hotel manager in Aswan, he said, 'I'll do a deal with you. If you, sir, agree to sit here till breakfast helping me with these editorials, I will get your charming wife and children into a hotel at once. I will also arrange that when your non-stop train to Cairo passes through Karnak tomorrow night at eleven fifty-eight the train will stop for your benefit and there will be a policeman in plain clothes on the platform with your passports.'

He proved – amazingly – as good as his word. My night's work with him on his editorials left me less than fresh for the family programme the next day; but that night our train did stop improperly at Karnak, and there on the empty platform was a muffled figure holding out our passports ...

I have scarcely mentioned Cairo itself but as there is plenty of literature on the marvels of Giza, Sakkara and so on, I will limit myself to two minor but less hackneyed memories. One day we took the children to the huge camel market at Imbaba. Camels are herded there in thousands from the Sudan 800 miles south, to be sold as meat. Seeing some obvious middle-aged Sudanese standing with a group of these unhappy and exhausted beasts, I went to greet them and discovered that they came from Geneina, my old imperial stamping-ground in Darfur. I told them in excited tones that I had been the *Mu'tamid* (Resident) there in 1951–52 before independence. 'Ah,' they said, 'so you're American.' (*Sic transit gloria...*)

My other unusual memory of Cairo is of the time we spent in the 'ACADEMY OF ESENCES' (*sic*), a big shop in the Muski *suq* selling natural medicines. Its walls were lined with row upon row of boxes labelled in Arabic with approximate English equivalents: everything from BRIMSTONE to VULTURES' TESTICLES, from TOOTHPICK SEEDS to CROWS NEST, from FISH'S GIFTS to ABYSSINIAN WORM. Even if the object of translating all these magic medicaments into English was simply to engage the curiosity of foreigners without expecting any resulting business from them, the shop was always full of well-dressed Egyptian customers buying vultures' testicles or whatever in small, scrupulously weighed heaps. So they must be regarded as effective – and perhaps they *are*. The owner himself alleged to us that 99 per cent of his medicines were powerful aphrodisiacs.

After three months we had to drag the children reluctantly away from Egypt and head for the Yemens (then two separate republics) for Jenny to pursue her indigo trail. After surviving sundry difficulties we got to Aden, where its struggling university, which I had reason to visit, saved the day for us in more senses than one. First they found a sort of bungalow on the campus that we could occupy. Their final act of kindness (to be related later) left us even more in their debt.

A great moment befell this old imperialist when we went one afternoon to bathe at a fine beach some way along the coast from Aden. On the way back – and this was at a time when the South Yemeni Marxist government forbade its citizens, on pain of police interrogation, from talking to capitalist foreigners – our taxi-driver suddenly said to me (in Arabic): 'I wish you British were back here.' 'Oh?' I said in some surprise, 'Why?' 'Because', came his reply, 'anything that's any good in Aden we got from you.' 'Oh, really? What sort of things do you mean?' 'Well,' he said, 'things like walking on the pavement [i.e. as opposed to the middle of the road] and ironing our trousers.' Walking on the pavement and ironing trousers – The Legacy of Empire!

Our main object, however, was to get to Beihan, several hundred miles away up on the edge of the Empty Quarter and rumoured to have been an important centre of the indigo industry. When providence in the form of a small Aden aeroplane finally enabled us to get there (no road existed), Beihan turned out to be scenically enchanting, quite apart from revealing in its small township one surviving and very active indigo dyer and such other delights as a huge square in which a number of camel-driven sesame-oil presses were operating. Expeditions outside the town to see this and that were hazardous as there had just been colossal rainstorms: the wadis were flowing and the fords through them were of uncertain depth. Fortunately the old van we were driven around in suffered nothing more terminal than a puncture – but a puncture 10 miles out and with no spare tyre. Providence luckily came chugging along after half an hour in the shape of an ancient lorry and gave us a lift. While we had been nervously awaiting some such miraculous dispensation, a long train of camels passed some way off, carrying (we liked to think) frankincense, for Beihan lies on the immemorial incense route from east to west.

Our return flight from Beihan to Aden after three memorable days was at best uncertain, and made more so by discovering when we woke at dawn that there had been more savage rainstorms overnight. Indeed, the sky was still zigzagged with lightning. The primitive airstrip was virtually under water and we were told that the twice-weekly plane from Aden, if it came at all, was unlikely to risk trying to land. If it didn't, we would miss our flight from Aden back to Sana'a the following morning. Providence was again on our side, and the plane landed (and took off again) successfully.

But before we could catch that flight to Sana'a I had to pay the bill for our sojourn in the university bungalow. I should explain that the rate of exchange of the local currency was wholly arbitrary and that, for example, a half-pint of the local beer cost £5. But even without my having indulged in alcohol, our bill when the manager showed it to me was for an impossible £800. He then made a phone call and, to my astonished relief, disclosed that the university was paying it. Yet another illustration of the generosity of the poor!

Further Travels with Jenny

CHAPTER 23

Off again: Morocco, Thailand and Laos

IN 1987 we sold Bradridge for over four times what we had paid for it and bought Uppincott Barton, a sixteenth-century farmhouse near Exeter. Though our intention had been to find a stone house with a slate roof not needing such constant maintenance as Bradridge did, characteristically we ended up in a thatched house of mud that needed even more.

Jenny was by now plunged even deeper into indigo and in April 1990 off we went overland to Morocco in a camper-van to pursue the relevant dyes and textiles in that country. Three curious incidents befell us on the trip.

One relates to our two brief stays in Tangier, in the spooky palace inherited by Michael Scott (Marnie's brother-in-law) from his law-lord father, who had been Chief Justice of Bombay. Built by the latter in Moroccan style on a prime hill site looking across the sea to Gibraltar, it consists of four wings, three storeys high, pointing to the four points of the compass, with of all things a mosque protruding in the centre. Michael and his wife Cherie occupied the east wing. We were allocated as much as we wanted of the south one and we established ourselves in a huge room on the second floor, barely furnished and with inconsequential plumbing in its bathroom. On a small cloth-covered table on one side stood an iron candlestick with a white candle in it. (My reason for mentioning it will appear later.) In the morning our hosts gave us coffee in their wing. Their kitchen was piled ceiling high with unwashed dinner services, including a number of coffee pots. From one of the latter Jenny was dismayed to pour herself not just coffee but two dead earwigs. Michael's mother had evidently lived an equally bizarre life, for he told us she had sustained herself almost entirely on meringues regularly imported from Piccadilly; and when Michael and Cherie took over the house and had unlocked the wing his parents had lived in, they found stacked in a cupboard countless cardboard boxes of meringues, still unopened but no longer savoury.

Michael's Tangiers friends who looked in for a gossip were also unusual, but I shall mention only Bruce Condé, whom I had met years back in Beirut, the stamp-collecting American convert to Islam and associate of the old Imam of Yemen. The Imam having awarded him several high appointments, he had written on the back of the envelope containing a letter he had sent to me in Baghdad his full title. It read, 'The Amir, Lieutenant-General al Haj Bruce Condé de Bourbon'. When I now teased him about this, his response was that since his Yemeni days he had almost become as well the King of an island off the coast of Japan, whose Queen (a Japanese princess) died just as he was marrying her. He was now living, a simple Haj Bruce Condé, in Tangier with no passport and two adopted Berber children. He was certainly an amazing raconteur with an amazing amount to recount. Detecting my scepticism, he supported his whole story by showing me the diaries he had scrupulously maintained since 1932.

Though it means jumping ahead, I revert to the table with its candlestick in the room we occupied. On our return three weeks later from southern Morocco we looked in, as arranged, for a final night. We were horrified to learn that eight days after we had left, our room had gone up in flames. The savage fire was judged to have started on the cloth on that table, but *the candle standing on it was the only thing in the room untouched!* Michael's throwaway explanation of the conflagration was 'spontaneous combustion' caused by the Arab who lived opposite the front door and who had often displayed vicious voodoo powers against him – killing, for instance, his healthy male housekeeper without direct contact. Forty-three rue Shakespeare (as the lane was oddly named) was certainly – for other reasons as well, not recorded here – the spookiest house I have ever lodged in.

When, after plenty of interesting happenings on the way south, we reached Goulemine, the most southerly inland town in Morocco (where Jenny hoped to discover some Blue Men from the Sahara in the camel market), we found that the handsome campsite advertised by the Moroccan Tourist Board was fictitious. Nor, we were told, was there anywhere in the town where foreigners were permitted to lodge. Then a teenage Moroccan drew me aside and said we would be most welcome to spend the night in his village 8 miles away, whose sheikh was married to his sister. The youth, Mawlood, guided us there, and when we had bedded the children down in the camper outside the sheikh's house, we were invited in to take tea. This is where the second of our curious experiences began. In the course of conversation with the sheikh about Blue Men and the nomad people of the desert, he remarked that he had lodging just then in one of his houses a blue sheikh who trekked up every year to sell to the merchants of Goulemine the crafts and products of his Riguebat tribe from the deserts farther south, exchanging them for grain. The sheikh added that last year the man's camels had eaten up everything in his garden, so this year he had lodged him and his camels in another of his houses with no garden. Would we care to visit him there? Yes, indeed – and there the magic started.

We were greeted in this other house by a sixty-year-old man in blue who kissed us unaffectedly on both shoulders and ushered us into a large mud-walled room. Round its walls hung dozens of rugs and on the floor lay innumerable objects displayed there for local merchants to come and barter for them. The room was lit by three candles, and while we sipped our tea, squatting on the ground, the Blue Man casually mentioned that we were the only Europeans he had ever set eyes on, and that he had never in his life ventured into Goulemine or any other town. And later, when the candles were burning out and Jenny shone her torch, he expressed a quiet interest in this phenomenon, remarking that it doubtless had a lighted candle in its barrel. Yet his poise, his dignity and his quiet confidence in his traditional desert lifestyle were magnetic. When we had drunk our tea, he suggested we might like to examine some of his goods, perhaps some of the trunkful of silver that sat beside him. One by one his stock-in-trade was slowly laid before us in the almost dark. Jenny ventured to take a snap of him sitting cross-legged among his wares. When her flash went off, he buried his face in his indigo shawl, crying '*Barq!*' (lightning).

The exhibition of his wares proceeded – not, he assured us, with any idea of business but just to see whether we found any of them interesting. If we did, he said, they should be placed in the wooden camel-milking bowl 'over there' for further study later. It must have taken a full hour for every object to be methodically placed before us. None of them in fact was of much interest, but out of courtesy Jenny picked out about twelve, which were duly deposited in the milking bowl. This was then drawn closer, and the twelve objects were laid out in a formal row in front of us, their value in terms of *ghararas* of grain being listed for us – just for our edification. Again we were assured there was no question of our having to buy any of them. We could see them in the dark only by the use of Jenny's small torch, and to add to the oddity of the scene I found myself ceremonially enveloped in a nomad's indigo turban, looking (Jenny whispered) like a proper idiot. The only way to end the ensuing silence was obviously to select some of the twelve and offer to purchase them for so many *ghararas*. Jenny gravely picked out some stone beads, an inlaid Koran teacher's stick and a grubby Bedouin smoking-pipe. The number of *ghararas* these represented was then translated by Mawlood into an alarmingly large sum of Moroccan dirhams, which we solemnly dug out of our wallets and handed to the sheikh with much dignified handshaking.

So summary an account scarcely conveys the magic of what was clearly a timeless traditional procedure, completed in two and a half impassive hours. An ingenious con, no doubt, but well worth suffering. As we took our leave, the blue nomad requested us to bring our children to receive his blessing in the morning. Six thirty a.m. was, said Mawlood, the proper time to conduct us to the camel market in Goulemine. So it was something of a scramble, but we made it. Our blue-clad friend was waiting at the door of his lodgings. Having kissed all four of us on both shoulders, he invited us in to conduct a further examination of his wares, over a cup of tea. This we were justified by Mawlood and his watch in declining. As we turned to go, he suggested there might be some possessions of our own we would care to offer as barter. Jenny meekly ran off and returned with some of the children's old clothes, some Woolworths clothes pegs and (to my dismay) our torch. These were gravely examined and laid in a neat pile by the sheikh, who went inside the house and returned to offer in exchange a worn leather cushion and a long carved tent peg whose additional use as a weaving aid was explained to us in detail. Jenny solemnly took back from the pile of our possessions Finella's anorak and (to my even greater relief) the torch. After mysterious mathematical calculations on his fingers the sheikh accepted the rest in exchange for just the tent peg, which now hangs on the wall at Uppincott. The farewells and blessings were finally accomplished and off we went with Mawlood to the camel market.

The market was disappointing. But on the way back the third of our bizarre Moroccan experiences occurred. Sitting next me as I drove the camper, Mawlood in all seriousness begged me for the hand of Finella in marriage. 'I am going to study culture at Agadir University,' he declared, 'and could then give her a good home in London or, if she preferred, we could live here in Goulemine. I come from an honourable family ...', and so on. Mawlood was a nice eighteen-year-old with impeccable manners who had been most helpful, but ... The most courteous response I could devise was to express gratification for the offer but explain (or allege) that the custom in England was for young ladies not to marry till they were twenty-one, which in Finella's case was not for another seven years. He was visibly disappointed, but he can at least take the credit of having made to Finella her very first proposal of marriage.

We had occasion the following year to visit Thailand – again following Jenny's indigo trail. In Bangkok we were guests of our old friends the Melhuishes (who were to figure even more generously in our lives seven years later) in their sumptuous Embassy. They had two pet otters that pattered around their drawing room and even up the stairs and into the bedrooms.

Out in the city itself the traffic was even more remarkable. For most of the day it constituted one vast stationary traffic jam; and this, to Ramsay's delight, made attendance at the National Day receptions of his diplomatic colleagues, none of which were within walking distance, out of the question. The city was also so desperately polluted that on one occasion Jenny virtually passed out on the street. As for the Thais themselves, with their courteous smile, neat clothes and rejection of anger, amiable as these characteristics are, they left me wondering what goes on behind the smile. I then read the standard Anglo-Saxon book on Thai manners. It told me that no Thai ever makes close friends since friendship entails the right to quarrel, and among Thais quarrelling is disallowed. Frankly I rather prefer the peace-seeking custom we ran into in Siwa a year or two back. A Berber family there, in whose charming mud house we had spent some time, kept a leafy/rooty twig (origin not established) tied between the ceiling beams of their kitchen.

It had, they explained, two remarkable qualities. It lived for ever, needing no water; and as long as you had it suspended in your house, it would prevent family quarrels. They kindly chopped off a bit for us, wrapping it in a piece of homespun, and we took it eagerly home. It seems to have vanished in the years that have followed, perhaps because we found that its magic wouldn't work with *our* family!

There were of course attractive aspects of Bangkok and of the lifestyle of its inhabitants, who largely move around by canoes on the city's canals. I couldn't help admiring the old lady we watched sitting unostentatiously on the ground and carving roses exquisitely out of carrots. (Who for?)

The Thai language, which seemed to consist of nothing but vowels, mostly nasalised, evidently makes it difficult for Thais to master other people's languages, though English is compulsory in schools from the age of twelve. The deputy head of their Foreign Office, whom we met at a dinner party of Ramsay's, had been five years at Marlborough College but spoke English very imperfectly. I was told that a Thai who is fluent in English can command a higher salary than a Prime Minister or senior General. It may be that salaries are a poor criterion of wealth among top Thai office-bearers since corruption is notoriously widespread, though barely mentioned. Anything as acrimonious as criticism is disallowed and all the judiciary can do is to question a man's 'unusual wealth'.

We were quite glad to leave the city and embark on ventures inland – notably to the Chiang Mai area in the north and then to Vientiane (the capital of Laos, where Ramsay was also accredited) to the east. Almost everywhere up-country we watched and exchanged smiles with thin men and women in conical hats bent double all day in the rice paddies. We tried our hand at the work, but enjoyed watching it more. Of all the *wats* (Buddhist temples) we visited as we meandered north, the most gripping was at Phunum. Its walls are covered from floor to ceiling with enchanting murals. The building is dated AD 1496. The murals are said to be of the same period, but since they include smartly dressed Thai ladies smoking cigarettes, this must be judged questionable. Moreover, the European traders arriving in paddle steamers to parley with the King are depicted wearing late eighteenth-century clothes. But nothing detracts from the charm of these huge paintings. The good are shown going to heaven and the bad to hell – a hell exactly like that of the Christian fundamentalists, flames, pitchforks and all. The 'angels' conducting the good are half bird, half woman, and are reinforced by a squadron of winged elephants. There are lots and lots of elephants in this part of Asia, but we saw none with wings. In these villages it was moving to see in the morning how many villagers were setting off quite a distance to the local *wat* as a matter of habit with huge pots of food to give to the monks (who may eat only before noon).

When we crossed into Laos, the huge and swollen Mekong river which forms the frontier was full of tree trunks but not (as in T. S. Eliot's 'The Dry Salvages') 'dead negroes' like the Mississippi. That might, I suppose, have been the case a few generations back for Laos had been the constant stamping-ground for bloodthirsty warlords for a thousand years – until the French came. Although the French evidently kept the peace, they reportedly did little else, preferring to keep Laos as a living museum for the holiday entertainment of their compatriots from nearby colonies. During the Vietnam War, we were informed, Laos received more American bombs per capita than any country did in the Second World War. Not that Laos was *at war* with America – it was simply that US bomber pilots were always instructed to empty the 'unexpired portion' of their bomb load in this area before returning to their base in eastern Thailand. It sounds incredible and I hope the story is nonsense.

Half Ramsay's small flat in Vieng Chan (more familiar as Vientiane) was rented to the Australian Embassy and shared a kitchen with the Save the Children Fund. We all fitted in somehow, however. The young American running the SCF kindly lent us his van for two days to explore up the flooded river. Laos is so poor that there was almost no transport in the country other than old Chinese bicycles, and no metalled roads outside the capital. The people, however, were conspicuously nice. But the only memorable *thing* we came upon, 20 miles from the town, was an amazing salt factory: an unbelievably medieval spectacle. It was based on two 200-yard rows of continuous thatched open-fronted sheds, huge logs being laid side by side throughout the entire length, pointing outwards. The logs were fired bit by bit in long narrow 'ovens' in which salt water, brought from God knows where, boiled and evaporated. The coagulated salt was continually picked up in very long-handled shovels by boiling-hot men and dumped in large wicker creels above the ovens to complete the drying process. Do I make myself clear? Actually the process mystified me at the time and mystifies me even more in retrospect.

Back at the flat we all hired Chinese bicycles and for twenty minutes, one behind the other, followed the fearless Ramsay in the pitch dark with no bicycle lights (and of course no street lamps) till we reached the one French restaurant. How we managed to avoid colliding with dozens of other lightless bicyclists was a mystery. The food was so excellent we felt indifferent to such dangers as we pedalled lightless home.

CHAPTER 24

Pursuing Indigo into Mali's Dogon Country

BACK home the completion of my book on *The End of Empire in the Middle East* took precedence for me over other things, as did for Jenny her PhD on *Indigo in the Arab World*. The former's publication was followed by that of her book for the British Museum Press on indigo worldwide, which received high praise. My own effort had at least one flattering consequence. This was that Professor William Roger Louis, the distinguished American specialist on Britain's imperial history (especially in the Middle East), reviewed it and wrote inviting me to contribute the Middle East chapter in the five-volume *Oxford History of the British Empire*, of which he had been appointed head editor. I rang him and asked in a suitably embarrassed voice what remuneration I could expect. 'Contributors', he replied, 'are not paid. It's a privilege to be invited.' I reflected on this 'privilege' many times during the two years' hard work it entailed. When the 120 contributors – all top academics from around the world except for myself, with nothing but a bogus war degree – assembled in Oxford to present their draft chapters and invite comments, the result in my case was unnerving. Lord Beloff, the doyen of imperial studies in England (though not directly involved in the Oxford *History*), raised his finger and said, 'Mr Balfour Paul's chapter is totally unacceptable!' Fortunately William Roger Louis in the chair signalled me to stay mum. It transpired that Beloff objected to what I considered my scrupulous impartiality in dealing with a First World War episode over which Arabs and Israelis have disagreed ever since. (Could the great Max Beloff, being Jewish, have been unconsciously a crypto-Zionist?) Roger Louis backed me up privately but asked me to rephrase the 'offending' passage so that the influential Beloff would cause the editors no further trouble. This was a vain hope for he caused trouble in a big way in the national press, this time on a general issue where he had my (reluctant) sympathy. I had been protesting for some time that the slant of the whole project was *too* hostile to the concept of British imperialism, the pendulum having swung over-far in that direction since Cambridge University published their more favourable version in the 1920s. Imperialism, I argued, was (like most things in life, past and present) a mixture of good and bad, and it was a historicist arrogance to understate the good there had been in it. Lord Beloff was equally critical of what he saw as the whole project's anti-imperial slant, and there was a good deal of public argument. Anyway, Volume 4 of the Oxford *History*, which contains my chapter, was published in October 1999.

Jenny and I set off in January 1997 to pursue her usual subject in West Africa (she had already been to remote south-west China and north-west India without me). She happened to have made the acquaintance in London of a remarkable dyer and weaver, Anita Whittle, who lived in the Gambia, the small river-mouth ex-colony of Britain. Her doctor husband, Hilton, ran Britain's Medical Research Centre on African Diseases based in Gambia's Banjul.

The reason we descended on the Whittles in Banjul was that they had volunteered to accompany us from the Gambia right up the Senegal river on the indigo trail, using Hilton's four-wheel drive and Anita's unique ability to speak the main local lingo, Wolof. After some days driving up the river from St Louis on its southern side, we decided to cross to the other bank and have a look at Kaedi, the biggest town in southern Mauritania. We parked our Land Rover at the Senegal frontier post, where a notice warned: '*Stationnement interdit pour voitures hippomobiles*', though the warning seemed unlikely to be understood by hippomobile (mule-cart) drivers. The ferry itself was a 20-foot canoe cut out of a single tree trunk and painted in bright geometrical patterns all over its sides. We had little trouble with the lonely *douaniers* and immigration officials occupying their respective straw shacks on the two sides of the river, but on our way on foot into Kaedi town a splendidly humiliating incident overtook me. On the assumption that in Mauritania, a member of the Arab League, Arabic was spoken, I volunteered to ask a group of citizens where we might find indigo dyers and I addressed a well-dressed man in my 'fluent Arabic' accordingly. His memorable reply was '*Monsieur, je ne comprends pas l'anglais*'. Hearty laughter from Jenny and the Whittles. Later, however, we learnt of a well-known indigo lady living in a village two miles away and got to her along with other cargo in a *voiture hippomobile* – to Jenny's great advantage.

The ferry canoe that took us back to the Senegal side was distinctly waterlogged, and Hilton Whittle, the expert on African diseases, adjured us to keep our feet out of the bilge water or we would risk catching bilharzia. On getting out, Hilton, unlike the rest of us, slipped straight into the bilge. It wasn't, however, bilharzia which overcame him when we finally reached Bakel, the last village before the frontier with Mali. Hilton had a habit, curious in a doctor, of buying and eating unappetising bits of meat stuck on sticks in the ground in every village market we went through, and we were not surprised when he fell seriously ill in the horrible hostelry that we shortly lodged in, in the remote oasis of Bakel. We thought, as did he despite all the drugs he swallowed and vomited up, that he was dying, though even he was uncertain what he was dying of. In despair we enquired whether there was a Senegalese doctor anywhere and heard that by chance the head army physician (and the only doctor) in the province lived near by. We dug him out and he came nobly to examine Hilton, diagnosing a combination of typhoid and amoebic dysentery. Whatever it was he gave him did some good and after four days Hilton was just able to travel on.

Bakel proved a fascinating relic of French colonialism – on a beautiful bend in the river, supervised by a 'Beau Geste' fort. The pavilion on an adjoining hill-top, which the great explorer René Caillié had occupied on his famous journey to Timbuktu in 1827, now bore a notice reading: 'CENTRE DE LECTURE ET D'ANIMATION CULTURELLE DE BAKEL'. It proved to be used just as a public loo, and no one could have practised 'Reading and Cultural Animation' in it, had anyone been so minded. But some of the people do good things. We were much impressed by a girl in Bakel running a crèche off her own bat and teaching letters, sewing and embroidery to her pupils. Anita offered to give them a lesson in English song and movement. So she taught them 'Roly Poly, Ever so Slowly, Roly Poly, Roly Poly, Faster and Faster, Faster and Faster, STOP!' A big success, and the infants responded by singing us '*Frère Jacques*'.

For our benefit the Whittles decided to take us across the border to Kayes in Mali before returning home. Having bought the necessary vaccination certificates (without the vaccination), they drove us through forests of baobab trees, the habitat of hornbills and baboons, to Kayes, where the textile hunt was productive. Kayes, the second city of Mali, is connected by rail, but not (amazingly enough) by road, to the capital city, Bamako. Jenny and I had to catch the 'express' from Dakar on the Senegalese coast to Bamako, due to stop in Kayes at 2.45 a.m. 'Catching' it was an experience in itself. All hotel rooms in Kayes were fully booked for a Malian conference, so we positioned ourselves on some seats in the lobby of an old French *auberge* near the station. Our attempt to buy train tickets in advance was fruitless. No one could do this until the express actually arrived and the ticket officer could determine how many empty seats there were. Every half-hour or so we went over to enquire whether there was any news of the express or indeed of the ticket officer. For the next twelve hours there was no news of either. The following afternoon both arrived simultaneously. There was only one ticket guichet and the crowd heaving round it, with me in the middle, was enormous. When I got to the front, the ticket-seller wouldn't accept French francs (though everywhere else in Mali happily did), so I had to extricate myself from the crowd to find a currency dealer, and then push back in. By the time I emerged again – and that thanks purely to a young Malian who managed somehow to squeeze himself to the front and buy our tickets for us – Jenny, watching the express snorting to be off, was almost frantic. But even armed with our first-class tickets we were refused permission by the commissaire to climb aboard without another pair of tickets for the 'air-conditioning supplement'. He had no suggestions as to how or where these might be obtained. Eventually I buttonholed a man in uniform who disappeared through the back door of the office. Later, just as Jenny and I were despairing of getting aboard before the train finally set off, he reappeared waving the vital documents.

It was 4 a.m. when we reached Bamako. The chaos was monumental. Fifty or more taxi-drivers screamed at the young man who had our heavy bags on his head to dump them in *their* taxi out of the fifty wedged together (inextricably, it looked) at the station entrance. They pulled the boy mercilessly this way and that, and for a few alarming minutes we lost sight of him. But somehow or other we and the bags ended up in the same taxi, which squirmed its way through its protesting rivals and wobbled us from purgatory to paradise. The latter took the form of a heavenly hostelry recently designed, built and opened by the phenomenal Aminata Traouré. This in every sense colossal lady had revived and improved single handed all the arts and crafts of Mali, opened a magnificent shop for them, and alongside it the best restaurant in the country. Like everything she did, the buildings she put up and the crafts she encouraged had to be in the vernacular, her aim being to get the Malians to recognise that their traditional styles were something to be proud of. One evening she invited us up to her private bedroom in the hotel to watch US President Clinton making his State of the Union address on the TV. She knew enough English to roar with laughter throughout at the absurdity (for an African) of everything he said.

We had meanwhile met up with a man Jenny had contacted before leaving home who was reportedly a knowledgeable guide. Adama Marra proved good fun, despite his passion for garlic in milk, and offered to accompany us throughout the rest of Mali, but the fee for his (admittedly most helpful) services was so high we restricted him to a week. The bus from Bamako went, like the tarmac, only as far as San, another sizeable market town on the river. We got a lift on a van to take us from there to the river causeway and had to push it part of the way when it conked out. But eventually we were rewarded by coming on a group of girls washing dozens of large 'mud cloths', for which Mali is famous, in the shallows and spreading them on the sandy bank where the colours changed as they dried. While we watched along came two young men, each pushing eight dogs, each dog at the far end of a 6-foot bamboo. They were driving them to market in San to be sold, the girls told us, for human consumption.

For the next 100 miles or more we had to choose between one or other of the town's two decrepit taxis. The one we chose – largely because of the entertaining objects and inscriptions almost blocking its driver's vision through the windscreen – kept breaking down every few kilometres during the week it carried us. Whenever this happened, our cheerful driver simply threw open the bonnet, unscrewed sundry bits of ironmongery, knocked them about with a hammer, screwed them in again – and mysteriously the engine stuttered into life, at least for another few kilometres.

In every village the poverty was startling but not, it seemed, dispiriting.

We watched women laboriously sewing, or rather riveting, broken old gourd bowls together (having first bored parallel rows of holes) rather than throwing them unthriftily away. Droughts are always occurring, and Adama Marra told us how during one of them he had worked for a foreign aid agency, touring the area in one of its vehicles. Along every track babies had been left by their starving parents in the hope that some aid agency vehicle would pick them up and take any that were still alive for treatment somewhere. It was, he said, the most awful experience he had ever had. The last village we bumped to ourselves was said to be the home of a very old indigo lady. We found her squatting by her tiny hut. She was so poor she had nothing on but a ragged loincloth. She couldn't remember when she last had something to eat but she talked readily enough of her past when she was a dyer and had a family. Then she crawled into her hut and emerged with a ravishingly beautiful indigo-dyed wedding robe – her one cherished possession. Quite rightly she wouldn't consider selling it. The aspirins Jenny gave her seemed to be welcomed even more than the money pressed into her hand.

In an area farther to the east we much admired the mud grain-stores. It was noticeable that some villages had beautiful mud mosques, some had unbeautiful churches (and pigs), and some had neither. There seemed to be no hostility between them – maybe the shared harshness of life had fostered a pragmatic sense of community. I did not feel that Christianity was 'right' here. If animism is doomed, a simple, comprehensive, social (and non-European) religion like Islam seemed more in keeping – and will doubtless swallow up the others anyway in the course of time. Indeed, it is already the dominant persuasion. On our subsequent twelve-hour bus journey from Mopti back to Bamako the driver stopped the bus at all Muslim prayer times, and everyone (except us) got out as a matter of course to pray together.

Twice during our wanderings we bumped into a curious feature of the childhood of Muslims in Mali. Recently circumcised boys, aged seven or eight, are obliged to go around in large groups in the forest for many months, out of contact with their kin and living off God knows what. Each boy carries with him a clapper device in the form of flat rings of gourd-skin mounted on a hand-held stick, the rings decreasing in diameter towards the top; when shaken, their clacking noise is instantly recognisable and is presumably intended to warn adults away. The philosophy behind this long exiling of small boys after circumcision escaped me, but there must be one.

The island of Djenné farther up the Niger and accessible only by ferry deserved a visit, for its mosque is the biggest mud building in the world, 80 yards square. But of its boasted fourteenth-century university, 'bigger than Oxford', there was no longer any visible evidence. Getting back next day to the mainland looked like a non-starter. When we reached the ferry point, there was a foul *haboob* blowing and the ferryman said he had run out of diesel and could not take anyone across. Fortunately another car arrived containing the American Ambassador. American Ambassadors have a certain clout in the Third World, and when this one told the ferryman that he 'had better *find* some diesel, or else … ', he quickly did! And on we went to Mopti.

Before we had left home we had been commissioned by David Goddard (of the Exeter Maritime Museum) to photograph every boat we saw on the upper Niger, since that was one of the few places where the planks of canoes, he said, were *sewn together with string* – the only working boats in the world that he had never seen himself. Thanks to deforestation there are now no trees left in Mali big enough to carve a decent-sized canoe out of a single trunk, so several have to be used and joined together. In the boat-building yard at Mopti, near the mouth of the harbour, we watched one such canoe under construction. The maker, however, had only reached the stage of joining the curved prow to the relevant half of the future boat. But this process too was fascinating. Having morticed all the end bits to fit together, he placed a piece of old cloth in the joints and glued the whole clamjamfry with a sludge made of the pounded fruit kernels of the carité tree* and the baobab tree mixed together. We were assured that boats glued together in this way remained in good condition for twenty-five years. The vertical stitching with strong string apparently gives extra flexibility amidships.

The huge loop-shaped harbour itself, fringed with countless stitched canoes (many of them double-deckers), bustled with activity. All over its sloping cobbled surround goods of every sort and smell were offered in heaps, the normal covering of rubbish being, as a rule, moved hither or thither first. Most extraordinary of all the wares on sale were the huge slabs of natural salt, the size of tombstones, brought initially by camel to Timbuktu from salt mines in the desert much farther north, where prisoners extract them in appalling conditions. From Timbuktu they were floated up the river by canoe to Mopti, humped up on arrival by small staggering men, and stacked on the slope like playing cards. These thousands of tombstones find their way somehow all over Mali, where the quality of their salt is regarded as infinitely higher than that of Saxa.

The Dogon country away to the south of Mopti was the final objective of our trip. Planning to get anywhere, now that we had said goodbye to Adama Marra, was not easy, but we luckily came across a splendid man (Jebreel) with a Peugeot to get us at least as far as Bandiagara. This was the market town on the high plain this side of the colossal escarpment along the bottom of which live the Dogon we wanted to see. The market kept us busy until we had to push on in the Peugeot. After an hour even the fearless Jebreel had to stop since the frightful track definitively ended.

---

* The fruit of the carité tree (which is peculiar to this part of Africa) is turned into an edible local butter (*shea*), also highly valued in Paris as the basis of an expensive face cream. The baobab has so many uses it is too valuable and holy to cut down.

Before we reached the edge of the escarpment we had a queer experience. In some unpronounceable village we were taken to visit its millet-beer shop. In it were three rather tipsy beer-makers in brown gowns like monks. They insisted on us sipping their product from a calabash 'as a mark of friendship'. One of the three turned out to be a psychic clairvoyant. Having studied Jenny's person, he gave her an amazing account of her past, present and future. His prophecies have already been partly fulfilled.

To reach and climb down the precipitous escarpment to the Dogon villages meant a three-hour walk, taking enough bottled water and other necessities for three days. Fortunately there were boys around only too glad to carry anything for a pittance. One of them, with 12 litre-bottles of water balanced in a box on his head, danced down 500 feet of vertical cliff without apparently the faintest difficulty or discomfort. I myself was happy to be considered too senile to carry more than my sponge bag.

Life was distinctly basic in the village down at the bottom where we stopped for the night. Sleep was not easy on bumpy beds of bamboo sticks, and cooking could be done only on a paraffin lamp and in the dark – our host having no paraffin to light his other one. Dawn, however, disclosed to us nearby both a beautiful mud mosque (more beautiful, we thought, than any we had seen elsewhere) as well as a stout old lady dyeing with indigo, which grew wild hereabouts. But I spent the following day feeling unwell on another bamboo bed in a particularly repellent house in the next village, while Jenny pushed on through the desert to Ende. In the afternoon I struggled up the lower slope of the impending precipice to examine the old thatched grain stores ranging along it. Above them in horizontal fissures in the cliff face could be seen what looked like big pots plastered over, said to have been constructed in the fifteenth century by the Tellem* (the people who reputedly preceded the Dogon) for burying their important dead. The people in this (animist) village told me that their own important ancestors were buried there too, in specially woven funeral robes, and that ceremonial sacrifices were still made in their honour. As a whole the Dogon were clearly losing many traditional peculiarities that have made their habitat a mecca for Western ethnologists and suchlike. We were glad to have seen something of some of the Dogon, however, and, in Jenny's case, to have recorded traditional crafts that will soon have vanished.

When we had struggled for three hours up the cliff and back to the track-end where Jebreel had said he would meet us with his Peugeot, there to our surprise he was. By nightfall he had got us back to Mopti – despite having to pay the police a bribe to be allowed past an otherwise purposeless

---

* These Tellem burial places were excavated in the 1980s by Dutch archaeologists. The textiles (most patterned in indigo) are the earliest dyed textiles in Africa, having survived since the fifteenth century.

roadblock outside the town. This was the only occasion on which he disclosed any knowledge of English, at least of unprintable English invective. Even so, he was the nicest and best-looking Malian we met.

On our return to Bamako, Jenny had instantly to prepare a lecture which she was suddenly asked to give to Mali's International Women's Association that very evening. (She had been advertised a week earlier as giving it, but no one had told *her*.) Not only had she lost her voice with a pestilential cold, but she found on arriving that she had to lecture in French. She went bravely ahead and had the curious experience of hearing her own dubious French simultaneously translated back into a sort of English for the benefit of the American Ambassadress sitting in the front row, who knew no French. What *she* made of it can only be conjectured.

Before we left we were keen to acquire for Hamish, now a keen percussionist, a *balafon*. The *balafon* is a sort of wooden xylophone, its foot-long 'keys' being scooped underneath to give the required note when struck with a leather drumstick; and beneath each wooden key small round gourds of descending sizes are attached as sound boxes. We were taken to the house of a *balafon*-maker and bought one he had just made. Since there was no way it could go with our baggage on the flight home, we took it round to the cargo manager of Sabena Airlines, an impressive young Malian. He told us just to leave it on his office floor and he would have it delivered, wrapped in blankets, to Exeter airport for a very modest charge. 'If it doesn't arrive in five days, ring me up!' It arrived, undamaged, and on our doorstep, in three.

A strange people, the Malians. The country is too poor to feed so many mouths, yet a man who breeds fewer than ten children feels ashamed; and even the poorest women deck themselves in voluminous Technicolor robes, whose necks are always made wide enough to fall provocatively off one shoulder. No one seemed to notice the exceptional filth, and ground-level drains trickled right through the huge vegetable market in Bamako, in between colourful women sitting on the ground selling their wares. The people as a whole were unaffectedly joky and good mannered, but it would take a thousand Aminata Traourés with plenipotentiary powers to alter their mind-set. Something similar might no doubt be said – by Aminata perhaps – of Middle America (or Middle England).

The following year we made another foray into Africa, this time to Namibia where Finella was now working. We had learnt (each time after the worst was over) that she had barely survived a series of dreadful diseases when walking and trucking up and down Africa on leaving school. The worst was cerebral malaria due to a rare allergy to quinine; luckily the Melhuishes, living in retirement in Harare, had rescued her from the small clinic she had been carried into in Bulawayo when she collapsed, temporarily paralysed and blinded, and nursed her back to health. In Cape Town she had been in hospital again, this time with tick-bite fever, but had impatiently discharged herself and travelled by bus for twenty-four hours to Swakopmund on the coast of Namibia, where she was working taking tourists and 'disturbed' children trekking in the desert. By the time we succeeded in getting there she greeted us looking, but not feeling, well, and on her return to Devon months later was found to have bilharzia, which the doctors had failed to diagnose in Cape Town.

Of the many excitements we enjoyed wandering around in Namibia I shall mention only four. One was the sensational game parks in the north. Dozens of wild beasts, including rhinos, assembled daily at dusk in order of precedence to quench their thirst in a pool, the whole process – from the approach until the final bending to drink – being conducted in a sort of slow motion, as though the animals were moving under water. The second was the gigantic nests of a remarkable bird, the social warbler, built in large trees further south. Many of these phenomenal bird houses were of the size and shape of bullocks, and one we measured was 15 feet long, 8 feet high and 7 feet wide. Hundreds and hundreds of these tiny birds were flying in and out of their downward-facing entrance holes; and what a staggering amount of grass they must collect to construct a city of this size. The third was a sight near our campsite at Twyfelfontein. A roadside notice said 'VISIT OUR GRAFT SENTER'. This proved to be the finest example of private enterprise in Namibia. It consisted of the bodywork of a crashed car bearing on its horizontal bits a display of very simple crafts – set up in the middle of nowhere by an enchanting couple. God knows whether they ever sold anything, except to us. The fourth was the prehistoric engravings of animals of all sorts and sizes on an outcrop of sandstone rocks at Twyfelfontein. What especially intrigued us was the artists' practice of drawing their hoof marks separately, below where their legs stopped. Was this for the education of children in a hunter-gatherer culture – a sort of Stone Age primary school?

CHAPTER 25

Dramas in India and Bangladesh

APART from our travels, in the nineties Jenny was writing and lecturing on indigo as well as contributing, with a group of Devonshire artists, to a succession of Michael Honnor's handmade books of colourful artists' prints. The first commemorated the quatercentenary of the poet-priest Robert Herrick, whom the stuffy ecclesiastical establishment of his day had exiled for years to a small Devonshire parish on the edge of Dartmoor. Each contributor chose one or two short extracts or poems of Herrick's. Here is one of the two four-line poems Jenny selected to illustrate:

> The Coming of Good Luck
>
> So good luck came and on my roof did light
> Like noyse-less snowe or as the dew of night,
> Not all at once, but gently, as the trees
> Are by the sun-beams tickl'd by degrees.

The second book, *A Printmakers' Flora*, commemorated wild flowers and their poetical colloquial names. Both very limited-edition books sold for high prices and the second was snapped up by the V & A Museum.

As for me, I had already started scribbling away at these memoirs, as well as writing some more 'Immortal Lyrics' (my term). Jenny thought well of my verses, and liked teasing me by quoting Wendy Cope:

> When they ask me Who's your favourite poet?
> I'd better not mention you,
> Though you certainly are my favourite poet
> And I like your poems too.

I did acquire a few other fans among those on whom occasional bundles were inflicted. And I received quite a number of prizes in 'national competitions', and gave a few poetry readings.

Steve Sims, a freelance writer and publisher in Crediton, decided to publish a collection of about hundred specimens of my poetry at his Cervisian Press. It eventually came out (with suitably quirky illustrations, mainly by Jenny) in November 2000 and had to be 'launched' by another reading. I chose the book's title, *A Kind of Kindness*, incidentally, from a passage in a poem I did not include in the collection, but I am still rather proud of the three relevant lines:

> Subject and object, boxed always in together,
> Slowly we reconcile our Selves to Us
> By a kind of kindness …

Meanwhile my three older daughters were firmly settled in three corners of Britain, between them bringing up my seven grandchildren; Cati (after four years in Catholic Guatemala, where her husband was training Presbyterian ministers) in Scotland, Ann in England and Alison (still a practising violinist) in Wales. Jamie was constantly travelling, working for Oxfam on their projects in East Africa. Finella, after a stint as 'galley slave' on a tall ship, had moved to Australia. Later she married – in typically unconventional style – Ian Gompertz, and set up her own equine establishment at Hamlet's Creek near Sydney. And Hamish's degree in music would lead to some entertaining posts in the show bands of huge American cruise liners in Alaska, Central America and the Caribbean.

The beginning of the new millennium found me accompanying Jenny on another of her distant indigo expeditions. This was to Bengal to explore anything left of the old Bengal Indigo Company's activities on both sides of today's India/Bangladesh frontier, using the illustrated manuscript journals of a certain Thomas Machell (b. 1824). These had been sold in the 1980s by an unmarried descendant of the Machell family to the British Library, where they remained, until Jenny heard of them, unread. How this attractive young man, who had (among many other things) worked for nine years as an assistant to an indigo planter in the 1840s, crossed Jenny's path and became the subject, and part author, of Jenny's proposed book about him will all be explained when she finishes it.

We had a stupendous month. Crossing from Calcutta to Bangladesh was an experience in itself. On the Indian side there was only one gloomy official to deal with all non-Indian travellers going in either direction. The poor man had to copy all passport details very slowly into four separate ledgers. It was a Kafka-like nightmare – especially for a group of despairing Thais, who could not communicate in anything but unintelligible Thai and had been in the queue for three whole days.

Once across we were met and looked after by friends – an irrigation expert and his wife, Stephen and Liz Bichieri-Colombi. At their flat in Jessore we were joined by Ruby Ghuznavi, a splendid Bangladeshi natural-dye enthusiast, who had flown from Dhaka to meet Jenny and talk dyes. She accompanied us on our three-day exploration up-river. Among the relics of the indigo industry (abandoned 140 years ago) our most exciting discovery was at Amjhupi. Climbing through a hole in one of the factory's still-standing outbuildings we found first an ancient chest full of old accounts, which alas turned out to be Bangladeshi tax records; but then, braving the snakes and ducking under swarms of large bats escaping from the adjoining room, what should we find in it but the original drying racks for indigo blocks (exactly like those in the Woad Museum near Toulouse). Jenny was over the moon.

When we crossed the frontier back into India we hired a taxi in the official taxi park to take us on the three-hour journey to Calcutta. The driver agreed to do a brief excursion first up-river to see whether anything was left of a major indigo factory at Mulnath described by Machell. This involved crossing a tributary river in a punt and then a longish walk. On getting back to the river we found large buffaloes with sweeping horns queueing up to cross with us on the punt. Fortunately we were given precedence. During the drive back to the frontier post, our driver turned unaccountably sour, and after lengthy discussion in the transport park he dumped our baggage and us in a shoddy-looking taxi with an unappetising driver and mate. We set off, and after a short distance the car stuttered to a halt. The driver fiddled under the bonnet and on we went for a mile, when the same thing happened again. After another 10 miles the engine conked out once more, and this time the driver declared, from under the bonnet, that it was not repairable by him. He advised us to get out in the hope that some other vehicle would come past on which we might thumb a lift. When we did so, the driver and his mate instantly slammed the bonnet shut, leapt into the car and drove off in a cloud of dust with our baggage in the boot. So there we were, abandoned by crooks in an uninhabited wilderness in the almost-dark. Fortunately we had always made a point of carrying our passports, money, and cameras in knapsacks on our backs, but everything else – all Jenny's drawings, notes, films, etc., as well as our clothing – was gone. After a minute or two of growing alarm a van did come past, whose helpful driver stopped and took us on board. We learnt later that a young Englishman had recently been given a drugged banana in this dangerously dacoit-infested area and, having passed out, had been dragged into the forest, robbed of everything and left there stark naked. Our fate was at least less disagreeable than his.

As we drove towards Calcutta we could find no sign of our own despoilers. On arrival we spent the hour after midnight (it was now Jenny's birthday too!) trying to get a helpful reaction from the officers in the main (Tolhalla) police station. They first told us we must go back to the area of the offence, on the grounds that it lay outside their geographical purview, and report to the police at Barasat, two hours' drive away. But they changed their minds when we marched out declaring that we would go straight off and complain to 'my colleague' the British High Commissioner. One of them ran out to call us back from our rickshaw. They then took a long statement and said they would pursue the matter. The frustrating process that followed for three days was made worse by their arresting the suspected thief and calling us in to identify him. He could scarcely walk as a result of their 'interrogation'

– and he was the wrong man. Number plates get switched around freely in the Indian underworld.

The evening of Jenny's birthday proved more enjoyable than its morning. We were invited to dine in the Calcutta Club, a grand legacy of Empire, by the Maharaja of Burdwan and his wife – Danny and (if you can believe it) Pussy. Maharajas still use the title, though it was officially abolished on India's independence. The invitation resulted from our having met a friend of his niece in Somerset. During the meal the Maharaja told us that his father had owned more square miles of territory than anyone else in the whole British Empire, maintaining dozens of palaces and twenty-six Hindu temples. He also mentioned that he had done a PhD at SOAS (the School of Oriental and African Studies in London University). When I asked what on, he replied without the trace of a smile, 'My subject was landownership in Bengal.' The family property had, of course, all been expropriated fifty years ago, resulting in hundreds of court cases.

But Danny and Pussy were enjoyable hosts. At one point Pussy went off from the table (to the loo, we supposed) and returned some minutes later bearing, touchingly, a birthday cake for Jenny in the form of a tiny chunk of gingerbread with a 2-inch stub of used candle on top – the only bits of cake and candle the kitchen staff had been able to rustle up.

Our base in Calcutta was the extraordinary Fairlawn Hotel, in a grubby lane, Sudder Street. It had been owned for fifty years by a pair of aged eccentrics who had 'stayed on', remaining more 'British' than anyone who hadn't. (This applied especially to the wife Violet, though she was in fact of Armenian origin.) The Fairlawn stands back from the lane behind a colourful jungle of potted and hanging plants; its walls are covered with photographs and similar memorabilia of often quite distinguished past lodgers – including a framed statement by Eric Newby (ironical or not) to the effect that the Fairlawn was 'his favourite hotel in the world'. A gong was sounded at meal times and guests not parading promptly were likely to be refused service. The food, generally tepid and served by grumpy waiters, was as execrable as the stuff that used to be provided in English boarding schools, and not remotely Indian. Lodging there, comfortably enough to be fair, was worth a guinea a minute, always under the intense but of course smiling scrutiny of Violet.

We were shown round both halves of the city, the imperial and the Indian, by Monish Chakraburti, a knowledgeable architect and conservationist. The walls in the Indian half were plastered everywhere with electioneering graffiti, notably the Communist Party's hammer and sickle. Across it were often written the words STAMP ON THIS SYMBOL. I presumed these had been added by the opposition but learnt from our guide that they meant 'When you vote, put your thumbprint against the hammer and sickle'. The endless small shops were either pharmacies or computer businesses; but in answer to a question Monish said there *was* one birth control shop, a tiny one which he showed us squeezed between two computer shops. Did people go there? we asked. Men go there in hundreds, he told us, in the belief that its purpose was to enable them to breed even more children.

The Indians have taken to computers in a big way, and I understand that even the British government now has the computerisation of its complicated finances done for it in India. I wished the Indians had taken in a similar big way to the arts of refuse disposal. A refuse disposal lorry did wobble down our hotel lane one day and we watched its workers shovelling up the muck and heaving their shovel-loads right over the top of their high-piled lorry so that it all fell down the other side and stayed there on the ground when they moved on.

With our Devon friend Anthony Harrison, we hired a 'dinghy' and had to push it through the muck on the river's edge, along the bank of which once ran the imperialists' immaculate esplanade. But once in the clearer middle of the wide river the sight of similar 'dinghies' propelling themselves hither and thither with one huge oar against the background of the glorious Haora suspension bridge was a spectacular reward.

We had meanwhile made the acquaintance of a remarkable Hindu lady, Amrita Mukerjee, who had collected indigo textiles in Nigeria and whose name had been given to Jenny before we left home. When we called on her in her Calcutta flat she decided to come with us on our explorations to the north, hiring for the purpose a commodious 4-wheel-drive Toyota. Before we set off she took us to dine in Calcutta's most exclusive restaurant with some like-minded friends. Apart from the exquisite Bengali food, the relative of the Mukerjees who owns and runs the restaurant delighted us with an account of her 'training'. The lecturer at some college of food science, where her parents sent her, spent hours teaching her students what she called 'The Broken Bowl Method of Housekeeping'. Under it, broken bits of every bowl a housekeeper smashed had to be ranged by her along a mantelpiece or kitchen shelf, and into each had to be placed money for different specific domestic requirements. Mastery of this valuable technique was essential for passing the final exam.

On our explorations we made, as in Bangladesh, good use of Thomas Machell's journal and drawings. When we were being led by the villagers to the site of one old indigo factory, Amrita in her voluminous sari wobbled enthusiastically along the narrow bunds of wet paddy fields and once fell in with shouts of laughter. Amrita had arranged with some Banerjee friends that we could spend our final night in their up-country retreat, though they wouldn't be there themselves. This was Plessey House, originally an indigo planter's residence, near the site of the famous victory at Plessey against the Mughals by which Clive (whose brother was a direct ancestor of Marnie's mother) had effectively seized control of India for Britain. The last indigo planter at Plessey, before the early Banerjees acquired the house, had died in it in 1809 and his tomb stood beside the river. Its inscription named him as John Ogilvie, who (as we learnt later) had started an indigo factory there when his sugar plantations in the West Indies had shown signs of collapse. By a curious coincidence (if it was no more than that) Marnie's uncle Sir Angus Ogilvy owed his wealth to a sugar plantation in the West Indies inherited from a direct ancestor. Could this have been the John Ogilvie (the name could be spelt in either way in those days) who died in Plessey House in 1809?

His house, enlarged by the Banerjees from a recognisably typical indigo planter's residence, was now surrounded by magnificent gardens. (A few months later this splendid house was severely damaged in the unprecedented floods of 2000. Much of its garden – along with the Ogilvie tombstone – was washed out of existence.) After our night in it we got up early to look round in the dawn light before setting off to search for another indigo factory described and drawn by Machell at Khabolya, near the Bangladeshi border. We were already getting low on petrol and discovered, when we had gone 10 miles along the main road, that there was a petrol workers' strike throughout Bengal and that all filling stations were shut. We tried the next one in vain and had almost run dry when Amrita noticed a merchant's shoddy workshop standing back from the road with three 40-gallon drums in its yard. When the owner was dug out it was established that the drums contained the right stuff, and after a powerful appeal from Amrita he reluctantly agreed to let us have a watering-canful. That wouldn't have got us far but the imperturbable Ram, our driver, quietly filled the watering-can over and over again unobserved until he had decanted enough to get us to our immediate objective (which was a long way off the main road) and then to Calcutta.

When we eventually located the old indigo planter's place, the only traceable relics were the base of the grand steps of the house and the tombs of this planter and his wife(?) – the name slabs had been removed long ago – hidden in a clump of bushes. If an up-country planter died on the job, as so many did (often of malaria or cholera), he had to be buried on-site since in that climate his corpse could not reach one of the grand old British cemeteries in Calcutta.

We might have ended in a local cemetery ourselves the previous evening. In order to reach Plessey House after visiting the ruins of Machell's first indigo factory, we had been told there was a short cut to our destination, though it would mean getting across a nearby river. We decided to go and see. When we reached the river as darkness fell we found the only way across it was by punt – not designed for carrying 4-wheel-drive Toyotas! The punt man said we could probably manoeuvre it on to a square of bamboos marginally bigger than the Toyota, balanced on a pair of small punts tied together, a few yards upstream. Amrita and Ram (and more hesitantly ourselves) thought this would be fun and imperturbably proceeded to nudge the vehicle little by little on to the bamboos. It *just* fitted. Thrillingly but hilariously we were punted across.

Our last day's excitements were not yet over. On arrival in Calcutta, Amrita took us first to call on the owner of Plessey House, and then to visit the flat of the great Indian film-maker and writer, Satyajit Ray, to whose son Sandip (also a film-maker) Amrita's sister is married. The great man himself was dead but his charming old widow and Amrita's sister welcomed us. His study was packed with books from floor to ceiling. The climax came, as we stood there admiringly, when the old lady untied a recently arrived parcel of books on a crowded table. What should it contain but copies of a new paperback edition of Satyajit's collected short stories, all written where we stood, entitled *Indigo*. And it began with a story of that very name. The old lady presented Jenny with a copy and movingly inscribed it. That night, as Jenny lay in bed in the Fairlawn, she read the 'Indigo' story, and was transfixed. It is a brilliantly spooky tale of a modern Indian who dosses down in an old indigo planter's house.

To restore ourselves after our exertions in low-lying airless Bengal we went off into the fresh and freezing air of the Himalayas, climbing the narrow wiggling mountain road that rose 7,000 feet to Darjeeling from the railway terminus on the plain below. No wonder the imperial Britons wanted Darjeeling as a summer resort, whatever the cost of constructing access to it by wheeled transport, horse-drawn at first and, at the end of the century, motorised. What was even more remarkable was their construction in 1881, beside the road and sometimes *on* it, of a 2-foot-gauge railway. This still runs today, using the original engine, a real museum piece. It takes nine hours to climb from the bottom to the top; and Anthony and Ski Harrison, whom we joined in Darjeeling, had ventured the whole way up in its ancient rolling stock. One afternoon Jenny and I took an hour's ride in it ourselves from Darjeeling to Ghoom, 7 whole kilometres. The engine runs (or walks) on coke, shovelled into its furnace non-stop from the front end. Every time it stopped, water was conveyed into its boiler via a rickety semi-circular length made of old petrol tins for several minutes. When it had drunk enough, a bell clanged to remind passengers to board again – avoiding if possible the mustard-coloured smoke spewing out from its funnel and everywhere else. It was a priceless journey – in every sense, for nobody invited us to buy tickets.

On a clear day you can see Kanchenjunga, the third-highest mountain in the world, from Darjeeling, and we were at least granted a brief glimpse of it in the snow. The inhabitants are ethnically different from the Indians down below, gentle Buddhists and mostly refugees from Tibet. Being poverty-stricken these refugees have had to sell off their few precious possessions to shopkeepers to be purchased in the tourist season by people with cameras and warm clothing, like us. In our own desire for warmth we replaced some of our stolen clothes with jerseys said to be of yak wool and other items, costing almost nothing.

But Indians did not apparently make shoes larger than size eight, so my cold feet had to continue flopping around in their (wet) open sandals.

In our blissful hotel, the famous Windamere, we were kept warm by hot-water bottles in the beds and coal fires alight all day in every public room and bedroom. On the hill-top behind it was a big Buddhist shrine, enveloped in millions of multi-coloured prayer-hankies strung from poles and from wires between the trunks of the tall surrounding trees. Groups of small brown monkeys were enjoying themselves by climbing unreproved up the cascades of prayer-hankies. In the centre the shrine itself contained a clay stove into which the thronging worshippers cast papers bearing (we supposed) confessions of their sins for the gods up above to give them absolution. It was all singularly moving.

We hired a taxi with the Harrisons to go farther east for a few hours to Kalimpong. The road drops thousands of feet to the River Teestria (beyond which shoot up the real Himalayas) and then climbs back up again to Kalimpong, a smaller and slightly lower version of Darjeeling. Along the precipitous flanks of the road huts of wood or tin projected, their lower ends suspended, as if by hind legs, on wobbly-looking poles. From our hotel in Kalimpong, owned by Mr and Mrs Macdonald (though they showed no physical evidence of Scottish origins), we walked up and down the town and drew pictures of a Buddhist monastery. Climbing to a higher monastery, we listened to monks chanting in a closed outbuilding, the leader singing while the rest droned a sort of pibroch noise. Nearby we passed a yard where a man was hanging what appeared to be white yarn, thick as string, over frames. It turned out to be the local string-like vermicelli being dried; and in an adjoining room another man was teasing it out and rolling it into little paper pokes, piled ceiling high in the corner for sale. An oldish man by the door had just bought a poke but insisted on presenting it to me with a smile – and went off home without his meagre supper. In Kalimpong everyone always smiled at us.

These were the last smiles I exchanged for some time. Having driven down the corkscrew road from Darjeeling to the flat lands below, I felt suddenly unwell. Just surviving the fourteen-hour train journey to Varanasi (Benares), I was swept into hospital by Jenny. The Heritage Hospital, we were assured, was the best in that huge and holy city. (I was in no mood to brood on what the less good ones might be like.) All its beds being full, I was wheeled in a trolley into the intensive care unit, pushed up against the feet of a man distinctly in need of intensive care, and put on a drip. The nice ward nurse, who had difficulty reading English, wrote me down in the medical record ledger as HUG GLEN, but none of the pretty nurses showed any inclination to do so, even after it was later changed to HUGH GRANT. The unexpected first question of the doctor who eventually came to examine me was, 'Do you play cricket?' Actually the doctors were splendid and carried out every sort of high-tech test including a brain scan, but found nothing, even in my brain, to cause further alarm.

It was evidently viral pneumonia. In retrospect I wouldn't have missed for anything my time in the Heritage Hospital, despite its non-operative mod. cons, the non-provision of any food and (when I was moved into a larger ward) the long nights of groaning, snoring and high-pitched Hindu from the beds around me. All that Jenny enjoyed was a quick visit to Varanasi's famous *ghats*, where thousands of citizens stood washing themselves and their clothes in the Ganges' chocolate-coloured water, despite the corpses of cows and occasionally humans floating past. After three days of this the East–West Rescue Centre in Delhi sent a Sikh doctor by air to fly me (and Jenny) there. It proved a splendid place manned by three excellent Sikh medicos; but all I shall record of them is the view they expressed – damning enough even if allowance is made for minority resentments – of India's dominant Hindu population. They described the Hindus as after nothing but money. Those that collected lots had 'no curiosity or interests' and spent it all on 'cream cakes for their wives and still bigger TV sets'. Much more alarming was the account given by one of them of the appalling destruction some years ago of the Sikhs' great temple at Amritsar, said to have been ordered by the Prime Minister, Mrs Gandhi. Our Sikh had been doctoring there at the time. Sikhs were being assassinated all round and he had had to hide inside a grand piano for three days. He had then escaped only thanks to the kindness of a Hindu colleague.

Delhi is said to be the second-most polluted city in the world (though it has improved since we were there). A month before this, when we flew there by Air Jordan on our way to Calcutta, its airport was under an impenetrable blanket of pollution. Its automatic landing system had broken down and we had to turn round to fly back for three hours, landing in Karachi. Karachi being in Pakistan, where Indians were unwelcome, no one was allowed to disembark. After another three hours we took off again. Lots of aircraft were now circling round above Delhi hoping a hole would appear in the blanket and enable them to land. We joined them. Then, seeing a small hole, our Jordanian pilot bravely dived through it and managed to land. We were then faced by the almost equally impenetrable blanket of Indian officialdom and barely managed to pierce it and climb on a train for Calcutta.

This time, however, Delhi was reasonably clear. When I was allowed up some days later, the city surprised me by the magnificence of its old (mostly Mughal) buildings, but also by one new one, the Bahai temple, one of the loveliest structures I have ever seen. But all this splendour was counterbalanced by the fact that half the city's inhabitants live wherever they can raise a bit of sackcloth or something slightly less porous over their wretched heads.

We spent an evening in the house of our old friends the Housegos, who had abandoned their respective professions ten years ago and set up in Delhi a textile factory, now employing three hundred Indians and selling all over the world. David capped our story of the theft of our baggage in Bengal by an astonishing one of his own. When he was the *Financial Times* correspondent in Asia he had flown to Madras to cover some happening four hours' drive south of it. He climbed into a taxi and set off. The driver soon stopped to fill up with petrol. While he was doing so, David went off for a pee. When he came back, his taxi had vanished – with all his baggage and vital documents in it. He made his way back to the taxi park and told his new driver to whizz south and see whether they could find the thieving offender anywhere. They drove for three hours, gave up the search and returned to the taxi park. And *there* was his original taxi. Its apologetic driver had driven south for three hours before he noticed that his passenger was not in the seat behind him! But in David's case, unlike ours, all his baggage was safe.

I will not describe Delhi's marvels, which thousands of tourists see. When the time came to catch our Air Jordan flight back to England, we were advised to get to the airport at 1 a.m. for its departure five hours later. We did so and joined the horde of would-be passengers. When we reached the check-in desk at 5.30 we were informed that owing to the usual overbooking our seats were no longer available and we should come again in ten days' time for the next Air Jordan flight that was not already fully booked. With great difficulty I found a taxi and back we went to the East–West Rescue Clinic, where the Sikhs welcomed us into an even nicer double room. The head one, Dr Chowla, magically fixed for us to fly in two days' time by Air India, upgraded free of charge to club class, and even arranged for a car to meet us at Heathrow and drive us to Devon – all at the expense of our insurers.

We made good use of our extra days, not least at the Kutab Minar complex just outside the city. It boasts the first and highest minaret in the Islamic world (Mughal, of course), but it provided an even more unexpected surprise. As we were walking out through the multiple colonnade erected by the Mughals out of decorated columns looted from the temples of other faiths during their invasion of India in the sixteenth century, Jenny suddenly said, 'Shut your eyes. Take two steps forward. Now open them!' When I opened them, there 2 feet in front of them was the head of a splendid 'Green Man'. ('Green Men' in south-west England, as well as medieval bench-ends, had been an obsession of mine for some years.) Then we found similar 'Green Men' on almost every column. It was from Jain temples that these particular columns had been looted. But how come that the Jain artists had carved 'Green Men' (with the familiar vines growing out of their mouths, etc.) thousands of miles from those in Europe and several centuries earlier? It was a splendid high ending to the ups and downs of our month's expedition.

I will just add the rather lower ending to another visitor's experiences in Delhi. This was Anthony Harrison. He had gone to look (as we too had done) at the famous Red Fort, a handsome antiquity on the central hill, and told me how, from the walkway up above, he had observed the 'mowing' of the lawn round the fort. Two men were *pulling* an old Atco with no motor by means of a rope tied to its front. Their dodge was evidently to show rich tourists how poor Indians were and to collect coins thrown to them in consequence. Anthony indicated with a gesture his unwillingness to contribute, and the disgruntled mowers, breaking into civilised English, shouted at him, 'Fuck off, you.'

CHAPTER 26

Following Footsteps in the Marquesas Islands and Southern India

EARLY in the new millennium, Finella had given me on my eighty-second birthday a card with a drawing of a donkey with spectacles. The likeness of this donkey to myself – as everyone (including me) agreed – was uncanny. It would, I feared, become even more acute in whatever 'donkey's years' remained for me. But my life still had much unexpected fun.

The first of the heavenly bits of the world revealed to me in my donkey's years was the Pyrenees. Jenny had been addressing a group of dye buffs near Carcassonne, and when that was over we drove up into those magical mountains for a sun-struck week of enchantment. All I will recall here is the final stanza of a poem they inspired in me:

On the Col de Peguère
The cowbells hanging in that white herd couched
Two miles off on the other hill
Make mediaeval music. No other sound,
No visible movement, breaks the still
Silence. Up here we'll neither see nor hear,
Till we have dropped right down the zigzag mountain,
The singing stream that guards it – a halbardier
Guarding his mounted lord and singing for him.
Cowbell and streamsong: in this mountain air
What man-made music could, my love, compare?

But even that week's benison could not compare with the two-month expedition round the world in early 2001, which Thomas Machell (see p. 297), with financial help from the British Academy, sent us on. All we had originally intended was to pursue Thomas's traces in southern India in the 1850s and then pop down to Sydney to see Finella before flying home. But our travel agent disclosed that it would be much cheaper to take round-the-world tickets and that this would also enable us to stop off anywhere we liked – for instance, he said, in French Polynesia. Jenny's heart gave a resounding thump, for the Marquesas Islands, which are part of French Polynesia, were the scene of

23 GBP in 2002 in Anaho Bay, Nukuhiva (where Robert Louis Stevenson
anchored and stayed for three weeks en route for Samoa).

a dramatic episode in Thomas Machell's life in 1844, but she had scarcely
imagined it possible that she could ever get there herself.

The Marquesas Islands could be reached only by a sixteen-day trip in a
monthly cargo ship from Tahiti, the Polynesian capital; but Tahiti was precisely
where round-the-world flights came down to refuel. The Marquesas lie 500
sea miles to its north-east, farther from a continent than anywhere else in the
world: indeed most atlases only show them in a 'box'. To get berths on the
cargo ship, the *Aranui*, and sail to this box ('Box ahoy!', as a friend of Jenny's
neatly put it) meant rearranging all our plans, reversing our direction round
the world and flying direct to Tahiti via Los Angeles.

Tahiti's capital, Papeete, proved to be an unappetising city bulging with
tourists. But the *Aranui* turned out a splendid old boat. Its early life had been
spent traipsing round the Baltic, but in its old age here it was, in Papeete,
manned entirely by Polynesians, brown and tattooed all over. Its captain was
the fattest man I have ever seen. He had to squeeze his tummy sideways
through all the ship's doors. But he was enormously jovial, and he formed
with others of the crew the uproarious ship's orchestra. To add to the trip's
attractions, we were the only British among some fifty polyglot passengers.

After a stop on one of the intervening atolls to see the production of its
unique black pearls, we eventually came in sight of the capital village of the
Marquesas in a spectacular bay on Nukuhiva, the main island. This was
the place to which in 1844 Thomas's sailing ship, having survived a terrifying

passage round Cape Horn, took coals from Newcastle(!) to fuel the new patrol boats of the French, who had invaded and colonised Polynesia two years earlier. (Since steamships could not then cross big oceans they put together small ones on the spot.) On arrival Thomas fell in love, not just with the island but more powerfully with Wyheva, the daughter of a local cannibal chief.

But Nukuhiva had a special attraction for me too, for this was where Robert Louis Stevenson first hit land on his voyage in 1888 on the schooner *Casco* from San Francisco in search of a climate that might prolong his tuberculous life. The Anaho bay where the *Casco* fetched up in the north-east of Nukuhiva island is now virtually uninhabited; but as an act of family *pietas* I was keen to touch my hat there. We managed to do this in a hired motor boat, holding on tight as it bounced through a big spumy swell. RLS thought the island beautiful beyond measure and spent three weeks there before pushing on, ultimately to Samoa, where six years later he died. His book *In the South Seas* was not his most admired work, perhaps because his criticisms of colonialism were not then fashionable, but it is a fine read. (One quote from it that I cherish is his description of the coconut palm as 'that giraffe among vegetables'.) So too is the book* by his mother, Margaret Stevenson née Balfour, who was one of his party and who had seldom ventured out of Edinburgh before. She felt so uniquely relaxed in the Marquesas that she went so far as to take off her thick stockings and prance barefoot on the beach hand in hand with a near-naked notable. RLS relates among much else the sad story of another Englishman, who told him, when they later met, how he (like so many others) had fallen in love with a Marquesan chieftainess. She had rejected his advances on the grounds that without tattoos he looked indecently naked. So he had got himself painfully tattooed from head to foot and presented himself again. This time the lady simply roared with laughter and sent him packing.

Another famous writer on the Marquesas in the middle of the nineteenth century was Herman Melville. In Nukuhiva he had illegally jumped the American whaler he was employed on and, to escape pursuit and punishment if caught, he had taken refuge with a wild tribe in the valley just over the hill from the harbour. In his book *Typee* (which in his lifetime sold much better than his later *Moby-Dick*) he too claims to have fallen in love with a tribal beauty – just two years before the same thing happened to Thomas. *Typee*, which had not been published when Thomas wrote his Marquesas journals, is a gripping story, part fact, part fiction. Thomas's account in his private journals

---

* *From Saranac to the Marquesas*, Methuen, 1903. It consists of letters to her sister Maria Balfour. The notes added by another member of the family, Graham Balfour (the first biographer of RLS), include a detailed account of Marquesan tattooing, carried out with a sharpened shark's tooth and a mallet, the colouring being prepared from the ashes of the candle-nut mixed with vegetable juices. All very painful.

of his own passionate affair is, we may be sure, wholly fact. All I will record of it is that his beloved Wyheva insisted on taking him to visit her father, having warned him that he hated Europeans since the French invaders had slaughtered his three sons. In the event the chief took to Thomas enormously and approved of the idea of their marrying. But the marriage was not to be, Thomas deciding sadly that he had to call it off as it would have meant staying there and abandoning his beloved widowed father.

RLS, as I said, did not die in the Marquesas, but another European prominent in a different field of art chose to do just that. This was Paul Gauguin. A typically naughty story is related of one thing he did on Ua Pou island. The local Bishop had refused to sell him a piece of land belonging to the Church unless he attended mass. So Gauguin reluctantly went to church every Sunday in order to buy the land. Once he had acquired it he never set foot in the church again, and got his revenge for having had to do so by painting a picture of the Bishop in the arms of his mistress and sticking it up outside his door on the main thoroughfare. When Gauguin died the Bishop refused permission for him to be buried in the cemetery but was forced to relent by the outcry from Gauguin's supporters. Gauguin had the last laugh too since the Bishop's own tomb is sited almost alongside Gauguin's.

During our own stay on Ua Pou there were very nearly some other deaths there. A small group of us had got ourselves driven in a Toyota to explore the 'Valley of the Kings'. This was where in the past a certain clan had set up its 'capital' because its rough and rocky bay was notoriously too dangerous for enemy clans to paddle into and attack them. On our dropping down the valley to the bay's small shingly beach, a bathe was decided on. 'Don't go in the middle of the bay,' our fat driver admonished us, 'there's a nasty undertow there. Keep to its left side.' Our four companions and Jenny plunged in where instructed. Not having a swimsuit with me I modestly intended to follow them in my skimpy underpants but had hardly undressed and turned round towards the water when Jenny and the others waded out looking mighty queer. They had very very nearly drowned. Had it not been for a slice of rock to which they had just managed to struggle and cling, they would have been. The fierce undertow had been sucking them out into the crashing surf. Jenny told me she had thought her end had come.

Back on board the *Aranui* Jenny continued sketching portraits of the captain and other members of the crew. The latter, wearing little but their tattoos (even on their bald heads), worked right through the night at every island unloading cargo and loading in exchange whatever an island had for export. Marquesans are not inclined by nature to such a thing as work, for which there is apparently no word in their language, but our ship's crew showed they were extremely capable of it. Since there are only two islands with jetties, the *Aranui* couldn't anchor closer to the others than about a half a kilometre. In such cases we passengers had to trans-ship to small whale boats and then wade the last 20 yards – all of us, that is, except the aged like me, who were carried in the cradling arms of the handsome sailors. Jenny was very jealous.

These precipitous islands are indescribably beautiful, especially in the changing lights that settle on them. RLS sets the scene better than I can: 'The land heaved up in peaks and rising vales; it fell in cliffs and buttresses; its colour ran through fifty modulations in a scale of pearl and rose and olive; and it was crowned above by opalescent clouds.' And he finishes his account of arriving in Anaho bay with these memorable words: 'The first experience can never be repeated. The first love, the first sunrise, the first South Sea island, are memories apart and touch a virginity of sense.'

On one of these virginal islands Jenny and some other younger braves indulged in a strenuous six-hour climb in pouring rain over the precipitous mountains to see the third-longest waterfall in the world. At its bottom it disappears behind a vast rock. Jenny and two other girls rashly swam through a hole in the rock to see what they could see in the pool beyond. What they fortunately didn't see (nobody having warned them of the danger) were the large lethally poisonous eels that apparently abound there. So this was Jenny's second lucky escape from death in the Marquesas.

The islands' inhabitants (those who have survived the evils brought to them over two hundred years by Europeans – alcohol, drugs, syphilis, etc.) were described by RLS as 'unquestionably the best-looking people in the world'. They are attractive for many minor reasons too. (For instance, not only the girls but the men too have the charming habit of wearing flowers in their hair, not out of vanity but just because they like to.) It was great to watch the men carrying sacks of copra (dried coconut meat) from piles on the shore for transfer to the *Aranui*. This meant plunging through 20 yards of surf with the sacks on their heads and hurling them into a cage on a bouncing whale-boat. Another delight was watching the manufacture of bark cloth on the one island, Fatuhiva, where the practice continues. Bark cloth is ingeniously made from the soaked and pounded inner bark of three different trees and was formerly the main Marquesan clothing. Today there is almost more of it – thanks initially to Captain Cook – in Exeter Museum than anywhere else. One more attraction of the Marquesas deserves a mention. Is there anywhere else in the world where mango trees grow wild and a 20-foot stick with a forked end lies under big ones, so that passers-by can dislodge and devour as many mangoes, almost as big as rugby balls, as they fancy?

The Marquesans, wherever they first came from, were clearly an adventurous lot. They are the ancestors of the Maoris of New Zealand, but I had no idea that they had once sailed away to make a colony of Easter Island, 1,000 miles south-east, centuries before it became a Chilean one, and that the famous Easter Island figures may well have been the offspring, so to speak, of the strange representations of ancestral gods (*tikis*) carved in stone by the

Marquesans in their own islands. They give off, as do the whole islands, a spiritual force, *mana*, still potently felt by the islanders and feelable even by visitors such as ourselves. We were shown quite a number of these *tikis*, the oddest being a horizontal female divinity giving birth. Below her head is carved in relief what Thor Heyerdahl (of *Kon-Tiki* fame) declared to be a llama; and partly on this he based his mistaken belief that Polynesia had been colonised from Peru. His 'llama', because of its long curled tail, is now regarded as a common-or-garden Marquesan dog.

I could go on for ever about the charms of these islands. When the time came we watched with heavy hearts as they faded behind us into the sunset. On arrival back in Papeete we ferried over to Moorea island and trekked out to Cook's Bay. The eighteenth-century Captain Cook was the one great British explorer who was recognised as a really fine man, though ultimately stabbed to death by a native of Hawaii. When RLS approached Anaho he wrote: 'It was with something perhaps of the same anxious pleasure as thrilled the bosom of discoverers that we drew near these problematic shores.'

Captain Cook, as he bravely picked his way through uncharted reefs into the Moorean bay that still bears his name, must certainly have experienced that thrill. It was only by the greatest luck that we succeeded in getting back in time to catch the ferry to Papeete and the flight to Sydney on the next stage of our journey. We waited a frantic hour for the old wooden bus that serves Cook's Bay almost as regardless of timetables as British railway operators. It was a huge relief when it eventually rumbled along and picked us up in the nick of time.

Finella was waiting for us at Sydney airport and drove us out to the log cabin she was then living in, 40 miles to the west, surrounded by animals of all kinds that she had rescued from the slaughterhouse. As for Sydney's famous Opera House, where we saw a fine performance of *Così fan tutte*, I remembered sitting next to a Scottish architect at a lunch in the Beirut Embassy forty years earlier. He told me he was on his way by request to Sydney to solve an awkwardness in the construction of the Opera House when its two magnificent main arches had failed by a few inches to meet at the top. He or some other genius must have solved the problem.

We flew on from this amazing city to Bombay for the original purpose of our expedition. Nine months earlier Jenny had been invited by a visiting Indian lady, Ratna Krishnakumar, who was interested in dye plants, to lunch with her in London. Ratna told her she would be glad to help and even accompany her round Kerala if she ever visited Bombay (where she lived). Jenny later let her know that we planned to do so in March 2001. But we hardly expected to be met on descending our aircraft gangway at Bombay in the small hours by a man in uniform, who whisked us past Customs and Immigration with a wave of the hand to a car with a uniformed driver. The driver took us straight to a posh block overlooking Bombay harbour and up to a flat on its twenty-first floor owned, we learnt, by Ratna and her husband. They were away themselves but a note left by Ratna bade us use the flat and the car and said she hoped to join us somewhere in the mountains of Kerala. We did not yet know that her husband had revolutionised many Tata industries in India, in addition to managing sixty five-star Taj hotels all over the world. He had done all this by getting recognised as one of India's few incorruptible top tycoons and by sacking any of his thousands of subordinates suspected of malpractice. We were to meet him on our return to Bombay a fortnight later as guests once more in the flat; and a most impressive personality he proved to be, as well as a devout Hindu intellectual. (He prayed at the shrine outside our bedroom door every day from 5 to 6 a.m. before setting off to his daily twelve hours' work.) He and Ratna whisked us off on that second arrival, smartened up as best we could, to a performance of nothing less than the Vienna State Chamber Orchestra, conducted by a world-famous Japanese. This took place in the magnificent ballroom of the nearby Taj Hotel and began with a demonstration of the Viennese waltz by twelve pairs of Indians trained (perhaps over-hastily) for the purpose. To add to the improbability of the occasion I found myself, despite the discomfort in my swollen right foot (which had been troubling me and a succession of doctors for the last fortnight), whirling round the ballroom floor, on and on, in an unprecedented Viennese waltz with Jenny.

That was the climax to a fortnight's waltzing, so to speak, round south-west India in the car provided by the Krishnakumars, accompanied as guide by the delightful Bency Issac, one of the managers of the Tata Coffee Company. We picked up all over the place the traces both of Thomas Machell in the 1850s and of Jenny herself in 1970. (After struggling alone round India and Ceylon aged eighteen, she too had suffered in Bombay from an infected foot, though she didn't do any Viennese waltzing on it.) When she now reached the Mysore area once more, she found one of the three Van Ingen brothers, who had spontaneously cared for her thirty years before and who were old even then, still alive and welcoming. The three were world-famous taxidermists in the distant past, and Jenny was now allowed to see the stupendous collection of their stuffed animals locked up in the 'trophy room' of the Maharaja's palace. The business had finally closed down and the surviving brother, aged over ninety, no longer practised the family art; but he still hunted (illegally), manufacturing in his bedroom his own cartridges out of home-made gunpowder.

The part of our wanderings in Kerala that relates to Thomas Machell I must leave to Jenny's own pen; but I did make a curious contribution. With my swollen foot I was laid up for a day or two in the Tata Coffee Company's luxurious guesthouse at Coorg up in the Malabar hills; and the consequent hold-up in our plans enabled us to meet over the lunch table a newly arrived pair of guests. They were the Swiss journalist Bernard Imhasly and his Indian wife, Rashna. She turned out to be a widely acclaimed psychotherapist who also occasionally does 'past life regressions'. After one look at Jenny she asked whether she might do one on her. The outcome of the exhausting three-day exercise that resulted was unbelievable, but outside my sphere ...

With Bency still guiding us we then drove down to the coast again, our first port of call being Tellicherry. This was where in the 1850s Thomas and his colleagues used to send by bullock-cart the coffee they grew away up in Coorg, for curing and export. The Portuguese mansion, alongside which still stands the old coffee-curing factory, contains in its upstairs hall the only punkah still operated in India. It is now worked by a small invisible motor hidden away where the punkah-wallah, also hidden away, used to spend his weary days. We ate our tiffin under it, Thomas-fashion. We explored everything in Tellicherry and I even engaged briefly in the cricket being played by some young Indians under the walls of the old Portuguese/Dutch fort (Jenny having declared to them that I had played for Oxford University!).

Our next stop was up in the mountains again – the highest in India except for the Himalayas – where Tata's tea-growing company operates, centred on Munnar. Ratna was waiting for us in its lavish guesthouse (originally, like other Tata guesthouses, a British planter's residence). Its sensational gardens overlooked endless tea plantations plunging and surging in all directions with groups of tea-pickers smiling out of them. (My father's Oodoowerry estate in Ceylon – see Chapter 2 – must have looked like this on a smaller scale.) In Munnar village Ratna set up ten years ago an establishment for the schooling and craft training of the physically or mentally handicapped offspring of Tata's tea-company employees; and very impressive it was. Ratna, wherever she happens to be in the world, rings up the teacher in charge of the centre every day, and everybody there worships her.

The only other institution in Munnar I will mention is the Plantation Managers' Club – once wholly British, now wholly Indian. In its bar – still marked 'Men Only' – we were struck by a massive array of hats on the wall. These, it was explained to us, were the hats of dozens of former British planters hung there on their retirement – but only if they had been planters for thirty-four years or more. Does the expression 'To hang up one's hat' derive from this old planters' club?

Down we drove to the coast again (having said goodbye to Bency), first to Cochin, which proved a most intriguing town. Tata's handsome guesthouse there looked after us handsomely. Up the street from it stands the house, still preserved and lived in, of the epoch-making Vasco da Gama, who was originally buried in the Catholic churchyard nearby.

In the town we visited the oldest synagogue in Asia. The man (a Roman Catholic) selling entry tickets told me there were now only seven adult Jews with four children living in Cochin. The synagogue itself, however, remains sensational and its internal decor fabulous. In a junk shop beside it we bought

24 Amazing fourteenth-century fishing nets at Cochin in Kerala.

an old brass doorknocker to add to the one I picked up in the Jewish quarter of Baghdad the morning after Saddam Hussein bulldozed it down. So both our doors at Uppincott now have Jewish brass doorknockers.

But the most memorable feature of Cochin is the long row of colossal fishing nets set up along the beach by the Chinese in the fourteenth century, restored by a local magnate in the sixteenth, and still worked twice daily when the tide is fully in. Each circular net, some 25 feet in diameter, is repeatedly lowered for a few minutes into the water by a complicated contraption of beams and ropes, looking like a gigantic praying mantis pouncing on its prey. It is then raised again by four strong men hauling, from the landward end of a wooden jetty, a rope that passes through a hole at the top of the main huge swing-beam. From the same hole descends vertically another rope to which are precariously tied, one below the other, ten big stones, heavy enough to balance the weight of the net contraption. The stones pile themselves up, as the operation is completed, on the jetty's far end. The whole Heath Robinson procedure is harder to describe than to operate; but the sight of these remarkable devices all at work was breathtaking. The catch, however, is miserably small nowadays – sometimes a net is absolutely empty – owing to the number of boats fishing much more profitably offshore all night. And these great praying mantises, seven hundred years of age, will surely soon be left to die. Thank goodness we were there in time to watch them still alive and pouncing.

On we went down the coast to Allepey (Allepuzha today). As soon as we entered it we were able to rejoin the ghost of Thomas Machell. He spent some days there in the 1840s on his voyage home from Calcutta in a series of Arab dhows, having learnt Arabic and adopted Arab dress. Jenny recognised instantly the house in its main street where Thomas had lodged. Much in Allepey was agreeably time-warped.

On getting back to our Cochin guesthouse in the late afternoon we learnt that two unmissable events would be happening that very night 60 miles inland. One was a performance of the ritual *Kathakali* play outside a grand Hindu temple; the other was a shadow-puppet performance in an isolated village 20 miles farther on. (We had been asked by a friend near Exeter, who is writing a book on the subject, to photograph any shadow puppetry we might come across.) We taxied out at once.

The *Kathakali* play, performed in sumptuous costume (but very slowly) in dumb-show to a drumbeat accompaniment, rehearsed the meeting of the divine Shiva and his impoverished old guru; and it was put on solely for the entertainment of the crowded local audience. The shadow-puppet affair was a total contrast. After dancing briefly round the village shrine and distributing 'seeds' to anyone present (including ourselves), the puppeteers disappeared behind the long screen in a shed erected for the purpose with a row of dim oil lamps behind it. We waited – and waited – expectantly. Only a small handful of the villagers were squatting or sleeping on the sand anywhere near, and we learnt that these performances are not designed for any local audience but purely and simply for witnessing by the gods. They, it was believed, would shower special grace on any village that staged them. After half an hour, around midnight, some fuzzy shadow figures began to appear on the screen, but they were impossible to photograph. This particular village, a visibly impoverished one, had somehow raised the money to hire performances on five successive nights. The villagers themselves, as stated above, did not watch any of them. One can only hope that they received a mysterious spiritual benefit. But is there anywhere else in the world where a spectacular display of this kind is expensively mounted in the absence of any human observer?

We got to bed in the small hours in our Cochin guesthouse, and in the morning, after a last rush up to the Chinese fishing nets, we flew to Bombay. Kerala had been an unforgettable experience from first to last, and it had brought Jenny what I had best call a strange new intimacy with Thomas ('Book ahoy!').

On this second visit to Bombay we met, as already mentioned, our bene-factor Krishnakumar. We could quickly understand how, with his drive and his omniscience, he was such an industrial star. His familiarity with English poetry was also rewarding for me, for he looked through the copy of *A Kind of Kindness* that we had given to Ratna and him, and said '"Matthew Five" is excellent, especially the last two lines.'

Back home, the only unexpected development in my own existence was that, having been encouraged by Jenny to enter the writers' competition in the 2001 Ways-with-Words festival at Dartington, I was awarded the first prize for a brief extract from these memoirs (the *Lob* language bit in Chapter 3). A curious consequence of this was that I found myself being interviewed on *Lob* by the BBC and broadcast on the late John Peel's *Home Truths* programme on Radio 4. Half the population of England apparently listen to this programme at 9 a.m. on Saturdays (though they pretend they don't) because that is when they do the washing-up of their Friday-night party dishes. The many kindly comments I received included the following from Venetia Porter of the British Museum's Islamic Department: 'My colleagues and I have decided to give up Arabic and learn *Lob*.' My performance, repeated on *Pick of the Week*, led to my being invited to Norwich to read some *Lob* and any other musical languages I liked on an art gallery programme entitled 'The Music of Language'. I gave them, in addition to a very brief piece of *Lob*, a Scots poem (inevitably 'Gin I was God') and a Latin one (Catullus's even more musical poem on Sirmio, almost the only piece of Latin I still have by heart). And I met there the remarkable Oliver Bernard, poet and translator of Rimbaud and Apollinaire, who has bought a lot of copies of *A Kind of Kindness* as presents for friends of his, mostly poets and critics. They all sent flattering comments. Robert Nye wrote in a letter to Oliver Bernard that if he hadn't just ceased to be *The Times*'s poetry critic, he would certainly have given *A Kind of Kindness* a review notice. And he added, a bit cryptically, 'Always a relief to find poems that are about something, and that have at best almost become the thing they are about ... Clever of him to have got through most of his life without being known.' A letter from Teresa Keswick, Prioress of a Carmelite nunnery, to whom Oliver Bernard had presented a copy, was so beautifully written that I feel compelled to reproduce a whole paragraph:

They are wonderfully useful. (Not perhaps the first adjective that springs to mind where poetry is concerned.) But I am a contemplative nun, which means that two hours of every day are spent in silent prayer. The foundress and reformer of the Carmelites, Teresa of Avila, recommends that during such times it is advisable to have close at hand a book of good, solid spiritual thinking, just in case one's own mind should be a blank. Which is where your poems come into their own. They are even good news in winter, when prayer-time takes place in the dark. Because they are still *there*; the fact that for a while they cannot be read is immaterial. Thank you very much for providing so much fun, so much interest, and so much appropriate sadness, which is a very long way from nostalgia, and a great deal more real.

On that note it will be sensible to end these reminiscences at last – but not before recording the climax of a tour through Scotland in September 2001. We drove all the way up to Orkney and Shetland. In the former we spent two luxurious nights in the huge Balfour Castle (a presumptuous rival to Pilrig) on

Shapinsay Island off Kirkwall. This was followed by a less luxurious night in a lonely B & B, as near the famous Old Man of Hoy as possible. As for the treeless Shetlands, our final aim was to get sight of Muckle Flugga, the most northerly of all the lighthouses built by the fearless Stevensons, on the edge of the Arctic. There was a fairly good road leading up to the north end of Unst, to serve the early-warning station recently set up there by the Ministry of Defence. We were rewarded, when the sun finally banished the thick clouds and took charge, with a magnificent view of Muckle Flugga from the top of the last cliff in Scotland, but I will not quote the love poem it inspired.

Two further enchantments were granted me not long after Muckle Flugga. One was in southern France, where we rented a cottage in Caunes Minervois owned by Carmen Callil, founder of the Virago publishing house. It was the perfect medieval French village, with its *abbaye* beside which I heard for the first time in my life a nightingale singing its heart out – and not only heard but, remarkably, *watched* it doing so for half an hour, silhouetted on a treetop. The other excitement was attending the wedding in Exeter of Toni Evennett and Jez Waites at which the Queen's personal piper, met quite by chance by one of the bridesmaids, had agreed to come and pipe. He had left the job that morning and flown straight down from Balmoral. He was full of uninhibited stories of his years with the Queen, with whom he enjoyed a unique status (like Victoria's John Brown), being more companion than employee.

During these years the world elsewhere was plunging into unspeakable horrors (New York on 11 September 2001, Afghanistan, Iraq and Darfur thereafter, and Palestine continually).

> *Audax omnia perpeti*
> *Gens humana ruit per vetitum nefas*

('So bold at daring everything/The human race rushes into forbidden wrong'). Horace wrote those lines two thousand years ago (Odes I.3), when human folly was far less unforgivable than it is today. Latin verse would be much easier if the order of the words were always (as here) dictated by the flow of the sentence. The confusion usually imposed on limping Classicists (like me) by the requirements of Latin scansion is, however, nothing to compare with the confusion imposed on limping Pacifists (also like me) and on the rest of the world by the devilish achievements of modern military technology.

Before signing off, two questions remain. First, what is my justification for writing my memoirs at all? Well, to the extent that they have become more and more a foreign travelogue, the corny excuse must be 'What do they know of England,/Who only England know?'. The earlier chapters did delve into a more distant era. We are all of us, of course, prisoners of our own past, however hard we try to escape from it into the present. I must be the only member of the family, brother Ian excepted, who is still 'imprisoned'

25 Jenny, Hamish, Finella and Glencairn (left to right) at the wedding of Toni
Evennett and Jez Waites in Exeter, 2004.

in the song that kept so many young British soldiers chirpy in the dark days
of 1940–43:

> We'll hang out the washing on the Siegfried Line
> If the Siegfried Line's still there.

It still echoes every day, silently as a rule, round my tonsils. Ian, who bravely
landed by glider beyond the Siegfried Line without much thought of hanging
his washing on it, at least received a Military Cross for his pains.

Second, who, I ask myself, will ever read these reminiscences other than older acquaintances for sentimental reasons? The only encouragement I can offer others to do so is to repeat the lines from Cicero quoted in my Introduction: 'Not to know what happened before you were born is to remain for ever a child.'

Index

Abu Dhabi, 204–5
Abu Simbel (Sudan), 248
Abu Sinn, Mohammed Ahmed, 128, 179, 180, 256
Abyssinia, 79
Adama Marra (in Mali), 292
Adams, Michael, 59, 252, 271
Aden, 279–80
Aerial Post (first ever 1911), 32
Aflaq, Michel (founder of Baathism), 221
Agedabia (Libya), 98–9
Al-Alamein, 79, 275–6
Albany Herald, 55
Algeria, 244–8
Allepey (Kerala, India), 317–18
Alsatian dog (as protector, Jordan), 228–9
Amesfield, 38
Amish people, Philadelphia, 259–60
Amjhupi (Bengal), 299
Amman (Jordan), 226–34
'Annie Laurie', 29
Antunez, Nemesio, 166, 170
Apollinaire, 248
Arabic language, 82
Arab–Israeli Six-Day War, 207
Arab–Israeli War (no. 3), 227–8
Arab League intervention in Gulf States, 199
Aranui, cargo ship, Polynesia, 310, 312
archaeology, 90, 114, 125, 131; Amman Institute of, 156, 257, 261; Jerusalem Institute of, 156
Argyll and Sutherland Highlanders, 73, 74, 75, 78, 83, 276
Armenians in Middle East, 258
Asmara (Eritrea), 80
Aswan (Egypt), 278
Atacama Desert (Chile), 166–7
Athens, 233
Auden, W. H., 10
Austin, John (Tutor, Oxford), 64
Ayer, Sir Alfred (Oxford), 58

Baalbek, 106–7
Baathism (in Iraq), 221–2
Baghdad, 215, 220
Bagnold (in Libya), 96
bagpipes, 43, 192
Bahai (Sudan–Chad frontier), 150
Bahrain, 201–7
Bakel (Senegal), 291
Balfour, Alfred Stevenson, 4, 27
Balfour, James, Professor, 6
Balfour, Margaret (of Pilrig), 6
Balfour, Millicent (aunt), 27
Balfour-Melville, Barbara (historian), 5
Balfour Paul, Sir James, 4, 6–15
Balfour Paul, John William (my father), 13, 21–4, 26, 39–40, 42, 45–6, 49, 54–6, 73, 113, 115, 166
Balfours of Pilrig, 4–6
Balsdon, Dacre 66–7
Bamako (Mali), 292, 296
Bangkok, 286–7
Bangladesh, 299–80
Barr, Greig, 62, 157
Barzani, Mustafa (Kurdish leader), 219
Beer, Patricia (poet), 262
bees, 231
Beihan (Yemen), 279
Beirut, 179–82
Benares, see Varanasi
Benevento, 113
Bengal, 299, 304
ben Zakour, Fathi (Tunis), 241, 248
Bernard, Oliver, 319
Bimbashi, 79
Bisharat, Mamdouh, 235
Blackwood's Magazine, 150
Blake, George, 186–7
Blunt, Sir Anthony, 188
bodyguards (Jordanian), 229
Boer War, 22–4
Bombay/Mumbai, 314, 318
Bordubordu (Masalati practice), 141

Bosra eski-Sham (Syria), 235
Boulos brothers (Beirut), 175–6
Brach (Fezzan), 52, 109
Brimelow, Sir Tom, 161–2
Budapest, 162
Bullard, Sir Reader, 209
Burdwan, Maharajah of, 301
Burnett, David and Betty, 91, 105–6, 113
Bussell, Lawrence, 127–8

Cairo, 100, 120, 274–6
Cakemuir Castle, 42, 45, 115, 130
Calcutta/Kolkata, 299–300
Cape Town, 76
CARE (in Egypt), 275
carpets, oriental, 188–9
Carswell, John, and his elephant, 179
Caunes, Minervois (France), 320
Cavalry Corps, Oxford University, 63
Ceylon, 21
Ceylon Mounted Rifles, 22–3
Chad (French Colony) policy, 139;
    Abéché (region), 139; Adré (district),
    139–40; Goz Beida (district), 142
Chawner, Frank, 53, 60
Chesney, F. F., 216–17
Chicken-fish (Aqaba), 231
Chile, 163–70; visit of Princess Marina
    of Kent, 164–5; National Ballet,
    165; nitrate mining, 166–7; Santiago
    museum, 165; Valparaiso (my visits
    to), 169–70
Cicero, xi, 322
Clark, William, 62, 131, 135
Cochin (Kerala, India), 316–18
Cockburn, Henry (in Edinburgh), 12
Cocos Islands, 45
Condé, Bruce, 283
Coorg (India), 315
Crawford, O. G. S. (archaeologist), 131
Ctesiphon Palace (Sassanian – Iraq), 217
curling, 10
currencies (Persian Gulf), 192–3
Customary Law (Sudan), 133
Cuzco (Peru), 166, 272–3

dambaris (locust wizards), 141
Darfur, 137–49; the Masalit Sultans,
    137–8; my *Short History of*, 140, 146;
    wild animals, 138–9
Darien Scheme, 5

Darjeeling (India), 304–5
Dartington Festival ('Ways with Words'),
    319–20
'Dead Reckoning', 96–7
Deane, H. H. (HHD), 81, 83–5, 87, 90,
    98, 105
de Gaulle, Charles (French President),
    171
de Grünne, Dominic, 262
De La Mare, Walter, 57
Delhi, 306
demobilisation (Jan. 1946), 115
demonstrations (anti-British, Sudan
    1947), 122–3
d'Erlanger, Leo, 241–2
Descartes and mandrakes, 171
dhows (Dubai), 194
Djanet (Algeria), 245–7
Djenné (Mali), 293
Dogon people (Mali), 294–5
Dubai (as Political Agent), 191–2 ;
    bagpiper, 192; gold trade to India,
    192–4; hat problems, 191–2; oil search
    begins, 193; Political Agent's job, 191
Duncan, Jock, 160; our musical comedy,
    Sunlight on Water, 160
Dunkirk, 74
Dunn, Douglas (poet), 254
Dupret, Marcel (Belgian Ambassador,
    Iraq and Morocco), 216

Easton, Richard, 168–9
Edinburgh, 3, 14
Egypt: Anglo-French invasion 1956,
    162–3; Karnak riots, 248; term's stay
    with Finella and Hamish 1989, 274
Eissa al Khalifa (ruler of Bahrain), 207
Elie, Fife, 37–45
Eliot T. S., 73
Elizabeth II, Queen; gifts and poetic
    tributes from abroad, 176–7; 'Kissing
    Hands' (as Ambassador), 163
Elliot, Nicholas, 185
Ennedi, my exploration of, 149–50
Erkowit (Sudan), 90, 92
Exeter University, ix; Research fellowship
    since 1979, 257; fund-raising for,
    267–8

Fairlawn Hotel, Calcutta/Kolkata, 199,
    301

'Fallen Angels', 163
Finella (daughter), 254, 296, 299, 305, 315
Flecker, James Elroy, *Hassan*, 254
Fonteyn, Margot, 178–9
Foreign Office, my training in, 158–9
'Freedom certificates' (Dubai), 191
Free French; in Fezzan, 109; in Kufra, 87–8; in Port Sudan, 209
Frey, Fr Jean (Iraq), 217

Gambia, 290
Gaspard, Dr Lorand (Tunisia), 241, 245
Gauguin, Paul (in Marquesas Islands), 312
Geneifa (Suez Canal), 77
Geneina (Darfur), 137–43
George II, King, xii
George V, King, 14
German language, 64
Germans, 13, 26
Gharian (Tripolitania), 99
ghosts, 13
Ghuznavi, Ruby (Bangladesh), 299
Gifford, Brig. J. (Comdr 12th Div. SDF), 103, 108, 112
Glencairn parish, 17, 23, 26–7
Glenluiart House, 17, 27, 29
Glenluiart Journal, 27–9
Glubb Pasha (Jordan), 105
Goddard, David, 203, 294
gold exports (from Dubai), 192–4
golf, one-armed championship, 55
Gondar Pass (Abyssinia), 83
Goremé (Turkey), 235
Grover, John (Sudan), 120, 123
Guadalupé (Spain), 257
guano (bird-dropping fertiliser), 167
Guernsey, 18–19
Guraan tribe (S. Libya), 150
Gurney, Oliver (Abyssinia), 83

Hahn, C. (Cocky), 210, 218
Haile Salassie, Emperor, his sister (Abyssinia), 85
Hamish (son), 258, 277, 299
Hanbury-Tenison, Robin (explorer), 169
Hardan al-Takriti (Iraq), 222
Harrison, Anthony, 304, 307
Hassaheissa (N. Gezira, Sudan) as DC, 130
Hassan, Crown Prince (Jordan), 227–8

'Haw-Haw, Lord', 74
Heath, Edward, PM, 226
Hemming, John (Royal Geographical Society), 263–4
Henderson, Bill, 137, 157, 209
Henderson, Nicko, 163, 165, 167
Heriot Row, Edinburgh, 7
Hilmi Samarra (Kirkuk Oil Co.), 210–11
Hitler, Adolf, 77–8
Hodgkin, Robin (Sudan and Oxford), 92–3, 114
Hourani, Albert, 188, 207
Housego, David and Jenny (in India), 306–7
Howe, Sir Robert (Gov. Gen. Sudan), 130
Huddleston, Gen. Sir Hubert, 90–1, 112
Hume, David (philosopher), 6
Hussein, King of Jordan, 226–8; and Arab–Israeli War 1973, 227; call on Prime Minister Heath, 226; his cricket XI, 234; party for Shah of Persia, 232
Huxley, Aldous, xii

Ian (my brother), 47, 238–9, 321
Imbaba (Cairo), 278
Imhasly, Bernard, 315
Imhasly, Rashna, 316
Inca, empire, religion etc. (Peru), 273–4
Indigo (Jenny's two books on), 264–5
Iran, coup attempt in Iraq, 222–3
Iraq, 215–23; Ambassador to (1969–71), 205–15; Baathists' rise to power, 221–2; Basra (Gellatly Hankey 1901), 219; Euphrates expedition 1835 (*see also* Chesney, F. F.), 217; expulsion of my Embassy, 223; Kurds in, 219; Lynch family, 216; National Museum, Baghdad, 220–1; Shatt al-Arab marshes, 219–20; *see also* Saddam Hussein
Israel, 155–6
Istanbul, 230–1

Jalo oasis (Cyrenaica), 98
James VI, King of Scotland, 5
Jenny (second wife), *see* Scott, Jenny
Jericho excavations, 165–6
Jerusalem, 102
Jordan, as Ambassador (1971–75), 226–34
Joseph, Hellen (Keith's wife), sculptress, 160–1

Joseph, Keith: All Souls rooms lent to me, 157; appointed Secretary of State for Wales, 160–1

Juma bint Mohammed (potter, Tunisia), 242

Jura (Scottish island, honeymoon with Marnie, 1951), 131–2

Kaedi (Mauritania), 290

Kalayan (Armenian archaeologist), 257–8

Kalimpong (India), 305

Karib, Abdullah (*Mamour*, Sudan), 123–4

Karnak, 248, 278

Kassala (Sudan), 85–6, 93

Kathakali (Hindu play), 318

Kayes (Mali), 291–2

Kenyon, Dame Kathleen, 155–6

Keswick, Teresa (nun), 319

Khartoum (1946), 120–9

Khartoum Museum (1978), 256

Khor Fakkan, misadventure (Indian Ocean), 192

Khudadad Khan (Odes to the Queen), 176–7

Kind of Kindness, A, 298, 318–19

Kirkbride, Diana, 181–2

Kirkuk, oil company, Iraq, 210–11

Kouklia (Cyprus, excavations), 144–5

'Krak des Chevaliers' (Syria), 106

Krishnakumar and wife Ratna (Bombay / Mumbai), 315–16, 319

Kufra (S. Libya); as Garrison Adjutant, 87, 94; market, 89, 95; salt-lakes, 89

Kurds (in Iraq), 219

Kutab Minar (nr Delhi), 307

Kutum (N. Darfur) as DC, 145–9

Laos, 287–8

Larkin, Philip (poet), 209

Lebanon, 172–89; Armenians in, 173–4; FO 'spy school', 174–5; PPS attempted coup, 174; traffic problems, 172–3

Lee, Laurie (poet), 229

Leptis Magna (Libya), 110

Libya, 87, 90, 94–9, 104–5, 255

Libyan police (1944), 96–7

Limerick, Lord, 255

Linplum, E. Lothian, 39–41

Little Boreland, Gatehouse of Fleet ('Wee Bee'), 135–6

Liverpool, 76

Liwa oasis (Abu Dhabi), 196–7

Lloyd George, Valerie, 63

'*Lob*' (our childhood language), 41, 43–5

Long Range Desert Group (LRDG), 87

Louis, Professor Wm Roger (Austin, Texas and St Antony's, Oxford), US expert on Britain in the Middle East, 289

Lovat Scouts, 113

Luce, Sir William, 130, 199, 201, 205

Lynch family, Iraq, 216

Lyon, King of Arms, *see* Balfour Paul, Sir James

Lyon's Tale, A, 8–15, 18

Lyons-Wilson, William (artist), 58–9

Maaloula (Syria), 234

Macbeth, 56

Macchu Picchu, 166, 273

Machell, Thomas, 299, 302–9, 311, 312, 315, 317–18

Macleod, Revd George, 7

Mahdi Tajer, 268

Makarios, Bishop (Cyprus), 145

Mali, 291–6; its mudcloth, 292

Margaret, Princess, visit to Tunisia 1976, 243–4

Maria Teresa dollars, 81–2, 84

Marib (Yemen), 266

Marina, Princess, of Kent, 164–5

Marquesas Islands (French Polynesia), 309–14

Mary Queen of Scots, 42

Masalit, 137–8

Maudling, Reginald (in Dubai), 200

May, General Sir Reginald, 31

McDermid, Gladys (governess), 39, 238

Medayin Saleh (Saudi Arabia), 233–4

Medinat Habu (Egypt), 277

Meidob crater and King (Darfur, Sudan), 146–7, 149

Melhuish, Ramsay, 231–2, 296

Melville, Herman, 311

Meteora (Greece) 237–8

Middle East Association, London, 253

migraines, 61

Milligan, Spike, 253–4

Mohammed ash-Sharqi (ruler of Fujeirah), 198

Moniaive, 14, 17, 24, 27, 38, 187

Monroe, Elizabeth, 207–8, 216

Monteith, Bill (William's son), 37, 45, 62, 102, 112, 135

Monteith, Revd John in Moniaive, 16, 17, 27; Hugh (son) on Scotland's Rugby XV, 29–30; Jack (son) killed at Loos, September 1915, 30; Maud (daughter), 31–2; William (son) killed at Loos, September 1915, 30

Monteith, Cynthia (Hugh's daughter), 31

Monteith, Muriel (my mother), 14, 23, 28, 30, 32–3, 103–4, 168, 182

Monteith, Muriel Cox (Aunt 'Moolie'), 37, 45

Monty (my brother), 26, 49

Mopti (Mali), 294

Moreland (Kinross), 41

Morocco, 283–6 ; Tangier, 283–4; Goulemine, 284–6

mosaics (Jordan and Tunisia), 242

motor cars invade Scotland, 1900, 9

Muckle Flugga (Shetlands), 320

Mukerjee, Amrita (Calcutta), 302–3

Munnar (Kerala, India), 316

Murray, Charles (poet), 54

Muscat, *see* Oman

Mussolini, Benito; medal struck for conquest of Egypt, 113; opts out of war, 102

Namibia, 296–7

Nannarone, Angelina, 65

Nazca Lines (Peru), 272

Neve, Margaret Ann, 18–20

Neve, William ('Nunc'), 17–18

Newbold, Sir Douglas (Sudan), 112–14

New York, 258–9

nitrates (fertiliser mined in Chile), 166–7

Noitgedacht, Boer War, 22

Nukuhiva (Marquesas Islands), 309–14

Officer Cadet Training Unit, at Colchester (1939), 71–3

Ogilvy, Marnie (my first wife), 131, 202; marriage in Haddington, 131; damages spine falling from horse, 132; our first child born (Ann), 134; our second child born (Alison), 147; collapses with polio, 155–6; our third child born (Cati), 167; our fourth child born (Jamie), 182; contracts fatal illness in Baghdad, 223

Oman, dramas in, 268–9

Oodoowerry tea-estate (Ceylon), 21, 23–5, 316

Order of the Thistle, 14

Ordugu (my Guraani guide in Ennedi), 149–50

Oulton, Harry (Sudan), 132

Oweinat rock paintings (Libya), 90

Oxford University, 53, 62–7; cricket and rugby trials, 53–4; Cavalry Corps, 63; my tutors 64

pacifism, 63

Palermo (Sicily), 251; puppet theatres, 251; Convento dei Capucini, 251–2; Taormina, 252

Palewski, Gaston, 253

Palmen, Inga, 166

pantomimes (in Edinburgh), 11

Papeete (Tahiti), 310, 314

Paris, 253

Parker, Michael (historian), 64

Parsons, Anthony, Britain's man in UN, 201, 259; death in August 1996, 203; joins me as Research Fellow, Exeter, 203; our host in New York, 258–9; personal adviser to Mrs Thatcher, 202; with me in Bahrain, 201

Paterson, James (artist), 17, 27

'Pauls of Glasgow' (grandfather's booklet), 4; Revd John Paul (19th cent.), 4, 16; Revd William Paul (18th cent.), 4; Revd William Paul (19th cent.), 15–16; Robert Paul, banker (18th cent.), 4

Pearl Harbor, 79

Persian exam, 208

Persian Gulf, 158, 190

Petra (Jordan), 105–6

'Phantoms' (World War II), 113

Philby, Kim, 182–7

Philby, St John, 183

piano lessons, 48–9

Piggott, Peggy (archaeologist), 128, 178

Pilrig House (Edinburgh), 5, 10

Plessey House (India), 302–3

polio, 155–6

Pompeii, 252

Powell, Gus (Kaimakam, SDF), 79–80

Poznan Trade Fair (Poland), 162

Pyrenees, 309

Qaboos (Sultan of Oman), 268
Qaddhafi, President of Libya, 108, 255
Qasimi rulers (Gulf): Saqr of Sharjah
   (expelled) 198–9; Saqr of Ras el-
   Khaima, 198

Raikes, Christine (artist, Devon), 261
Rashad (Sudan), 135
Rashid al-Maktoum, Ruler of Dubai,
   196–7, 267–8
Read, Sir Herbert and Lady, 238
Reagan, Johnny (English Cowboy), 114
Reed, Henry (poet), 73–4
Robertson, Sir James (Sudan), 120
Rome (1945), 113
Rommel, General (German, Libya), 79
Rufa'a, Sub-district N. Gezira (Sudan),
   128
Russian Orthodox Bishop of Tyre &
   Sidon, 176

Sacsawayman (Peru), 272
Saddam Hussein (Iraq), 3, 220, 221–3
St Antony's College, Oxford, 207–11
St Catherine's Monastery, Sinai, 276–7
St Cuthbert's church, Princes Street,
   11–12
St Petersburg, 12
St Simeon Stylites, Basilica, Syria, 235–6
Sami Abdulrahman (Kurdish Minister,
   Iraq), 210
Sana'a (Yemen), 263–4, 266–7, 280
Santiago Museum (Chile), 165
Sarafand, staff school (Palestine), 105
Satyajit Ray (Indian film-maker), 304
Sayed Sa'eed (Sultan of Muscat &
   Oman), 205–7
Scaife, Christopher (Lebanon and
   London), 179
Scarampi, Aleramo (Italy and Chile), 168
scorpions, 94, 138
Scott, Frank and Jill (Jenny's parents),
   231, 258
Scott, Jenny (my second wife): her first
   arrival in Amman, 229; our marriage
   in Brixton, Devon, 231
Scott, Michael, 179–81, 283
'Scrap' (my brother), 26, 43, 48, 51–2, 67,
   113, 239
seals, Antarctic, conference on, 224
Seamer, Jake (Sudan and Marlborough),
   129

Sebkha (Fezzan), 109
Sedbergh School, 21, 50–61
Senegal, 290–1
Sennar (Sudan), 123–4
Serenissima Travel Ltd, 271–4
Shaban, Professor M. A., 257, 263, 268–9
shadow puppets (Kerala), 318
Shakhbut, ruler of Abu Dhabi, 204–5;
   expelled from rulership, 204; settles in
   Muhammerah (Iran), 205; returns to
   live at home, 205
Shatt al-Arab (Iraq), 219–20
'sheikhly system' (Gulf), 207
Shemlan (FO 'Spy School', Lebanon),
   174–5
Shereen, Ismail and Hussein (Egypt),
   113, 275
Shihooh tribe (Musandam, Oman), 194–5
Sidki-Bevin Protocol on Sudan, 122
Sikhs (in Delhi), 306–7
Simms, Capt. (Bimbashi, Sudan), 81
Sims, Steve (writer and publisher), 298
sinusitis, 89–90, 114
Siwa oasis (Egypt), 275–6
Sleimani, Fatma (Algeria), 243
Smith, G. B. (Headmaster, Sedbergh),
   51–2
Smith, Kenneth, 62, 65, 126, 159
Smith, Lionel, 116
Smith, Sir Tom, 57–8
'So' tribe (Chad), 142
Spalding, Ian, 100–2
Spence, Basil (architect), 26
Squubbery Jimpo ('Squubbo'), 41
Stark, Freya (explorer), 179
Stevenson, Robert Louis Balfour (RLS),
   4, 5, 262, 311–14; his father, Thomas,
   4, 5; his mother, Margaret, 311; In the
   South Seas, 311, 313
Stratheden, SS, 76
Suakin (Sudan), 91–2
Sudan, Anglo-Egyptian Condominium,
   119
Sudan Defence Force, 77–108; ranks
   (Turkish) used in, 79, 80; 2 MMG
   Group (Abyssinia and Libya), 29, 84,
   93, 102, 105; 12 Division (Libya), 103,
   108
Sudan Plantations Syndicate, 125;
   ginneries destroyed by fire, 134
Sudan Political Service, 112, 119

Sudanisation of British jobs, 147
Suez, Anglo-French invasion, 162–3
Suez Canal, 77
Sydney (Australia), 314
Symonds, Julian, 66
Syria, 235

Tangier (Morocco), 283–4
Taormina (Sicily), 252
Tassili rock-paintings (Algeria), 245–7
Tellicherry (India), 316
tennis: at Bamborough, 1878, 14; at
    Kassala, 1947, 93–4; Suzanne Lenglen
    at Gleneagles, 1924, 40
Termessos (Turkey), 237
Ternström, Margareta, 242, 259
Thailand, 286–7; Bangkok (as guests of
    the Melhuishes), 286; Chang Mai, 287;
    wats (Buddhist temples), 287
theatre, Sir James BP's passion for, 10
Thesiger, Wilfred, 146, 150, 219, 269–70
Thorpe, Jeremy (in Dubai), 199
Tillicoultry (Scotland, in World War II),
    73
Titicaca, Lake (Peru), 272
Tolhalla Police, Calcutta, 300
Tommy-Martin, Henriette, 243
Touareg, 246–7
Traouré, Aminata (Mali), 292, 296
Trewin, J. C., 135
Tripolitania, 98, 110
Troglodytes (Libya), 99
Trucial States (brief history), 190
Tullibole (Kinrosshire), 15
Tunis, as Ambassador (1975–77), 240–4;
    magnificent Residence, 240, 242;
    occupation of residence by Gen.
    Alexander in 1944, 240; visit of
    Princess Margaret (1976), 243–4
Turkey, 235–7

Ua Pou (Marquesas Islands), 312
Um Sunut excavations (Sudan), 125
Union, Act of (England and Scotland), 5

UN Security Council, 259
Ur, Royal Burial, 220

Valparaiso (Chile), 169–70
Varanasi/Benares (India), 305–6; Heritage
    hospital, 303
Victoria, Queen, 14, 19
Vidler, Denis (Sudan), 120, 130, 163
Vientiane (Laos), 288; salt factory, 288

Wadi Halfa, 94
Wad Medani (Sudan), 120, 121, 123, 255
Waterloo, 19
weddings of my daughters, 261
West Yorks Regiment, 76
Wetheral, Lime House (Prep School),
    46–7
Wheeler, Lady (archaeologist), 156
Whittle, Hilton and Anita (Gambia,
    Senegal), 290–1
'Wi Tin Po', 66
Wolfe, Humbert (poet, lecturer), 56–7
Women's Rural Institutes (Scotland), 48
World War I, 26
World War II, 76–116 ; outbreak in 1939,
    67; summary of years 1940–43, 77–9;
    end of war with Italy, 102

Yemen (North and South), 262–3, 271;
    Aden, 272–80; Beidha, 265; Beihan,
    279; Hadramaut, 272; Marib, 266;
    Zabid, 265; see also Sana'a
Yid Fatima (silver talisman), 243, 277

Zabbaleen (rubbish collectors, Cairo), 274
Zabid (dyeing centre, Yemen), 265
Zaghawa tribes (N. Darfur, Sudan), 147
Zatopek (Czech athlete), 161
Zayed Al-Nahayan appeals for ouster of
    Shakhbut, 203; in Bureimi, 197; my
    fund-raising attempts, 267; takes over
    rulership of Abu Dhabi, 205;
Zein, Queen-mother in Jordan, 233
Zionism, 109